GW00659142

Evaluating Scientific Evidence

Scientific evidence is crucial in a burgeoning number of litigated cases, legislative enactments, regulatory decisions, and scholarly arguments. *Evaluating Scientific Evidence* explores the question of what counts as scientific knowledge, a question that has become a focus of heated courtroom and scholarly debate, not only in the United States, but also in other common law countries such as the United Kingdom, Canada, and Australia. Controversies are rife about what is permissible use of genetic information, whether chemical exposure causes disease, whether future dangerousness of violent or sexual offenders can be predicted, and whether such time-honored methods of criminal identification (such as microscopic hair analysis) have any better foundation than ancient divination rituals, among other important topics. This book examines the process of evaluating scientific evidence in both civil and criminal contexts and explains how decisions by nonscientists that embody scientific knowledge can be improved.

Erica Beecher-Monas teaches at Wayne State University Law School. She received her M.S. in Anatomy/Cell Biology from the University of Miami School of Medicine and J.D. from the University of Miami School of Law. She earned an LL.M. and a J.S.D. from Columbia University School of Law. Prior to entering academia, she clerked for the Honorable William M. Hoeveler, U.S. District Court Judge in the Southern District of Florida, and was an associate at Fried, Frank, Harris, Shriver and Jacobson in New York. She writes in the areas of judgment and decision making, with applications to scientific evidence and corporate governance, and has been published in numerous law reviews.

The Law in Context Series

Editors: William Twining (University College London)
and Christopher McCrudden (Lincoln College, Oxford)

Since 1970, the Law in Context Series has been in the forefront of the movement to broaden the study of law. It has been a vehicle for the publication of innovative scholarly books that treat law and legal phenomena critically in their social, political, and economic contexts from a variety of perspectives to bear on new and existing areas of law taught in universities. A contextual approach involves treating legal subjects broadly, using material from other social sciences and from any other discipline that helps to explain the operation in practice of the subject under discussion. It is hoped that this orientation is at once more stimulating and more realistic than the bare exposition of legal rules. The series includes original books that have a different emphasis from traditional legal textbooks, while maintaining the same high standards of scholarship. They are written primarily for undergraduate and graduate students of law and of the disciplines, but most also appeal to wider readership. In the past, most books in the series have focused on English law, but recent publications include books on European law, globalization, transnational legal processes, and comparative law.

Books in the Series
Anderson, Schum & Twining: *Analysis of Evidence*
Ashworth: *Sentencing and Criminal Justice*
Barton & Douglas: *Law and Parenthood*
Beecher-Monas: *Evaluating Scientific Evidence: An Interdisciplinary Framework for Intellectual Due Process*
Bell: *French Legal Cultures*
Bercusson: *European Labour Law*
Birkinshaw: *European Public Law*
Birkinshaw: *Freedom of Information: The Law, the Practice and the Ideal*
Cane: *Atiyah's Accidents, Compensation and the Law*
Clarke & Kohler: *Property Law*
Collins: *The Law of Contract*
Cranton, Scott & Black: *Consumers and the Law*
Davies: *Perspectives on Labour Law*
De Sousa Santos: *Toward a New Legal Common Sense*
Diduck: *Law's Families*
Eloworthy & Holder: *Environmental Protection: Text and Materials*
Fortin: *Children's Rights and the Developing Law*
Glover & Thomas: *Reconstructing Mental Health Law and Policy*
Gobert & Punch: *Rethinking Corporate Crime*
Goodrich: *Languages of Law*
Harlow & Rawlings: *Law and Administration: Text and Materials*
Harris: *An Introduction to Law*
Harris: *Remedies, Contract and Tort*
Harvey: *Seeking Asylum in the UK: Problems and Prospects*
Hervey & McHale: *Health Law and the European Union*
Lacey & Wells: *Reconstructing Criminal Law*
Lewis: *Choice and the Legal Order: Rising above Politics*
Likosky: *Law, Infrastructure and Human Rights*
Likosky: *Transnational Legal Processes*
Maughan & Webb: *Lawyering Skills and the Legal Process*

Continued after the index

Evaluating Scientific Evidence

An Interdisciplinary Framework
for Intellectual Due Process

Erica Beecher-Monas

Wayne State University Law School

CAMBRIDGE
UNIVERSITY PRESS

CAMBRIDGE UNIVERSITY PRESS
Cambridge, New York, Melbourne, Madrid, Cape Town, Singapore, São Paulo

Cambridge University Press
32 Avenue of the Americas, New York, NY 10013-2473, USA

www.cambridge.org
Information on this title: www.cambridge.org/9780521859271

First published 2007

Printed in the United States of America

A catalog record for this publication is available from the British Library.

Library of Congress Cataloging in Publication Data

Beecher-Monas, Erica, 1949–
Evaluating scientific evidence : an interdisciplinary framework for intellectual due process / Erica
Beecher-Monas.
   p.   cm. – (The law in context series)
Includes bibliographical references and index.
ISBN-13: 978-0-521-85927-1 (hardback)
ISBN-10: 0-521-85927-1 (hardback)
ISBN-13: 978-0-521-67655-7 (pbk.)
ISBN-10: 0-521-67655-X (pbk.)
1. Evidence, Expert – United States.   2. Forensic sciences – United States.   3. Evidence, Expert.
4. Forensic sciences.   I. Title.   II. Series: Law in context.
KF8961.B44   2007
347.73'67 – dc22   2006017094

ISBN-13   978-0-521-85927-1 hardback
ISBN-10   0-521-85927-1 hardback

ISBN-13   978-0-521-67655-7 paperback
ISBN-10   0-521-67655-X paperback

For
my father, Sidney Monas,
with love and gratitude
for his inspiration.

Contents

Acknowledgments   *page* xi

    Introduction   1
1   Triers of science   4
2   What is intellectual due process?   17
3   A framework of analysis   36
4   Toxic torts and the causation conundrum   57
5   Criminal identification evidence   94
6   Future dangerousness testimony: The epistemology of
    prediction   122
7   *Barefoot* or *Daubert*? A cognitive perspective on vetting
    future dangerousness testimony   146
8   Future dangerousness and sexual offenders   155
9   Models of rationality: Evaluating social psychology   168
10 Evaluating battered woman syndrome   203
    Conclusion   232

Index   239

Acknowledgments

This book owes so much to so many mentors, colleagues, students, and friends that it would be impossible to thank them all. Many of the formative ideas in this book were first articulated in law review articles and at talks given at various conferences, and the editors and attendees were extremely helpful in developing my initial thoughts. Many discussions about neuroscience and biological systems had their genesis over the dinner table with neuroscientist Edgar Garcia-Rill and his scintillating wife, Catherine. I greatly appreciate feedback on my writing from Cambridge editor, author, and mentor, William Twining, as well as Deirdre Dwyer, Philip Dawid, Terence Anderson, Theresa Beiner, and Tom Sullivan. For practical advice, editorial assistance, and unflagging support, I thank John Karr.

Evaluating Scientific Evidence

Introduction

Scientific evidence pervades modern legal decisions, whether the decision is made in the courtroom, during the regulatory process, or through legislation. The question of what counts as scientific knowledge has become a focus of heated courtroom and sholarly debate, not only in the United States but also in other common-law countries such as the United Kingdom, Canada, and Australia. Controversies are rife about what is permissible use of genetic information, if chemical exposure causes disease, and whether future dangerousness of violent or sexual offenders can be predicted, among other important topics. Many time-honored methods of criminal identification, such as hair analysis, voice spectography, and bitemark identification, to name a few, have turned out to have no better foundation than ancient divination rituals. This book examines the process of evaluating scientific evidence in both civil and criminal contexts and explains how decisions by nonscientists that embody scientific knowledge can be improved. This is a timely and important subject for anyone interested in the impact of law and science on society.

Evaluating Scientific Evidence: An Interdisciplinary Framework for Intellectual Due Process emphasizes the unifying themes of probabilistic reasoning, hypothesis testing, and interdisciplinarity, and it is intended to provide the guidance that judges and the lawyers advising them need to make scientifically legitimate admissibility determinations. Moreover, scholars who turn to interdisciplinary arguments are confronted with an urgent need for a framework to evaluate scientific argument.

Evaluating Scientific Evidence is intended to provide this guidance to scholars, judges, lawyers, and students of law. The heuristic it proposes consists of five parts and emphasizes underlying principles common to all fields of science. To meet the requirements of intellectual due process, anyone evaluating scientific information must be able to do five things: (1) identify and examine the proffered theory and hypothesis for their power to explain the data; (2) examine the data that supports (and undermines) the proffered theory; (3) employ supportable assumptions to fill the inevitable gaps between data and theory; (4) examine the methodology; and (5) engage in probabilistic assessment of the link between the data and the hypothesis. To demonstrate how using this heuristic would improve the evaluation of the scientific evidence at issue, my book uses real examples of recorded courtroom battles and scholarly debates as to what counts as valid science.

In the United States, both the category and the content of scientific knowledge are controversial. During little more than the past decade, in a trio of landmark cases beginning with *Daubert v. Merrell Dow Pharmaceuticals, Inc.,* the U. S. Supreme Court placed the burden of an early evaluation of the validity of scientific testimony – called "gatekeeping" – squarely on federal trial judges. An amendment to the Federal Rules of Evidence followed in short order and – although many states continue to apply a rule under which only a scientific consensus is required for admissibility and others use some combination of these approaches – scientific validity has become and remains an important question.

In Great Britain, the *Sally Clark* case has similarly ignited controversy over the use of experts testifying about science, a debate that has prompted the reopening of hundreds of cases.

Notwithstanding its significant alteration to the legal landscape, the U.S. Supreme Court has done little to guide judges in the necessary assessment. *Evaluating Scientific Evidence* argues that because most scientific studies and the conclusions culled from them are imperfect, the assessment process needs to include more than a knowledge of optimal experimental design. No study is perfect, no matter how well designed. What judges and lawyers – and anyone attempting to understand the validity of scientific information – need to know is not how to design the best scientific study but how to assess an imperfect one. Assessing imperfect studies – that is, the scientific validity of conclusions drawn from imperfect knowledge – is precisely the goal of the heuristic provided in this book.

Although a substantial literature about scientific evidence has appeared in the past decade, most of these treatises have discussed discrete areas of scientific evidence and their attendant problems in litigation. They have not offered a discussion of unifying principles that can make sense of areas beyond the topics they specifically address. In its novel approach, *Evaluating Scientific Evidence* takes a more philosophical bent that is intended for a broader audience and that addresses the underlying principles of scientific argument in a unifying manner.

Throughout, *Evaluating Scientific Evidence* draws on the rationalist tradition in evidence sholarship and its main epistemological assumptions. A tradition of aspirational rationality in the legal system is the inspiration for this book. Recognizing that concerns about evidence and inference are not limited to law and that issues of logic, probability, and knowledge are common to many disciplines, any study of scientific evidence inevitably becomes a multidisciplinary subject. In this book, common themes of logic, probability, and knowledge are emphasized and fine-tuned to scientific information used in legal decision making.

The premise of *Evaluating Scientific Evidence* is that critiquing scientific information in both civil and criminal systems is within the capability of judges, lawyers, and scholars, armed with the framework for analysis that this book provides. In presenting an updated philosophy of science, examining the relationship between facts and values, and exploring the question of how nonscientists properly can use scientific information to make sound and persuasive arguments and decisions, it takes a global perspective on how courts evaluate scientific evidence and builds on the comparative enterprise to address normative structures for the valid use of scientific information within the framework of the rule of law.

The heuristic advanced and applied in *Evaluating Scientific Evidence* draws from the U.S. Supreme Court's guidelines; the Federal Judicial Center's *Manual for Scientific Evidence*; guidelines proposed by the U.S. Environmental Protection Agency to assess scientific validity; the philosophy of science; and my own experience as a research scientist. The intention of this book is to offer insights into scientific process that will produce legal judgments and decisions that are intellectually defensible and fairer to the litigants. In doing so, it aims to put the interdisciplinary use of scientific information on a solid and reliable foundation. Its contention is that understanding the process of science and the nature of probabilistic reasoning will enable the proper use of science in the courts. This work carries on the tradition of Law in Context and complements other publications in the series (including Twining's *Rethinking Evidence* and Anderson and Twining's *Analysis of Evidence*, as well as Eggleston's *Evidence, Proof and Probability*, now out of print).

Those in our legal systems with responsibility for judgments and decisions are far from the only outsiders who must evaluate scientific evidence. Scientists working outside of a given field routinely critique each others' work. By taking information gleaned from one discipline and applying it to another, scientists' new insights make developments in science possible. Scientists can do this, even without intimate knowledge of the type of research being discussed, because underlying all scientific disciplines are common understandings about probabilistic and analogy-based reasoning. Even nonscientists can learn this kind of reasoning. By emphasizing the unifying themes of probabilistic reasoning, hypothesis testing, and interdisciplinarity, this book will guide legal participants to formulate scientifically adequate legal arguments and will illustrate the process through critique of a number of areas in which scientific information is invoked in legal argument. Empowering judges and lawyers to reliably evaluate the science confronting them can only enhance credibility of the judicial process, soundness of scholarly debate, and – in the end – a proper functioning of law.

1

Triers of science

Scientific evidence is an inescapable facet of modern litigation. It is fundamental to criminal justice and to civil litigation. What counts as science, however, who gets to make this decision, and how they should go about it are all hotly contested. Nor is this contest limited to the United States. The issue of scientific reliability is a hot topic in England and other Commonwealth jurisdictions, as well as in continental European systems.

In the United States, legislatures, federal, and many state courts have placed the responsibility for evaluating the validity of scientific testimony squarely on judges.[1] Other states continue to use a general-consensus standard for scientific validity, in which it is the scientific community that makes that decision.[2] In those jurisdictions where judges must evaluate scientific validity, the result is that judges – traditionally triers of law, occasionally pressed into service as triers of fact – now must also be triers of science in cases where experts proffer scientific evidence.

Predictably, not everyone is pleased with this new state of affairs, and many question judicial competence in this area. Years after *Daubert v. Merrell Dow Pharmaceuticals, Inc.*[3] and the subsequent amendments to the Federal Rules of

---

1 The Federal Rules of Evidence, amended in response to *Daubert v. Merrell Dow Pharmaceuticals,* 509 U.S. 579 (1993), now provide (in relevant part) that

> If scientific, technical, or other specialized knowledge will assist the trier of fact to understand the evidence or to determine a fact in issue, a witness qualified as an expert . . . may testify . . . if (1) the testimony is based upon sufficient facts or data, (2) the testimony is the product of reliable principles and methods, and (3) the witness has applied the principles and methods reliably to the facts of the case.

Fed. R. Evid. 702.

2 This general-consensus standard is usually referred to as the *Frye* test, from *Frye v. United States,* 293 F. 1013 (D.C. Cir. 1923), explaining that scientific testimony must "be sufficiently established to have gained general acceptance in the particular field in which it belongs."

3 509 U.S. 579 (1993). In a series of three revolutionary cases, the U.S. Supreme Court radically transformed the jurisprudence of expert admissibility determinations, with results that are reverberating throughout the judicial system. In *Daubert v. Merrell Dow Pharmaceuticals, Inc.,* the U.S. Supreme Court laid the groundwork for this transformation by requiring district court judges to evaluate the scientific validity and "fit" of expert testimony. In *General Electric Co. v. Joiner,* the Court reiterated the standards, expounded on its notion of "fit," and explained that although the standards for admissibility had changed, the traditional abuse of discretion standard of review

Evidence made federal judges responsible for assessing scientific validity, judges and lawyers are still grappling with the fact that they can no longer merely count scientific noses[4] but must instead analyze whether expert testimony meets the criteria of good science. Many judges, however, are stymied by the science component of their gatekeeping duties, focusing instead on rules of convenience that have little scientific justification. As a result, judges make unwarranted decisions at both ends of the spectrum: by rejecting even scientifically uncontroversial evidence that would have little trouble finding admissibility under a general-consensus standard and by admitting evidence that is scientifically baseless. But judges need not be unarmed for these decisions.

The U.S. Supreme Court gave judges some rudimentary guidelines in *Daubert* and its progeny, outlining the notions of scientific validity and fit. In addition, the Federal Judicial Center publishes a reference manual (periodically updated) for evaluating scientific evidence, outlining basic theory and optimal practices in a given field.[5] Courses have sprung up to help familiarize judges with scientific issues, and the trial court may appoint its own experts for advice.[6] Federal regulatory agencies like the U.S. Environmental Protection Agency (EPA) also have useful guidelines. These are particularly salient because, like judges, most agency decision makers are not trained scientists, yet they must make creditable scientific validity assessments. Despite these attempts at guidance, however, no coherent conceptual framework has emerged to guide the legal treatment of scientific knowledge. This book seeks to provide that framework.

Throughout this book, I argue that judges are capable of providing intellectual due process to litigants on issues of scientific evidence but that an integral part of that process is the requirement that judges explicitly give the basis for their decision in the form of written opinions, educate themselves about the kinds of evidence before them, and make default assumptions that are justifiable on scientific and policy grounds. The underlying principles of reasoning are not different in law and science, although context and culture determine their application. When discussing rationality, I include inductive, deductive, and abductive reasoning because all three forms are important tools in analysis. In short, for deductive argument to be valid, the truth of the premises must guarantee the truth of the conclusion;

had not. Finally, in *Kumho Tire*, the Court explained that not only do judges have to evaluate the scientific validity of testimony based on the traditional "hard" sciences, they must also evaluate the validity of expert testimony based on the "soft" sciences, such as engineering, handwriting analysis, and psychology. The U.S. Supreme Court, through these three seminal cases, has mandated that federal judges evaluate the validity of such evidence.

4 Before *Daubert*, the federal courts overwhelmingly applied a consensus standard for admissibility. This was the standard of *Frye v. United States*, 293 F. 1013 (D.C. Cir. 1923), explaining that scientific testimony must "be sufficiently established to have gained general acceptance in the particular field in which it belongs."

5 See THE FEDERAL JUDICIAL CENTER REFERENCE MANUAL ON SCIENTIFIC EVIDENCE (1994).

6 FED. R. EVID. 706.

the paradigmatic form of the deductive argument is the Aristotelian syllogism.[7] By inductive reasoning, I mean both inductive generalization, involving probabilistic generalization from the particular, and inductive analogy, in which one concludes that some particular instance will have the aggregate characteristics given in the premises.[8] Exemplary reasoning is sometimes referred to as abduction.[9] The theory of abduction was introduced by Charles Sanders Peirce to explain how scientists select a relatively small number of hypotheses to test from a large number of logically possible explanations for their observations.[10]

To aid nonscientists in this complex reasoning process, I set out a framework for analysis of scientific argument in Chapter 3. The heuristic proposed in Chapter 3 consists of five basic parts and emphasizes the underlying principles common to all fields of science. To meet the requirements of such intellectual due process, I suggest that judges (and the lawyers and scholars who educate them about their cases) must be able to do five things: (1) identify and examine the proffered theory and hypothesis for their power to explain the data; (2) examine the data that supports (and undermines) the expert's theory; (3) use supportable assumptions to fill the inevitable gaps between data and theory; (4) examine the methodology; and (5) engage in probabilistic assessment of the link between the data and the hypothesis.

What's wrong with counting scientific noses?

When scientific evidence surfaces as the focus of a courtroom dispute, it neither should – nor can – be left to the scientists to decide. Determining legal admissibility based on the scientific community's assessment of validity is troubling in both theory and practice. The rule of law is often described as a search for truth in a system that aspires to rationality.[11] Although the meanings of truth and rationality are subject

---

7 *See* DAVID A. SCHUM, EVIDENCE AND INFERENCE FOR THE INTELLIGENCE ANALYST, Vol. I, 18–21 (1987), offering an elegant explanation of inductive, deductive, and abductive reasoning and the process of logical inference.

8 *See* STEPHEN F. BARKER, THE ELEMENTS OF LOGIC, 381–82 (8th ed., 1990).

9 For an article describing the process of legal reasoning by analogy as a species of abduction, see Scott Brewer, *Exemplary Reasoning: Semantics, Pragmatics, and the Rational Force of Reasoning by Analogy*, 109 HARV. L. REV. 923, 947 (1996), where he argues that "abduction is a disciplined (albeit, in contrast to deduction, not a rigidly guided) form of inference; . . . it has a substantial degree of rational force; and . . . it plays a vital role in exemplary, analogical reasoning, just as it does in explanatory and justificatory reasoning in science and other fields of inquiry."

10 CHARLES S. PEIRCE, PHILOSOPHICAL WRITINGS OF PEIRCE, 150–6 (Justus Buchler, ed., 1955).

11 *See* Scott Brewer, *Exemplary Reasoning: Semantics, Pragmatics, and the Rational Force of Reasoning by Analogy*, 109 HARV. L. REV. 923, 929 (1996), explaining that the "normative order constituted by the legal system, informed by 'rule of law' principles as well as by many others, aspires to be rational in significant ways." Asserting truth and rationality goals tends to make people nervous in a postmodern world, where people doubt the achievability of truth, where many believe truth is contextual, and different perspectives on truth abound. *See, e.g.*, DENNIS PATTERSON, LAW AND TRUTH 150 (1996), characterizing postmodernism as emphasizing the idea that "no practice or discourse enjoys a privileged position vis-a-vis others" and asserting that "truth in law is a matter of forms of legal argument." Some postmodern scholars ditch the concept of law as a

to debate in an open society, a structured reasoning process relating sensory input to theoretical explanation is fundamental. This requires accurate information and justifiable inferences. It is the necessity of a structured reasoning process that argues for a gatekeeper to assess the scientific validity of expert testimony. The object of demystifying scientific argument and making it more accessible to lawyers and judges is not to transform lawyers and judges into amateur scientists[12] but to help them resolve a legal policy issue: whether, given the state of knowledge about a particular scientific hypothesis proffered by experts, that hypothesis is useful in resolving a legal dispute. The purpose of the admissibility inquiry is not to decide whose expert is correct but whether the expert can provide information to help the factfinder resolve an issue in a legal case. This is a decision that is quintessentially legal. In sum, the reason we need gatekeepers is to ensure that the statements offered into evidence comport with permissible legal theories, embedded as they are in cultural systems of belief, assumptions, and claims about the world. Although what we seek to know are the facts, facts are inevitably theory-laden.[13] Therefore, in an adversary system, it is the judge whose role it is to manage coherence by reference to what is relevant to the legal determination.

Nor is this an impossible task to place on the judge. Requiring judges to act as evidentiary gatekeepers – analyzing proffered testimony for the soundness of its underlying theory, technique, and application, and analyzing that testimony in light of the issues posed by the case – does not seem like an insurmountable judicial task. After all, judges are supposed to direct legal proceedings based on logical analysis and considered judgment. Moreover, judges are far from the only outsiders who must evaluate scientific evidence. Scientists who work outside of a given field critique each others' work all the time – that is how science advances: by taking information gleaned from one discipline and applying it to another.

search for truth entirely, seeing it rather as a contest for power. *See, e.g.,* Carrie Menkel-Meadow, "The Trouble with the Adversary System," 38 WM. & MARY L. REV. 5, 13 (1996), arguing that the adversary system is not a search for truth but a contest, the goal of which is to win. Just because our attempts to discover the truth may be only relatively successful, just because we may have different perspectives on what is truth, it does not mean the search should be abandoned or that the effort to improve the process unavailing. For an amusing and enlightening explanation of why both visions (i.e., law as truth search and law as contest) may be correct, *see* Arthur A. Leff, *Law and,* 87 YALE L. J. 989, 1005 (1978), acknowledging that although the adversary system "does seem more or less well adapted to providing the more or less accurate data needed for the rational operation [of the system and is] largely capable of answering the question 'what happened' at the legally relevant time," there are important ways in which it is also a contest.

12 Chief Justice Rhenquist expressed this concern in his dissent in *Daubert,* where he worried that the majority was forcing judges "to become amateur scientists in order to perform [their] role." *Daubert,* 509 U.S. 601.

13 *See, e.g.,* THOMAS S. KUHN, THE STRUCTURE OF SCIENTIFIC REVOLUTIONS, 200 (2d ed., 1970), arguing that the manner in which science develops is largely determined by values and experience shared by the scientific community; Willard V. Quine, "Epistemology Naturalized" in *Ontological Relativity and Other Essays,* 83 (1969), explaining the "reciprocal containment" of "epistemology in natural science and science in epistemology." Thus, a commitment to empiricism does not preclude the understanding that knowledge and theory are inseparable.

This is possible, even without intimate knowledge of the type of research being discussed, because underlying all scientific disciplines are common understandings about probabilistic and analogy-based reasoning.

The framework provided here is based on unifying themes common to scientific thinking of all stripes. Understanding the language and structure of scientific argument and the way "science" is produced provides an invaluable tool in deciphering the logic behind scientific testimony. The framework proposed here is intended to resolve some major issues on which the courts are still foundering. Even nonscientists can learn this kind of reasoning. By emphasizing the unifying themes of probabilistic reasoning, hypothesis testing, and interdisciplinarity, this book seeks to provide the guidance legal participants need for scientifically adequate legal arguments. It illustrates the process through a critique of a number of areas in which scientific information is invoked in legal argument.

Not only is counting scientific noses bad for theoretical reasons, it does not work well in practice either. In practice, the general-consensus standard devolved into a meaningless exercise because it was nearly always possible to define the expert's field so narrowly that consensus by a cohort of the expert's was virtually guaranteed. Thus, the general-consensus standard often resulted in a cursory inquiry into the expert's credentials without any screening of the substance of the testimony. In this way, voiceprints, bitemark and handwriting analysis, and a whole cornucopia of questionable exercises masquerading as science crept into litigation.

Admissibility of expert testimony Pre-*Daubert*

Daubert[14] emerged against the backdrop of immense public controversy about the perceived flood of "junk science" that, according to some popular critics, threatened to inundate the courts.[15] For years, *Frye v. United States*[16] was the predominant standard for the admissibility of scientific evidence. *Frye* was a murder case involving expert testimony based on an early version of the polygraph technique, which the court found inadmissible because polygraph testing had not achieved general acceptance in the relevant scientific community. The *Frye* test asked whether the proffered expert polygraph evidence – including the conclusions reached – was generally accepted in a relevant community of experts. *Frye* thus offered a standard of admissibility based on the general acceptance of the proposed testimony by a relevant community of experts and permitted peer review and publication to substitute for any attempt at analysis by the court.

Although a majority of courts in the United States applied the general acceptance standard, its results were anything but uniform. Some courts applying the general

---

14 *Daubert v. Merrell Dow Pharmaceuticals, Inc.*, 509 U.S. 579 (1993).

15 *See, e.g.*, PETER HUBER, GALILEO'S REVENGE: JUNK SCIENCE IN THE COURTROOM (1991), castigating the use of "junk science" in the courts. Huber's exposé itself came under attack as a form of junk science because it relied on anecdotal evidence. *See* Kenneth J. Cheesboro, *Galileo's Retort: Peter Huber's Junk Scholarship*, 41 AM. U. L. REV. 1637, 1651, rejecting Huber's work as factually incorrect and the product of faulty legal analysis.

16 293 F. 1013 (D.C. Cir. 1923).

acceptance test did little more than "count noses," while others performed in-depth analyses. Thus, the apparently straightforward standard provoked a number of controversies. For one thing, it frequently was unclear which facets of the testimony or underlying rationale had to be generally accepted. For another, the *Frye* standard failed to account for the phenomenon that much knowledge slips into general acceptance without any careful examination, especially where that knowledge has been accepted for a long time. Most controversial of all, however, was the *Frye* test's substitution of peer consensus and publication for any detailed analysis by the court. In effect, this permitted nonjudicial actors to make what is essentially a judicial policy decision and deflected responsibility away from the judge.

Consequently, at a time when scientific evidence was becoming increasingly important in resolving legal disputes, the standards for its courtroom use were anything but certain. Not surprisingly, criticism of the legal system's ability to cope with scientific evidence mounted. Among the various solutions proposed were separate science courts, special administrative tribunals, and an interdisciplinary council established to advise the courts. It was against this background that the U.S. Supreme Court granted certiorari in *Daubert*.

The *Daubert* analysis

Daubert v. Merrell Dow Pharmaceuticals, Inc. was a civil case involving claims that Bendectin, a morning-sickness remedy that the plaintiffs' mothers had taken during pregnancy, had caused the plaintiffs' limb-reduction birth defects. The evidence at issue consisted of epidemiological reanalyses, in which data obtained in previously published studies was reanalyzed and proffered to support the plaintiffs' claims. The trial court found the plaintiffs' proffer insufficient to withstand the defendants' motion for summary judgment because it did not meet with general acceptance in the field to which it belongs. The Ninth Circuit affirmed, holding an expert opinion inadmissible absent general acceptance of the underlying technique, and the U.S. Supreme Court granted certiorari to resolve "the proper standard for the admission of expert testimony."

The U.S. Supreme Court dispatched the general acceptance test in a few paragraphs, finding it an "austere standard" that was superseded by adoption of the Federal Rules of Evidence in 1975. The Court explained that the two-pronged test of Rule 702 requires judges to assume a gatekeeping role by inquiring into the reliability of the evidence and its helpfulness to the jury. This requires the trial judge to conduct an independent inquiry into the scientific validity, reliability, and relevance of the proposed testimony. To guide this scrutiny, the Court outlined four nondefinitive factors: the trial judge should consider whether the theory can be and has been tested, its error rate, whether it has been subjected to peer review and publication, and whether it has met with general acceptance in the scientific community.

Many judges question judicial abilities to assess scientific validity. Chief Justice Rehnquist, for example, in his *Daubert* dissent, felt the majority was requiring district judges to become "amateur scientists." On remand, the Ninth Circuit's Judge Kozinski was openly sarcastic about the feasibility of the effort.[17] Notwithstanding such skepticism, however, many judges have risen amply to the occasion. A fair number of them were engaging in a validity analysis long before *Daubert* required it,[18] thus demonstrating that judges can indeed learn to think like scientists, or at least become adept at recognizing faulty logic when they hear it.

In the years since *Daubert*, the results admittedly have been uneven. Judges comfortable with analyzing scientific validity before *Daubert* continue to do so; those who are too discomforted by the new analysis are finding ways to circumvent it. Some of the avoidance techniques include the erection of barriers by insisting the evidence meet requirements that have little to do with its inherent logic. For example, in the *Daubert* remand, Judge Kozinski added an unwarranted and illogical new admissibility factor that he found to trump those listed by the U.S. Supreme Court: whether the research was conducted independent of the litigation. Even Judge Kozinski recognized the problematic nature of his new factor for criminal evidence, where most of the research involved is generated only for litigation. There is virtually no other "market" than litigation for identification tests.

Although the ostensible difference between *Frye* and *Daubert* is that the gatekeeping responsibility has been explicitly shifted to the judge from the scientific community, it is unclear whether the practical consequence of this difference will mean that cases will be decided differently using the *Daubert* analysis than they were under *Frye*. Some skeptics contend that *Frye* and *Daubert* essentially are indeterminate and cannot account for the results in particular cases. Other critics contend that *Daubert* has changed little about the way courts handle scientific evidence other than changing the label. At least one major survey of judicial competence to evaluate scientific evidence has been conducted, which concluded that judges lack the scientific literacy necessary to do so.[19] However, such criticism fails to consider the changes that criminal laboratories are already beginning to undertake as a result of the increased scrutiny of laboratory protocols and techniques. In addition, the scientific validity of previously accepted identification techniques is now being challenged with some success. Absent the heightened scrutiny required under *Daubert*, it is doubtful that such changes would have emerged.

---

17 *Daubert v. Merrell Dow Pharmaceuticals, Inc.*, 43 F. 3d 1311 (9th Cir.), *cert. denied*, 116 S. Ct. 189 (1995).

18 For example, Judge Becker of the Third Circuit employed a validity test for determining admissibility of scientific evidence in *United States v. Downing*, 753 F. 2d, 1224 (3rd Cir. 1985), cited by the U.S. Supreme Court in *Daubert*.

19 *See* Sophia Gratowski et al., *Asking the Gatekeepers: A National Survey of Judges on Judging Expert Evidence in a Post-Daubert World*, 25 Law & Hum. Behav. 433, 452 (2001), surveying state court judges and concluding that although most judges – in both *Daubert* and non-*Daubert* states – believed that the role of gatekeeper was appropriate irrespective of the state standard for admissibility, "judges have difficulty operationalizing the *Daubert* criteria and applying them, especially with respect to falsifiability and error rate."

Daubert has caused a profound change in the rhetoric of judicial analysis and has focused the law on the necessity of a test for the admissibility of scientific evidence that considers the evidence itself and not merely the conclusions of a witness. Courts must now at least go through the motions of examining the scientific validity of proffered evidence. Obviously, some courts are more adept at the required analysis than others, and some courts are notably recalcitrant in performing it at all. Nonetheless, the level of the debate has changed. No longer is it enough to obtain the approval of a cohort of the expert's cronies willing to vouch for the technique. Even in state courts that have eschewed the *Daubert* standard in favor of general consensus, courts are beginning to examine the substance of the testimony. At the very least, *Daubert* has focused attention on the importance of examining the underlying theory and technique rather than just the proffered conclusion. The U.S. Supreme Court has made it explicit that examining the logical basis of expert reasoning is what judges should be doing when they make the admissibility decision, rather than merely polling professional opinion.

What's happening in other common-law countries?

Canada

Canadian courts have cited *Daubert* with approval, and analysis of expert testimony appears increasingly to be based on judicial gatekeeping.[20] In *Mohan*,[21] the Canadian Supreme Court set out four criteria for admissibility: relevance, necessity, absence of an exclusionary rule, and proper qualifications for the expert. Subsequent cases have referred to *Mohan* as being in parallel with *Daubert* in imposing gatekeeping criteria on judges regarding the reliability of expert testimony.[22]

English law

Under English law, expert-opinion testimony is admissible on matters of specialized knowledge, on which the court would be unable properly to reach a conclusion unaided.[23] As in the United States, experts may be court-appointed or

---

20 *See, e.g., R. v. Murrin,* 181 DLR (4th) 320 (1999), approving *Daubert.* The Canadian Supreme Court, although not adopting *Daubert,* has discussed reliability as an essential facet of the relevance criteria for expert testimony. *See R. v. Mohan,* 89 CCC (3d) 402 (1994), reliability is part of the relevance determination.

21 *R. v. Mohan,* 89 CCC (3d) 402 (1994).

22 *See, e.g., R. v. J.* (J-L), 37 C.R. (5th) 203 (2000), referring to judge as a gatekeeper and citing *Daubert* with approval as being in parallel with *Mohan.*

23 Law Reform Committee, Seventeenth Report, 1970 Cmnd. 4489, 6 ("Seventeenth Report"); Civil Procedure Rules 1998 (Eng.). Under the new civil procedure rules, parties are encouraged to select an expert jointly and the court may direct discussions between experts to identify expert issues and attempt to reach an agreement (Rule 35, Civil Procedure Rules 1998 [amended 2001]). In criminal procedure also, an expert may give an opinion "on any relevant matter which forms part of his professional expertise . . . and to draw upon technical information widely used by members of the expert's profession." Criminal Justice Act 2003 (Eng.), ch. 44, Explanatory Notes. *See also* Mike Redmayne, *Expert Evidence and Criminal Justice,* 140 (2001), arguing that the rule in *R. v. Turner,* 1 QB 835 (1975), primarily used to exclude psychological testimony, is based on the concept that for

adversarial.[24] As long as the expert is qualified, however, there is little inquiry into the reliability of the science or techniques the expert espouses.[25] A number of controversies over the misuse of scientific information has erupted in criminal cases, however, and precipitated the formation of the Royal Commission on Criminal Justice,[26] which has acknowledged problems with the trial process but, nonetheless, left the admissibility inquiry as a question of expert qualification. This solution has not stilled the controversy, which recently flared up again in the Sally Clark[27] case, in which a mother was convicted of murdering two of her apparently healthy children, who had died suddenly as infants. The prosecution's expert, a pediatrician, testified that it was extremely rare for two children in a family to both die of sudden infant death syndrome (SIDS). The expert testified that the rate of double SIDS deaths in a family were about 1 in 73 million.[28]

Sally Clark was convicted of smothering her two infants. The expert was not a statistician, nor was one involved in the trial. On appeal, although two expert statisticians were employed for the defense, and wrote reports exposing the prosecutor's fallacy, the court dismissed the appeal, declining to let them testify, and concluding that "any error in the way in which statistical evidence was treated at trial was of minimal significance."[29] On a second appeal, based on newly discovered evidence of infection that the pathologist had failed to disclose, Sally Clark prevailed. The outcry over the unreliability of the pediatrician's statistical testimony, however, has caused the Criminal Cases Review Commission to undertake a review of more than two hundred cases involving parental murder of a child, as well as thousands of cases in which a custodial parent has lost parental rights, based on this kind of testimony.

Australia and New Zealand

Australia and New Zealand, like England, have no explicit requirements that judges scrutinize expert testimony for reliability. Following a number of controversies

---

expert testimony to be admissible, it must be helpful to the court or to the jury in its deliberations. This is similar to the requirement of Rule 702 of the U.S. Federal Rules of Evidence that to be admissible, the testimony must "assist the trier of fact." Federal Rules of Evidence 702. The U.S. federal rules go farther, however, in also requiring a reliability analysis.

24 Under Order 40 of the Rules of the U.S. Supreme Court, parties may cross-examine court-appointed experts and offer one witness in rebuttal. Seventeenth Report, 8. As in the United States, however, courts have made little use of the power to appoint an expert. *Id.*

25 *See, e.g.,* Mike Redmayne, *Expert Evidence and Criminal Justice,* 95 (2001), noting that "[t]he closest thing to a reliability-based rule in English law is the rule that an expert must have appropriate qualifications."

26 The Royal Commission on Criminal Justice, Report Cm. 2263 (HMSO 1993), considering whether changes were needed in the role of experts in criminal proceedings.

27 *EWCA Crim,* 1020 (2003).

28 For a discussion of the case and an explanation of why the expert's use of statistics was fundamentally wrong, *see* Deidre Dwyer, "The Duties of Expert Witnesses of Fact and Opinion: *R. v. Clark (Sally),*" 7 EVIDENCE & PROOF 264 (2003).

29 *See* Philip Dawid, *Statistics and the Law* in EVIDENCE (John Swenson-Wright, et al., eds. 2006) (forthcoming; Cambridge University Press).

involving questionable scientific testimony, the Australian legislature enacted evidence rules in 1995 modeled on the 1975 U.S. Federal Rules of Evidence.[30] In particular, Section 79 is based on Federal Rule of Evidence 702, and both incorporate a knowledge requirement. However, the new legislation does not impose a duty to scrutinize expert testimony for scientific validity. Under the Australian rules, emphasis is on the judge's duty to weigh probative value against unfair prejudice.[31] That does not foreclose a judge from scrutinizing scientific validity, but it does not encourage it either. As in the United States, both pre- and post-*Daubert*, those judges who wish to engage in scrutinizing can certainly find ample justification to do so.[32] The problems that remain are encouraging those who are not such enthusiastic gatekeepers into taking this role seriously and giving them the tools with which to do it.

New Zealand also is engaged in legislative reform; but in both Australia and New Zealand, the admissibility of expert testimony appears to be governed by common-law requirements that the testimony be based on specialized knowledge, outside the common knowledge of the factfinder, and that the facts supporting the testimony also be admissible.[33] Although the courts may sometimes use this last factor as a reliability screening device, there is no requirement that they do so, and the results are uneven. Some New Zealand courts have applied the equivalent of the *Frye* test,[34]

---

30 *See* Ian Freckelton, *Judicial Attitudes Toward Scientific Evidence: The Antipodean Experience*, 30 U.C. DAVIS L. REV. 1137, 1176 (1997), "In 1995, the federal and New South Wales jurisdictions . . . passed new evidence legislation, intended to be model legislation comparable to the United States 1975 Federal Rules of Evidence."

31 Sections 135 and 137 of the Evidence Act provide for the exclusion of evidence where its probative value is outweighed by unfair prejudice. Evidence Act, Austl. C. Acts No. 2 §§ 135, 137 (1995).

32 For example, in *Makita (Australia) Pty Ltd. V. Sprowles* (2001) 52 NSWLR 705, [85], Heydon J. stated the admissibility of expert testimony under the Evidence Act to be as follows:

> In short, if evidence tendered as expert opinion evidence is to be admissible, it must be agreed or demonstrated that there is a field of "specialised knowledge"; there must be an identified aspect of that field in which the witness demonstrates that by reason of specific training, study or experience, the witness has become an expert; the opinion proffered must be "wholly or substantially based on the witness's expert knowledge"; so far as the opinion is based on facts "observed" by the expert, they must be identified and admissibly proved by the expert, and so far as the opinion is based on "assumed" or "accepted" facts, they must be identified and proved in some other way; it must be established that facts on which the opinion is based form a proper foundation for it, and the opinion of an expert requires demonstration or examination of the scientific or other intellectual basis of the conclusions reached: that is, the expert's evidence must explain how the field of "specialised knowledge" in which the witness is an expert by reason of "training, study or experience," and on which the opinion is "wholly or substantially based," applies to the facts assumed or observed so as to produce the opinion as propounded. If all these matters are not made explicit, it is not possible to be sure whether the opinion is based wholly or substantially on the expert's specialised knowledge. If the court cannot be sure of that, the evidence is strictly speaking not admissible, and, so far as it is admissible, of diminished weight.

33 *See R. v. Perry*, 49 *A. Crim. R.*, 243, 249 (Ct. Crim. App. N. S. W., 1990), the admissibility of opinion evidence depends on the admissibility of the facts on which the opinion is based.

34 *See R. v. C.S.*, 11 C.R.N.Z. 45, 47 (H.C., 1993), excluding psychological testimony about child sexual abuse victim behavior patterns because not "firmly founded upon accepted scientific research."

while others have rejected it.[35] In attempting to clarify the standard for admissibility of forensic hair and blood analyses, the New Zealand High Court – after considering not only New Zealand precedent but also admissibility standards in England, Australia, Canada, and the United States – chose a flexible reliability standard emphasizing that "[t]o be helpful, the evidence must pass a threshold which can conveniently be called the minimum threshold of reliability."[36] The court did not, however, offer any guidance about how to apply the required threshold.

Why not let the jury decide?

Even assuming – as I argue – that the legal system is the proper locus for deciding admissibility questions and that judges are capable of handling the validity inquiry, there is still a major question that must be answered. Why do we need gatekeepers? This is a question on which even the U.S. Supreme Court is divided. The Court in *Barefoot*[37] – as a constitutional matter – thought that the adversary system could be relied on to present enough information to jurors so that they could sort reliable from unreliable expert testimony. The *Daubert* Court thought – as an evidentiary matter – that expert testimony needed to be screened for relevance and reliability first. Which approach gets us closer to the goals of the rule of law?

Epistemology – the study of the nature and grounds of knowledge – has an important bearing on this question. From an epistemic vantage point, the question of whether we need judges to act as gatekeepers depends on whether gatekeeping actually promotes better, that is, more accurate and more rational, decision making in the context of a particular social practice: here, the context of legal proceedings.[38] Judges and juries must make decisions that have a number of alternative solutions, the choice of which will vary based on the information presented, and they must make these decisions within a limited time frame. This is the definition of complex decision making and it has implications for the quality of the judgment reached. People use shortcuts in evaluating complex information, and scientific testimony is

---

35 *See R. v. R.*, 11 C.R.N.Z. 402, 405 (H.C., 1994), refusing to examine either general acceptance or validity of repressed memories of abuse.

36 *R. v. Calder*, No. 154/94, 7 (N.Z.H.C., April 12, 1995).

37 *Barefoot v. Estelle*, 463 U.S. 880 (1983), refusing to exclude future dangerousness testimony as a constitutional matter. The *Barefoot* decision was based on constitutional grounds and the *Daubert* decision was evidentiary, so *Daubert* did not overrule *Barefoot*. As a matter of logic, however, it is difficult to reconcile the rationale of *Barefoot* with that of *Daubert*. This issue is more fully discussed in Chapter Seven.

38 The question asked by social epistemology is what norms work best under the real-world limits of a particular social practice. *See* Brian Leiter, *The Epistemology of Admissibility*, 1997 BYU L. Rev., 803, 809, suggesting two lines of inquiry: "paternalism," whether substituting judicial screening will enable jurors to make more accurate decisions; and "ought equals can," that is, whether shortcomings in cognition will preclude either judges or jurors from making an accurate decision.

quintessentially complex information. Empirically, juries have difficulty in assessing scientific testimony.[39] So do judges.[40]

However, although judges are just as prone to use unconscious shortcuts as juries, there are a number of factors that counteract this tendency in judges. First, the structured-reasoning process undertaken in a *Daubert* inquiry improves performance in cognitive tasks.[41] Second, judges are repeat players in the way that

39 *See* Daniel A. Krauss and Bruce D. Sales, *The Effects of Clinical and Scientific Expert Testimony on Juror Decision Making in Capital Sentencing,* 7 PSYCHOL. PUB. POL'Y & L., 267, 270 (2001), research suggests that jurors are incapable of differentiating more scientifically valid expert testimony from less accurate testimony. *See also* W. Kip Viscusi, *Jurors, Judges, and the Mistreatment of Risk by the Courts,* 30 J. LEGAL STUD. 107, 135 (2001) (finding that judges were "less prone to over-estimate low probability events" than jurors); Sonja J. Ivkovac & Valerie P. Hans, *Jurors Evaluation of Expert Testimony: Judging the Messenger and the Message,* 28 LAW & SOCIAL INQUIRY 441, 442–443 (2003) (examining jurors' reactions in civil trials and concluding that expert characteristics as well as the substance and style of the testimony contributed significantly to the impact of such testimony on jurors). *But see* Theodore Eisenberg, et al., *Judge-Jury Agreement in Criminal Cases: A Partial Replication of Kalven & Zeisel's* The American Jury, 2 J. EMPIRICAL LEGAL STUD. 171–207 (2005) (finding high agreement between criminal judge and jury in evaluating complex evidence).

40 In a study of state court judges, Sophia Gatowski and her colleagues found that although judges overwhelmingly endorsed a gatekeeping role for judges even in those states following the general-consensus standard, a fair percentage of them could not apply the standards correctly. *See* Sophia Gatowski, et al., *Asking the Gatekeepers: Results of a National Survey of Judges on Judging Expert Evidence in a Post-Daubert World,* 25 LAW & HUM. BEHAV., 433 (2001), finding that with respect to the most important inquiries, falsifiability and error rate, 35 percent of judges' explanations of falsifiability were unequivocally wrong, 10 percent were wrong in their assessment of error rate, and 86 percent gave error rates that were equivocal. For a critique of courts' post-*Daubert* handling of scientific evidence, *see* M. Kovera & B. McAuliff, *The Effects of Peer Review and Evidence Quality on Judges' Evaluations of Psychological Science: Are Judges Effective Gatekeepers?,* 85 J. APPL. PSYCHOL. 574–86 (2000) (finding judges may be insensitive to experimenter bias or absence of controls); Veronica B. Dahir, et al., *Judicial Application of Daubert to Psychological Syndrome and Profile Evidence,* 11 PSYCHOL., PUB. POL'Y & L. 62 (2005) (finding a "strong tendency for judges to continue to rely on more traditional standards such as general acceptance and qualifications of the expert when assessing psychological syndrome and profile evidence"). In a study undertaken by the Rand Institute for Civil Justice of 399 federal district court opinions between 1980 and 1999, the authors found a significant rise in the proportion of evidence excluded post-*Daubert*. *See* Lloyd Dixon & Brian Gill, *Changes in the Standards for Admitting Expert Evidence in Federal Civil Cases Since the* Daubert *Decision,* RAND INSTITUTE FOR CIVIL JUSTICE REPORT (2001). However, the Federal Judicial Center, in two surveys of federal district court judges, and one survey of attorneys, found that, although there was a marked increase in scrutiny of expert testimony post-*Daubert*, judges identified general acceptance, peer review and insufficient theory testing as problematic in only 8% of the excluded evidence, and error rate as problematic in only 2%, suggesting that the *Daubert* factors were not being employed by the judges in their scrutiny. *See* Carol Kafka, et al., *Judge and Attorney Experience, Practice and Conclusions Re: Expert Testimony in Federal Civil Trials,* 8 PSYCHOL., PUB. POL'Y & L. 309 (2002). A study of criminal cases similarly found that there was a "lack of discussion devoted to the four *Daubert* criteria" in either trial or appellate court opinions. Jennifer L. Groscup, et al., *The Effects of* Daubert *on the Admissibility of Expert Testimony in State and Federal Criminal Cases,* 8 PSYCHOL., PUB. POL'Y & L. 339 (2002).

41 *See, e.g.,* Christopher Jepson, et al., *Inductive Reasoning: Competence or Skill,* 3 BEHAV. & BRAIN SCI. 494, 498 (1983), discussing studies indicating that training in reasoning improves performance dramatically; Richard E. Nisbett et al., *Teaching Reasoning,* 238 SCI. 625, 630 (1987), advocating formal training in the "rules underlying reasoning." Training is much more effective for pragmatic applications of reasoning than for abstract principles. *See* Patricia W. Cheng, et al., *Pragmatic Versus Syntactic Approaches to Training Deductive Reasoning,* in RULES FOR REASONING, 186 (Richard E.

juries are not. Repeat exposure to the decision-making task – at least in the presence of feedback – can improve performance.[42] Third, judges are accountable, at least in some respects. They must present the bases for their decisions, and those bases are subject to scrutiny and to being overruled by a higher court. Accountability, which is difficult to achieve for group judgments like those made by the jury, is more effective for individual decision makers like trial judges.[43] Individual judgments under conditions of accountability are more likely to be careful and thoughtful.[44] These studies indicate the soundness of judicial screening for relevance and reliability.

This is no denigration of the jury. The judge should perform this function not because judges are innately more thoughtful or responsible than jurors but because a structured inquiry into scientific validity for which they will be held accountable forces judges to engage in what cognitive psychologists refer to as "active, open-minded thinking."[45] A basic insight of the common-law system is that a structured-reasoning process improves judgment. Thus, in allocating the decision process between judge and jury, and to give litigants the process that is due, methodologies (such as the rules of evidence) need to be employed routinely and consistently in a process reasonably designed to ascertain the truth.

Nisbett, ed. 1993) noting that "the near total ineffectiveness of purely abstract training in logic contrasts dramatically with the ready ease with which people seem able to apply a naturally acquired pragmatic reasoning schema," and noting that people "who received a brief training session on the obligation schema improved markedly on selection problems interpretable in terms of that schema."

42 *See, e.g.,* Jonathan J. Koehler, *The Base Rate Fallacy Reconsidered: Descriptive, Normative and Methodological Challenges*, 19 BEHAV. & BRAIN SCI. 1, 6, citing studies showing that people learned to use base rates more effectively after receiving feedback about their errors from their experience; for example, physicians who learned the low base rate of pneumonia from their practice experience relied heavily on the base rate when making diagnoses, and auditors "learned and used the base rate for financial statement errors most easily by directly experiencing those errors"; but cautioning that "personally experienced base rates were used only by those who also experienced the relationship between the base rate and the diagnostic information."

43 *See* Kenneth L. Bettenhausen, *Five Years of Groups Research*, 17 J. MGT. 345, 361 (1991); Shelley E. Taylor, *The Social Being in Social Psychology*, in VOL. I, HANDBOOK OF SOCIAL PSYCHOLOGY, FOURTH EDITION, 76 (Daniel T. Gilbert et al., eds., 1998).

44 *See* Kenneth L. Bettenhausen, *Five Years of Groups Research: What We Have Learned and What Needs to Be Addressed*, 17 J. MGT. 345, 361 (1991), citing studies demonstrating that people in groups of sixteen who shared responsibility for the judgment task "used less complex judgment strategies than subjects working alone," although "multiple judges who expected to justify their judgments worked as hard as individual judges."

45 JONATHAN BARON, THINKING AND DECIDING, 191–92 (3d ed., 2000), defining active open-minded thinking as willingness to consider new evidence and opposing arguments before reaching a conclusion; and, specifically, (1) engaging in a search that is thorough in proportion to the question; (2) having confidence that is appropriate to the amount and quality of thinking done; and (3) being open to other possibilities.

2

What is intellectual due process?

The rule of law is often described as a search for truth in a system that aspires to rationality.[1] The rule of law is also conceived as a vital safeguard from the paradox of freedom in democracies, in which the strong – physically or economically – if not restrained from preying on the weak, defeat the freedom that enabled them.[2] An integral component of this vision is – at least in the United States and for criminal trials elsewhere in the former Commonwealth countries – the jury.[3] The jury system, which provides a structure for citizen participation and brings the voice of the community into the process of legal decision making, is a key feature of the separation of powers doctrine.[4] At the same time, the bifurcation of

---

1 *See* Scott Brewer, *Exemplary Reasoning: Semantics, Pragmatics, and the Rational Force of Reasoning by Analogy*, 109 Harv. L. Rev. 923, 929 (1996), explaining that the "normative order constituted by the legal system, informed by 'rule of law' principles as well as by many others, aspires to be rational in significant ways." Asserting truth and rationality goals tends to make people nervous in a postmodern world, where people doubt the achievability of truth, where many believe truth is contextual, and different perspectives on truth abound. *See, e.g.,* Dennis Patterson, Law and Truth, 150 (1996), characterizing postmodernism as emphasizing the idea that "no practice or discourse enjoys a privileged position vis-a-vis others" and asserting that "truth in law is a matter of forms of legal argument." Some postmodern scholars ditch the concept of law as a search for truth entirely, seeing it rather as a contest for power. *See, e.g.,* Carrie Menkel-Meadow, *The Trouble with the Adversary System*, 38 Wm. & Mary L. Rev. 5, 13 (1996), arguing that the adversary system is not a search for truth but a contest, the goal of which is to win. However, just because our attempts to discover the truth may be only relatively successful, just because we may have different perspectives on what is truth, does not mean that the search should be abandoned or that the effort to improve the process unavailing. For an amusing and enlightening explanation of why both visions (law as truth search and law as contest) may be correct, *see* Arthur A. Leff, "Law and," 87 Yale L. J. 989, 1005 (1978), acknowledging that although the adversary system "does seem more or less well adapted to providing the more or less accurate data needed for the rational operation [of the system and is] largely capable of answering the question 'what happened' at the legally relevant time," there are important ways in which it is also a contest.
2 *See* Karl R. Popper, The Open Society and Its Enemies, 124 (5th ed., 1966), discussing the paradox of freedom; William Twining, Theories of Evidence: Bentham and Wigmore, 89, 90 (1985), explaining the truth theory of adjudication as the foundation of good government and remarking that "justice absolutely depends upon it."
3 *See* R. Simon, The Jury: Its Role in American Society, 6–7 (1980), describing the role of popular participation in the administration of justice.
4 *See generally,* Charles W. Wolfram, *The Constitutional History of the Seventh Amendment*, 57 Minn. L. Rev. 639, 653–71 (1973), discussing the jury as a popular check on the three branches of government.

decision-making duties between judge and jury has consequences, a primary one being the restriction on the information that the jury will be given and able to use for its determination.

One hotly debated area in this bifurcation has been the use of expert witnesses and the necessity of judicial screening for validity of the expert's science before permitting experts to testify. For scientific evidence, the question now is whether the testimony has met the standards and methods of science.[5] Even in state courts that have eschewed the *Daubert* standard in favor of the old general acceptance rule, there is increased concern with scientific validity. In this chapter, I suggest some reasons why the judge is the appropriate decision maker for this issue and why, from a cognitive standpoint, it is important to the goal of rationality that the judge perform this screening function.

A fundamental tenet of evidentiary principles is that only facts having relevance – rational probative value – should be admissible in the search for truth.[6] The common law's long-standing requirement that judges act as gatekeepers, screening irrelevant information from the jury; explaining the basis of their reasoning; and justifying that basis is the cornerstone of a system that aspires to rationality.[7] This system requires accurate information and justifiable inferences. Although what we seek to know are the facts, facts are inevitably bound up with theory. In an adversary system, this is why it is the judge's role to manage coherence by reference to what is relevant to the legal determination. This cornerstone, it turns out, has support in cognitive psychology.

Even federal judges, with their life tenure, are subject to political pressure, a point that worried the framers and was a subject of discussion during the ratification debates. *See id.* at 695–96. The jury was expected to restore community values to what might otherwise become arbitrary decision making. *See* B. SCHWARTZ, THE BILL OF RIGHTS: A DOCUMENTARY HISTORY, 3–16 (1971), discussing the function of the jury as a bulwark against tyranny.

5 *See generally,* ARTHUR FINE, THE SHAKY GAME: EINSTEIN, REALISM, AND THE QUANTUM THEORY (1986), asserting that questions about the truth claims of science must be answered by reference to the methods and standards of science.

6 The doctrines of relevance and probativity are expressed as follows under the Federal Rules of Evidence:

"Relevant evidence" means evidence having any tendency to make the existence of any fact that is of consequence to the determination of the action more probable or less probable than it would be without the evidence. (Fed. R. Evid. 402)

And:

Although relevant, evidence may be excluded if its probative value is substantially outweighed by the danger of unfair prejudice, confusion of the issues, or misleading the jury, or by considerations of undue delay, waste of time, or needless presentation of cumulative evidence. FED. R. EVID. 403

A corollary is that all facts that have rational probative value should be admissible unless forbidden under a competing concern of the justice system (e.g., the improper uses of state power implicated in the exclusionary rule). *See* Twining, note 2, p. 152.

7 *See* Brewer, note 1, p. 929, exploring the rational force of reasoning from precedent, given that the "normative order constituted by the legal system, informed by 'rule of law' principles as well as by many others, aspires to be rational in significant ways."

Accurate information as a prerequisite to rationality

Many of the rules of evidence are based on a concern for accuracy. Witnesses with first-hand knowledge about the circumstances and people involved in a legal dispute are brought in to testify about their observations. Because they might lie, the witnesses are required to take an oath. Cross-examination is further designed to probe the accuracy of their statements.

Scientific experts, however, are allowed to testify and, unlike other witnesses to offer opinions, not because they have observed anything about the parties or the dispute for themselves but because they have knowledge about how the world works. With regard to scientific experts, the concern for accuracy is not only that they will lie or exaggerate (although they are also required to take an oath) but also whether their observations are accurate; and, whether – given the state of knowledge about a particular scientific hypothesis a scientific expert may offer – that hypothesis is useful in resolving a legal dispute.[8] The purpose of the admissibility inquiry is to decide whether the expert can provide information to help the factfinder resolve an issue in the case. That is, the judge must decide whether a descriptive claim about the world has sufficient indicia of reliability (i.e., the concern for accuracy) and relevance to the case at hand (i.e., the concern for rationality) to enter the courtroom.

Structured reasoning and empirical correspondence as rational prerequisites

The twin rule-of-law goals of truth and rationality mean that rationality does not operate in a closed system. Instead, rationality inevitably refers to the real world.[9] Justice and rationality only have meaning in the context of our underlyng goals.[10] The requirements of coherence and correspondence are both prerequisites of a framework for justice.

---

8 Bear in mind that the judge does not have to decide whether a given scientific hypothesis is actually correct. Rather, what the gatekeeper must determine is whether there are good grounds for the expert's testimony. Once this determination has been made, it remains the jury's province to decide which set of battling experts has the most persuasive argument.

9 Descriptive claims, to be valid, must correspond to the natural world, offer a logical explanation, be falsifiable, and open to critique. *See* Karl R. Popper, The Logic of Scientific Discovery, 276–281 (5th ed., 1992); Susan Haack, Defending Science Within Reason 94–95 (2003) (explaining science as "continuous with everyday empirical inquiry."

10 In other words, the legal system can only be understood as an institution that implements the system of democratic governance we have chosen. Of course, even accepting a correspondence and coherence theory of rationality does not mean that all rational minds will agree on what justice requires. On the contrary, more than one theory can always be supported by the data. *See* Willard V. Quine, *Epistemology Naturalized*, in Ontological Relativity and Other Essays, 69 (1969), explaining that the underdetermination of theory by evidence means that more than one theory will always be supported by the data.

Bounded rationality

One of the key insights of cognitive psychology is that the use of heuristics – mental shortcuts – is a pervasive and constructive tool that humans employ to make sense of a complex world.[11] Lately, heuristics have been given a "bum rap" by being lumped together with "biases."[12] Heuristics, however, are a characteristically human way of processing information. They can be extraordinarily helpful, as I hope to demonstrate throughout this book. Indeed, some "satisficing" heuristics may be superior to rational algorithms in complex-decision contexts.[13] Simplifying heuristics are especially useful in making complex decisions[14] such as those confronting legal decision makers.

When cognitive psychologists refer to heuristics, however, they generally mean a largely unconscious method of processing information that can result in poor judgment and decisions with less than optimal consequences.[15] Virtually everyone agrees that sometimes heuristics can get in the way of optimal decision making.[16]

11 *See* Gerd Gigerenzer & Daniel C. Goldstein, *Reasoning the Fast and Frugal Way: Models of Bounded Rationality*, 103 Psychol. Rev. 650, 651, proposing models of bounded rationality that replace unrealistic views of the mind. This model of human decision making is further discussed and evaluated in Chapter 9.

12 *See, e.g.,* Jeffrey L. Rachlinski, *Heuristics and Biases in the Courts: Ignorance or Adaptation*, 79 Or. L. Rev. 61, 61 (2000), explaining that the brain's limited ability to process information leads people to rely on mental shortcuts, which "leaves people susceptible to all manner of illusions: visual, mnemonic, and judgmental"; James A. Fanto, *Quasi-Rationality in Action: A Study of Psychological Factors in Merger Decision-Making*, 62 Ohio St. L.J. 1333, 1343 (2001), noting that people "exhibit various biases that prevent or distort rational calculation"; Jon D. Hanson and Douglas K. Kysar, *Taking Behavioralism Seriously: The Problem of Market Manipulation*, 74 N.Y.U. L. Rev. 632, 633 (1999), observing that "cognitive illusions – sometimes referred to as "biases" – are not limited to the uneducated or unintelligent, and they are not readily capable of being unlearned."

13 Satisficing is a term coined by Herbert Simon to mean those cognitive abilities that best enabled people to survive and reproduce. *See* Gerd Gigerenzer and Daniel C. Goldstein, *Reasoning the Fast and Frugal Way: Models of Bounded Rationality*, 103 Psychol. Rev. 650, 650 (1996), explaining that "proponents of the heuristics and biases program, who concluded that human inference is systematically biased and error prone," are mistaken about the degree of error induced by this method of reasoning because in real-world situations characterized by "multiple pieces of information, which are not independent, but redundant," the complexity of the task makes satisficing algorithms superior for most tasks.

14 By complex, I mean decisions that have a number of alternative solutions, a quantity of information on which each alternative is based, and some time pressure. *See, e.g.,* John W. Payne, et al., The Adaptive Decision Maker 34 (1993), noting that "as decisions become more complex, people will tend to use simplifying heuristics."

15 For terminology in this area, *see* Gregory Mitchell, 91 Geo. L. Rev. 67, 79–80 (1999), defining judgment as "the process of perceiving and cognitively integrating stimuli to form a global evaluation about something" and decision as "the expression of a preferential choice" expressed in words, action, or a commitment to a course of action.

16 *See, e.g.,* Robyn Dawes, *infra* n. 23, at 497, explaining that if actual decision making violates certain principles of rationality "systematically (not just as a result of unreliability or 'error'), this deviation is termed an anomaly – if the people who violate these principles simultaneously accept them as ones that they believe should govern their decision making"; Gerd Gigerenzer, *The Bounded Rationality of Probabilistic Mental Models*, in Rationality: Psychological and Philosophical Perspectives (K. I. Manktelow and D.E. Over, eds., 1993), presenting a process theory of overconfidence bias successfully predicting conditions under which overestimation occurs. Notably, even Professor Mitchell, who derides as "misleading" the equation of heuristics and biases with

Some errors are the result of computational limitations,[17] some are the result of memory restrictions, and others are more motivational in nature. All of these errors can lead to drastically poor decisions under the right circumstances.[18]

Although some scholars contend that these biases are artifacts of the experimental setting, virtually no one believes that rational choice models of human decision making reflect reality.[19] Where people make judgments under conditions of uncertainty (i.e., where there are no clear answers), they are particularly likely to use shortcuts.[20] People using these heuristics may be behaving rationally in the sense of conserving time, but their decisions differ from what the rational-actor approach of economics would have predicted. Judgmental accuracy may also be impaired.

Across cultures, although human memory and attention are limited because of brain structure and function, people tend to make inferences as though both were infallible, resulting in cognitive shortcuts. These are unconscious processes and doubtless enable people to make decisions that are fast and, on average, accurate enough.[21] It also keeps people from being paralyzed into inaction.[22] Although this

error in legal judgment, concludes that "[t]he interesting and important question for empirical research on legal judgment and decision-making is not whether judges or jurors ever fall prey to systematic biases and errors in their reasoning – some surely do – but rather what contexts foster good and bad reasoning." Gregory Mitchell, *Mapping Evidence Law*, 2003 MICH. ST. L. REV. 1065, 1082. This chapter offers an analysis of the allocation of decision making between judge and jury that demonstrates how gatekeeping requirements foster good reasoning.

17 *See, e.g.,* GERD GIGERENZER, CALCULATED RISKS: HOW TO KNOW WHEN NUMBERS DECEIVE YOU (2003) pp. 242–43; training students to draw conclusions from numbers is more successful if they are taught to translate probabilistic statistics into frequentist representations.

18 *See* Philip E. Tetlock and Richard Boettger, *Accountability: A Social Magnifier of the Dilution Effect*, 57 J. PERSON. & SOC. PSYCHOL. 388, 388 (1989), explaining that people "use different information-processing strategies in different situations" so that, for example, the pressure to justify one's views may actually magnify the dilution effect.

19 *See, e.g.,* Bernard Grofman, *On the Gentle Art of Rational Choice Bashing*, in INFORMATION, PARTICIPATION, AND CHOICE, 239, 240 (Bernard Grofman, ed., 1993), "Only an idiot (or an economist) would claim that rational choice models can explain all of human behavior." For more about evaluating the underlying science of cognitive (sometimes called social) psychology, *see* Chapter 9.

20 These "quirks" are often called heuristics and biases, but whatever they are called, the idea is that people take cognitive shortcuts as a strategy for processing information. *See,* JOHN W. PAYNE, ET AL., THE ADAPTIVE DECISION MAKER 2 (1993) explaining that strategies for processing information vary from the rational choice model when people are faced with complex choice problems with many alternatives. These are not irrational responses, although the resulting decision may be less than optimal. *See id.,* noting that "people have multiple goals including to be accurate and the desire to conserve cognitive resources." Although some people exhibit these quirks more than others, and in some contexts more than others, the unconscious tendency of most people to take these cognitive shortcuts has been well documented in a number of situations applicable to jury decision making. Understanding these tendencies and how to counteract them can vastly improve the way information is presented by experts and understood by juries.

21 *See* Gerd Gigerenzer and Daniel G. Goldstein, *Reasoning the Fast & Frugal Way: Models of Bounded Rationality*, 103 PSYCHOL. REV. 650, 651, 655 (1996), designing and empirically testing satisficing algorithms of bounded rationality against statistically rational algorithms to solve real-world problems of limited knowledge and finding that the satisficing algorithms scored the highest proportion of correct inferences in the shortest time.

22 *See, e.g.,* SHELLEY E. TAYLOR, POSITIVE ILLUSIONS: CREATIVE SELF-DECEPTION AND THE HEALTHY MIND, 212–14 (1989), noting that the only people who do not suffer from over-optimism bias about their chances for success in the future are the clinically depressed.

may confer an evolutionary advantage to humans as a species, it does not lead to optimal decision making in all situations.[23] In other words, the satisficing strategies that people adopt to solve complex problems with limited resources may have long-term value for humans as a species, but they can also lead to errors in judgment.

A structured reasoning process improves judgment

Decisions that are less than optimal because of satisficing strategies can be improved. People benefit from decision aids.[24] Training in reasoning dramatically improves performance.[25] People can be taught to think correctly and to retain this knowledge.[26] People are capable of sound reasoning if the information is presented to them correctly.[27] Identifying the conditions under which the use of otherwise helpful heuristics may result in biased (i.e., less than optimal) decision making provides insight into structuring legal decision making in such a way as to minimize these biases.

Making the probabilistic nature of an evaluation task explicit, for example, tends to reduce the frequency of base-rate errors.[28] Moreover, training is much more effective for pragmatic applications of reasoning than for abstract principles.[29] Further, repeat decision making in the presence of unambiguous feedback also improves judgment.[30]

23 *See, e.g.,* Robyn M. Dawes, *Behavioral Decision Making and Judgment,* in Vol. 1, HANDBOOK OF SOCIAL PSYCHOL., 497, 497 (Daniel T. Gilbert et al., eds., 4th ed., 1998), explaining that if actual decision making violates certain principle of rationality "systematically (not just as a result of unreliability or 'error'), this deviation is termed an anomaly – if the people who violate these principles simultaneously accept them as ones that they believe should govern their decision making."

24 Payne et al., p. 7, using the example of supermarket price unit information, which consumers tended to ignore until the format was changed, making the information more available by ranking unit prices from lowest to highest.

25 Christopher Jepson, et al., *Inductive Reasoning: Competence or Skill,* 3 BEHAV. & BRAIN SCI., 494, 498 (1983), discussing studies; Richard E. Nisbett et al., *Teaching Reasoning,* 238 SCI. 625, 630 (1987), advocating formal training in the "rules underlying reasoning."

26 *See* GIGERENZER, CALCULATED RISK, pp. 242–43, describing the successful training of students in making correct statistical inferences.

27 *See* Jonathan J. Koehler, *The Base Rate Fallacy Reconsidered: Descriptive, Normative and Methodological Challenges,* 19 BEHAV. & BRAIN SCI. 1, 15, citing studies demonstrating that when information is presented in certain ways, people are capable of sound probabilistic reasoning.

28 *See* Gerd Gigerenzer, *From Tools to Theories: A Heuristic of Discovery in Cognitive Psychology,* 98 PSYCHOL. REV. 254–67 (1991).

29 *See* Patricia W. Cheng, et al., *Pragmatic Versus Syntactic Approaches to Training Deductive Reasoning,* in RULES FOR REASONING, 186 (Richard E. Nisbett, ed. 1993), noting that "the near total ineffectiveness of purely abstract training in logic contrasts dramatically with the ready ease with which people seem able to apply a naturally acquired pragmatic reasoning schema" and noting that people "who received a brief training session on the obligation schema improved markedly on selection problems interpretable in terms of that schema."

30 *See, e.g.,* Jonathan J. Koehler, *The Base Rate Fallacy Reconsidered: Descriptive, Normative and Methodological Challenges,* 19 BEHAV. & BRAIN SCI. 1, 6, citing studies showing that people learned to use base rates more effectively after receiving feedback about their errors from their experience. For example, physicians who learned the low base rate of pneumonia from their practice experience relied heavily on the base rate when making diagnoses, and auditors "learned and used the base rate

In addition, accountability, which refers to the expectation that one may have to justify one's actions, can sometimes improve judgment.[31] Accountability for the decision-making process to an unknown audience that the decision maker views as legitimate may assist people who know that they will be held accountable beforehand in making better decisions by engaging in preemptive self-criticism, as long as there exist formal decision rules that can correct the mental processes involved.[32] On the other hand, accountability does not always aid decisions. Accountability actually increases the effects of some kinds of cognitive biases.

For example, the tendency to pick a less ambiguous alternative when given a choice between options differing in uncertainty regarding the potential outcomes is made worse under conditions of accountability.[33] Accountability tends to increase the confirmation bias, a tendency for decision makers to seek evidence that confirms an initial judgment,[34] which is troubling because confirmation bias is also magnified through group polarization. If the jurors share an initial view of the best decision, the group will seek information to support that decision.[35] Once a decision has been made, accountability may increase cognitive dissonance effects.[36]

The dilution effect

Jurors who are presented with expert testimony that has not been scrutinized for scientific validity may have a difficult time sorting the wheat from the chaff. A cognitive bias known as the dilution effect occurs when people are presented with complex information, some of which is relevant to the decision task and some of which is irrelevant.[37] The probability that a particular choice will be made should not

---

for financial statement errors most easily by directly experiencing those errors"; but cautioning that "personally experienced base rates were used only by those who also experienced the relationship between the base rate and the diagnostic information."

31 Jennifer S. Lerner and Philip E. Tetlock, *Accounting for the Effects of Accountability*, 125 PSYCHOL. BULL. 255, 255 (1999), reviewing the literature on accountability.

32 The necessary conditions are, principally, "an audience (a) whose views are unknown, (b) who is interested in accuracy, (c) who is interested in processes rather than specific outcomes, (d) who is reasonably well-informed, and (e) who has a legitimate reason for inquiring into the reason behind participants' judgments." *Id.*, p. 258. Lerner and Tetlock explain that while process accountability increases both accuracy and calibration (the correlation between accuracy and confidence), outcome accountability decreases calibration and increases judgment inconsistency, but they also note that "there is no reason to suppose that all kinds of PA [process accountability] work the same." *Id.*

33 Lerner and Tetlock, p. 264, observing that a well-defined probability is preferred to an ambiguous probability holding expected values constant, and that this tendency is exacerbated under accountability.

34 David M. Sanbonmatsu et al., *Overestimating Causality: Attributional Effects of Confirmatory Processing*, 5 J. PERSONALITY & SOC. PSYCHOL. 892, 897 (1993), describing a tendency for decision makers to seek out information that confirms their initial hypotheses.

35 F. D. Schultz-Hardt et al., *Biased Information Search in Group Decision Making*, 78 J. PERSONALITY & SOC. PSYCHOL., 655, 659–60 (2000), studying middle managers.

36 *Id.*, p. 665, studying increased commitment to a group decision.

37 Some of the classic work on the dilution effect was that of Philip E. Tetlock and his coauthors. *See, e.g.,* Philip E. Tetlock et al., *The Dilution Effect: Judgment Bias, Conversational Convention, or*

vary with the amount of information available, nor should irrelevant information enter into a judgment.[38] But it does.[39] The dilution effect occurs when irrelevant information dilutes relevant information, leading to less accurate judgments than when only relevant information was available.[40]

In studies of this effect, participants responded differently to stories detailing the same phenomenon but containing different amounts and kinds of information.[41] Although the probability that a particular choice will be made should not vary with the number of irrelevant facts available, irrelevant information that should not enter into a judgment nonetheless creeps in. When people are asked to judge whether someone else has a particular characteristic, such as aggressiveness, their judgments tend to be more focused (and accurate) when they are presented with only relevant information; even when details are obviously irrelevant, they still appear to affect judgment.[42] Physical attractiveness of the defendant should not affect the verdict, for example, but a number of jury studies have shown a "leniency shift" toward an attractive defendant but not for unattractive defendants.[43]

Two heuristics are thought to underlie the dilution phenomenon: the representativeness heuristic and the norms of social discourse. In the first explanation, the dilution problem arises because irrelevant information obscures what is relevant. The representativeness heuristic is one in which people rely on representative patterns – stereotypes – in reaching a decision.[44] Rational choice and Bayes theorem predict that rational people will consider the statistical probability that an event will occur and update it with particularized specific information. In fact, however,

a Bit of Both?, 26 Eur. J. Psych., 915, 916–17 (1996), citing studies demonstrating that "linking diagnostic with nondiagnostic evidence produced more regressive predictions than people would otherwise have made."

38 See Naresh K. Malhotra, Information Load and Consumer Decision Making, 8 J. Cons. Res., 419, discussing studies on information-load effects.

39 See Dawes, note 23, p. 537, noting that even "someone who has a strong opinion based on very strong evidence may be influenced to "moderate this opinion by exposure to a flurry of uninformative information."

40 See John Castellan, Jr., Multiple-Cue Probability Learning with Irrelevant Cues, 9 Org. Behav. & Hum. Performance, 16, 26 (1973), study participants were unable to ignore irrelevant information even after a large number of trials.

41 See Henry Zuckier, The Dilution Effect: The Role of the Correlation and the Dispersion of Predictor Variables in the Use of Nondiagnostic Information, 43 J. Pers. & Soc. Psychol., 1163 (1982).

42 See Dawes, note 23, pp. 532, 537, "Dilution effects occur when evidence that does not distinguish between hypotheses in fact influences people to change their mind."

43 Dennis J. Devine, et al., Jury Decision Making: 45 Years of Empirical Research on Deliberating Groups, 7 Psychol. Pub. Pol'y & L., 622, 679 (2001), citing mock jury studies by Izzett & Leginsski (1974) and McCoun (1990); Kerr, supra note 65, p. 710, describing the McCoun (1990) study and finding its conclusion that dilution effects are greater among juries than individual jurors to be consistent with computer analyses.

44 Daniel Kahneman and Amos Tversky, Subjective Probability: A Judgment of Representativeness, 3 Cognitive Psychol. 430 (1972). These shortcuts are not consciously employed but operate on a subliminal level to affect decision. Id.

people ignore base rates[45] and overestimate the correlation between what something appears to be and what it is, adhering to stereotypes. For example, in assessing the career of a person described as overbearing, aggressive, rude, and skilled at rhetorical argument, people will refer mentally to known stereotypes rather than population base rates.[46] People think by association and respond to patterns – even infants recognize shape patterns.[47] This is a characteristic of human thought and undoubtedly speeds up the thinking process, but it has a downside.

The social-norms heuristic (which is a second postulated reason for the dilution effect) hypothesizes that, in a testing context, people focus on social cues and assume that the experimenter would not be presenting them with information unless they were expected to consider it.[48] People may believe that the information provided to them in such a context is relevant and appropriately specific. Under this rationale, jurors, who understand that information is being screened in this way, may be especially prone to the dilution effect. Experts (like judges) are less likely to suffer

45 The base rate is the frequency of a given subject in the population. For example, if a sample of 100 people consists of 70 lawyers and 30 engineers, the base rate of lawyers is 70 percent and of engineers is 30 percent. Knowing only that, if you were asked the occupation of any given person, you would be wise to answer "lawyer." It is interesting that most people do not. In a study in which subjects were divided into two groups, both of which were told that 100 people were either lawyers or engineers, one subject group was told there were 70 lawyers and 30 engineers, the other group that there were 30 lawyers and 70 engineers. Both groups were given thumbnail descriptions of the people written by psychologists, designed to be nondiagnostic with respect to occupation. *See* Richard E. Nisbett et al., *Teaching Reasoning*, 238 Sci., 625 (October 30, 1987). In both groups, the subjects based their answers on stereotypes rather than population base rates.

46 Amos Tversky and Daniel Kahneman, *Availability: A Heuristic for Judging Frequency and Probability*, in Judgment Under Uncertainty: Heuristics and Biases 1124 (Daniel Kahneman et al., eds., 1982). There is an ongoing debate between Kahneman/Tversky and Gigerenzer about whether this is a reasoning error, with the focus of the disagreement on interpretations of probability. *See, e.g.,* Gerd Gigerenzer, *The Bounded Rationality of Probabilistic Mental Modes*, in Rationality: Psychological and Philosophical Perspectives, 284, 291–97 (K.I. Manktelow and D.E. Over, eds., 1993), arguing that you cannot assign probabilities to unique events and that, therefore, there is no normative basis for assigning error to stereotyping, and suggesting errors are eliminated by asking questions in terms of frequencies rather than in terms of probabilities and increasing the use of random sampling. Daniel Kahneman and Amos Tversky, *On the Reality of Cognitive Illusions*, 103 Psych. Rev. 582, 582–83 (1996), acknowledging that representation in terms of absolute frequencies improves accuracy but citing studies to demonstrate that people nonetheless perceive correlations that do not exist and that "some significant judgmental biases are not readily corrected by the observation of natural frequencies." For purposes of this discussion, it is enough to note that both sides agree that information is rarely presented to decision makers in a form – frequency – that is optimal for accuracy.

47 *See, e.g.,* Roger Lecuyer and Christine Cybula, *Categorization of Geometric Figures Composed of Three or Four Elements by 3-Month-Old Infants*, Current Psychol. Cognition 221, 221–44 (2000), noting studies showing that infants recognize geometric patterns; Dawes, note 29, p. 534, explaining the problems of representativeness and pseudodiagnosticity as probabilistic fallacies.

48 *See* Tetlock et al., *infra* note 96, p. 916, observing that "far from representing an error, the dilution effect may constitute a rational response to the interpersonal and institutional demands that impinge on individual perceivers."

from dilution effects because repeat exposure in the presence of feedback increases the ability to filter irrelevant from relevant information.[49]

There is some evidence that group processes decrease the dilution effect.[50] This is true, however, only if the resulting bias is nonsystematic – that is, if each member ignores different information. When the irrelevant information plays into commonly held stereotypes, it may skew the decisions in a systematic fashion. The dilution effect explains the harmful consequences of simply permitting the jury to hear expert testimony and then try to sort out its relevance for themselves without initial judicial screening for relevance and reliability.

Egocentric biases: self-interest and cognitive dissonance

A well-documented bias of individuals is a tendency to overrate their abilities and their control over events, at least when the questions are difficult and the decision makers have no prior experience in making such decisions.[51] Across cultures, people appear to overestimate their ability to provide correct answers to questions.[52]

---

49 Although this effect is made worse if the decision maker is accountable, because the decision maker searches for all evidence – even irrelevant evidence – that might possibly have bearing on the solution, judges are explicitly cued to the task of screening for relevance, which ought to minimize that effect. Philip Tetlock and Richard Boettger, *Accountability: A Social Magnifier of the Dilution Effect*, 57 J. PERS. & SOC. PSYCHOL. 388 (1989).

50 *See* Gigone and Hastie, *infra* note 66, p. 155.

51 *See* Gerd Gigerenzer, *The Bounded Rationality of Probabilistic Mental Models*, in RATIONAL-ITY: PSYCHOLOGICAL AND PHILOSOPHICAL PERSPECTIVES, 284, 297–300 (K. I Manktelow and D. E. Over, eds., 1993), noting the results of two decades of research showing that test participants were overconfident when judging the correctness of their answers to difficult general-knowledge questions, but that when they were directed to assess their correctness with reference to their prior experience in answering similar general-knowledge tests, their overconfidence disappears. The problem for jurors is that they do not have any such reference points when it comes to assessing the defendant's dangerousness. The major determinant of overconfidence is the difficulty of the question. *See* Lyle A. Brenner, et al., *Overconfidence in Probability and Frequency Judgments: A Critical Examination*, 65 ORG. BEHAV. & HUMAN DECISION PROC. 212, 213, observing that "the major (though not the sole) determinant of overconfidence is the difficulty of the questions." Overconfidence has been observed in a number of predictive tasks, including physicians' predictions of disease, economists' forecasts of recession, and players' predictions of their opponents' moves. However, as one researcher points out, we do not know if the kind of question domain makes a difference or "whether there are simply some domains in which we tend to exaggerate the accuracy of our knowledge or judgment (not in others)." Robyn M. Dawes and Matthew Mulford, *The False Consensus Effect and Overconfidence: Flaws in Judgment or Flaws in How We Study Judgment?*, 65 ORG. BEHAV. & HUMAN DECISION PROCESSES 201, 210 (1996). Nonetheless, although we do not know whether results in the general-knowledge questions are equally applicable to the decision the jurors make in capital sentencing, if our goal is to improve accuracy, we should implement ways of minimizing such effects.

52 *See* Gregory Mitchell, *Why Law and Economics' Perfect Rationality Should Not Be Traded for Behavioral Law and Economics' Equal Incompetence*, 91 GEORGETOWN L. J. 1, 137–38 (2002), citing studies showing that – with the exception of Japanese and Singaporeans – Asians are even more overconfident than Westerners.

People tend to believe that their judgments are correct.[53] In addition, the social environment of the jury deliberations may increase overconfidence because greater overconfidence has been demonstrated in people acting within small social networks.[54] These networks are characterized by having three to fifteen members (a characteristic that juries – normally twelve members – share); with someone in a central, coordinating position (here, the judge); and weak contact with outsiders (juries are typically told not to discuss the case with anyone).

There are numerous explanations for overconfidence bias, and each of these has implications for jury decision making and emphasizes the importance of judicial screening of expert testimony for accuracy. For example, one explanation for overconfidence is that people "confuse easily drawn inferences for easily remembered facts."[55] Another is the possibility that people selectively focus on evidence that is consistent with their first impression and ignore inconsistent evidence.[56] A third is that people's overconfidence is a buffer against anxiety.[57] Moreover, cognitive dissonance theory suggests that people tend to take further actions that justify and reinforce decisions that they have already made.[58] For example, gamblers and voters are more confident after they have placed their bets or votes than they were before.[59]

The dynamics of group decision making

Legal decision making at trial has two aspects: individual, in the person of the judge, and group, in the form of the jury. Although there is strong evidence that group decisions are better than individual decisions when evaluating information that has a demonstrably correct solution, most decisions that juries are called upon to make

53 *See* Hart Blanton, et al., *Overconfidence as Dissonance Reduction*, 37 J. Expt'l Soc. Psychol. 373, 373 (2001), citing studies asking people to evaluate their ability in solving laboratory problems and showing that "people think that they can solve problems that they cannot, think that they have made progress toward correct solutions when they have not, and think that they have drawn correct conclusions when they have not."

54 *See* Joshua Klayman, et al., *Overconfidence: It Depends on How, What, and Whom You Ask*, 79 Org. Behav. & Human Dec. Proc. 216, 243 (1999), finding an overall bias toward overconfidence, particularly in small social networks.

55 Blanton, et al., *supra* note 53, p. 374, citing studies.

56 *See* Eddie Harmon-Jones and Judson Mills, *An Introduction to Cognitive Dissonance Theory and an Overview of Current Perspectives on the Theory*, in Cognitive Dissonance: Progress on a Pivotal Theory in Social Psychology, 3–33 (Eddie Harmon-Jones and Judson Mills, eds., 1999), citing studies demonstrating that people selectively seek information that will decrease expected postdecision dissonance.

57 *See* Jeff Greenberg et al., *Why Do People Need Self-Esteem? Converging Evidence that Self-Esteem Serves an Anxiety Buffering Function*, 63 J. Personality & Soc. Psychol. 913, 913–21 (1992), arguing that self-deception sustains the illusion of control and diminishes anxiety.

58 *See* Leon Festinger, A Theory of Cognitive Dissonance (1957). Festinger's theory provoked a great deal of controversy, but the empirical basis for it appears to have survived the controversy. *See, e.g.*, Dawes, note 23, pp. 557–61, 561, detailing the controversy and concluding that "cognitive dissonance theory is resilient."

59 *See* Blanton, et al., note 53, p. 374, arguing that "overconfidence reflects the motive to maintain a view of the self as a knowledgeable perceiver who makes sound judgments" (citing studies).

do not have clear answers.[60] Complex decisions are not necessarily improved by group processes. Moreover, when the individuals in a group share a particular bias, group processes tend to magnify its effect.[61] Group final judgment depends both on where the individual members begin deliberation and the processes in which the group combines preferences to define a group decision.[62] Group-polarization effects have been demonstrated for attitudes toward capital punishment, judgments about facts, and perceptions about people.[63]

In group decisions, although random errors in assessing information tend to cancel each other out, systematic biases may be amplified.[64] Individual biases and group dynamics are thus both important facets of the decision-making process. Although both individual and group decision making are subject to biases – that is, decisions about what and how information is relevant[65] – there are some characteristics of group decision making that emphasize the importance of protecting the jury from irrelevant information that exacerbates biases and providing instructions that can guide the group's reasoning process. Group decisions are better than individual decisions when evaluating information that has a demonstrably correct solution.[66] The reason for this is that the errors of individuals in assessing information tend to cancel each other out.[67] Thus, I am not arguing that the jury should be replaced in criminal or civil trials or in capital sentencing proceedings. I am suggesting that the confluence of systematic errors requires that judges carefully screen information that the jury will use to make its collective decision.

The argument that collective decision making should cancel out judgmental errors does not work for systematic biases.[68] Instead, collective processes under

60 *See* Daniel Gigone and Reid Hastie, *Proper Analysis of the Accuracy of Group Judgments*, 121 PSYCHOL. BULL. 149, 149 (1997). As Gigone and Hastie explain, "groups performing tasks that involve solutions that are not easily demonstrable tend to perform at the level of their average members." *Id.*

61 *Id.*, p. 159.

62 Kerr, et al., *infra* note 65, p. 694.

63 Paul E. Jones and Peter H. Roelofsma, *The Potential for Social Contextual and Group Biases in Team Decision-Making: Biases, Conditions and Psychological Mechanisms*, 43 ERGONOMICS 1129, 1144 (2000), discussing the "overwhelming number of studies" demonstrating group polarization.

64 *See* Gigone and Hastie, *supra* note 60, p. 159, observing the cancellation of uncorrelated errors in group decision making.

65 Norbert L. Kerr, et al., *Bias in Judgment: Comparing Individuals and Groups*, 103 PSYCHOL. REV. 687, 714–15 (1996), defining bias as reflecting "decisions about whether and how to use information" and demonstrating that "groups will amplify bias under some conditions but attenuate it under others"; Chip Heath and Rich Gonzalez, *Interaction with Others Increases Decision Confidence but Not Decision Quality: Evidence Against Information Collection Views of Interactive Decision Making*, 61 ORG. BEHAV. & HUM. DEC. PROC. 305, 323 (1995), concluding that individual interactive decision making exhibits similar characteristics to group consensus decision making).

66 *See* Daniel Gigone and Reid Hastie, *Proper Analysis of the Accuracy of Group Judgments*, 121 PSYCHOL. BULL. 149, 149 (1997).

67 *Id.*, p. 159, observing the cancellation of uncorrelated errors in group decision making.

68 *See* Norbert L. Kerr et al., *Bias in Judgment: Comparing Individuals and Groups*, 103 PSYCHOL. REV., 687, 713–14 (1996), noting that although the law of large numbers suggests that random errors will cancel each other out in collective decisions, it will not do so for systematic errors.

certain conditions skew the decision away from judgmental accuracy.[69] These conditions are precisely those a jury faces in making its determination – for example, where there is no clearly shared framework for defining right or wrong answers.[70]

Rather than achieving a compromise solution that reflects the average of the members' initial position, groups often polarize; that is, the group will make a more extreme decision than the individuals' initial positions would have predicted.[71] The result is that group decisions may move toward an extreme position instead of the middle of the individually held antecedent positions. For polarization to occur, there must be an initial leaning of the group in a particular direction.[72] There are a number of explanations for this tendency, such as social comparison theory (i.e., people tend initially to espouse opinions less extreme than their true opinion because they fear being labeled deviant, and once they realize that others have more extreme opinions, they shift theirs to their true value); persuasive arguments theory (i.e., explaining group polarization on the basis of a pool of arguments drawn from discussion among the group members); self-categorization theory (i.e., group members define the social identity of the group and then modify their positions to conform with it); social influence network theory (i.e., a network of interpersonal influence); and social decisions schemes (i.e., the distribution of initial opinions specifies the relative influence of the alternative initial positions of group members).[73] But, whatever the explanation, if the context is one in which a systemic bias can be predicted, group polarization may magnify the effect.

Essentially, if the group members already have a predilection in attitude, group dynamics intensify the predilection and result in a more extreme judgment.[74] For example, when there is an underlying norm endorsing capital punishment, individuals would attempt to signal that they shared the group attitude.[75] This

69 *Id.*, pp. 714–15, citing studies.
70 *See*, e.g., Garold Stasser et al., *The Social Psychology of Jury Deliberations: Structure, Process and Product*, in THE PSYCHOLOGY OF THE COURTROOM, 221–56 (Norbert L. Kerr and Robert Bray, eds., 1982), jury studies.
71 *See*, e.g., Daniel J. Isenberg, *Group Polarization: A Critical Review and Meta-Analysis*, 50 J. PERSONALITY AND SOC. PSYCHOL. 1141, 1141 (1986), noting that "an initial tendency of individual group members toward a given direction is enhanced following group discussions."
72 *See* Noah E. Friedkin, *Choice Shift and Group Polarization*, 64 AM. SOC. REV. 856, 857–59 (1999), explaining the concept of group polarization in terms of a choice shift, which occurs "when, after a group's interaction on an issue, the mean final opinion of group members differs from the members' mean initial opinion . . . in the opposite direction of the initial inclination of the group."
73 *See id.* discussing alternative explanations.
74 As Noah Friedkin explained,

    A choice shift is said to occur when, after a group's interaction on an issue, the mean final opinion of group members differs from the members' mean initial opinion. Group polarization is said to occur when the choice shift is in the same direction as the mean initial opinion. . . .

    Friedkin, at 857.
75 *See* ROBERT S. BARON ET AL., GROUP PROCESS, GROUP DECISION, GROUP ACTION, 73 (1992), discussing the process of polarization; Baron and Roper, pp. 528–30, hypothesizing that members strive to show adherence to group norms.

results in a kind of competition, but because no one can be sure exactly what the average is, the value moves in the direction favored by the group norm. This effect has been observed in studies where the group categorized itself as either risk-taking or cautious. Group decisions were observed to polarize in the risky direction by stereotypically risk-seeking groups and in the cautious direction by self-perceived cautious groups, although risky and cautious individuals tended to shift away from their individual predilection.[76]

Apparently, this polarization phenomenon is a function of group discussion.[77] One explanation for group polarization is that groups have an internal culture that prefers some values over others.[78] During discussion, group members attempt to signal their adherence to these group norms, but because they do not know ahead of time the level of group adherence to these norms, the result is a competition that shifts the initial preferences to a more extreme level.[79] This means that if group members share a particular bias, group dynamics may intensify its impact.[80] People wish to be perceived favorably by the group, so they adjust their expressed opinion in line with their image of the group position, an image already polarized because of its prototypical nature.[81]

Another explanation for the polarization effect is that the initial declaration of the individual's position was more moderate than the position the individual really held.[82] During group deliberations, as the individual realizes the group position is more extreme, the individual is freed to express these more extreme views. In this explanation, there is not really a shift in underlying attitudes but merely an increased willingness to express previously held views. Both this and the prior explanation are social comparison theories, suggesting that group polarization occurs when high-status members of the group hold more extreme views than the mean.[83] Thus, if the jury foreperson or other influential member has a predilection for a particular view, that may shift the group decision. Instead of fracturing the group into opposing

76 John C. Turner, et al., *Referent Informational Influence and Group Polarization*, 28 BRIT. J. PSYCHOL., 135, 143 (1989), noting that "defining the shared characteristics in advance will ensure that arguments/positions/ members in line with the stereotype will tend to be perceived as more representative of the group as a whole and hence more persuasive and valued."

77 ROBERT S. BARON ET AL., GROUP PROCESS, GROUP DECISIONS, GROUP ACTION, 73 (1992), noting the "process whereby group discussion tends to intensify group opinion, producing more extreme judgments among group members than existed before the discussion."

78 *See* Robert S. Baron and Gard Roper, *Reaffirmation of Social Comparison Views of Choice Shifts: Averaging and Extremity Effects in an Autokinetic Situation*, 33 J. PERSONALITY & SOC. PSYCHOL. 521, 528–30 (1976).

79 *See* Glen S. Sanders and Robert S. Baron, *Is Social Comparison Irrelevant for Producing Choice Shifts?* 13 J. EXPT'L SOC. PSYCHOL. 303, 311 (1977).

80 *Id.*, p. 304.

81 JOHN TURNER ET AL., REDISCOVERING THE SOCIAL GROUP, 156 (1987).

82 Isenberg, *supra* note 71, p. 1142.

83 G. R. Goethals and M. P. Zanna, *The Role of Social Comparison in Choice Shifts*, 37 J. PERSON. & SOC. PSYCHOL., 1969 (1979).

views, polarization is a consensual shift further in the direction of the group's initial tendency.[84]

Yet another explanation for group polarization is the persuasive arguments theory.[85] Here, the deciding factors are the number and persuasiveness of the arguments mustered in support of a given position. This theory also relies on a notion of underlying group orientation. Under this theory, group polarization occurs when there is a disproportionately large number of persuasive arguments in the direction the group is leaning.[86]

In mock-jury studies,[87] polarization around the question of guilt or innocence has been well documented.[88] In interactive groups, rather than responding to

84 James H. Liu and Bibb Latane, *Extremization of Attitudes: Does Thought and Discussion-Induced Polarization Cumulate?*, 20 BASIC & APP. SOC. PSYCHOL. 103, 103 (1998), noting the difference between popular conceptions of polarization and those of social scientists.

85 Eugene Burnstein and Amiram Vinokur, *What a Person Thinks upon Learning He Has Chosen Differently from Others: Nice Evidence for the Persuasive Arguments Explanation of Choice Shift*, 11 J. EXPT'L SOC. PSYCHOL. 412 (1975), discussing shifts in choice even without discussion, based on knowledge of others' preferences.

86 *See* Eugene Burnstein and Amiram Vinokur, *Persuasive Argumentation and Social Compromise as Determinants of Attitude Polarization*, 13 J. EXPT'L SOC. PSYCHOL. 315 (1977), polarization as a result of informational influence.

87 Mock-jury experiments are frequently castigated as lacking the real-world context of jury deliberations. *See, e.g.,* Michael J. Saks, *What Do Jury Experiments Tell Us About How Juries (Should) Make Decisions?*, 6 S. CAL. INTERDISC. L. J. 7–8 (1997), noting the differences between live trials and mock-jury studies but explaining that the real issue is whether such differences affect generalizability of the study results. In many cases, however, the results of experimental research and studies involving real juror interviews coincide. *See* Neil Vidmar and Shari S. Diamond, *Juries and Expert Evidence*, 6 BROOK. L. REV. 1121, 1166 (2001), noting that "the experimental research related to juries and experts produces conclusions consistent with the studies involving juror interviews" and concluding that jurors "generally make reasonable use of complex material, utilizing the expert testimony when it is presented in a form that they can use." In the polarization studies, the mock jurors were interviewed about their initial determinations, deliberated, and reached a consensus that tended to be more extreme than the initial interviews suggested. *See* Norbert L. Kerr et al., *Bias in Judgment: Comparing Individuals and Groups*, 103 PSYCHOL. REV., 687, 705 (1996), describing mock-juror studies showing a polarization effect in which jurors were exposed to evidence, deliberated in 12-person juries, and provided post-deliberation guilt judgments; ROGER BROWN, SOCIAL PSYCHOLOGY, 227–29 (2d ed., 1986), citing studies. For an article contending that even computers experience group polarization when "fed with the same noisy input and confronted with the same environmental distributions," *see* Klaus Fiedler, *Explaining and Simulating Judgment Biases as an Aggregation Phenomenon in Probabilistic, Multiple-Cue Environments*, 103 PSYCHOL. REV. 193, 198–99, 211, discussing group polarization as resulting "from aggregation alone whenever one of two opposite attitudes is dominant," a finding "consistent with the repeated empirical finding that polarization occurs only after unconstrained, extended discussion."

88 *See* ROGER BROWN, SOCIAL PSYCHOLOGY, 227–29 (2d ed., 1986), collecting studies. Very diverse groups tend to diminish this effect, according to James Fishkin's experiments demonstrating an absence of polarization effects in groups composed of highly diverse individuals. Although juries generally are diverse in many respects, capital juries are not heterogeneous: in order to serve on the jury, jurors must be willing to support the death penalty (in the appropriate case, as the voir dire usually instructs juries). It might be less polarizing to have a diversity of opinions about the legitimacy of the death penalty. *See* Devine et al., *supra* note 43, p. 693, citing evidence from the Capital Jury Project that capital juries tend to polarize toward death rather than life, seemingly contradicting the strong leniency bias observed in mock-jury studies.

information against their position by modifying their position or lowering their confidence, researchers have found that group members' interaction increases peoples' confidence in their decision in a way that is not justified by increased accuracy.[89] Instead, group members frequently fail to respond to the information presented.[90]

Another anomaly of groups is that its members tend to put less effort into a task than they would if acting alone. "Social loafing" is the term used to describe the observed phenomenon that individuals put less effort into a group decision than into an individual decision. The classic experiments have to do with physical exertion, such as rope pulling, shouting, and clapping; at all these tasks, group output tends to be less than the sum of the individuals' efforts when performing the same task alone.[91] This work has been extended to judgment tasks, with similar results.[92] The reasons given for such social loafing have to do with lack of accountability, inability to measure individual input, and lack of control over the output. When, for example, test participants were told that they (individually) would have to justify their judgments, they exerted as much cognitive effort as individual judges.[93] We do not, however, ask juries to justify their opinion. Thus, the jury's difficult task – making complex decisions on the basis of unfamiliar information – may become overwhelming to the individual jurors with a less careful result than had an individual been responsible.

89 *See* Chip Heath and Rich Gonzalez, *Interaction with Others Increases Decision Confidence But Not Decision Quality: Evidence Against Information Collection Views of Interactive Decision Making*, 61 ORG. BEHAV. & HUM. DEC. PROC. 305, 306 (1995), arguing that interaction does not cause people to assess the available information differently but merely to develop more coherent ratio-nales for their choices and beliefs. Heath and Gonzalez studied interactive decision making – individual decisions made after consultation with the group – and distinguished it from group decision making on the basis that groups must reach a consensus and the "aggregation procedure may hide or distort changes in individual preferences." *Id.*, 307. Jury decision making has facets of both interactive and group decision making; although the end product must be a consensual decision, in order to avoid a hung jury, each juror must individually agree and each can hold out until persuaded. Moreover, Heath and Gonzalez conclude that consensus decision making is not the only kind of group decision that exhibits the characteristics of groupthink. *Id.* at 323. The characteristics of groupthink, "'discount[ing] warnings and other forms of negative feedback that, taken seriously, might lead the group members to reconsider their assumptions'... provide a remarkably satisfying description of the phenomenon ... of individual decision makers interacting in a social environment." *Id.*

90 *Id.* at 305.

91 *See* Bibb Latane, et al., *Many Hands Make Light the Work: The Causes and Consequences of Social Loafing*, 37 J. PERSONALITY & SOC. PSYCHOL. 822, 823 (1979). Although social loafing has been documented under diverse conditions, it appears to disappear under conditions of accountability. For example, social loafing is virtually eliminated when people are told that their individual production will be measured, even when working in groups. *See* Kenneth L. Bettenhausen, *Five Years of Groups Research: What We Have Learned and What Needs to Be Addressed*, 17 J. MGT. 345, 361 (1991).

92 Bettenhausen at 360–61, citing studies showing that people who shared responsibility for a complex judgment task put less cognitive effort into the task than individuals working alone.

93 Kenneth H. Price, *Decision Responsibility, Task Responsibility, Identifiability, and Social Loafing*, 40 ORG. BEHAVIOR & HUMAN DEC. PROC. 330–45 (1987).

Judicial screening

There are a number of reasons that judicial gatekeeping – that is, screening for accuracy before permitting expert testimony – makes for more accurate judgments.[94] As Robert Burns explains, the question that should be asked with regard to admissibility is whether the evidence at issue would throw the jury "off track" in its goal of reaching the public truth.[95] The dilution effect explains the importance of screening irrelevant information from jury decision making. People participating in experiments expect that information given to them for the purpose of making a decision is relevant.[96] Similarly, jurors, who have experienced judicial screening when objections are made at trial, may expect that whatever information they are given is relevant to their task.[97] When it is not, the decision will be less accurate than had such evidence been excluded.

Judges, however, are aware that they are hearing both relevant and irrelevant information, and they are accountable to their reviewing courts. The dilution effect disappears when people are made accountable for their judgment – as judges are by judicial review – as long as the decision maker knows that both relevant and irrelevant information is being presented.[98] Even when you tell unaccountable individuals (and jurors are unaccountable because they never need to explain the reason for their decision[99]) that they are receiving both relevant and irrelevant information and that they need to sort through it to reach their decision, the dilution effect occurs.[100]

---

94 As discussed earlier in this chapter, to call something an "accurate" judgment is a normative statement that raises complex issues about what we know, how we know it, and what our goals are. In the context of the goals of a capitol juror, for example, the jury appears to focus on the goal of determining whether this defendant would kill again if released. Interviews with capitol jurors reflect this overwhelming concern. *See* William J. Bowers and Benjamin D. Steiner, *Death by Default: An Empirical Demonstration of False and Forced Choices in Capital Sentencing*, 77 Tex. L. Rev. 605, 609 (1999), discussing the Capital Juror Project. The arguments of lawyers and legal scholars that the question ought to be whether the defendant will pose a threat to other inmates or prison personnel are beside the point. My point is simply that in light of their goal, the presentation of irrelevant – unscientific – expert testimony makes their determination less accurate.

95 Robert Burns, A Theory of the Trial (2001).

96 *See* Philip E. Tetlock et al., *The Dilution Effect: Judgment Bias, Conversational Convention, or a Bit of Both?* 26 Eur. J. Psych. 915, 916–17 (1996).

97 For example, Tetlock and his coauthors found that even when test participants were told that the information was randomly generated from a computer and contained both relevant and irrelevant information, they still made more regressive estimates given the irrelevant information. *Id.* at 926.

98 *Id.* at 930–31, demonstrating that "the dilution effect disappears among accountable subjects who were explicitly told that conversational norms did not apply because the information they had been given had been randomly selected from a computer database ... [or] conversational norms were explicitly deactivated."

99 Even if one assumed that jurors were accountable, in the sense that they must render a public decision and may have to explain their reasons to friends and family, it is only the accountability to unknown audiences that appears to affect the care with which information is scrutinized. *See* Philip E. Tetlock, *Accountability: A Social Magnifier of the Dilution Effect*, 57 J. Personality & Soc. Psych., 388, 388 (1989), defining accountability.

100 *See* Tetlock, et al., note 96, p. 931, demonstrating that "explicitly deactivating conversational norms was not sufficient to eliminate the dilution effect among unaccountable subjects."

Irrelevant and inaccurate information throws group decisions off track even more than it does individual judgment. Thus, the dilution effect suggests that merely presenting evidence that counters the misinformation may not be enough.

Moreover, judges are experts (in the sense that they make repeat decisions) in the presence of feedback. People who repeat the decision-making process many times in the presence of feedback regarding their accuracy (as judges do because of the appellate process) are more likely to make accurate judgments. Judges get more feedback than juries through the appellate process and through legal scholarship and commentary. Expertise tends to decrease both technical errors and the consideration of irrelevant information. Experts – such as judges – trained in decision rules (e.g., the analysis required under *Daubert*) tend to make better judgments about validity than laypeople – jurors, for example – who are unaware of these rules.[101] As noted previously, training can improve reasoning. Judges, who have extensive training in legal analysis and, post-*Daubert,* in reasoning about expert testimony, can be expected to make better evaluations of such testimony than untrained jurors. In addition, although the overconfidence bias may afflict experts more than novices, groups are more prone to it than individuals.[102]

Further, accountability can significantly improve the quality of some kinds of judgment.[103] Individual judgments under conditions of accountability are more likely to be careful and thoughtful than group judgments without individual accountability.[104] Judges are accountable not only to their superior courts but also to a wider audience of legal scholars and practitioners who will comment on their decision. Accountability to an unknown audience enhances careful decision making.[105] People who know that they will have to justify their decisions ahead of

---

101 *See* Lerner and Tetlock, note 31, p. 263, explaining that accountability, which may attenuate biases resulting from lack of effort or self-critical awareness, has no effect on judgment tasks requiring knowledge of formal decision rules that are unfamiliar to the decision maker.

102 *See* Philip E. Tetlock, et al., *Assessing Political Group Dynamics: A Test of the Groupthink Model,* 63 J. PERSONALITY AND SOCIAL PSYCHOL. 403, 419 (1992) (performing multiple regression analysis of various collective decision processes and concluding that there was ample support for the groupthink hypothesis first advanced by Irving Janis).

103 *See* Shelley E. Taylor, *The Social Being in Social Psychology,* in Vol. I, HANDBOOK OF SOCIAL PSYCHOLOGY, 4th ed., 76 (Daniel T. Gilbert et al., eds., 1998): "Accountability for one's inferences produces more thorough and more elaborate processing that takes account of more information and that is, at least sometimes, more accurate than processing that occurs in the absence of accountability." Because the conditions of judicial gatekeeping review are precisely those that increase accuracy, it is the judge who should be the locus of the decision about admissibility of expert testimony rather than the jury.

104 *See* Bettenhausen, note 91, p. 361, citing studies demonstrating that people in groups of 16 who shared responsibility for the judgment task "used less complex judgment strategies than subjects working alone" although "multiple judges who expected to justify their judgments worked as hard as individual judges."

105 *See* Lerner and Tetlock, note 31, p. 256, explaining that "people often seek approval from their respective audience" and that if "audience views are known prior to forming one's own opinion, conformity becomes the likely coping strategy" and the result is likely to decrease rather than increase accuracy as it does when the audience is unknown.

time, as judges do, perform better cognitively.[106] Moreover, when the accountability review evaluates the process resulting in the judgment rather than the outcome, such process judgments are improved under conditions of accountability.[107] The gate-keeping decision of the judge is reviewable primarily for its process rather than its outcome, so one would expect a more careful and critical evaluation of the evidence than could be expected from jurors, who at most may have some outcome accountability in terms of possible negative consequences from their community.

Conclusion

Daubert[108] is unequivocal that relevance in the context of expert testimony means scientific validity. Relevance is not "merely" a matter of evidentiary rules, it is a requirement of due process and fundamental fairness, both requirements of the rule of law. Contrary to the U.S. Supreme Court's contention in *Barefoot*,[109] the adversary process cannot be trusted to sort out the reliable from the unreliable evidence. Instead, as the Court explained in *Daubert*, the requirement that expert testimony be helpful to the jury, "supported by appropriate validation – i.e., 'good grounds,' based upon what is known," is a condition of relevance.[110] This is the task of the judge and the rule of law emphasis on rationality underscores why this should be so.

---

106   *Id.*, p. 257, noting that while post-decisional accountability leads to self-justification rather than self-criticism and thus poor decision performance, people who know they will be held accountable before engaging in the judgment task tend to be highly self-critical and more accurate.

107   *Id.*, p. 258, citing studies showing that "accountability for decision outcomes – rather than decision processes – would increase the escalation of commitment to prior courses of action ... [while] [p]rocess accountability, by contrast, would (a) lead decision makers to engage in more even-handed evaluation of alternatives, and (b) decrease the need for self-justification."

108   *See Daubert*, 509 U.S. 583.

109   *Barefoot*, 463 U.S. 900.

110   *Daubert*, 509 U.S. 590–91.

3

A framework for analysis

To function as gatekeepers, judges must decide whether the scientific expert's testimony is valid scientific knowledge, which *Daubert* explained as knowledge grounded in scientific method.[1] Although most of us have heard the term "scientific method,"[2] expecting judges to decide whether expert testimony has been derived from its criteria – without more guidance – seems a stretch. As commonly understood, scientific method means taking an idea about how things work, framing it in a testable hypothesis, and testing the hypothesis to see if it holds true, all measured and expressed in mathematical (i.e., probabilistic) terms. However, despite the U.S. Supreme Court's reference to the scientific method as the cornerstone of scientific knowledge, its existence is debatable. First, there is no monolithic scientific method. Karl Popper, the preeminent philosopher of science cited by the *Daubert* Court, thoroughly debunked any such notion.[3] There is no all-inclusive set of rules that can be applied to science to determine its validity.[4] Differences arise among

---

1 *See Daubert v. Merrell Dow Pharmaceuticals, Inc.*, 509 U.S. 579, 589 (1993).
2 Webster's defines "scientific method" as:

> [P]rinciples and procedures for the systematic pursuit of knowledge involving the recognition and formulation of a problem, the collection of data through observation and experiment, and the formulation and testing of a hypothesis.

WEBSTER'S NINTH NEW COLLEGIATE DICTIONARY (Mish et al., eds., 1990).
3 *See* KARL R. POPPER, THE LOGIC OF SCIENTIFIC DISCOVERY 276–281 (5th ed., 1992).
4 Occasionally, commentators will argue that Koch's Postulates or Hill's can be used as criteria for good science. *See, e.g.,* KENNETH R. FOSTER AND PETER W. HUBER, JUDGING SCIENCE: SCIENTIFIC KNOWLEDGE AND THE FEDERAL COURTS, 28 (1997). But, while these respected canons are unquestionably useful in designing optimal experiments, they cannot – and were not intended to – be used as a checklist for sound science. *See* Austin Bradford Hill, *The Environment and Disease: Association or Causation?* 58 PROC. ROYAL SOCIETY OF MED. 295, 295–300 (1965). Hill's postulates require consideration of strength of association; consistency with other scientists' results; specificity of association, temporality, biological gradient, or dose-response curve; biological plausibility; coherence; and analogy with similar evidence. *See* Foster and Huber, at 28, noting that "[m]ost scientists would agree that evidence satisfying all Koch's postulates establishes a compelling case" for causation, but explaining that they are neither necessary nor sufficient conditions for inferring causation. Koch was a bacteriologist who outlined ten criteria for causation, including (1) higher prevalence of disease in exposed than unexposed populations; (2) those with the disease should have had more exposure to the agent than healthy populations; (3) experiments should demonstrate increased incidence of disease in exposed over unexposed populations; (4) temporality; (5) linear dose-response curve; (6) biological plausibility; and a number of other factors relating to immune responses. *See* Alfred

scientists in different disciplines, and even within the same discipline, with respect to the amount of evidence that is needed to support a theory. Instead, there are many methods and many procedures. The only essential ingredient for good science – and, hence, the only overarching method – is that science must be open to critique and revision.[5]

Purportedly, the scientific method is a way to ensure objectivity; however, the scientific method is no guarantee of objectivity. Although empirical content is fundamental to science, it is no more true of science than law that facts exist independent of value.[6] Mere observation of the world does not lead to scientific knowledge.[7] Observation must be informed by theory.[8] Science is a creative enterprise.[9]

S. Evans, *Causation and Disease: The Henle-Koch Postulates Revisited*, 49 YALE J. BIO. AND MED. 175 (1976), explaining that these postulates "were not regarded as rigid criteria by Koch himself and should not be today."

5 *See* KARL R. POPPER, THE LOGIC OF SCIENTIFIC DISCOVERY, 279 (5th ed., 1992). This willingness to be continually critiqued is what Popper called "falsifiability," a concept that the U.S. Supreme Court emphasized in *Daubert*. *See Daubert*, 509 U.S. at 593.

6 *See* KARL R. POPPER, THE MYTH OF FRAMEWORK, 8 (M.A. Notturno, ed., 1994); WILLIAM L. TWINING, RETHINKING EVIDENCE, 107 (1990), discussing the rationalist tradition in evidence scholarship and its main epistemological assumption that the purpose of adjudication is to discover an objectively knowable truth. "[T]he notion of "fact" in adjudication is more problematic than the orthodox view suggests. . . . Thus it is misleading to suggest that legal enquiries into questions of fact are value-free."

7 *See* MICHAEL POLANYI, PERSONAL KNOWLEDGE: TOWARDS A POST-CRITICAL PHILOSOPHY 161 (1958), "Factuality is not science. Only a comparatively few peculiar facts are scientific facts, while the enormous rest are without scientific interest."

8 *See* KARL R. POPPER, THE LOGIC OF SCIENTIFIC DISCOVERY, 480 (1959). A striking example is given by a leading scientist:

[E]ven the so-called "fact" that a star is located in a certain position in the heavens is a consequence of Einstein's theory which determines how much light may deviate from a straight line.

Stephen G. Brush, *Prediction and Theory Evaluation: The Case of Light Bending*, 246 SCI. 1124 (1989).

9 Although we think of scientific facts as having been discovered rather than fabricated, the etymology of the word "fact" is from the Latin, *facere*, which means to make. *See* KARIN D. KNORR-CETINA, THE MANUFACTURE OF KNOWLEDGE: AN ESSAY ON THE CONSTRUCTIVIST AND CONTEXTUAL NATURE OF SCIENCE, 3 (1981). As one scientist explained, "Most of the reality with which scientists deal is highly preconstructed, if not wholly artificial." *Id.* For an excellent discussion of how theory and fact intertwine, *see*, generally, HAROLD I. BROWN, PERCEPTION, THEORY AND COMMITMENT: THE NEW PHILOSOPHY OF SCIENCE (1979). As an initial matter, the availability of funding for particular experiments – clearly, a social phenomenon reflecting exigencies of politics and demand – determines which theories will be examined and which data analyzed. In addition, what we know is inextricably a social process. *See* MICHEL FOUCAULT, POWER/KNOWLEDGE, SELECTED INTERVIEWS AND OTHER WRITINGS, 69 (1980), "Once knowledge can be analyzed in terms of region, domain, implantation, displacement, transposition, one is able to capture the process by which knowledge functions as a form of power and disseminates the effects of power." Further, what will count as truth is a matter of negotiation between various factions that have a stake in the matter. Thus, the definition of "scientific" fact "must be sought through interpretation of the changing borders and territories of what is taken as science." *See* Thomas F. Gieryn, *Boundaries of Science* in HANDBOOK OF SCIENCE AND TECHNOLOGY STUDIES, 417 (Sheila Jasanoff et al., eds., 1994). For example, the feminist critique of science examines the boundary shifts in what counts as science toward the masculine and away from the feminine so that not only are women underrepresented in science, but scientific research also underrepresents women.

To make matters more difficult for anyone seeking a set of rules for science, not only is science about more than a mere accumulation of facts, but just as "facts" are intertwined with subjective values in legal decision making,[10] scientific conclusions are also based on subjective judgments made at key points ranging from the initial decision to study a particular phenomenon through the collection, categorization, and interpretation of data.[11] Interpreting experiments is neither a simple nor a disinterested process.[12] On the contrary, scientific paradigms are – like legal paradigms – socially constructed through a process of discussion and consensus-building about theories, experimental methods, instrumentation, and validation. That does not make them any less reliable.

Nor does it follow from the consensual nature of the enterprise that scientific conclusions are completely indeterminate. Acknowledging that science is a creative process does not imply that everything is up for grabs. The consensus of rational opinion is constrained by nature. There are shared perceptions of validity.[13] The shared perceptions regarding how to determine experimental and technical validity provide some constraints, just as shared perceptions of accepted judicial methodology provide restraints on judicial activism.

Something that legitimately can be defined as science has persisted despite radical changes in content. Explicitly acknowledging the subjective element present in all scientific methodologies opens for questioning the underlying assumptions of a particular scientific argument. To determine what is really at stake when experts disagree, it is necessary to examine those underlying assumptions.

Regardless of whether the scientific method exists in practice, people – scientists and nonscientists alike – frame their arguments about scientific issues as though

---

10 *See, e.g.,* WILLIAM L. TWINING, RETHINKING EVIDENCE, 107 (1990), noting that "triers of fact are regularly and unavoidably involved in making evaluations.... [I]t is misleading to suggest that legal enquiries into questions of fact are value-free."

11 *See* THOMAS S. KUHN, THE STRUCTURE OF SCIENTIFIC REVOLUTIONS, 200 (2d ed., 1970), explaining that scientists are engaged in a creative endeavor based on shared assumptions about the nature of the world rather than in generating objective knowledge. Thomas Kuhn's philosophy of science provides useful insight into the sociology of scientific paradigm change. Paul Feyerabend's critique of Kuhn's work forced Kuhn to modify his stance somewhat but not to withdraw his position entirely. *See, e.g.,* Paul Feyerabend, *Consolations for the Specialist* in CRITICISM AND THE GROWTH OF KNOWLEDGE, 209 (Imre Lakatos and A. Musgrave, eds., 1970); Thomas S. Kuhn, *Second Thoughts on Paradigms* in THE STRUCTURE OF SCIENTIFIC THEORIES, 459 (Frederick Suppe, ed., 1977).

12 Although the systematic testing of proposed explanations of reality is a basic feature of scientific process, it is the theoretical construct, the hypothesis, which precedes experimentation. *See* Kuhn, pp. 25–31. An example of this is the emptiness of the data-dredging experiments, in which computers were employed to elicit huge quantities of "facts" that no one has yet been able to make sense of. *See, e.g.,* Patricia K. Woolf, "Deception in Scientific Research" in *AAAS-ABA National Conf. of Lawyers and Scientists, Project on Scientific Fraud and Misconduct, Report on Workshop Number One,* 78 (1988).

13 That is, even if there is no set of inflexible "rules" for judging the validity of a scientific argument, there are criteria for formulating and testing scientific ideas. *See* Karl R. Popper, *Realism and the Aim of Science* in POSTSCRIPT TO THE LOGIC OF SCIENTIFIC DISCOVERY, 420 (W. W. Bartley III, ed., 1983). Testing internal consistency of the theory, consistency of the theory with other theories, and consistency with the empirical data is crucial. *Id.* Most important, science must continually question and criticize all its theories, continually refining its explanations.

it does. Even Popper did not dispute that there are good methods in science. He merely cautioned against sanctioning any rules that would exclude alternate forms of inquiry. Thus, scientists continue to describe their evaluation process generally in terms of scientific method, despite their skepticism.

Moreover, even without a single, universal, scientific method, there is a consensus about certain basic principles.[14] Probabilistic assessment of data, independent verification of new procedures, and concern over false positives are fundamental to scientific argument in every discipline. Metaphor is also basic to scientific understanding in every field.[15] In addition, quantum physics has added the insight that precise prediction of future behavior is impossible; the most that can be predicted is the probability of various behaviors (e.g., the exact position of electrons cannot be determined). The implications of complexity theory – that complex systems consist of interacting parts capable of shaping themselves into organized fluctuating patterns – are replacing deterministic notions of causation.[16] These ideas form the background of much modern scientific discourse. Thus, the reality of scientific method is a common understanding of probabilistic reasoning; the importance of testability, interdisciplinarity, and rationality; and an emphasis on the explanatory power of a proposed hypothesis.

Probabilistic reasoning

Underlying modern science – especially science involving complex systems like biological systems – is probabilistic reasoning.[17] By probabilistic reasoning, I mean a way of thinking about the physical characteristics of an object or event.[18] I do

14 *See* ALAN G. GROSS, THE RHETORIC OF SCIENCE, 32 (1990), noting that although most procedures have limits and, therefore, detractors and that no method is universally accepted, argument nonetheless proceeds from certain basic understandings about these procedures.

15 *See Id.*, p. 47 (1990). Scientific models should be understood as metaphor. *See* MICHAEL R. MATTHEWS, SCIENCE TEACHING: THE ROLE OF HISTORY AND PHILOSOPHY OF SCIENCE, 205 (1994), observing that "[a] good deal of science method courses are devoted to practice in the use of metaphor and models." Indeed, Lakoff and Johnson argue that metaphor is indispensable to reasoning in any human endeavor. *See* GEORGE LAKOFF AND MARK JOHNSON, METAPHORS WE LIVE BY, 221 (1980), arguing that the process of reasoning involves building metaphors and contrasting these with other inconsistent metaphors.

16 For an overview of complexity theory, *see* M. MITCHELL WALDROP, COMPLEXITY: THE EMERGING SCIENCE AT THE EDGE OF ORDER AND CHAOS (1992).

17 *See* Ian Hacking, *Was There a Probabilistic Revolution 1800–1930?* in THE PROBABILISTIC REVOLUTION: IDEALS IN HISTORY, Vol. I, 45 (Lorenz Kruger et al. eds., 1987), arguing that "today our vision of the world is permeated by probability." Probabilistic reasoning does not mean, however, that you can say a theory is more or less probable. *See* KARL R. POPPER, OBJECTIVE KNOWLEDGE: AN EVOLUTIONARY APPROACH, 55 (1981). Rather, it refers to an understanding that our world is run by rules of chance.

18 What I am calling probability here is what Popper referred to as "propensity." *See* Karl R. Popper, *Quantum Theory and the Schism in Physics* in POSTSCRIPT TO THE LOGIC OF SCIENTIFIC DISCOVERY, 159–60 (William W. Bartley III, ed., 1992), describing the physical world as "changing propensities for change" and explaining that "all properties of the physical world are dispositional, and the real state of a physical system, at any moment, may be conceived as the sum total of its dispositions – or its potentialities, or possibilities, or propensities." *See* Andreas Kamlah, *The Decline of the LaPlacian*

not mean subjective probabilities as prediction about whether a theory is true or not.[19] In other words, if we are speaking about the probability of a male president dying in office, it can reflect the consideration that the president is one of a group of males living in a particular geographic locale, or the consideration of other specified risk conditions (i.e., the frequentist approach) or it can mean one's belief in its likelihood (i.e., the subjectivist approach).[20] Although scientists may attach subjective probabilities to their conclusions, for modern scientists, probability is a physical quantity.[21] The paradigm for modern science is a frequentist one.[22]

The definition of probability is complex because probability theory arose as a solution to problems involving games of chance and swiftly was extended to decision theory.[23] Thus, the word *probabilistic* has two faces: it can connote chance or belief.

Theory of Probability in THE PROBABILISTIC REVOLUTION, Vol. I, note 17, p. 112, observing that, to some extent, the two senses of probability are indecipherable.

19 *See* IAN HACKING, THE EMERGENCE OF PROBABILITY, 14 (1975), noting that "[t]he propensity to give heads is as much a property of the coin as its mass, and the stable long run frequency found on repeated trials is an objective fact of nature independent of anyone's knowledge of it, or evidence for it." Of course, to some extent, even the notion of probability as a physical property contains subjective elements. As Heisenberg explains, "the probability function contains the objective element of tendency and the subjective element of incomplete knowledge" (quoted by Hacking, 148). But "the probability of getting a head from this coin" may have – in addition to an objective state about the tendency of the coin – subjective implications due to a lack of knowledge about whether it is a fair coin or not. Heisenberg considered this mixture of statements an essential feature of quantum theory. But that is an entirely different meaning from degree of belief. Some scientists may also be subjectivists. Carnap, for example, was a subjectivist. *See* IMRE LAKATOS, MATHEMATICS, SCIENCE AND EPISTEMOLOGY, PHILOSOPHICAL PAPERS Vol. I (John Worrall and Gregory Currie, eds., 1978). To some degree, Lakatos was also a subjectivist, recognizing that "some speculative genuinely epistemological theory connecting scientific standards with versimillitude is necessary to avoid turning science into an uncritical game," IMRE LAKATOS, THE METHODOLOGY OF SCIENTIFIC RESEARCH PROGRAMMES, PHILOSOPHICAL PAPERS Vol. II, 163 (John Worrall and Gregory Currie, eds., 2d ed., 1980).

20 The example is Colton's. *See* THEODORE COLTON, STATISTICS IN MEDICINE, 63 (1974).

21 Under the older (i.e., Bayesian or LaPlacian) paradigm, probability denoted a degree of expectation. *See* Colton, note 20, p. 71, noting that although many prominent scientists subscribe to Bayesian ideas, "it will be a long time before the Bayesian methods supplant the methods of statistical inference currently pervading the scientific literature."

22 *See* Hacking, note 19, p. 12. Under this paradigm, Kamlah explains that the operative question is, "If I make measurements of the same kind, how often in the long run can I get an estimated value that is equal to the true value within certain limits of error?" One no longer asks, "What is the probability that the mean value of my measurement is equal to the true value of the quantity within certain given limits of error?" *See* Kamlah, note 18, p. 112. Note, however, that although probability within a science is explicable in terms of relative frequency, the concepts of relative frequency and probability are not identical. *See* RICHARD B. BRAITHWAITE, SCIENTIFIC EXPLANATION: A STUDY OF THE FUNCTION OF THEORY, PROBABILITY AND LAW IN SCIENCE, 120 (2d ed., 1960). Hempel, for example, attempted to amalgamate testability concepts with subjective probability by claiming that repeated testing increases the probability that a theory will be true. *See* CARL G. HEMPEL, PHILOSOPHY OF NATURAL SCIENCE, 33–46 (1966). But an empirical frequency is simply not the same thing as the degree of rational belief. *See* Popper, note 18, p. 147, explaining propensity theory in quantum physics.

23 *See* Hacking, note 19, p. 11. Probability theory became explicitly linked with subjective belief when Pascal invented decision theory by making a wager about the existence of God. *Id.* Decision theorists in legal-evidence scholarship employ this branch of probability theory (and generally refer to their stance as Bayesian). *See, e.g.,* DAVID A. SCHUM, EVIDENCE AND INFERENCE FOR THE

For a scientist, probability reflects chance regardless of belief. In consequence, it is a nonsequitur to say that a theory is more likely than not to be true.[24] Scientists understand that there is simply no way to prove a theory true or even probable.[25] Although a theory can be disproved, the most that can be said of its truth is that a particular theory has withstood criticism and provides the best explanation of the data.[26]

Probabilistic reasoning encompasses the idea that statistical laws are fundamental to scientific explanation.[27] Statistical inference, with its concepts of probability and randomness, is basic to scientific discourse and forms the cornerstone of data analysis as well as the basis for causation and other explanatory arguments.[28] That there are regularities in processes with random or chance elements is an idea fundamental to science. Any observation of regularity in complex systems – any model, or "law" of nature – depends on statistical theorems that describe the behavior of large samples of objects. Normal distribution,[29] significance

INTELLIGENCE ANALYST, Vol. I, 101–02 (1987). For an explanation of decision theory (and its limitations), *see* Mark J. Machina, *Decision-Making in the Presence of Risk*, 236 SCI. 537 (1987).

24 *See* Popper, note 17, p. 40. Many scientists vehemently believe in their theories. My point is that they understand that there may be a disconnect between their belief and reality. *See* Hacking, note 19, p. 14, recognizing that the majority of practitioners ignore the distinction between the two types of probability.

25 *See* Stephen F. Lanes, *Error and Uncertainty in Causal Inference* in CAUSAL INFERENCE, 173, 182 (Kenneth J. Rothman, ed., 1988). "The uncertainty in causal inference is attributable to the fact that we cannot establish that an association is val*id*." *Id.*, p.185. An unidentifiable error may exist and it may cause the observation. *Id.* The most that can be expected of strength of association, the shape of a dose-response curve, and the level of statistical significance is that they affect subjective beliefs. *Id.* Truth, in other words, must be distinguished from its fallible signs. *See* Lakatos, *Programmes*, note 19, p. 108, explaining that "a proposition may correspond to a fact but there is no infallible way to establish this correspondence."

26 As Suppes explains, "probability theory is designed to discover and to analyze partial causes in complex situations for which a complete causal analysis is not feasible." PATRICK SUPPES, A PROBABILISTIC THEORY OF CAUSALITY, 8 (1970).

27 *See* Lorenz Kruger, *The Slow Rise of Probabilism: Philosophical Argument in the Nineteenth Century* in THE PROBABILISTIC REVOLUTION, Vol. I, *supra* note 17, p. 59.

28 *See* MICHAEL O. FINKELSTEIN AND BRUCE LEVIN, STATISTICS FOR LAWYERS, 107 (1990). As Suppes explains, "the concept of independence is one of the most profound and fundamental ideas, not only of probability theory but of science in general." Suppes, note 26, p. 109. Two events, A and B, are independent when $P(A/B) = P(A)$. *See* DAVID A. SCHUM, THE EVIDENTIAL FOUNDATIONS OF PROBABILISTIC REASONING, 150–51 (1994). The concept of independence asserts that discrete biological or physical events, like coin tosses, have no memory of time and place. *See* Lynn A. Steen, *The Science of Patterns*, 240 SCI. 611 (1988). In other words, knowing whether the coin toss yielded heads or tails last time will not help predict what the next coin toss will yield. *See* FREDERICK MOSTELLER ET AL., PROBABILITY WITH STATISTICAL APPLICATIONS, 8 (2d ed., 1970). On the other hand, an idealized "fair" coin has a probability of yielding heads on any given toss of $1/2$ and when n such coins are tossed, the probability that all land heads is $(1/2)$ to the nth power. *Id.*, 31. Even after ten heads have appeared in a row, however, the probability of a tail grows no larger. *Id.* The coin cannot change its probability because it has no memory. Equally important is the concept of a random variable, which is a variable whose value is a number determined by the outcome of an experiment, such as the number of heads when three coins are tossed. *Id.*, pp. 171–72. For definitions and explanations of these concepts, *see* generally Mosteller.

29 Normal distribution is the theoretical probability distribution sometimes referred to as Gaussian distribution or, more commonly, as the bell curve. *See* Colton, note 20, pp. 81–84. The normal distribution is determined by two quantities: its mean and standard deviation.

levels,[30] and power[31] are all key concepts in the biological sciences. Also important is the idea that false positives are disfavored in all scientific fields; that is, scientists attempt to minimize the probability of claiming an effect when there is none.[32]

Not only does probabilistic reasoning rely on statistical concepts of randomness and chance, but probabilistic assessments employ assumptions, taking it as given that all knowledge is incomplete.[33] Background assumptions are pervasive and inevitable. Every branch of science (including statistics) employs background assumptions to proceed. No experiment can be performed without using assumptions. But which assumptions are justified? Within a particular theory, or model, scientists agree on a set of basic premises.[34] These are assumptions that have an empirical and consensual basis, and they operate like rebuttable presumptions act in the law: under most circumstances, scientists will rely on these background assumptions, but in some circumstances, the assumptions will be demonstrably false, and then the scientist needs to explain the discrepancy.[35]

Because theories cannot be verified or validated, only falsified, theories must be evaluated in relative terms. Data (from experiment or observation), theory,

---

30 Statistical significance is set by convention at a level of significance, or p-value, of 0.05 (which corresponds to a confidence level of 95 percent). See Shayne C. Gad and Carrol S. Weil, *Statistics for Toxicologists* in Principles and Methods in Toxicology 435 (A. Wallace Hayes, ed., 1989) [hereinafter *Principles and Methods*]. If the p-value is 0.01, the evidence is said to be highly statistically significant. See Stephen E. Fienberg et al., *Understanding and Evaluating Statistical Evidence in Litigation*, 36 Jurimetrics J. 1, 22 (1995). The object of statistical significance tests is to keep the scientist from asserting a positive effect when the effect may actually be due to chance. See David Ozenhoff and Leslie I. Bodin, *Truth & Consequences: Health Agency Responses to Environmental Health Problems*, 12 Sci., Tech. & Hum. Values, 70, 73–74 (1987). "By rejecting a hypothesis only when the test is statistically significant, we have placed an upper bound, .05, on the chance of rejecting a true hypothesis." Fienberg et al., p. 22. Another way of explaining this is that it describes the probability that the procedure produced the observed effect by chance. If the test is not statistically significant, it may be because either the results were due to chance or the test lacked the power to discern a difference between the null hypothesis and the proposed effect.

31 Power is the probability of a test rejecting the null hypothesis (i.e., that there is no effect) when the alternative hypothesis is correct. See David H. Kaye and David A. Freemen, *Reference Guide on Statistics* in Federal Judicial Center, Reference Manual on Scientific Evidence, 381 (1994). Power increases with the size of the study and with the degree of difference from the null hypothesis (i.e., the more extreme the alternatives, the better the power). See Fienberg et al., note 30, p. 22. Power will, therefore, be an issue for small studies of low effects – precisely those most likely to be proffered in toxic tort cases. Thus, separate studies of small numbers of subjects may not yield statistically significant results simply because each test may lack the power to discern the null hypothesis of no effect from patterns of illness that are not extreme. See Fienberg et al., note 31, p. 22 (using employment discrimination as a hypothetical example).

32 See Colton, note 20, p. 128.

33 See Stephan F. Lanes, *The Logic of Causal Inference in Medicine* in Causal Inference, 65 (Kenneth J. Rothman, ed., 1988). This is the idea behind Lakatos's revised theory of falsification in which a series of theories, rather than a single theory in isolation, is subjected to critique and a new series is preferable if it increases the empirical content of the explanation. See Lakatos, *Programmes*, note 19, pp. 32–4.

34 Collective judgment about which background assumptions are warranted and under what circumstances is not static; it is subject to revision, and this collective judgment forms what Lakatos calls a "research programme." See Lakatos, *Programmes*, note 19, pp. 47–52.

35 Kuhn points out that sometimes the anomalies are just ignored, but when too many accumulate, the theoretical framework (or research programme, as Lakatos called it) collapses and is replaced by a new framework (or programme). See Kuhn, note 12, pp. 81–85.

contingencies, and assumptions are juxtaposed to provide an explanation of the way things work. The operative question is which theories explain the data, not which data establish the theory. Causal inference is a matter of explanation. Scientists often critique each others' explanations, and must persuade other scientists that their reasoning in making these juxtapositions is sound. This discourse among scientists is what I refer to as scientific argument. This is the foundation of probabilistic reasoning.

Testability, criticism, and rationality

Popper's philosophy of science has had a marked impact on the way scientists think about what they do. Although Popper is certainly not the most recent philosopher of science, nor is he uncontroversial, subsequent philosophers of science have had to respond to his ideas.[36] Key elements in his thesis are the importance of a theory's testability, openness to critique, and rationality. All of these ideas have been challenged as insufficient to explain what really goes on in science, but they nonetheless remain central to scientific argument.[37] Moreover, they are useful ideas for judges faced with the task of assessing scientific validity.[38]

As the U.S. Supreme Court acknowledged in *Daubert*, testability is a key precept. Affirming the importance of empirical content to scientific theory, this concept asserts that what makes a hypothesis scientific is that it can be provisionally corroborated or falsified by observation and experiment.[39] The articulation of what the testing means is also critically important.[40] Popper explained that the scientist's task is continually to criticize and reassess scientific theories in light of new theories and data. The greater the empirical content of a theory, the stronger the theory because it is more open to testing and more easily falsifiable.

---

36 Popper's work has been criticized as inadequately accounting for the growth of scientific knowledge. *See, e.g.,* Lakatos, *Programmes,* note 19, p. 9; Paul Feyerabend, Against Method: Outline of an Anarchistic Theory of Knowledge, 93–98 (1978). More recently, philosophers of science have focused on what they call "realism." *See* Richard N. Boyd, "Constructivism, Realism, and Scientific Method" in Inference, Explanation, and Other Frustrations: Essays in the Philosophy of Science, 131 (John Earman, ed., 1992), stating that theories explain the real world, they are true descriptions of reality, even if we can never be sure of what ultimate reality is. Nonetheless, the arguments of science are based on the precepts that Popper identified as falsifiability, interdisciplinarity, and rationality. *See,* e.g., Gross, note 15, pp. 26–27. Thus, while those philosophers of science often disagreed with each other, there are many areas of common understanding and each offers insights about particular aspects of the validity determination.

37 For example, Ayer's critique of falsifiability is that refutations, like confirmations, presuppose certain conditions. *See* A. J. Ayer, Language, Truth and Logic, 38 (2d ed., 1959). But this critique fails to undermine Popper's insight that although it is possible in principle to refute a theory, it is not possible even in principle to prove a theory true.

38 As Lakatos explained, theories cannot be appraised without some theory of the growth of knowledge. *See* Lakatos, *Mathematics,* note 19, p. 159.

39 *See* Francisco J. Ayala, *Biology as an Autonomous Science,* 56 Am. Sci., 207, 207 (1968). A theory can only be provisionally corroborated at any given point in time; further testing may reveal hitherto undiscovered flaws that refute it. *See* Popper, note 36, p. 121.

40 *See* Lakatos, *Mathematics,* note 19, p. 110, explaining the fundamental precepts of what he calls "demarcationists" among whom he includes himself, Popper, Russell, and Liebniz, among others.

As a corollary to the idea of falsification, the hypothesis being tested must have precise logical consequences that are incompatible with alternative hypotheses.[41] The effects of variables other than the ones being tested for (i.e., so-called secondary variables) must be either controlled or known (as in an experiment) or explicitly assumed (as in observational studies of human populations). The importance of a control group or a null hypothesis is that a researcher is exposing the chosen hypothesis to the possibility of falsification. If the data do not refute the proposed hypothesis, it may be (provisionally) valid.

In addition, the concept of testability includes the idea that the data obtained by testing or observation must be accounted for in a proposed model.[42] A model is a metaphor, an analogy to something more familiar. The most common scientific metaphors (or models) in current use are the pump and the computer, and many disparate systems are described in terms of these metaphors. The heart, for example, is commonly described as a pump; the brain is described as a computer.[43] These metaphors are useful but – to some degree – inaccurate. Nonetheless, they illustrate some important ideas.

The concept of testability has been challenged on several fronts. Many scientists ignore the principle in practice. The concept itself ignores the problem of identifying underlying assumptions.[44] Testability assumes a laboratory science paradigm of methodology: it has to be stretched to encompass epidemiology, with its reliance on statistical inference.[45] Further stretching still is required for psychology and the

---

41 Thus, "[s]cience advances toward truth (though never arriving at certainty) by a combination of bold conjecture and severe criticism." Gieryn, note 9, p. 395.

42 See Ayala, note 39, p. 207. This was not originally part of Popper's philosophy but rather reflects an extension of his work by later philosophers of science such as Lakatos and Kuhn, who were troubled by the importance of what Popper called "auxiliary hypotheses" – that is, assumptions and their implications for falsifiability. See Naomi Oreskes et al., *Verification, Validation, and Confirmation of Numerical Models in the Earth Sciences*, 263 Sci. 641, 644, n.19 (1994), observing that scientists routinely modify their models to fit recalcitrant data.

43 See, e.g., Harry Levin, *The Cognitive Revolution in Psychiatry*, 236 Sci. 683 (1983), describing computer as metaphor for human information processing.

44 See Imre Lakatos, *Falsification and the Methodology of Scientific Research Programmes* in Criticism and the Growth of Knowledge, 91 (Imre Lakatos and Alan Musgrave, eds., 1970), arguing that the asymmetry Popper proposed between falsification and corroboration is much less significant than he thought. In fact, some commentators have argued that using falsifiability as a criterion for good science would render much of modern science unscientific. See, e.g., Alan F. Chalmers, Science and its Fabrication, 18 (1990), contending that if the criterion of falsifiability is "formulated sufficiently strongly to have some force, then physics would fail to qualify as a science." Growth in scientific knowledge occurs, according to the critique, not because of falsification alone but because the scientific community observes empirical evidence apparently falsifying the original hypothesis and then tries to formulate auxiliary hypotheses to explain away the apparent anomaly. See Feyerabend, note 37, pp. 197, 220. Eventually, more and more empirical data must be explained by way of these auxiliaries as exceptions to the theory.

45 Testability may not be an adequate notion for psychology and other social sciences where retrospective observational studies rather than controlled experimentation are the norm. Indeed, Popper was explicitly using the concept to differentiate between "true" empirical science and what he considered the pseudosciences of economics (Karl Marx was the particular target of Popper's ire) and psychology (Freud was singled out in Popper's polemic). Karl R. Popper, Conjectures and Refutations: The Growth of Scientific Knowledge (1992). Even these fields, however, have criteria for validity that need to be examined for coherence and rationale. The use of empircal

social sciences. Nonetheless, it remains a fundamental requirement in distinguishing between mere conjecture and scientific process. Moreover, testabililty does not stand alone as the sole criterion for distinguishing science from pseudoscience.

In addition to testability, Popper believed diversity of dialogue to be imperative. Instead of a narrow focus, Popper believed that the interaction of various scientific disciplines was important to the growth of knowledge. He believed that scientific inquiry could only benefit by listening to interdisciplinary voices.[46] Science aims at high informative content. The more the different fields of science interact to test their ideas against each other, the more we will know about the world.[47] Using studies from many disciplines is thus an important facet of scientific argument.

The force of rationality is a third tenet of Popper's philosophy of science. Popper's idea of rationality was based on comparing ideas. Popper asserted that a background in science should not be a necessity for understanding scientific ideas.[48] He thought that ideas, including scientific ideas, ought to be tested in a public forum. For Popper, science could be distinguished from myth by its openness to critique and modification in the light of criticism.

Explanatory power

The strength of a scientific theory is its ability to explain what happened. Empirical support for this explanation may take many forms. Multiple avenues of deductive reasoning based on persuasive data are what leads to scientific acceptance of a theory. Thus, scientists gather all the information available to support a biologically plausible theory. An important part of scientific argument is juxtaposition of theory and data, and the way data were obtained and analyzed. Methodology must

---

data, statistical description, openness to critique, and their coherence with the underlying theory are indicia of validity in these fields also. The U.S. Supreme Court made this point in *Kumho Tire*, where it emphasized that *Daubert* analysis must be applied even to fields such as engineering and psychology. *See Kumho Tire v. Carmichael*, 526 U.S. 137 (1999).

46 Karl R. Popper, *Normal Science and its Dangers* in CRITICISM AND THE GROWTH OF KNOWLEDGE, 57 (Imre Lakatos and Alan Musgrave, eds., 1970), arguing that science progresses through communication of rival scientific systems.

47 An important example of this interdisciplinarity is the rapid spread of chaos theory and principles of nonlinearity across a broad spectrum of scientific disciplines, including chemistry, physics, and biology. *See* Celso Grebogi et al., *Chaos, Strange Attractors, and Fractal Basin Boundaries in Nonlinear Dynamics*, 238 SCI. 632 (October 30, 1987).

48 In this idea, Popper differed radically from elitists such as Polanyi and Feyerabend, who stressed the notion that only a privileged elite can understand science. *See* Lakatos, *Mathematics*, note 19, pp. 113, 127. Thus, a theory is not better for Popper just because a scientific elite prefers it but because the ideas have withstood severe criticism and offer a better, more persuasive, rational explanation that is higher in empirical content than rival theories. *See* Lakatos, *Mathematics*, note 19, pp. 228–42, arguing for clear theses in science "where logic can assist criticism and help to appraise the growth of knowledge." Lakatos's solution to the dilemma was to examine not a single theory in isolation but rather theories in conjunction with each other to determine whether the new series explains at least some of the anomalies unexplained by the predecessor series. *See* Lakatos, *Programmes*, note 19, pp. 94–95. In other words, the new theory must explain the partial success of its predecessor and also something more.

comport with scientific norms of good practice.[49] Data must be analyzed in statistically acceptable ways. The most that can be said is that one theory is superior to another (because of its explanatory power, or persuasiveness), not that it is "true." It is superior if it offers a better metaphor, if it accounts for most if not all the known data in a more persuasive way.[50] In addition, the theory must be capable of accommodating newly discovered information.[51] It is around these basic principles that any heuristic must be framed if it is to be useful in assessing scientific arguments. Scientific method, insofar as it exists, consists of a common discourse about probabilistic assessment, testability, and explanation. How can these themes be teased into a useful heuristic to solve the validity puzzle?

There are five basic things a judge should consider in making the decision to let an expert testify. First, the judge must come to grips with the underlying theory and hypothesis. The second requirement in order to determine whether the theory is supportable is that the judge must examine all the available information – human studies, animal studies, cellular, and chemical structure – in concert. In this vein, it is useless – and unscientific – to expect a single study to uphold an entire explanation. Third, where there are information gaps (which are inevitable), they should be filled with scientifically justifiable default assumptions. Statistical inferences need to be examined in light of the biological "story" being presented, and the underlying assumptions assessed for coherence. Fourth, an inquiry into the methodology (including the laboratory or observational methods as well as statistical methodology) and whether it conforms to generally acceptable practices in the field is imperative. Finally, the judge must be able to put all this information together in such a way as to make a decision about how well the four previous steps mesh with the conclusion the expert espouses.

What's the theory? examining explanatory power

What's the theory? What's the hypothesis? And what's the difference? Expert testimony is proffered to support a theory. Theories are the starting point for scientific analysis. The difference between theory and hypothesis is a matter of degree: the

---

49 This brings into focus the principle of scientific reliability. Reliability in science refers to the reproducibility of results. Just because results are reproducible, however, does not mean they are correct. Kuhn provides the example of early studies purporting to show the existence of "phlogiston," a substance that was thought to cause fires. *See* Kuhn, note 11, pp. 148–49, accounting for the replacement of the phlogiston theory with Lavoisier's chemical theory as a paradigm shift, caused when so much data anomalous to the theory accumulates that it causes a crisis in the way scientists perceive the interrelationships of theory, terms, concepts, and relationships. The results of the phlogiston experiments could be reproduced, but the underlying theory was wrong. *Id.* On the other hand, if results are irreproducible, that suggests something is wrong with the methodology.

50 Lakatos explained that "[a] hypothesis, however novel in its intuitive aspects, will not be allowed to be proposed, unless it has novel empirical content in excess of its predecessor." Lakatos, *Programmes*, note 19, p. 142.

51 *See* Popper, note 3, p. 279, explaining that accommodating newly discovered evidence is the hallmark of valid theorizing.

theory has achieved more testing and refinement (and, therefore, acceptability) than has a hypothesis.[52] As noted previously, judges cannot decide whether a scientific theory or hypothesis is correct. Neither can scientists. Instead, anyone making a decision about whether a given theory/hypothesis is "valid" can only decide whether a given theory is adequately supported by facts and logic to be reliable, either as evidence at trial, or – in the case of a scientist – as a basis for further experimentation. Understanding science as a process of idea construction rather than mere description makes it possible to examine the logic of the ideas about which the expert proposes to testify and how they are rationally related to what they are supposed to show.

Knowing what the underlying theory is – and whether it makes sense – is the first step in this process. Analysis of all the available biological information is the key to knowing whether each of the analytic steps "fits" together to make a coherent whole. In a toxic tort case, for example, the underlying theory on the most general level is that exposure to chemicals can cause illness or birth defects; less broadly, that a particular chemical can cause specific illness or birth defects; and, at the level of specific causation, that certain chemicals to which plaintiffs were exposed caused the plaintiffs' disease or birth defects. In a criminal case where identification is the issue, the theory is that each individual has unique identifying characteristics (e.g., DNA, fingerprints, handwriting) shared by relatively few other people, that these characteristics can be measured, and that the frequency with which these characteristics appear in the general population is quantifiable.

Identifying the theory is deceptively simple, although courts rarely stop to explain what theory underlies the expert's testimony. Assessing the theory's validity – that is, determining whether each of the steps fits together to make a coherent whole – is more difficult, and courts routinely get it wrong. Scientists use their data as building blocks for their analogies. Assessing the aptness of the analogy requires attention to the data; understanding assumptions, methodology, hypotheses, and theory; and weighing the strength of the links between them. Underlying all of this is the understanding that biological processes are complex interactions that can only be understood in probabilistic terms. A good theory accommodates most or all of the available evidence. It explains data that appear to refute it. Examining all the available data is, therefore, key to deciding whether the theory explains the phenomenon well enough to be admissible.

Examine all the available data

Many courts – including the U.S. Supreme Court in *Joiner* – mistakenly require that each study support the entirety of the expert's hypothesis.[53] This is a fundamental

---

52 *See* Popper, note 36, p. 121, stating that if a hypothesis repeatedly withstands testing, it may become accepted as theory.
53 The U.S. Supreme Court in *Joiner* made this mistake when, rather than assess how the various studies in conjunction supported the expert's hypothesis, it rejected each study seriatim as unable

misconception about the scientific process. No single study should be expected to show all this information, nor should the supporting data be limited to one particular field of inquiry. Complex scientific inferences are rarely based on a single type of study; rather, consistent association in several types of studies combined with a causal mechanism consistent with a biological theory is the hallmark of a justifiable inference. Not only are many steps necessary to build a theory, but each step is itself built on a theory that is based on many steps, and so on. Moreover, experimental studies using different methodologies (e.g., in vivo animal studies, in vitro tissue-culture studies, and structure-activity relationship studies) have inferential synergy. That is, together the studies have a far greater inferential force than if taken separately. Of course, not all evidence will corroborate the expert's hypothesis, and the expert should be able to explain contradictory or conflicting data. A sound biological explanation would be drawn from many well-performed studies of humans, animals, cells, general metabolic processes, and chemical structure.[54] Each of these kinds of studies provides different information contributing to an understanding of the other studies and how they fit within the explanatory theory.

Many courts refuse to apply this kind of analysis, mistakenly believing that it is a "methodology result[ing] from the preventive perspective that the agencies adopt in order to reduce public exposure to harmful substances."[55] On the contrary, this approach is not used only in preventive agency determinations. It is the most widely used methodology of the scientific community and has firm scientific support. Moreover, courts should not confuse risk assessment with risk management.[56]

to justify the expert's causation conclusion. See General Electric Co. v. Joiner, 522 U.S. 136, 146–7 (1997).

54 See, e.g., RONAN O'RAHILLY AND FABIOLA MULLER, HUMAN EMBRYOLOGY & TERATOLOGY, 8–9 (2d ed., 1996), explaining the importance of animal studies to understanding human development; JAMES L. SCHARDEIN, CHEMICALLY INDUCED BIRTH DEFECTS, 24–33 (2d ed., 1990), discussing use of structure-activity studies, pharmacokinetics, animal models, and in vitro methods for studying birth defects; Barbara D. Beck et al., The Use of Toxicology in the Regulatory Process in PRINCIPLES AND METHODS, note 30, p. 25, observing that "the rational approach is to examine all sources of information in the evaluation of toxic chemicals; A TEXTBOOK OF MODERN TOXICOLOGY, 6–7 (Ernest Hodgson and Patricia E. Levi, eds., 2d ed., 1997), explaining the interrelatedness of toxicology with other sciences. This is the approach used by the EPA in assessing the risk of cancer or birth defects presented by various chemicals, as well as by the International Agency for Research on Cancer (IARC), the World Health Organization, and the NTA. In this respect, the agencies have it right.

55 Allen v. Pennsylvania Engineering Corp., 102 F.3d, 194, 197 (5th Cir.1996). In Allen, the plaintiff's experts sought to testify that plaintiff's exposure to ethylene oxide had caused his brain cancer, relying on imperfect epidemiological studies, animal studies, and cell biology data, none of which standing alone was sufficient to explain the plaintiff's illness. Id. Despite the recognized connection between ethylene oxide exposure and other kinds of cancers, of which the judge took judicial notice, a "suggestive" link between the chemical and brain cancer demonstrated by the epidemiological studies, animal studies showing brain tumors developed in rats after exposure to the chemical, and cell biology studies showing the chemical to have "mutagenic and genotoxic capabilities," the court found that the "paucity of epidemiological evidence, the unreliability of animal studies, and the inconclusiveness of cell biology combine to undercut the expert testimony" and was therefore inadmissible. Id. 196–7.

56 Although EPA risk characterization assessments should not necessarily be adopted as dispositive in toxic tort litigation, there is nothing inherently biased about the methodology used in reaching the

That is, the EPA may decide that a chemical has only a slight possibility of being carcinogenic (i.e., the risk assessment) and nevertheless decide to regulate it to protect public health so that people are exposed at only very low levels (i.e., risk management).[57] Assessing the cumulative force of all the available information does not require adoption of unrealistic assumptions.

Most important, assessing the cumulative force of all the available information "recognizes the growing sophistication of research methods, particularly in their ability to reveal the modes of action of carcinogenic agents at cellular and subcellular levels as well as toxicokinetic and metabolic processes."[58] Science accommodates change. Judges too should accommodate changes in research. Although human studies may be the most relevant in assessing the effect of a given chemical on human beings, animal studies and information about the physical, structural, and chemical properties of a suspected agent can also yield important information about its risk to humans.

The more complete the picture presented by these various studies, the better the decision maker can assess the expert's conclusions.[59] However, all the pictures are incomplete. How to tell whether conflicting data and gaps in the information provided by the studies are fatal to the expert's proffered testimony or weaken the expert's position is a matter of carefully evaluating these uncertainties. In litigation, this means that the party espousing scientific evidence (usually the plaintiff in toxic tort actions, the prosecutor in criminal cases) will have to show how the individual studies on which the expert relies are linked together analytically with the inferences the expert wishes the court to draw.[60] But it also means that experts must be permitted to proffer studies other than human studies in support of their hypotheses.

---

risk characterization. *Cf.* Ellen Relkin, *The Sword or the Shield: Use of Governmental Regulations, Exposure Standards and Toxicological Data in Toxic Tort Litigation*, 6 Dick. J. Envtl. L. & Pol'y 1, 4 (1997), cautioning against wholesale adoption of risk assessment models.

57 *See* U.S. Environmental Protection Agency, "Proposed Guidelines for Carcinogen Risk Assessment" (hereinafter EPA Proposed Guidelines), 61 Fed. Reg. 17960, 17965 (1996). Although an expert's unexplained adoption of agency risk characterizations should be viewed critically by trial judges because they may be based on underlying default assumptions meant to protect the public, that does not mean the entire methodology should be categorically dismissed. Such a rejection fails to recognize that most agency determinations are based on scientific probability assessments, not on worst-case scenarios, and therefore may realistically assess the environmental risk. Indeed, the EPA's Proposed Guidelines explain that while initial assessments may be "worst case" in their default assumptions, subsequent risk assessments based on more complete information will replace the initial assessments as the data become available.

58 *See* EPA Proposed Guidelines, p. 17960.

59 *Id.*

60 *See, e.g.,* Judge Posner's analysis in *Rosen v. Ciba-Geigy Corp.*, 78 F.3d, 316, 319 (6th Cir. 1996), where he castigates the expert for attempting to infer precipitation of plaintiff's heart attack from a nicotine overdose based on animal studies showing that nicotine can contribute to the formation of plaque. As Judge Posner correctly pointed out, the expert had failed to distinguish between long- and short-term effects in reaching his conclusion and had failed to explain how a nicotine overdose (purportedly caused by wearing defendant's nicotine patch while smoking) could precipitate a heart attack. *Id.*, 319.

Use assumptions to fill the gaps

The reliance on assumptions within the heuristic may strike many legal readers as a departure from legal concepts of causation. In science, however, background theories and assumptions underpin any theory, hypothesis, or experiment. Being able to identify and critique these background assumptions is key to understanding scientific explanation.

As explained previously, facts alone, even scientific facts, are not knowledge. They become scientific knowledge only in conjunction with coherent answers to the following questions: What range of facts is worth investigation? What is the proper way to investigate them? What do the results of the investigation mean? Assumptions and theory permeate all these considerations. Values and judgment are involved with each step of the process; it is not necessarily that one expert is "right" and the other "wrong," but rather that, relying on different assumptions, they have each reached a separate, contradictory, but equally valid interpretation of the available information.[61]

The phenomenon of battling experts is not confined to the courtroom. Different approaches to data analysis may lead to radically different conclusions, depending on the researcher's underlying assumptions and strategies. Even in a controlled randomized study, two investigators from the same team can reach opposite conclusions.[62] It is "often not that one researcher is right and the other wrong, but that different assumptions, implemented through different analytical strategies, can produce conflicting results."[63] These (often unstated) assumptions must be analyzed by anyone trying to assess whether the expert's conclusion is a valid interpretation of the studies on which the expert relied.[64] It is important for the courts to be able to identify assumptions made in the studies because which assumptions are warranted

---

61 The *Hall* court's appointed expert explained the importance of inference-drawing, observing that it is not necessarily that one witness is right and the other wrong but rather that both can validly draw different inferences from the same data. *Hall v. Baxter Healthcare*, 947 F. Supp. 1387, 1447 (D. Or. 1996), observing that "both [plaintiffs' and defendants' experts' inferences] are based on scientifically valid data . . . arriv[ing] at somewhat different positions as a result of different, but legitimate, interpretations of the results." Curiously, the court did not respond to this explanation.

62 This is precisely what happened in the clinical trials of antibiotic treatment for "glue-ear," a common childhood ailment. *See* Andrew W. Osterland, *A Child's Guide to Medical Ethics*, FINANCIAL WORLD, August 16, 1994, p. 54, chronicling the disagreement between Drs. Erdem Cantekin and Charles Bluestone over whether antibiotics are effective in treating otitis media.

63 *See* George D. Smith, *Increasing the Accessibility of Data; Making Medical Research Data Available for Study Increases the Validity of the Research*, 308 BRIT. MED. J., 1519, 1519 (1994). One of the assumptions at stake in the otitis media controversy between Drs. Cantekin and Bluestone may have resulted (at least according to Cantekin) from bias stemming from drug-company funding of the studies. *See* Osterland, *id.*

64 One common mistake that judges make in assessing scientific testimony is to assume that the expert who relies on a particular study must adopt the study's conclusion. This is a fallacy because it is the underlying data – no doubt in conjunction with the underlying data from other studies – that has been used to reach a different but – absent any errors in reasoning – equally valid conclusion. "Science as we know it would not exist if scientists did not defend their theories, by criticizing either the assumptions that go into the design of an experiment that supposedly refutes their theories, or the alternative theories that are proposed as replacements for their theories." Warren Schmaus,

is an important basis of scientific argument and, therefore, is crucial to assessing the expert's theory.

Gaps in scientific knowledge are inevitable, not fatal flaws.[65] Making assumptions to fill gaps in scientific knowledge is a normal and necessary part of scientific analysis.[66] Most theories are built on sets of assumptions that follow a model (i.e., a metaphor), which varies somewhat from the actual process being studied but which nonetheless is a useful explanation.[67]

Appropriate inferences in the context of litigation should be based not only on the concerns of scientists but also on judicial policy concerns. Thus, the criteria for basic assumptions should be ensuring scientific validity; minimizing significant errors in estimating risks; maximizing incentives for safety research; and creating an orderly, predictable, and trustworthy process. Merely rejecting studies as "too speculative," as many courts dismissively call them, without explaining the basis for rejecting the underlying assumptions is not enough.[68] Intellectual due process requires explicit acknowledgment of the assumptions used – or rejected – by the court and the reasons for the court's determination. The next chapters of the book discuss default assumptions upon which sound judicial validity determinations should be based in a number of key areas of litigation.

Examine the methodology

Methodology is the way an experiment (or series of experiments) is conducted and refers to the process of gathering, measuring, and reporting data. Evaluating the data and the methodolgy through which it was obtained is an important aspect of assessing validity. To test an articulated scientific hypothesis, the scientist must design an experiment: a series of observations calculated to corroborate (or falsify) the

---

"An Analysis of Fraud and Misconduct in Science" in *AAAS-ABA National Conf. of Lawyers and Scientists, Project on Scientific Fraud and Misconduct Report on Workshop Number One 89* (1988).

65 Inferences based on general scientific knowledge about phenomena are not only acceptable, they are also unavoidable. *See* National Research Council, *Risk Assessment in the Federal Government: Managing the Process* (1983).

66 As one scientist explained,

> All scientific work is incomplete whether it be observational or experimental. All scientific work is liable to be upset or modified by advancing knowledge. That does not confer upon us a freedom to ignore the knowledge we already have, or to postpone the action that it appears to demand at a given time.

Hill, note 4, p. 295.

67 *See* National Research Council, note 65, p. 28. Of course, the metaphor needs to be apt. Metaphors are helpful explanatory tools only to the extent to which they are consistent with the evidence. And the evidence – that is, data – must have been produced through observations meeting certain standards. This is where the U.S. Supreme Court's emphasis on protocols and error rates comes in. *See Daubert v. Merrell Dow Pharmaceuticals, Inc.,* 509 U.S. 579, 594 (1993).

68 For cases rejecting studies as too speculative without analyses *see,* e.g., *Moore v. Ashland Chem. Co.,* 151 F. 3d, 269, 279 (5th Cir. 1998); *Allen v. Pennsylvania Engineering Corp.,* 102 F.2d, 194, 197 (5th Cir. 1996).

theory.[69] In designing an experiment, the researcher must decide how large a sample must be used to give statistically significant results. In addition, the researcher attempts to control the experiment so a minimum of variables impinge on discovering a proposed causal association. Any description of the methods used in a study should include the reason for their selection.

The major task of experimental design in laboratory sciences is to rule out excess variables, to rule out possibilities, and to manipulate the balance of choices. Reliability, experimental controls, and statistical analysis are all important facets of methology. In determining whether an experiment has yielded "reliable" data, a scientist looks at factors that relate to the control exerted over the experiment. Among those suspect practices that should set off warning bells are use of "historical controls," which are control subjects used in previous experiments.[70] Each time a study is performed, there should be controls in place so that extrinsic variables are accounted for. Background "noise" that could affect the experiment must be eliminated as much as possible (e.g., the laboratory and its equipment must be clean to prevent contamination of the procedure) or taken into account (i.e., human error means that no experiment can ever be performed perfectly).[71] By performing a number of experiments and determining how far the results deviate from each other and from those expected under the theory, the scientist determines the study's reliability.

Principles of experimental design differ widely from field to field in science: some fields require more exacting protocols than others.[72] Although perfection is unachievable and it may be necessary to stray from the standards, the expert should be able to account for this, giving adequate reasons for the variance. For example, in toxicology studies generally, the experiment will be designed to hold all variables constant except for the exposure to the chemical in question. The implicit assumption is that any changes observed will be due to the chemical. This, of course, is not always true, because of individual variation in the animals used, but the experimenter attempts to minimize such variations (by using genetically similar strains of mice, for example). In a good study, a range of doses should have been used in order to understand when a dose has no measurable effect. This is the

---

69 Actually, as Popper pointed out, the scientist can at most demonstrate that the data provisionally corroborate the theory.

70 The use of historical controls was the reason the *Hall* court's appointed immunology expert rejected one of the studies relied on by plaintiffs' expert. *See Hall v. Baxter Healthcare Corp.*, 947 F. Supp. 1387, 1462 (D. Or. 1996).

71 Patrick Suppes calls the background noise problem "ceteris paribus conditions" and acknowledges that "[d]etailed information about the distribution of physical parameters characterizing the experimental environment is not a simple matter to incorporate in models of data and is usually not reported in the literature; roughly speaking, some general ceteris paribus conditions are assumed to hold." Patrick Suppes, *Models of Data* in Logic, Methodology and Philosophy of Science: Proceedings of The 1960 International Congress, 258 (Ernest Nagel et al., eds., 1962).

72 Protocols offer a way of standardizing methodology and address such aspects of methodology as experimental conditions, reliability, and controls. *See* Fienberg et al., note 30, p. 17.

dose-response relationship, which is important in extrapolating the data to human beings. There are standards of appropriate laboratory practice, and the design of an experiment, or a series of experiments, should incorporate these standards or provide a logical basis for disregarding them.[73] There also are standards for clinical medicine, which are somewhat different from the standards of research science. In every field, however, the experiment must be designed so that the results can honestly be attributable to the data. In general, the standards require that scientists develop and follow a protocol, use extensive quality-control measures, and submit to outside audits of their studies.[74]

Courts in criminal cases have the most difficulty dealing with laboratory standards and protocols because criminal laboratories are largely unregulated and – with the notable exception of DNA evidence – much of what passes for criminal evidence lacks any empirical support. In toxic torts, on the other hand, courts frequently have gone to the opposite extreme, requiring strict adherence to conventional methodology. The important question for the judge in either civil or criminal trials is whether the experimental conditions and data really show what the expert says they show. When the study relied upon has been designed soundly from a statistical viewpoint, followed the protocols for such studies in their field, observed proper control techniques, and the technique used has demonstrated its reliability, the methodology is sound.

Putting it all together: assessing expert conclusions for admissibility

The last step in the heuristic involves putting together answers to the four previous inquiries (into the expert's theory, empirical support, assumptions, and methodology), Scientists distinguish unsupported propositions from valid hypotheses by looking at all the information that is marshaled in support; how well contrary information is addressed; and the coherence of the hypothesis, theory, and methodology. Judges and lawyers, however, must resolve the admissibility question:

---

73 For experiments in clinical medicine and drug testing, Good Laboratory Practices and Good Clinical Practices are the most widely used of these guidelines and are part of government contracts for clinical testing; similar guidelines are used in other countries. These formal guidelines are not applicable to basic scientific research, where the methods are new or have modified existing protocols; nonetheless, there are fundamental protocols in all fields, and departures from them must be explained. In the context of DNA testing, this concern over laboratory controls has been the focus of litigation in numerous cases. *See*, e.g., *People v. Simpson,* No. BA097211 (Cal. Super. Ct., October 3, 1996); *People v. Marlow,* 41 Cal. Rptr., 2d 5 (Cal. Ct. App. 1995), defense experts complained of the lack of duplicate testing, lack of controls, failure to accurately measure results, and performance on proficiency tests; and *State v. Bogan,* 905 P.2d 515 (Ariz. Ct. App. 1995), blind testing of *seed* pods found in defendant's truck and at the crime scene made tests more reliable.

74 *See,* e.g., *Good Laboratory Practice,* 40 C.F.R. § 160 (1999); *Good Clinical Practice: Consolidated Guideline,* 62 *Fed. Reg.* 25692 (1997); AOAC International, *Official Methods of Analysis of AOAC International* (Patricia A. Cunniff, ed., 16th ed., 1999).

Is the expert's conclusion based on sound science?[75] In essence, for legal actors, this is a two-part question: Are the studies the expert relied upon relevant to the expert's conclusion; and is the expert's conclusion relevant to resolving an issue in the case (i.e., do they meet the requirement of "fit")? The first relevance inquiry requires an examination of whether the expert has corroborating empirical support for the proffered conclusion; and whether the expert has the data that do not support the conclusion. The question of "fit" involves an inquiry into whether the proffered studies add empirical content to the legal hypothesis. Do they add a piece to the puzzle picture? Do the proffered studies add anything to the expert's explanation of how things work? The question of empirical support requires examining the tests the hypothesis has undergone in terms of variety and methodology, with an eye toward those tests that might have been performed but were not. The reason for any absence of testing must also be taken into account. For example, in toxic torts, chemical manufacturers have a strong disincentive to engage in safety research that may provide information that could later be used against them. Tests that would be helpful in establishing the causation hypothesis may be absent. In other contexts, however, absence of testing may indicate a flaw in the expert's reasoning. For example, in the criminal context, expert failure to test the theory of individualization severely undermines the strength of much identification evidence.

One caveat: The question of whether there is sound support for the expert's conclusion is made more difficult by the way scientists articulate their conclusions.[76] This applies to the individual studies relied upon as well as to the expert's ultimate conclusion. For courts seeking certainty to justify their determinations, it is very frustrating to hear that a hypothesis can only be empirically tested, it can never be proven true. Unfortunately, however, there is no method of discovering the absolute truth in science. Indeed, there is no method of ascertaining whether a hypothesis is even probable. The most that can be asked is that the theory be consistent internally, consistent with other theories that have withstood repeated critique, and consistent with the data. In other words, what science offers is not the truth, not certainty, but explanation.

In addition to the inability of a truthful scientist to say whether a proffered hypothesis is "probable," the language of scientific conclusions poses another problem for judges. Because the goal of scientists is to exclude false positives – to

---

75 The task for the judge in an admissibility determination is not to determine whose evidence is most persuasive and exclude the evidence pointing the other way but rather to decide whether the evidence reasonably supports the expert's hypothesis. *See, e.g.,* Thomas J. Mack, *Scientific Testimony After* Daubert: *Some Early Returns From the Lower Courts,* 30 TRIAL 23, 28–30 (August 1994), noting that conflating sufficiency with admissibility, although mistaken, is widespread among the federal courts. For cases conflating the standards, *see Conde v. Velsicol Chemical Corp.,* 24 F.3d 809, 814 (6th Cir. 1994); *Hall v. Baxter Healthcare, Inc.,* 947 F. Supp. 1387, 1397 (D. Or., 1996); *In re* Hanford Nuclear Reservation Litig. 1998 WL 775340, at ∗140–41 (E.D. Wash. 1998); and *National Bank of Commerce v. Dow Chem. Co.,* 965 F. Supp., 1490, 1530 (E.D. Ark. 1996).

76 *See,* e.g., *Allison v. McGhan Medical Corp.,* 184 F.3d, 1300, 1315 (11th Cir. 1999), excluding evidence because the expert was willing to testify to "association" but not "causation."

avoid claiming there is an effect when there is none – scientific conclusions are couched in tentative phrases.[77] "Association" is preferred to "causation."[78] Thus, failing to understand that causation, like other hypotheses, can never be proven true, courts may reject as unreliable even evidence that easily meets scientific criteria for validity.[79]

It is equally nonsensical to discard a study just because it concludes differently from the testifying expert.[80] Experts can draw diametrically opposed conclusions about a perfectly valid study. That does not mean that one of the experts has drawn an invalid conclusion or that any conclusion would be speculative. It is more likely that the experts have used different underlying assumptions to fill the information gaps. This is in no way illegitimate or even unusual. It is not up to the judge to decide between battling experts; the admissibility determination is whether there is support for the hypothesis. As long as the study's data support the expert's hypothesis, the expert can justifiably rely on it. Thus, the expert's reasoning rather than the conclusions of the various studies relied on should be the focus of the inquiry. Unfortunately, because they fail to understand the language of scientific conclusion-drawing, courts frequently exclude expert testimony on this basis.[81]

Another problem posed by the language of scientific conclusion-drawing is that many published studies conclude that more research needs to be done.[82] Experts relying on such studies are apt to be confronted with exclusion because the judge finds theses studies irrelevant to the expert's testimony (i.e., failing to meet the "fit" requirement) as too speculative. This reflects ignorance of the research enterprise. It is not surprising that scientists publishing the results of their studies in scientific journals conclude that more research needs to be done. Of course it does.[83] There

---

77 *See*, e.g., *Hall,* 947 F. Supp. 1447, court-appointed epidemiology expert explaining that "in epidemiological science the odds are stacked against incorrectly rejecting the null hypothesis."

78 *See*, e.g., *Merrell Dow Pharmaceuticals, Inc. v. Havner,* 953 S.W.2d, 706, 727 (Tex. 1997), noting that the "discipline of epidemiology studies associations, not 'causation' per se."

79 *See Wright v. Willamette Industries, Inc.,* 91 F.3d 1105 (8th Cir. 1996), requiring proof of actual exposure at a level known to produce harm.

80 *See*, e.g., *General Electric Co. v. Joiner,* 522 U.S. 136, 145 (1997), rejecting study of workers at an Italian capacitor plant who had been exposed to PCBs because, although the authors "noted that lung cancer deaths among ex-employees at the plant were higher than might have been expected, . . . there were no grounds for associating lung cancer deaths. . . . and exposure." *See also Kelley v. American Heyer-Schulte Corporation,* 957 F. Supp., 873, 877 (W.D. Tex. 1997), rejecting because reasonable epidemiologist would not rely on study to find evidence of a causal relationship; *Cavallo v. Star Enterprise,* 892 F. Supp., 756, 763 (E.D. Va. 1995), finding that study did not establish link between exposure and illness.

81 *See*, e.g., *Rutigliano v. Valley Bus. Forms,* 929 F. Supp., 779, 785 (D. N.J. 1996), warning "against [the] use of medical literature to draw conclusions not drawn in the literature itself", *aff'd* 118 F.3d 1577 (3d Cir. 1997); *National Bank of Commerce v. Dow Chemical Co.,* 965 F. Supp., 1490, 1517 (E.D. Ark. 1996), excluding expert testimony that was based on studies that did not "go to the same extent as the opinions she would put before the jury."

82 *See*, e.g., *Kelley v. American Heyer-Schulte Corp.,* 957 F. Supp., 873, 877 (W.D. Tex. 1997), excluding report suggesting that "further research was necessary before firm conclusions could be drawn."

83 *See* Chalmers, note 44, pp. 125–26, observing that objective opportunities created by the work of other scientists and social forces – like funding – are what drives science.

are always gaps in our knowledge, and scientists are anxious to pursue the quest of filling them. How else to continue adding to the communal puzzle? How else to convince funding authorities to continue to support the effort? Good research tends to generate more research, if the funding can be found. It is thus irresponsible for a judge to exclude testimony merely because a study relied on concludes that more research needs to be done.

So what makes an explanation scientifically sound? High empirical content is important.[84] But, given the unavoidable gaps in our knowledge, how much empirical content ought a judge to demand for admissibility? There are a number of theories about evaluating evidence under uncertainty, each contributing important insights.[85] The following inquiries may prove helpful to judges having to decide whether there is sufficient empirical support to admit the expert's theory into evidence.[86] First, for each proffered study, how valuable is each study on its own? What piece of the hypothetical puzzle does each study provide? How sound is the methodology underlying each study? What are the areas of uncertainty the study fails to address? Given the knowledge of the first study (or set of studies), how much more support does the second study (or set of studies) add to the expert's hypothesis? What information gaps does it fill? How much does the second study (or set of studies) explain in the absence of the first study (or set of studies)? How rare or unexpected are the results of each of the studies?[87] In addition to the extent and strength of empirical support, consistency within the theory, with other current theories, and with all the available data is also an important consideration, as are the acceptability of underlying assumptions, whether each of the proffered studies is methodologically sound, and whether each contributes toward a plausible explanation.[88]

84 *See* Popper, note 36, p. 252, arguing the importance of empirical corroboration.
85 *See* Peter Tillers, *Mapping Inferential Domains*, 66 B.U. L. Rev., 883, 890 (1986), describing Bayesianism, Baconian rationalism, fuzzy set theory, and story theory as complementary systems and arguing that "diverse models of inference are both permissible and necessary."
86 *See* David A. Schum, Evidence and Inference for the Intelligence Analyst, Vol. II 192–93 (1987), suggesting questions that may be helpful in evaluating inferences drawn from evidence.
87 The unexpectedness of results may lead one to question methodology, but if the methodology and assumptions are sound, it may signal a robust theory. *See* Popper, note 3, pp. 57–58.
88 *See*, e.g., Schum, note 86, pp. 124–33, asserting that the art of valid conclusion-drawing consists in answering six questions: What did you expect? What do you know from the evidence? What does "believable evidence" mean? How consistent is the evidence? Can the value of any evidence be enhanced or suppressed? What's missing?

4

Toxic torts and the causation conundrum

It is in the arena of toxic tort cases that the "battle of the experts" has been the most vicious, protracted, and well publicized, at least in the United States. In the United Kingdom, Canada, Australia, and New Zealand, there are few toxic tort cases brought and far less controversy about the use of experts.[1] In civil law countries such as the Netherlands, where experts are appointed by the court on mutual agreement of the parties and prepare a joint report, disagreements are rarely aired in court.[2] But in the United States, toxic torts have been a battleground about what counts as science in the courtroom, and this issue propelled both *Daubert* and *Joiner*[3] into the U.S. Supreme Court.

Because of long latency periods and symptoms common to many diseases, proving causation in toxic torts nearly always involves the use of scientific experts, and courts are often stymied by their gatekeeping responsibilities in this arena. The courts have particular difficulty with several major issues, including statistical analysis, the admissibility and evaluation of animal studies, the impact of cumulative studies, and the conflation of admissibility with sufficiency. The underlying reason that courts appear to founder in this area is that causation – an essential element for liability – is highly uncertain, scientifically speaking, and courts do not deal well with this uncertainty.

---

1 Because there are relatively few tort cases brought in these countries, the controversy about what counts as science has emerged there primarily in the criminal context. The absence of civil juries and socialized medicine or national health insurance systems may be contributing factors. In addition, fee-shifting rules, a general prohibition on contingency fees, the rarity of punitive damage awards, and the general unavailability of joint and several liability in these countries may also have something to do with the paucity of toxic tort cases brought.

2 For an article discussing the Netherlands' experience with toxic torts in Halcion, asbestos, and diethylstylbestrol (DES) cases, *see* Petra van Kampen and Hans Nijboer, *Daubert in the Lowlands*, 30 U.C. Davis L. Rev. 951, 985 (1997), observing that the use of mutually agreed-upon experts who issue a joint report and are regarded as assistants to the court serve to prevent conflicts from reaching the court.

3 *Daubert* involved claims that the plaintiffs' birth defects were caused by the anti-nausea drug, Bendectin. *Daubert v. Merrell Dow Pharmeceuticals, Inc.*, 509 U.S. 579 (1993). *Joiner* involved claims that the plaintiff's lung cancer had been promoted by his exposure to the defendants' PCBs, which the plaintiff sought to support by expert testimony founded on two animal studies and four epidemiology studies. *See General Electric Co. v. Joiner*, 522 U.S. 136 (1997).

Scientific uncertainty about causation stems from a number of factors. Background rates of a given disease (e.g., cancer) in the general population make it difficult to establish a causal linkage between exposure to a potentially disease-causing agent and the disease. In addition, the exact mechanism of many diseases – like cancer – is still unknown, and many factors may be involved.[4] Further, because empirical experiments on humans are seldom possible (for ethical or feasibility reasons), many levels of uncertainty exist for toxicity studies. The uncertainties do not keep scientists from considering the studies valid.[5] Judges, on the other hand, frequently exclude testimony as invalid based on the same uncertainties that scientists accept as inevitable. This makes general causation testimony (i.e., whether a given agent is capable of causing a particular disease) the subject of intense admissibility disputes.

Specific causation (i.e., whether this particular plaintiff's disease was the result of exposure to the agent at issue) adds another layer of uncertainty. No matter how persuasive epidemiological or toxicological studies may be, they could not show individual causation, although they might enable a (probabilistic) judgment about the association of a particular chemical exposure to human disease in general. This brings into focus an important consideration underlying any scientific evidence: Attributing causation for a particular individual is not a scientific but a legal finding. Even if epidemiologists and toxicologists are able to identify correlations between exposure to a given chemical and a disease, their summary statistical statements apply only to the group studied, not to the individual members of the group. And even if a physician's diagnosis attributes the plaintiff's disease to a given agent, there is still a great deal of attendant uncertainty. That does not mean judges should exclude scientific testimony until more certainty appears. An overall assessment of the probabilities enables rational decisions even under conditions of uncertainty.

Are there scientific criteria that judges can use for causation determinations?

One set of criteria frequently proposed are the criteria of Austin Hill.[6] But Hill himself explained that his criteria were not to be used in this way. Koch's postulates

---

4 Most diseases are caused by many factors, and rather than speaking of one cause, scientists are more likely to refer to a causal network. *See, e.g.,* Mel Greaves, *Cancer Causation: The Darwinian Downside of Past Success?* 3 LANCET 244–45 (2002), noting that "Cancers are a collective of some hundreds of cellular disorders of differing origins and degrees of malignancy" and proposing a causal network for cancer risk.

5 Indeed, epidemiologists rely on a number of operational criteria that explicitly acknowledge the probabilistic nature of attributable risk. That is, epidemiologists conceive of causation as a matter of degree, rather than a dichotomy, and use certain criteria in making this assessment. *See,* generally, GERRY P. QUINN AND MICHAEL J. KEOGH, EXPERIMENTAL DESIGN AND DATA ANALYSIS FOR BIOLOGISTS (2002).

6 *See* Austin Bradford Hill, *The Environment and Disease: Association or Causation?*, 58 PROC. ROYAL SOCIETY OF MED, 295–300 (1965). These operational criteria include (1) strength of association in statistical terms; (2) dose-response effect – that is, higher frequency of disease with higher doses; (3) temporality: hypothesized cause must precede disease; (4) consistency of findings with other studies; (5) biological plausibility (i.e., support of the theory from biological sciences); (6) coherence

for inferring causation of disease by microorganisms are sometimes proposed as bases for scientific validity.[7] These simplistic frameworks are not useful criteria for admissibility, however, because they – like the guidelines of the Federal Judicial Center's *Reference Manual* – are unachievable. Few studies could (or should) hope to meet all the criteria. Not only do scientists recognize that no studies could meet all the criteria, differences arise among scientists in different disciplines, and even within the same discipline, with respect to the amount of evidence that is needed to justify causation. For example, consistency of the observed effect is a criterion most scientists would deem important, but it may be absent even where there is a strong causal link, such as the link between smoking and lung cancer, which, although strong, is not inevitably observed. Although it might be persuasive to find that there was a consistent specific association between exposure and a particular disease, such association is rarely observed.[8] Dose-response curves are important, but the absence of a linear response does not necessarily destroy the causal inference, although it does indicate a more complex relationship between the agent and disease.[9] Temporality is the one criterion that is universally recognized as a prerequisite for causation, and everyone agrees that it alone is not enough.[10]

Although scientists, like judges, often apply rules of thumb in assessing argument, there are well-recognized caveats, exceptions, and countervailing notions that may make them inapplicable. Lumping studies in categories according to their persuasiveness (roughly analogous to the rankings of legal authority) may simplify decision making, but things are not really as simple as such a hierarchy suggests. Empowering one type of information or one kind of study to the exclusion of another makes no scientific or evidentiary sense. Each of the canons has a counterpoint. Each type of methodology has inherent strengths and weaknesses, as does each particular study. In sum, scientists recognize that what matters most is the explanatory power of the proffered theory and how well the data support the theory, and what available data undermine it. Nonetheless, it is helpful to recognize the following rules of thumb when attempting to understand scientific arguments about causation.

(with regard to the natural history of the disease); and (7) specificity of association (i.e., disease rare outside of the exposure). These factors must be considered together rather than as a checklist.

7 Koch was a bacteriologist who outlined criteria for causation, including (1) higher prevalence of disease in exposed rather than unexposed populations; (2) those with the disease should have had more exposure to the agent than healthy populations; (3) experiments should demonstrate increased incidence of disease in exposed over unexposed populations; (4) temporality; (5) linear dose-response curve; (6) biological plausibility; and a number of other factors relating to immune responses. *See* Alfred S. Evans, *Causation and Disease: The Henle-Koch Postulates Revisited*, 49 Yale J. Bio. & Med. 175 (1976), explaining that these postulates "were not regarded as rigid criteria by Koch himself and should not be today."

8 This factor is often referred to by the courts as a "signature" disease, although most courts recognize that it is not a prerequisite for admissibility.

9 The Federal Judicial Center's *Reference Manual* agrees on this point, noting that although the presence of a linear dose-response relationship strengthens the inference of causation, its absence should not be taken to weaken it.

10 Just because most dead women are postmenopausal does not necessarily mean that menopause is fatal, for example.

Statistical analysis: numbers count

As discussed in Chapter 3, statistical analysis and probabilistic thinking are key to understanding the validity of scientific studies. Two kinds of statistical analysis may be used in scientific argument: descriptive and inferential. Descriptive statistics describe the data and include concepts such as mean and standard deviation. Inferential statistics are used in drawing conclusions, as in epidemiology, where inferences are made about the general population from a single study. There are some rules of thumb to simplify this analysis; however, as with all such rules, there are important caveats and exceptions.

Generally speaking, large samples (i.e., studies involving a large number of subjects) are better than small ones, and more studies are better than fewer. There are statistical reasons for these preferences for large and repeated studies. Repeating studies a number of times enables the researcher to identify and reject mistaken data that are the result of random[11] or systematic error.[12] With some variability, researchers expect the data to cluster about the mean in a characteristic manner.[13] The standard deviation indicates how far two particular data points deviate from the mean. So when the sample (study) is small, using few individual measurements, the variance[14] and standard deviation increase and the confidence intervals widen.[15] This decreases the power (or sensitivity) of the test to detect changes.

Power refers to the probability that the study for the hypothesis being tested will reject the alternative hypothesis (that there is an effect) when it is false. Power increases with the size of the study.[16] The validity of experimental design depends on the power (or sensitivity) of a test to detect the response for which the researcher is looking.

Relative risk is similarly a determination that requires a minimum sample size in experimental design.[17] In epidemiology, very large sample sizes are necessary to

11 Random errors are beyond the control of the researcher; they are unaccountable fluctuations in the data that are generally accounted for by statistical methods. *See* GERRY P. QUINN AND MICHAEL J. KEOGH, EXPERIMENTAL DESIGN AND DATA ANALYSIS FOR BIOLOGISTS (2002).

12 Systematic error is caused by improper experimental procedure or design and can be corrected if the cause of error is determined. Determining whether an error is random or systematic is not easy, of course, and is one reason proper experimental design includes running a number of tests to gather the same data. "[A] widely used standard is Chauvenet's criterion, which states that if the probability of the value deviating from the mean by the observed amount is 1/2 N [where N = the number of values obtained] or less, the data should be rejected." STUART L. MEYER, DATA ANALYSIS FOR SCIENTISTS AND ENGINEERS 17 (1975).

13 The mean of a batch of numbers lies somewhere in the middle of the data.

14 Variance is the square of the standard deviation.

15 The confidence interval is an estimate for a quantity in a population. Thus, when only a few data points are used, there may be statistical significance for rejecting the null hypothesis, but the confidence intervals detract from the study's conclusions.

16 Power also increases with the degree of difference from the null hypothesis (i.e., the more extreme the alternatives, the better the power).

17 Statistical tests, such as significance and relative risk, depend on the size of the population, which means that in large populations, even small differences may be statistically significant, whereas in small populations, even a large effect may not be statistically differentiated from chance. For an excellent explanation of epidemiological principles, *see*, generally, KENNETH J. ROTHMAN AND

detect a 50 percent increased incidence of disease (for a relative risk of two).[18] Thus, in general, a large study's findings will be more persuasive than those of a small study.

Statistical significance is a statement about the frequency with which a particular finding is likely to arise by chance.[19] Confidence limits indicate the values within which a certain percentage of all data are likely to fall. Hypothesis testing – that is, testing the hypothesis of some effect against the null hypothesis of no effect – consists of determining if two (or more) groups of data differ from each other at a predetermined level of confidence. If a study shows statistical significance, that is grounds for rejecting the null hypothesis.[20] In other words, the association is

---

SANDER GREENLAND, MODERN EPIDEMIOLOGY (2d ed., 1998). The relative risk (RR) is equal to the risk in exposed populations divided by the risk in unexposed populations. *See* Richard W. Clapp and David Ozonoff, *Environment and Health: Vital Intersection or Contested Territory?*, 36 AM. J. L. & MED. 189, 209, explaining that "when the RR = 2.0, the risk in the exposed population is double that of the unexposed." The confidence interval around the RR expresses how stable the estimate is in repeated experiments. *Id.*, 210. A 95 percent confidence interval is equal to the range of numbers that would include the real risk 95 percent of the time if the study were repeated. *Id.*, noting that "A relative risk of 1.8 with confidence interval of 1.3 to 2.9 could very likely represent a true relative risk of greater than 2.0, and as high as 2.9 in 95 out of 100 repeated trials."

18 *See* Philip E. Enterline, *Epidemiologic Basis for the Asbestos Standard*, 52 ENVTL. HEALTH PERSP. 53 (1983), noting that a sample of at least a thousand individuals would be necessary to detect a 50 percent increase in deaths from asbestos. Relative risk (or odds ratio), which statistically describes the measured strength of association between a disease and a risk factor, is an important concept in epidemiological studies. *Relative risk* is an epidemiological term defined mathematically as the probability that an individual's injury was caused by exposure to a particular agent. See DAVID E. LILIENFELD AND PAUL D. STOLLEY, FOUNDATIONS OF EPIDEMIOLOGY, 200–202 (3d ed., 1994). It is defined as the percentage of risk in the exposed population attributable to the agent under investigation. Any relative risk greater than 1.0 shows some increase of risk in the exposed population; a relative risk of 2.0 is a doubling of the risk.

19 As prominent epidemiologist Sander Greenland explains the concept of statistical hypothesis testing, "'Nonsignificance' at the 0.05 level (P > 0.05) means one and only one thing: That, assuming the null hypothesis AND perfect study validity, there is a reasonable probability (at least 5%) of observing data as or more discrepant from the null as the data that were observed (where discrepancy is measured by a test (statistic)." Sander Greenland, *The Need for Critical Appraisal of Expert Witnesses in Epidemiology and Statistics*, 39 WAKE FOREST L. REV. 291, 294 (2004). A result that fails to meet a predetermined level of statistical significance means that the null hypothesis cannot be rejected, not that it is correct. Conversely, "it also means one cannot reject the hypothesis that there is an effect." *Id.*, 296, noting that absence of evidence is not evidence of absence.

20 The null hypothesis is defined as the hypothesis that there is no association of exposure to disease. This is far from an uncontroversial position in epidemiology, where this kind of "privileging" of the null hypothesis may result in distorting the logic of causal attribution by refusing to acknowledge that all hypotheses are conjectural and should be evaluated for their explanatory power rather than by some (perhaps misleading) rule of thumb. *See, e.g.,* PETER B. MEDAWAR, ADVICE TO A YOUNG SCIENTIST, 73 (1979), explaining that any hypothesis is conjectural and should be evaluated in light of alternative hypotheses and refuting evidence. For example, the International Agency for Research on Cancer classifies chemicals according to a gradation of the evidence for cancer causation rather than a dichotomatous (i.e., yes/no) classification. *See* IARC, *IARC Monographs on the Evaluation of Carcinogenic Risks to Humans: Vol. 7,7 Some Industrial Chemicals,* 41–42 (2000), distinguishing between and requiring evidence of no effect rather than no evidence of effect before classifying a chemical as "probably not carcinogenic." Ambiguous evidence – that is, inability to reject the null hypothesis – is not the same as evidence that there is no effect.

unlikely to be due to chance. Lack of statistical significance means that the null hypothesis cannot be rejected; it does not mean that there is no association.

It is important to remember that association of agent and disease does not prove causation even under the best of circumstances, such as a well-conducted epidemiological study. The results of scientific studies can only tell us how frequently exposure to the agent would be associated with disease as a matter of chance. Probabilities are ways to set limits for decisions about whether an association between two variables exists. Although the choices about the appropriate degree of conservatism to employ in making a decision about causation may vary with the context, scientists are already very conservative, in that scientific analyses are oriented to rejecting false positives.[21]

Even with these widely accepted rules of thumb, statistical analyses (and their uses) are far from cut and dried; they are often the subject of lively debate. Understanding statistical assumptions made in extrapolating data from studies is often critical to evaluating the validity of a study's announced results.[22] Scientists routinely examine how statistical methods were used when critiquing each others' work. These critiques have some frequently recurring themes.

First, errors abound in the use of statistics, and courts need to be aware of this potential for error.[23] Second, statistical significance is a choice, not a fixed requirement. A scientist may have good reasons for choosing a different value than the standard 0.05 level. Third, statistical significance must be interpreted together with

---

21 Scientists attempt, whenever possible, to control and eliminate inaccuracies and explicitly attempt to minimize Type II (beta) error, the probability of failing to reject a false hypothesis. *See* T. COLTON, STATISTICS IN MEDICINE, 128 (1974). To accomplish this, scientists demand 95 percent confidence intervals and corresponding p-values of 5 percent before they consider their studies to have statistical significance. *See* Shayne C. Gad, *Statistics for Toxicologists* in PRINCIPLES AND METHODS IN TOXICOLOGY, 285 (A. Wallace Hayes, ed., 4th ed., 2001).

22 For example, in a formaldehyde risk assessment case, the two sides disputing formaldehyde safety were sharply divided over which of several sets of figures generated by an agreed-upon multistage mathematical model was the appropriate choice. *See UAW v. Pendergrass*, 878 F.2d, 389, 394 (D.C. Cir. 1989), reviewing OSHA's formaldehyde standard and remanding to the agency for a better explanation or a new risk estimate. The maximum likelihood estimate, an average calculation of risk showing a convex dose-response curve at low doses, was advocated by the agency, whereas the upper confidence limit, a risk-averse calculation that is linear at low doses (and therefore shows a higher response at low doses than does the maximum likelihood estimate) was advocated by the plaintiff. *Id.* at 395. The agency had selected a multistage mathematical model for purposes of extrapolating from the positive data on rats exposed to high levels of formaldehyde, which assumed there was no exposure below which formaldehyde would have no carcinogenic effect. *Id.* The problems arose over how to interpret the results of the model, a dispute over logical inferences and assumptions. The choice between linearity and convexity also implicated assumptions regarding whether the effect of the chemical in question enhances risks from other background carcinogens (entailing linearity) or acts independently (entailing convexity). The court noted that although the agency "acknowledged the truth of facts that appear to compel it to assume linearity at low doses in its risk assessment [i.e., the synergy of background wood dust and formaldehyde] . . . [I]t then proceeded either to discard the resulting estimates or at least give them comparatively scant weight," a failure of logic that necessitated remand to the agency. *Id.*, 395–6. On remand, OSHA lowered its formaldehyde standard to 0.75. *See* 29 C.F.R. § 1910.1048(c) (1999).

23 *See, e.g.,* Colton, note 21, p. 12, citing a study in which 73 percent of the published papers in three of the "most frequently read medical journals" contained significant statistical errors but concluding that statistics is nonetheless important to scientific argument.

biological significance (i.e., biological relevance). That is, unless the agent affects the body's function in some important way, statistical significance is meaningless.

Some common statistical errors include making inappropriate inferences based on questionable statistical techniques, failing to report contradictory evidence, and choosing statistical or graphing techniques that make the data look better than they are. Only by examining the data can the conclusions drawn by the studies be verified. The inquiry should be directed toward questioning whether the data were "trimmed" to favor a certain outcome and making sure that the results "were not the product of over-enthusiastic data torture." (As the old saw has it, if you torture statistics long enough, they'll tell you anything you want to hear.) Data that are "too good" are as suspect as data that are absent or do not fit the conclusions at all.

One might well ask: If statistical studies are error-prone or methods so controversial, why admit them? The answer is that they are a crucial part of scientific inference and can yield important insights if they are correctly done and based on viable assumptions. Examining statistical inferences in an expert's report or proffered testimony may appear a tall order for a lawyer or a judge, but statistical errors are fundamentally errors in logic.[24] At a minimum, lawyers and judges who are involved with admissibility determinations need to know enough to suspect a study's conclusions if either standard deviation or confidence intervals are large, indicating that the study included too small a number of observations (or data points) or that the method used to measure the data was imprecise.

The second issue that the courts need to recognize in statistical reasoning is that the numbers scientists frequently use, either to show that there was some effect (i.e., 0.05 is the conventional figure for statistical significance) or the magnitude of the effect (i.e., doubling of the risk as indicated by a relative risk of 2), are not magic.[25] They are functions of the size of the study. As noted previously, power varies with sample size, and the power of a hypothesis is the probability of correctly rejecting the null hypothesis when it is false. The level of statistical significance is set by the investigator in light of the acceptable Type I error rate (i.e., the error of rejecting the null hypothesis when it is true; a false positive). The higher the level of significance, the lower the power. The tradeoff is that the lower the false positives, the higher the false negatives will be, and while the legal consequence of privileging false positives is to decrease the chance that someone will recover whose health problem was not caused by exposure to the agent in question, the downside

24 By "logic" in statistics, I mean both Aristotelian deductive reasoning and inferential reasoning. For a concise introduction to the use of statistics in epidemiology, *see* Clapp and Ozonoff, note 17, pp. 204–11.

25 *Cf. Allison v. McGhan Med. Corp.*, 184 F.3d 1300, 1315, n.16 (11th Cir. 1999), upholding the district court's ruling excluding expert testimony based on a study with a relative risk of 1.24; *Hall v. Baxter Healthcare*, 947 F. Supp. 1387, 1403 (D. Or. 1996), upholding exclusion of testimony absent a showing of relative risk of 2 or above; *Sanderson v. Int'l Flavors & Fragrances*, 950 F. Supp. 981, 999–1000 (C.D. Cal. 1996), excluding expert testimony based on studies with relative risk less than 2.

is the likelihood that someone whose health was adversely affected will have the courthouse doors slammed in his or her face.

Third, and most important, an emphasis on statistics does not mean that scientists can ignore the context. Small studies can have vast biological significance (i.e., they may show health effects that matter) even without statistical significance, and epidemiological studies failing to make the judicially mandated relative risk of 2 may be extremely significant, biologically speaking.[26] Both biological significance and statistical significance are important to reasoning about biological systems. Judges are thus mistaken to categorically exclude testimony based on studies that fail to meet statistical significance of 0.05 or a relative risk of 2.[27] If a variety of studies in different disciplines shows association of agent and disease, scientists can make valid causal inferences even in the absence of statistical significance. The greater the number and diversity of confirming observations, the more likely it is that the theory or model is not flawed.

Statistical significance, a function of the size of the study, may be present in the absence of biological significance. Conversely, biological significance may be present in the absence of statistical significance. This is because the way a given chemical works in terms of its absorption, distribution, and metabolism is as important as the statistical attributes of the study. An example of biological significance in the absence of statistical significance is a rare tumor type appearing after chemical exposure in more animals than expected but too few to be statistically significant. The results of such a study are by no means irrelevant and should not be excluded. On the other hand, statistical significance without biological meaning is also possible; for example, where damage is commonly associated with a contemporaneous increase in three biochemicals, a statistically significant rise in just one may be biologically meaningless.

26 Some federal courts are beginning to acknowledge this precept. *See, e.g., Miller v. Pfizer*, 196 F. Supp. 2d, 1062, 1079 (D. Kan. 2002), recognizing that whereas most courts consider a relative risk of 2.0 a benchmark for admissibility, that reasoning is flawed. State courts, however, continue to demand a relative risk of 2.0. *See, e.g.,* in re *Lockheed Litig'n*, 115 Cal. App. 4th 558 (2d Dist. 2004), upholding exclusion of testimony relying on studies that failed to meet RR=2; *Graham v. Lautrec Ltd.,* 2003 WL 23512133, slip op., Mich. Cir. Ct., July 24, 2003, expert testimony based on studies with RR< 2 inadmissible; *In re Hanford Nuclear Reservation Litig.,* No. CY-91-3015-AAM, 1998 WL 77534, at *8 (E. D. Wash. August 21, 1998, requiring a relative risk of two – a doubling of the risk – for admissibility; and *Barrow v. Bristol-Meyers Squibb Co.,* No. 96–689-CIV-ORL-19B, 1998 WL 812318 at *23 (M. D. Fla, October 29, 1998) requiring studies to show a relative risk of two for admissibility.

27 For courts making this error, *see, e.g., Merrell Dow Pharmaceuticals, Inc. v. Havner,* 953 S.W.2d, 706 (Tex. 1997), under Texas equivalent of *Daubert,* rejecting any other level of statistical significance than 5 percent); *Kelley v. American Heyer-Schulte Corp.,* 957 F. Supp. 873 (W.D. Tex. 1997), rejecting testimony based on studies failing to show statistical significance; *Allen v. Pennsylvania Engineering Corp.,* 102 F.3d, 194 (5th Cir. 1996), rejecting testimony in the absence of statistical significance; *LeBlanc v. Merrell Dow Pharmaceuticals, Inc.,* 932 F. Supp. 782 (E.D. La. 1996), rejecting testimony based on studies failing to show statistical significance; and *Ambrosini v. The Upjohn Co.,* Civ. A. No. 84–3483, 1995 WL 637650 (D.D.C. October 18, 1995), rejecting epidemiological testimony failing to demonstrate a statistically significant association. *See also General Electric Co. v. Joiner,* 522 U.S. 136, 145(1997); and *Hall v. Baxter Healthcare Corp.,* 947 F. Supp. 1387, 1398 (D. Or. 1996).

Some commentators have attributed the causation conundrum in the courts to the differing burdens of proof in science and law.[28] In law, the civil standard of "more probable than not" is often characterized as a probability greater than 50 percent.[29] In science, on the other hand, the most widely used standard is a 95 percent confidence interval (corresponding to a 5 percent level of significance, or p-level).[30] Both sound like probabilistic assessment. As a result, the argument goes, civil judges should not exclude scientific testimony that fails scientific validity standards because the civil legal standards are much lower. The transliteration of the "more probable than not" standard of civil factfinding into a quantitative threshold of statistical evidence is misconceived. The legal and scientific standards are fundamentally different. They have different goals and different measures. Therefore, one cannot justifiably argue that evidence failing to meet the scientific standards nonetheless should be admissible because the scientific standards are too high for preponderance determinations.

First, most excluded scientific evidence is not excluded because it fails to meet statistical significance tests but because judges fail to appreciate the inevitably uncertain nature of scientific proof and because they refuse to assess all the available data. In other words, they require a higher standard for validity than do scientists themselves by excluding studies that scientists routinely include in their analyses. Even for the small subset of studies rejected for failing to meet the requisite level of statistical significance, the argument misapprehends the proper basis for admissibility. It is not because science standards are too high; instead judges are insisting on standards that scientists recognize to be impossibly high.

28 *See Carnegie Commission on Science, Technology and Government, Science and Technology in Judicial Decisionmaking: Creating Opportunities and Meeting Challenges*, 28 (1993), noting that "decisions that appear to be based on "bad" science may actually reflect the reality that the law requires a burden of proof, or confidence level, other than the 95 percent confidence level that is often used by scientists to reject the possibility that chance alone accounted for the observed differences."

29 *See* Richard Lempert, *Symposium: Probability and Inference in the Law of Evidence: I. Theories of Inference and Adjudication: The New Evidence Scholarship: Analyzing the Process*, 66 B.U. L. REV. 439, 451 (1986), observing that "the preponderance of the evidence standard is thought to mandate a verdict for the plaintiff whenever his case as a whole is more likely than not (i.e., has a greater than 0.50 chance) to be true." A number of scholars argue that this is a mischaracterization, that what is really meant is that the decision maker has been persuaded to believe the proponent, whatever the probability of the event at issue. *See, e.g.,* Vern R. Walker, *Probability, Inference and Warranted Factfinding*, 62 BROOK. L. REV. 1075, 1078 and n.14 (1996); ALVIN PLANTINGA, WARRANT: THE CURRENT DEBATE, 3–5 (1993); Ronald J. Allen, *The Nature of Juridical Proof*, 13 CARDOZO L. REV. 373, 416 (1991). The U.S. Supreme Court explained that the goal of the legal preponderance standard is to cause the litigants to "share the risk of error in roughly equal fashion." *Herman & McLean v. Huddleston*, 459 U.S. 375, 390 (1983), citing *Addington v. Texas*, 441 U.S. 418, 423 (1979). Professor Walker argues that the goal is not really the equal distribution of errors but rather the equal treatment of similar evidence. *See* Walker, p. 1108, explaining that "the errors will not be distributed equally . . . unless the proportion of plaintiff verdicts equals the proportions of meritorious cases." Professor Walker argues that the real reason for choice of preponderance as the civil standard is that courts are dependent on the parties to produce evidence and, in this institutional context, the use of a mid-range decision value for factfinding creates an incentive to produce adequate evidence.

30 This 95 percent confidence level is the criterion that study data must meet before rejecting the possibility that the results are due to chance.

Equating confidence intervals with burdens of persuasion is simply incoherent. The goal of the scientific standard – the 95 percent confidence interval – is to avoid claiming an effect when there is none (i.e., a false positive).[31] Scientists using a 95 percent confidence interval are making a prediction about the results being due to something other than chance. Judges, on the other hand, are simply charged with assuring that testimony does not rely on incoherent probability assignments, internal contradictions, or mathematical miscalculations, and the underlying studies must describe reality as accurately as possible. But to say that probably true means that the probability of being true is more than 50 percent is wrong. The judge is not making a prediction concerning the relative frequency of accurate outcomes in repeated litigations. We have no way of knowing what the real probability is of a cause-and-effect relationship. Thus, the standpoint of the argument is incorrect. It assumes we are looking back with the knowledge of what is an accurate outcome when all we can know is whether the evidence points toward an increased risk of association.

In addition, equating the legal and scientific standards is mistaken in that it assumes a common view of the strengths and weaknesses of a particular study. Scientists and judges do not have such a common viewpoint, however, because the legal process makes it difficult to assess the strengths and weaknesses of a particular study.[32] As a result, evidence that is uncontroversial to scientists – for example, the applicability of animal studies to humans – appears highly contingent in court. Because of the probabilistic nature of scientific facts, based as they are on underlying

31 The object of statistical significance tests is to keep the scientist from asserting a positive effect when the effect may actually be due to chance. *See* David Ozenhoff and Leslie I. Bodin, *Truth & Consequences: Health Agency Responses to Environmental Health Problems*, 12 Sci. Tech. & Hum. Values, 70, 73–74 (1987). Statistical significance is set by convention at a level of significance, or p-value, of 0.05 (which corresponds to a confidence level of 95 percent). If the p-value is 0.01, the evidence is said to be highly statistically significant. *See* Stephen E. Fienberg et al., *Understanding and Evaluating Statistical Evidence in Litigation*, 36 Jurimetrics J. 1, 22 (1995). As Fienberg explains, "By rejecting a hypothesis only when the test is statistically significant, we have placed an upper bound, 0.05, on the chance of rejecting a true hypothesis." *Id.* Another way of explaining this is that it describes the probability that the procedure produced the observed effect by chance. If the test is not statistically significant, it may either be because the results were due to chance or because the test lacked the power to discern a difference between the null hypothesis and the proposed effect. Power increases with the size of the study and with the degree of difference from the null hypothesis (i.e., the more extreme the alternatives, the better the power). Power will, therefore, be an issue for small studies of low effects – precisely those most likely to be proffered in toxic tort cases. Thus, separate studies of small numbers of subjects may not yield statistically significant results simply because each test may lack the power to discern the null hypothesis of no effect from patterns of illness that are not extreme.

32 *See* Joseph Sanders, *From Science to Evidence: The Testimony on Causation in the Bendectin Cases*, 46 Stan. L. Rev. 1, 45 (1993), noting the problem of the "one-eyed factfinders" who, lacking "depth perception," tend to give all scientific evidence "equal value and relevance." Professor Sanders observed that in the litigation over the antinausea drug Bendectin, factfinders "learned little about the accumulation of scientific knowledge" because the lawyers spent their time trying to undermine the credibility of the witnesses. *Id.*, p. 47. *See* also Margaret A. Berger, *Eliminating General Causation: Notes Towards a New Theory of Justice and Toxic Torts*, 97 Colum. L. Rev. 2117, 2128 (1997), noting that "the deconstructed evidence all tends to sound alike."

assumptions, litigation makes the data appear more controversial than they actually are, creating an impression of conflict even when there is little disagreement in practice. Although this lack of depth perception may affect both parties equally before a jury, it has a disparate impact on the proponent in admissibility determinations. The proponent, after all, must convince the judge that the testimony is scientifically valid. Creating an impression of conflict will make the judge suspect even evidence commonly relied on by those in the scientific community, to the disadvantage of the party seeking admissibility.

Finally, equating statistical significance with the legal burden of proof is mistaken because it confuses whether there is any effect at all with the magnitude of any effect that may exist. Statistical significance can measure only the first consideration: whether there is an effect at all. The second consideration – magnitude of effect – is instead measured by relative risk. *Relative risk* is an epidemiological term referring to the proportion of disease in exposed versus unexposed populations. While significance testing characterizes the probability that the relative risk would be the same as found in the study if the results were due to chance, a relative risk of 2 is the threshold for a greater than 50 percent chance that the effect was caused by the agent in question.

However, just because it is mistaken to equate statistical significance standards with legal burdens of proof does not imply that evidence failing to meet statistical significance parameters or relative risk of 2 should be categorically excluded either. Judges are not justified in excluding evidence that does not meet the 0.05 level of statistical significance (corresponding to a 95 percent confidence level) or a relative risk of 2.[33] On the contrary, as one scientist explained, "statistical significance testing is a mechanical process that debases measurements into the qualitative and sometimes misleading categories of 'significant' or 'not significant.'"[34] Making chance the primary explanation for any set of observations without thinking about what the best explanation might be is sloppy, leading to both under- and over-inclusiveness.[35]

---

33 *See, e.g., Kelley v. American Heyer-Schulte Corp.*, 957 F. Supp. 873 (W.D. Tex. 1997), requiring statistical significance; *Allen v. Pennsylvania Engineering Corp.*, 102 F.3d, 194 (5th Cir. 1996), rejecting studies that failed to demonstrate statistical significance; *LeBlanc v. Merrell Dow Pharmaceuticals, Inc.*, 932 F. Supp. 782 (E.D. La. 1996), requiring statistically significant epidemiologic studies; *Merrell Dow Pharmaceuticals, Inc. v. Havner*, 953 S.W. 2d, 706 (Tex. 1997), rejecting evidence that was not statistically significant; but *see Williams v. Hedican*, 561 N.W. 2d, 817 (Iowa,1997), holding the trial court had overemphasized the need for statistical significance; and *Berry v. C.S.X. Transportation, Inc.*, 704 So. 2d, 633 (Fla. App. 1997), rejecting argument that only statistically significant associations should serve as the basis for causation opinions.

34 Kenneth J. Rothman, *Significance Questing*, 105 ANNALS OF INTERNAL MEDICINE 445, 445 (September 1986).

35 *Id.* Dr. Rothman explains that the unthinking use of statistical significance as a screening device leads to both under- and over-inclusiveness, making real effects appear to be due to chance and, conversely, making events that are really due to chance appear to have a real cause-and-effect relationship. As an example of over-inclusiveness, he gives the example that the probability of winning more than a million dollars in a state lottery twice within a short time is small enough to reject the null hypothesis, but that dual jackpots are better explained by chance. *Id.,*

Using statistical significance (or relative risk) as a screening device for admissibility is a mistake because rigid tests of statistical significance may actually reveal less about the data than other types of data analysis.[36] For example, if there are multiple studies showing a small but consistent effect, scientists tend to believe that in itself is significant.[37] In that way it is under-inclusive. Conversely, statistical significance in the absence of biological plausibility results in over-inclusiveness. In sum, the unthinking use of statistical significance (or confidence intervals) as a prerequisite for admissibility makes little sense.

Humans first: the courts' unwarranted rejection of animal studies

Types of studies are also ranked according to rules of thumb. For human disease, a common assumption is that human studies are the most relevant. That is because studies offering the most analogous data to the hypothesis the expert espouses are the most persuasive.[38] So, human studies come first in the hierarchy when what is at issue is an effect on humans.[39] But there are numerous kinds of human studies, and each of these is also ranked according to a rule-of-thumb hierarchy. In this general hierarchy, clinical double-blind studies are best,[40] cohort studies[41] come next, with case-control studies[42] fairly close behind, and

---

p. 446. His point is that "an algorithm for inference cannot substitute for thinking about the problem." *Id.*

36 *See* Steven N. Goodman and Richard Royall, *Evidence and Scientific Research*, 78 Am. J. Public Health, 1568, 1568–74 (1988); Charles Poole, *Beyond the Confidence Interval*, 77 Am. J. Pub. Health, 195, 195–99 (1987); and W. Douglas Thompson, *Statistical Criteria in the Interpretation of Epidemiologic Data*, 77 Am. J. Pub. Health, 191, 191–94 (1987).

37 *See* Jennie A. Frieman et al., *The Importance of Beta, The Type II Error and Sample Size in the Design and Interpretation of the Randomized Control Trial: Survey of 71 'Negative' Trials*, 299 New Eng. J. Med., 686, 690 (1978).

38 *See Wade-Greaux v. Whitehall Labs. Inc.*, 874 F. Supp. 1441, 1454 (D.V.I., 1994), recognizing the hierarchy of studies in teratology, in which in vivo mammalian studies are accorded more weight than nonmammalian studies, and within mammalian species, primate studies are accorded more weight, whereas in vitro studies have the least force of persuasion.

39 The EPA recognizes this hierarchy, with caveats. *See, e.g.*, U.S. Environmental Protection Agency, Proposed Guidelines for Carcinogen Risk Assessment (hereinafter *EPA Proposed Guidelines*), 61 *Fed. Reg.* 17960, 17972 (1996), noting that "when available human data are extensive and of good quality, they are generally preferable over animal data and should be given greater weight." The EPA, however, emphasizes the importance of considering all the evidence in addressing the likelihood of human carcinogenic effects of an agent and the conditions under which such effects may be expressed.

40 The "gold standard" is the human clinical trial, used by the U.S. Food and Drug Administration (FDA) in its approval process, in which participants are randomly separated into groups receiving either the drug being studied or a placebo, and neither the researchers nor the participants know who is in which group.

41 In cohort studies, the researcher identifies two groups of individuals, exposed and unexposed; follows the groups for a length of time; and the number of individuals who develop the disease is statistically analyzed.

42 Case control studies compare a group of individuals with a particular disease with a control group that does not have the disease.

case reports bring up the rear.[43] Courts seem to have little difficulty with these assumptions.[44]

Another default assumption that the courts routinely make is that epidemiology studies on particular groups of human beings can be generalized to apply to the population as a whole. [45] The EPA also makes this default assumption in its risk assessment, although the EPA recognizes its limitations. This is a useful and supportable default assumption when the studies observe a toxic effect from exposure to a particular agent.[46] However, when no effect is observed, this result cannot be generalized. Not only are epidemiologic studies notoriously bad at observing small effects in human populations, but the effects also may differ significantly on different human populations.[47] Epidemiologic studies usually have low power to detect and attribute responses from a healthy population to other potentially sensitive exposed populations. In other words, courts are on sound scientific footing when they generalize positive epidemiological studies to the population as a whole but not when they do so with negative studies.

Although courts may prefer human studies, each of the various kinds of human studies has its own inherent weaknesses. Clinical double-blind studies are rarely, if ever, available for litigation purposes. In environmental epidemiology studies, a major limitation is the lack of exposure information, with respect to the exact chemical species and actual concentrations of exposure. Often complex exposures

---

43 Case reports are anecdotal filings describing "the temporal relation between an exposure and a disease." *See* Troyen Brennan, *Helping Courts with Toxic Torts: Some Proposals Regarding Alternative Methods for Presenting and Assessing Scientific Evidence in Common Law Courts*, 51 U. Pitt. L. Rev. 1, 46, note 192 (1989). Because there are few controls, courts tend to disparage these reports and give them little weight. *See, e.g., Hall v. Baxter Healthcare*, 947 F. Supp. 1387, 1411 (D. Or. 1996), finding that because "case reports lack controls," they have little scientific merit. Although this may be sound reasoning if case reports are the only evidence available, in conjunction with other evidence, case reports may be quite valuable.

44 *See, e.g., Allison v. McGhan Medical Corp.*, 184 F. 3d, 1300, 1316 (11th Cir. 1999), observing that "controlled, population-based epidemiological studies" were more persuasive than case reports; *Tyler v. Sterling Drug Co.*, 19 F. Supp. 2d, 1239, 1240 (N.D. Okla. 1998), admitting epidemiology testimony and case reports but excluding animal studies; *In re Breast Implant Litig.*, 11 F. Supp. 2d, 1217, 1230 (D. Colo. 1998), finding that "case reports and animal studies can be used to generate hypotheses about causation, but not causation conclusions."

45 *See, e.g., Tyler*, 19 F. Supp. 2d, 1239; *Arnold v. Dow Chemical Co.*, 32 F. Supp. 2d, 584 (E.D.N.Y. 1999); *Sy v. United Parcel Service General Services Co.*, No. Civ. 94–1464-FR, 1999 WL 39550 (D. Or. January 22, 1999); and *Hand v. Norfolk So. Ry. Co.*, No. 03A01–9704-CV00123, 1998 WL 281946 (Tenn. Ct. App. June 2, 1998), *Daubert*-like standard.

46 For example, epidemiology studies of worker populations would miss the effects of lead exposure on peripheral nerve function that is observed in young children. *See, e.g.*, U.S. Public Health Services, Centers for Disease Control, *Preventing Lead Poisoning in Young Children: A Statement by the Centers for Disease Control* (1991). Adults, on the other hand, are considerably more susceptible to the renal toxicity of mercury and fluorides than are children or the elderly. *See* E. J. Calabrese, *Pollutants and High Risk Groups* (1978).

47 *See* Enterline note 18, 93–97, explaining the need for relatively large increases in disease given the sample sizes generally available for investigations, using the example that it would require a large population yielding a thousand deaths on the Peto model to detect a 50 percent excess in deaths from lung cancer at an asbestos level of 2 fibers per cubic centimeter of air.

are involved, making it difficult to pinpont a causal association. Because the type of study judges would prefer experts to rely on probably does not exist in any given case, information from a variety of sources will have to be assessed in conjunction to decide whether there are good grounds for the experts' theory of causation.[48]

Excluding everything but human (i.e., epidemiologic) studies for causation is a legal policy rather than a scientific determination. Scientists recognize that all living organisms share a common biology.[49] This common biology leads to marked similarities in the responsiveness of cellular and subcellular structures to toxic agents. Nearly all of the chemicals recognized to cause cancer in humans also cause cancer in animals.[50] The target organs of animals and humans are frequently the same in these studies. Moreover, animal studies are often superior to the available epidemiologic data available because of the lack of controls endemic to epidemiologic studies, the difficulty in designing and analyzing such studies, and their costliness. In some ways, animal studies are better than human studies because they have more controls and greater sensitivity.[51] Animal studies are more persuasive than epidemiology for demonstrating small increases of risk. To understand the mechanisms of many diseases, animal studies are imperative. Although animal studies require extrapolation to be applicable to human beings, such extrapolation is a routine part of scientific analysis.[52]

The rule of thumb for ranking animal studies for their explanatory power in human applications is that primates are more persuasive than other mammals, which are more persuasive than birds, which are more persuasive than reptiles, and so on down the evolutionary (i.e., phylogenetic) tree. But this is not always the case. Assumptions based on phylogenetic grounds – that primates are

---

48 *See National Bank of Commerce v. Dow Chemical Co.*, 965 F. Supp. 1490, 1507–1508 (E.D. Ark. 1996), listing five "well-established methodologies" that could be used to assess the validity of the expert's causation hypothesis as structure-activity relationships, in vitro studies (analyzing the agent's effects on cells or tissues maintained in tissue culture), animal studies, epidemiological studies and secular trend data, but nonetheless declining to admit the plaintiff's expert testimony primarily because the only extant epidemiological study showed no developmental effect on the babies that had been exposed in utero.

49 *See* Bernard D. Goldstein and Mary Sue Henifin, "Reference Guide on Toxicology," in *Federal Judicial Ctr.* 201, noting that "among mammals, more than sufficient common organ structure and function readily permits the extrapolation from one species to another in most cases." Of course, if there is a fundamental difference in organ structure or function between the species studied and humans, these need to be accounted for. For example, rats do not have gallbladders, so they cannot be used to test the effects of chemical on human gallbladders.

50 *See* International Agency for Research on Cancer, "Preamble," in 63 *IARC Monographs on the Evaluation of Carcinogenic Risk to Humans* 9, 17 (1995).

51 *See* MICHAEL A. KAMRIN, TOXICOLOGY: A PRIMER ON TOXICOLOGY PRINCIPLES AND APPLICATIONS, 54 (1988). By sensitivity, toxicologists mean the ability of a test to detect changes in the animal's health.

52 *See* "Proposed Guidelines for Carcinogen Risk Assessment," 61 FED. REG. 17967. Regulatory agencies typically place greater weight on animal studies than they do on epidemiologic studies because animal studies are better controlled. Extrapolations must be properly performed, as must all parts of a given methodology. It is important, therefore, that the expert be able to explain the basis for the extrapolation used. Assuming that the extrapolations are explained and properly performed, however, there is no reason to categorically deny admissibility to animal studies.

closer phylogenetically to humans and, therefore, tests done on them are the most relevant – can be misleading. Sometimes the dog's metabolism of a drug will be closer to human metabolism than the monkey's.

Of course, animal studies have their own limitations, primarily having to do with extrapolating results from animals to humans and from high to low doses. The point is that animal studies are not "second best." Each type of study has its strengths and its weaknesses. Live animal studies, in vitro studies, and structure-activity reports – as well as human studies – all provide important information about the association of chemicals and disease. The strengths and weaknesses of various kinds of studies complement each other, and judges are simply not justified in categorically rejecting certain types of studies without examining the evidence as a whole.

With a few notable exceptions,[53] judges universally have difficulty understanding the persuasive impact of animal studies.[54] Animal studies are performed by exposing animals to a particular chemical and extrapolating the results to humans using what is known about the structure, function, and metabolism of the particular chemical and the similarity of the actions of the chemical in the animals studied and in human beings. No modern scientist seriously questions their relevance as long as the animal studies are part of a larger story in which chemical structure, absorption, metabolism, distribution, and physiologic analogy are a part. Extrapolations link the results in animals to human applications.[55] Information about biological similarity

53 See, e.g., In re Paoli Railroad Yard PCB Litig. 35 F.3d, 717, 779 (3d Cir. 1994). In the Paoli PCB litigation, the Third Circuit reinstated the excluded animal studies despite defendants' argument that "test animals are often very sensitive to chemicals due to . . . physiological, biological and metabolic pathways which are different than those in humans." Id., 779. In Paoli, unlike Joiner, the expert was permitted to testify that the animals studied (monkeys in Paoli) have similar sensitivities to PCDFs, a chemical similar to PCBs. Id., 779–80.

54 Post-Daubert courts often exclude expert testimony in toxic tort cases studies simply because the uderlying tests relate to animals rather than humans. See, e.g., Raynor v. Merrell Pharmaceuticals, Inc., 104 F. 3d, 1371, 1375 (D.C. Cir. 1997), requiring human experiments or epidemiological data; Wade-Greaux v. Whitehall Labs. Inc., 874 F. Supp. 1441, 1430 (D.V.I. 1994), finding human studies necessary for admissibility, aff'd 46 F.3d, 1120 (3d Cir. 1994); Hall v. Baxter Healthcare Corp., 947 F. Supp. 1387, 1410–11 (D. Or. 1996), finding animal studies "taken alone, are unreliable predictors of causation in humans"; Merrell Dow Pharmaceuticals, Inc. v. Havner, 953 S.W. 2d, 706, 729–30 (Tex. 1997), rejecting animal studies as unreliable under Texas equivalent of Daubert. For example, in Nelson v. American Sterilizer Co., 566 N.W. 2d 671 (Mich. Ct. App. 1997), the court excluded expert testimony that the plaintiff's liver disease was caused by exposure to chemicals used in sterilizing medical equipment merely because the animal studies the expert relied on were high-dose rather than low-dose studies. This appears to be a fundamental misconception about the validity of animal studies.

55 Extrapolation from rodent studies to human cancer causation is universally accepted as valid (at least by scientists) because "virtually all of the specific chemicals known to be carcinogenic in humans are also positive in rodent bioassays, and sometimes even at comparable dose and with similar organ specificity." Bernard Weinstein, Mitogenesis Is Only One Factor in Carcinogenesis, 251 SCI. 387, 388 (1991). The corollary to this is that the validity of the extrapolation depends on knowing the similarities in the disease-producing mechanisms of the studied chemical in the animals and human beings. See, generally, EDWARD J. CALABRESE, PRINCIPLES OF ANIMAL EXTRAPOLATION (1983). Extrapolating from animal studies to birth defects (i.e., teratogenesis) in humans is more controversial because of the 165 agents believed not to be human teratogens, 41 percent were shown to have an effect on at least one animal species and only 28 percent were negative in all animal species; nonetheless, of thirty-eight known human teratogens, thirty-seven

and chemical structure and function (including its interaction with other chemicals and the way the chemical acts in the body) is unquestionably important.[56] Even where such information is absent, however, extrapolation can provide the missing link.[57]

Extrapolating animal models to humans

Scientists widely assume that positive toxic effects in animal studies indicate a similar effect in humans. That does not mean that it is always true, and the utility in toxic tort litigation of animal studies designed for regulatory risk assessment is a frequent topic of legal controversy. What it does mean is that, absent information to the contrary, it is a sound default assumption.[58] It is an appropriate default because most of the data we have shows that to be the case. Therefore, a logical assumption for the courts would be that, in the absence of data to the contrary, animal studies can be extrapolated to humans.[59]

produced an effect in at least one species. *See* Michael D. Green, *Expert Witnesses and Sufficiency of Evidence in Toxic Substances Litigation: The Legacy of Agent Orange and Bendectin Litigation*, 86 Nw. U. L. Rev. 643, 655 (1992), noting that monkeys, however, are relatively good human predictors because 80 percent of the human nonteratogens had no effect on monkeys.

56 Some courts are aware of the significance of extrapolation. *See In re Paoli.*, 35 F. 3d at 743, explaining the "fit" requirement that "in order for animal studies to be admissible to prove causation in humans, there must be good grounds to extrapolate from animals to humans, just as the methodology of the studies must constitute good grounds to reach conclusions about the animals themselves." It was the lack of such an explanation that caused the plaintiff's dismissal in *Joiner* and made the majority remark that the proffered studies were linked together by nothing more than the *"ipse dixit"* of the experts. *General Electric Co. v. Joiner*, 522 U.S. 136, 146 (1997).

57 Extrapolation in science is similar to a rebuttable presumption in law. That is, in the absence of contrary evidence, one is entitled to make certain assumptions. These assumptions must be justifiable on scientific and policy grounds. One such policy in the toxic tort context is to place the burden on chemical manufacturers to rebut inferences of causation because they have the resources to engage in research about their products if they choose to rebut these presumptions as inapplicable. This policy would circumvent the need that a number of commentators have cited of ditching the entire causation requirement for toxic torts. *See, e.g.,* Dec. No. 549/9512, 1998 WL 2000559 (Ont. W.S.I.A.T.), 1998, Carswell Ont. 6404, in which a Canadian workplace tribunal discussed the interplay of expert uncertainty and burdens of establishing causation in tort and workplace injuries with respect to the admissibility of expert causation testimony. There, the issue was whether an inference of work-relatedness of the decedent's non-Hodgkin's lymphoma (NHL) could be drawn even though the experts disagreed on causation, and neither could arrive at a definite conclusion that the workplace exposure to alpha radiation either caused or did not cause the decedent's disease. The panel concluded, after careful and thoughtful analysis of the proffered expert testimony, that although the plaintiff's expert could not say definitively that radiation could cause NHL, the causal connection was not medically implausible and that, because there was little evidence about the effects of radiation exposure, a jury was entitled to hear what evidence there was and weigh the experts' competing explanations.

58 The courts' widespread rejection of animal studies is based on a failure to accept the scientifically uncontroversial default assumption that metabolic pathways in animals are generally similar to those in humans.

59 The arguments against using animal studies as evidence of general causation include the physiological differences between the animals studied and humans; the high dosages ordinarily used in such studies, in contrast to the low dosages typically at issue in toxic tort cases; and laboratory conditions. These are valid objections. These objections, however, are not dispositive because high-dosage extrapolations from animals to humans can provide realistic indications of causal

Despite the obvious differences between humans and laboratory animals, bio-chemical and metabolic processes carried out in most organs are similar. All of the chemicals recognized to cause cancer in humans also cause cancer in animals.[60] Chemicals that cause birth defects in humans generally also cause them in animals. The results for other kinds of diseases show a similar pattern, although they are studied less frequently. If there are data showing the opposite, then the validity of discarding the default becomes a question of whether the data supporting the contrary inference is stronger than that supporting the default.

Moreover, animal studies have a number of advantages: laboratory conditions permit the researcher to have better controls over the experimental conditions, high dosages more accurately reveal the presence of a dose-response relationship, and the time required to conduct an animal study is much shorter. Thus, because there are so few good epidemiologic studies available, animal studies are often the primary source of information regarding the impact of chemicals. Differences in metabolism, body size, dose, life span, and other factors can and should be accounted for, but courts should not categorically reject animal studies.

There are two fundamental types of extrapolation from animals to human: qual-itative extrapolation (if a chemical causes an effect in one species, will it also cause it in humans?) and quantitative (or dose-response curve; that is, the level at which the chemical will have an effect). Although the qualitative extrapolation is well accepted by scientists, there is ongoing debate over how to estimate the magnitude of a dose producing a similar effect in animals and humans. Nonetheless, animal testing of chemical effects predicts human toxicity in all but 10 percent of comparisons.[61] Thus, for judges having to assess the validity of expert conclusions about human disease using animal studies to support their arguments, the important thing to remember is that animal studies are vital to understanding human disease.

Extrapolating high doses to low doses

One corollary assumption to the applicability of animal studies to human pop-ulations is that high-dosage studies can be extrapolated to the low dosages more

---

relationships in humans as long as the animal studies are supplemented by information regarding chemical structure; how the chemical is absorbed, metabolized, and distributed in the body; and as long as there is a physiologic analogy in the species studied. For an outline of methods of extrap-olation, *see* Gary P. Carlson, *Factors Modifying Toxicity* in TOXIC SUBSTANCES AND HUMAN RISK: PRINCIPLES OF DATA INTERPRETATION, 47 (Robert C. Cardiff and Joseph V. Rodericks, eds., 1987). It is a mistake for the courts to reject this assumption because one of the bases of legal causation is a conclusion on the basis of the available information that if the exposure event recurs, it will increase the chances of the injury recurring. *See* Guido Calabresi, *Concerning Cause and the Law of Torts: An Essay for Harry Kalven, Jr.*, 43 U. CHI. L. REV. 69, 71 (1975). Probabilistically speaking, that is what animal studies are designed to show.

60　International Agency for Research on Cancer, note 50, pp. 9, 17.

61　*See* Michael A. Dorato and Mary J. Vodicnik, *The Toxicological Assessment of Pharmaceutical and Biotechnology Products* in *Principles and Methods*, note 21, p. 193, stating that pharmacodynamics of an agent are more predictable than its pharmacokinetics.

commonly found in environmental exposure. The prevalent understanding of scientists is that high dosages for short periods are (roughly) equivalent to low dosages over extended periods.[62] In addition, as animal species become larger in size, they also become more sensitive to short-term toxic effects.[63] Humans can be many times more sensitive than experimental animals.[64] As a rebuttable presumption, in the absence of data, it makes sense to adopt the prevalent view that high-dosage studies validly can be extrapolated to the low dosages of most environmental exposures.[65]

Biological damage processes (as we currently understand them) fall into two broad classes, implying either threshold or nonthreshold responses.[66] For systemic toxicants, the threshold-response theory asserts that there is a level of exposure below which there is minimal chance for an adverse effect. Under this hypothesis, there must be multiple cells injured before an adverse effect is experienced, and the rate of injury must exceed the rate of repair. Courts are familiar with this theory and frequently reject expert testimony where the plaintiff's exposure level is unknown, citing Paracelsus's maxim that the dose determines the poison.[67] As long as the dose is small enough, the threshold theory says that adaptive processes will repair any damage.[68] Under the threshold theory, the default used is a margin of exposure

---

62 See, e.g., R. L. Melnik et al., Cell Proliferation and Chemical Carcinogenesis, 7 MOLECULAR CARCINO-GENESIS, 135, 135–8 (1993). But see Philip H. Abelson, Risk Assessment of Low Level Exposures, 265 SCI. 1570 (1994), urging the development of low-level tests because linear extrapolation implies that "no dose, however small, is safe" and "[e]xamples of instances in which these assumptions are invalid are becoming numerous."

63 See ANIMAL MODELS IN TOXICOLOGY, 826 (Christopher P. Chengelis and Shayne C. Gad, eds., 1996), noting that the higher sensitivity of larger species may be due to increases of available target tissues and decreases of metabolic rate as size increases and observing that humans may be more sensitive than any test species.

64 See Dorato and Vodicnik, note 61, p. 193, observing that "humans can be as much as 50 times more sensitive on a milligram/kilogram basis than experimental animals."

65 The overwhelming consensus when it comes to correlating an observed dose-response curve to a relationship at lower doses is to use a linear model. See EPA Proposed Guidelines, note 39, p. 17,968. This view should not be accepted merely because it is prevalent, of course, but because although the theory is falsifiable and subjected to testing, it remains the best explanation for the observed data.

66 See D. Cooper Rees and Dale Hattis, Developing Quantitative Strategies for Animal to Human Extrapolation in PRINCIPLES AND METHODS, note 21, p. 276.

67 Paracelsus was a Renaissance alchemist who believed in the doctrine of signatures – to cure a liver ailment, for example, treat it with an herb shaped like a liver. See IAN HACKING, REPRESENTING AND INTERVENING: INTRODUCTORY TOPICS IN THE PHILOSOPHY OF NATURAL SCIENCE, 42 (1983). Paracelsus earned his place in the history of medicine by using chemicals (like mercury) to treat diseases. Id. Why modern courts cite his maxim without understanding his theory is a perplexing question. See, e.g., National Bank of Commerce v. Dow Chemical Corp., 965 F. Supp. 1490, 1506 (E.D. Ark. 1996), citing Paracelsus for the concept that "toxicity is a function of dose"; Cartwright v. Home Depot U.S.A., Inc. 936 F. Supp. 900, 906 (M.D. Fla. 1996), same; Cavallo v. Star Enterprise, 892 F. Supp. 756, 769 note 27 (E.D. Va. 1995); Carroll v. Litton Sys., Inc. No. B-C-88–253, 1990 WL 312969 *96 (W.D.N.C. October 29,1990), citing Paracelsus for the idea that "all substances are poisons and the right dose differentiates between a remedy and a poison."

68 Notably, however, what we once thought were the threshold levels for some toxic agents like lead appear to be lower than we once believed. For example, in the 1970s, the threshold for lead absorption was 40 micrograms per milliliter of blood; by the late 1990s, it had been lowered to 10 micrograms per milliliter of blood, and the Centers for Disease Control now takes the position that no threshold has been determined regarding lead's harmful effects on children's learning or

analysis in which the ratio between the environmental exposure and the lowest observable effect level is computed.

Nonthreshold effects, on the other hand, are characteristic of diseases (like some cancers) that are caused by genetic mutations. The linear-effects theory explains that "even a single molecule of a DNA-reactive substance has a small but non-zero chance of setting in motion a chain of events leading to mutagenesis or carcinogenesis."[69] However, not all cancers are the result of genetic mutations, so some carcinogens may have threshold effects.[70]

Unfortunately, even if we find the threshold theory of biological responses persuasive, there is usually not enough information to demonstrate either threshold or nonthreshold responses (for both cancer and other diseases). A biologically based or case-specific model for the observed range and for extrapolations below that range would unquestionably be the better approach. Frequently, however, such information is missing and, in its absence, a linear default approach is the best we can do.[71] As a policy matter, a linear presumption in toxic tort cases is fairer to plaintiffs, who rarely know their exposure level.[72]

---

behavior. *See* Pamela A. Meyer et al., *Surveillance for Elevated Blood Levels Among Children – United States 1997–2001*, MORBIDITY & MORTALITY WEEKLY REP., September 12, 2003, p. 2.

69 Rees and Hattis, note 66, p. 277.

70 Polychlorinated biphenyls and dioxins are thought to be examples of such carcinogens.

71 In Popperian terms, the competing linearity and threshold theories have to be evaluated in light of the severity of criticism each has withstood (or can withstand). Even if the theory has been refuted, one needs to keep testing until one gets a better explanation. Thus, Newtonian physics worked well enough until Einstein proposed a better explanation. The *EPA Proposed Guidelines* suggest, in the absence of data supporting a case-specific or biologically based model, that a curve-fitting model be used for the observed range of data and a linear model for extrapolating to the unobserved range. *EPA Proposed Guidelines,* note 39, p. 17,968. The *Proposed Guidelines* explain that the linear approach is to draw a straight line between a point of departure from the observed data. *Id.*, p. 17,969. Although the received wisdom is that linear dose-response assumptions are conservative (i.e., protect the public health), there is evidence that they may actually underestimate risk at low doses. *See* Leslie Roberts, *Is Risk Assessment Conservative?* 243 SCI. 1553 (1989), citing studies on vinyl chloride.

72 For a policy argument in favor of placing the burden on defendant manufacturers to come forward with contrary information, *see* Berger, note 32, pp. 2124–25, 2145; Wendy E. Wagner, *Choosing Ignorance in the Manufacture of Toxic Products*, 82 CORNELL L. REV. 773, 780 (1997). For cases excluding expert testimony where plaintiffs did not know their exposure level, *see, e.g., Conde v. Velsicol Chemical Corp.,* 24 F. 3d, 809, 810 (6th Cir. 1994), excluding expert testimony that chlordane, an acknowledged carcinogen, applied in a manner that violated federal criminal law, caused plaintiffs' injuries where testimony was based on animal studies that used high-dosage levels rather than the low-dosage levels to which plaintiffs' were exposed; *Chikovsky v. Ortho Pharmaceutical Corp.,* 832 F. Supp. 341, 345–46 (S.D. Fla. 1993), excluding testimony where the expert did not know how much Retin-A was absorbed by the plaintiff or the dosage level at which Retin-A becomes unsafe for pregnant women; *Schmaltz v. Norfolk & Western Ry. Co.,* 878 F. Supp. 1119, 1122 (N.D. Ill. 1995), excluding testimony where the expert did not know how much herbicide the plaintiff had been exposed to; *Cavallo v. Star Enterprise,* 892 F. Supp. 756, 773 (E.D. Va. 1995), finding testimony inadmissible because the expert could not identify the plaintiff's exposure levels or a dose-response relationship with respect to the jet fuel at issue; *National Bank of Commerce v. Dow Chemical Co.,* 965 F. Supp. 1490, 1518, 1552 (E.D. Ark. 1996), discrediting plaintiff's expert testimony because defendants' expert proffered a single epidemiology study showing no effects, even though the plaintiff offered evidence to show the study's results were inconclusive

In addition, the threshold-dose notion is scientifically shaky for carcinogens because, among other reasons, it is impossible to demonstrate mathematically a no-effects level.[73] Further, there is no empirical or theoretical basis for determining the level at which this threshold may occur. Nonlinear approaches, therefore, should be limited to those situations in which adequate data on the mode of action (i.e., how the chemical affects bodily processes and the progression of disease) show that linearity is not reasonable. Thus, in the absence of information to the contrary, a nonthreshold response is generally assumed by scientists.

Courts struggle with extrapolation issues.[74] Whether animal studies designed for regulatory risk assessment can be used in toxic tort litigation is the subject of ongoing legal debate.[75] Physiological differences (or, as one court remarked, "humans are not rats"[76]); the high dosages ordinarily used in such studies, in contrast to the low dosages typically at issue in toxic tort cases; and laboratory conditions are all contentious areas of litigation. Although there is some validity to these objections, they are not dispositive. High-dosage extrapolations from animals to humans are

because it involved only five subjects, who were exposed to unknown pesticides at unknown levels.

73 See R. W. Hart and L. Fishbein, *Interspecies Extrapolation of Drug and Genetic Toxicity Data* in Toxicological Risk Assessment, Vol. 1, 3–40 (D.B. Clayton et al., eds., 1985), explaining major arguments against threshold dose.

74 For example, in *Nelson v. American Sterilizer Co.*, 566 N.W. 2d 671 (Mich. Ct. App. 1997), the court excluded expert testimony that the plaintiff's liver disease was caused by exposure to chemicals used in sterilizing medical equipment merely because the animal studies the expert relied on were high-dose rather than low-dose studies. This appears to be a fundamental misconception about the usefulness of animal studies. However, this may be another lawyering failure, as the court does point out that the plaintiff's experts provided no understandable scientific basis for their extrapolations. The failure of the plaintiff in *Joiner* to provide the basis for extrapolating results of the animal tests appears to be the basis of their exclusion. The court responded to the plaintiff's argument that it should not categorically exclude animal studies by pointing out the failure of the expert to draw a convincing analogy from these studies to human causation. See *Joiner*, 118 S. Ct. 518. In the *Paoli* PCB litigation, the Third Circuit reinstated the excluded animal studies despite the defendants' argument that "test animals are often very sensitive to chemicals due to . . . physiological, biological and metabolic pathways which are different than those in humans." *In re Paoli RR Yard PCB Litigation*, 35 F. 3d 717, 779 (3d Cir. 1994). In *Paoli*, unlike *Joiner*, the expert was able to testify that the animals studied (monkeys in *Paoli*) has similar sensitivities to PCDFs, a chemical similar to PCBs. *Id.*, 779–80.

75 Courts sometimes categorically reject agency findings for purposes of tort litigation as having been developed for regulatory purposes rather than litigation and thus needing a lower standard of proof. See, e.g., *Allen v. Pennsylvania Engineering Corp.*, 11 *Toxics L. Rep (BNA)*, 866 (January 15, 1997), rejecting the EPA's "weight of the evidence" methodology. There is little rationale for this bias against hazard characterization (as opposed to level-of-exposure methodology, which may have a preventive bias) because EPA carcinogenic risk assessment explicitly characterizes the level of hazard gleaned from all the biological information available as "known/likely," "cannot be determined," or "not likely" to be carcinogenic to humans. See *Proposed Guidelines for Carcinogen Risk Assessment, Abstract*. Moreover, the EPA uses the same "more probable than not" standard to reach its risk assessments as is used in civil litigation. *Id.* Although EPA risk assessments should not be adopted as dispositive in toxic tort litigation, there is nothing inherently biased about the methodology used in reaching the risk characterization.

76 *International Union, United Auto., Aerospace & Agric. Implement Workers of Am. v. Pendergras*, 878 F. 2d, 389, 394 (D.C. Cir. 1989).

commonly used by toxicologists to provide realistic indications of causal relationships in humans. This is a cornerstone of scientific research.

Although there are always a few scientists who urge caution in the wholesale adoption of animal studies, they are a distinct minority. No modern scientist seriously questions their relevance as long as the animal studies are supplemented by information regarding chemical structure; how the chemical is absorbed, metabolized, and distributed in the body; and there is a physiologic analogy in the species studied.[77] The courts, however, have not yet caught up with this understanding and repeatedly reject testimony based on animal studies.

Extrapolating to different target organs

Not only must the results of high-dosage animal studies be extrapolated to the low dosages common to human exposure, but the studies also may show that a different organ was affected in the animal studies than in the plaintiff. Whether the organ affected in the studies (called the target organ) may be extrapolated to a different organ in human beings is controversial. Most of what we know shows that the organs affected should be the same.[78] There is typically a close correspondence between the target organ in human studies and at least one of the animal species studied.[79]

There are, nonetheless, distinct differences in the way various tissues react across species. Thus, there are justifications for adopting the assumption that either the affected organs must be the same or that they may be different. The EPA has adopted the default position that with respect to cancer, in the absence of data, it does not matter which organ is affected; if the animal develops cancer in any organ, the agent is assumed to be generally carcinogenic in humans.[80] Under this assumption, demonstrating the development of lung cancer in mice would be admissible to show human causation in any organ. Because we know so little about cancer causation, there is justification for this as a workable but questionable assumption with respect to cancer.

At the same time, although the EPA asserts that this position protects the public health and minimizes false negatives,[81] judicial decision makers must strive to minimize both false negatives and false positives. A more justifiable assumption for the legal system would be that, unless there is evidence showing a range of target organs, the target organ affected in animal studies should be the same as that affected in the

---

77 *See* JAMES L. SCHARDEIN, CHEMICALLY INDUCED BIRTH DEFECTS 27 (1993), observing that "not a single chemical exists that is teratogenic in humans that has not produced malformations in rodents" and noting that confirming studies in multiple species increases confidence in the results; "International Agency for Research on Cancer, Preamble" in 63 *IARC Monographs on the Evaluation of Carcinogenic Risks in Humans,* 17 (1995).

78 *See EPA Proposed Guidelines,* note 39, p. 17,967, most target organs are concordant at one or more sites across species.

79 *See* J. Huff, *Chemicals and Cancer in Humans: First Evidence in Experimental Animals,* 100 ENVTL. HEALTH PERSP., 201, 204 (1993).

80 *See EPA Proposed Guidelines,* note 39, p. 17,967.

81 *See id.,* pp. 17,967–68.

injured plaintiff.[82] This is more defensible for admissibility determinations because the metabolic route will usually be similar in animals and humans. Thus, the target organ ordinarily should be similar. If the expert relies on animal studies showing an effect on different organs than those affected in the plaintiff, the studies ought to be inadmissible in the absence of further explanation.

Route of exposure extrapolation

A further extrapolation involves deciding whether exposure to a chemical in one manner (e.g., through the skin) is the equivalent to exposure in a different manner (e.g., by ingesting it). This is the route of exposure extrapolation. The three main exposure routes in humans, either alone or in combination, are ingestion, inhalation, and dermal absorption. The route of administration of a chemical in laboratory animals may be different from the exposure of the plaintiff: the chemical may have been injected into the animals, for example, whereas the human plaintiff's skin may have been exposed to the chemical.

No matter what the route of exposure, the critical measurement in a toxicological study will be the bloodstream concentration of the chemical.[83] That is because the level of chemical in the target organ is generally a function of its concentration in the blood.[84] Aside from local effects at the site of contact,[85] a toxic substance can cause injury only after it is absorbed by the body.[86] Absorption, regardless of the

---

82 That is, animal studies showing an agent's toxic effects on the lungs should not be assumed by judges to be relevant to the issue of whether the plaintiff's pancreatic cancer was caused by the agent, unless the expert can provide other studies showing a different metabolic pathway in humans that would make it likely that the agent would affect the lungs in mice and the pancreas in humans.

83 *See* Andrew Gordan Renwick, *Toxicokinetics – Pharmacokinetics in Toxicology* in *Principles and Methods*, note 21, pp. 106–107, explaining that the slope of the plasma-concentration time-curve is a key measurement in toxicological studies. Moreover, if dosage is adjusted so equivalent serum concentrations are maintained, interspecies "differences in response tend to disappear." Steven E. Mayer et al., *Introduction; the Dynamics of Drug Absorption, Distribution, and Elimination* in THE PHARMACOLOGICAL BASIS OF THERAPEUTICS 26 (Goodman and Gilman et al., eds., 6th ed., 1980). Thus, absorption is equivalent to the appearance of the substance in the circulation, and the rate of absorption can be determined from the plasma concentration time-curve of the chemical in question.

84 *See* FRANK C. LU, BASIC TOXICOLOGY: FUNDAMENTALS, TARGET ORGANS, AND RISK ASSESSMENT, 23 (3d ed., 1996).

85 A local effect is one that occurs at the site of first contact with a chemical. *See* Curtis D. Klaassen, "Principles of Toxicology" in Goodman and Gilman, note 83, p. 1605. An example of local irritation is the injury to the skin caused by exposure to tetramethyl lead. *Id.* A systemic effect is one that occurs after absorption and distribution of the chemical. The two categories are not mutually exclusive and, for example, tetramethyl lead causes both local effects at the site of contact and systemic effects on the central nervous system. *See id.* Most toxic substances produce systemic effects. It is when substances have a predominantly local effect that the portal of entry (i.e., skin, gastrointestinal tract, or respiratory tract) affects the frequency of tissue reaction. Because most toxic tort cases involve systemic rather than local effects, the assumption that the route of exposure is of minimal importance is a sound one. If, on the other hand, the defense can demonstrate either predominantly local effects or that the systemic effects of the chemical in question are route-dependent, then the default presumption would be refuted.

86 *See* Lu, note 84, p. 13.

site of contact, is dependent on solubility.[87] Thus, for example, asbestos (which is relatively insoluble) has a greater effect when inhaled than when ingested because the particles stay in the lungs longer (and therefore dissolve more) than they do in the gut.[88] But, if solubility differences are accounted for, the route of exposure makes little difference. Although extrapolation from one exposure route to another can be accounted for mathematically through physiologically based pharmacokinetic models, such models themselves use many assumptions and simplifications and are more accurate where data are available with respect to exposure level and toxic effect.[89] In the absence of such information, therefore, a fair assumption is that exposure routes are equivalent.

In assessing the differences in the way the chemical agent was applied to the body in the animal studies and in exposed humans, the default assumption used by the EPA is that, for carcinogens, exposure by one route is equivalent to exposure by another route. This is because as long as the internal dose is the same, there is no reason to suspect the chemical agent will act differently if it were absorbed into the body through the skin or taken internally. The metabolism of the internal dose will be the same.[90] In other words, measurement of plasma concentrations gives proof of absorption and exposure.

Not only does this assumption protect the public health to some degree, it also offers the soundest scientific explanation of how things work.[91] Principles of absorption and distribution are similar in all mammalian species.[92] Almost every toxicant can pass through every portal of entry, although there may be differences in rate.[93] Unquestionably, data are needed with respect to absorption characteristics and toxicity across routes.[94] Development of scientifically based principles, procedures, and data for route-to-route exposure extrapolations would undoubtedly improve

---

87 *See* Mayer et al., note 83, p. 5.
88 *See* William E. Pepelko, *Effect of Exposure Route on Potency of Carcinogens*, 13 Reg. Toxicol. & Pharm., 3, 11 (1991).
89 *See* Kannan Krishnan and Melvin E. Anderson, *Physiologically Based Pharmacokinetic Modeling in Toxicology* in *Principles and Methods*, note 21, p. 174, arguing that appropriate equations representing each exposure pathway adequately account for exposure route differences.
90 *See* Rees and Hattis, note 68, pp. 275–309. This is particularly true for carcinogenic chemicals, where dose route has little effect.
91 *See Animal Models in Toxicology*, note 63, p. 9, explaining that the important factor is access to the circulatory system; W. E. Pepelko, *Feasibility of Route Extrapolation in Risk Assessment*, 44 Brit. J. Indus. Med., 649 (1987), explaining the necessity of route extrapolation and the use of uncertainty factors when environmental exposure differs from experimental route of exposure.
92 *See Animal Models in Toxicology*, note 63, p. 8, citing Avram Goldstein et al., Principles of Drug Action: The Basis of Pharmacology 129–217, 227–300 (1974). There are metabolic rate differences, but most of these can be accounted for mathematically.
93 *See* Ernest Hodgson and Patricia E. Levi, *Absorption and Distribution of Toxicants* in A Textbook of Modern Toxicology, 27 (Ernest Hodgson and Patricia E. Levi, eds., 2d ed., 1997), explaining that "few, if any, chemicals will be excluded from entry" to the body because of the route of exposure.
94 *See Summary Report of the Workshops on Principles of Route-to-Route Extrapolation for Risk Assessment* in Principles of Route-to-Route Extrapolation for Risk Assessment 2–3 (Timothy R. Gerrity and Carol J. Henry, eds., 1990).

their validity. But, in the absence of such information, the default assumption of equivalence is the soundest scientific explanation.

In addition, the assumption makes sense for judicial decision making from a policy standpoint of encouraging manufacturers to engage in safety research.[95] If manufacturers wish to demonstrate that there is no equivalence in exposure routes, they are in the best position to produce the data to verify it.[96] They are in a better position to produce the necessary data than are consumers because they are in the business of producing and testing the chemical.[97] From a policy perspective, placing such a burden on plaintiffs without access to research facilities makes little sense. Thus, use of the exposure-route-equivalence default assumption is an efficient allocation of resources, placing the cost on the party most able to assume it.

Cumulative impact of scientific evidence

Human and animal studies are by no means the only types of research scientists rely on to assess a causal nexus. Farther down in hierarchical persuasiveness than (in vivo) animal studies are (in vitro) tissue-culture studies designed to examine the effects of agents on isolated cells, bacteria, organs, or embryos. These tests are very useful to determine the effect of a chemical at the cellular level. Courts are even less comfortable when experts rely on these studies than they are with in vivo animal studies.[98] Yet, these studies are invaluable in understanding metabolic processes at the cellular level. If such studies have been performed, they add explanatory power to the expert's hypothesis. Courts should not reject them out of hand but instead consider the information they provide about metabolic processes in assessing the admissibility of testimony based on such studies, in consort with other studies.

---

95 Pharmacokinetic information on most chemicals is simply not available. See William E. Pepelko and James R. Withey, *Methods for Route-to-Route Extrapolation of Dose*, 1 TOXICOLOGY & INDUS. HEALTH, 153, 159 (1985).

96 Most chemicals on the market have never been tested for safety. It does not seem unfair, therefore, once safety has become an issue, to place the burden of producing evidence about the chemicals they market on those who profit from them, at least to the extent of refuting a presumption of route equivalence. This is a particular concern where for most routes of exposure "little is known about absorption characteristics, the potential for portal-of-entry effects, and the potential for first-pass metabolic effects for most compounds," and yet those compounds are marketed widely. *Summary Report of the Workshops on Principles of Route-to-Route Extrapolation for Risk Assessment* in *Principles of Route-to-Route Extrapolation for Risk Assessment*, note 94, p. 3.

97 Thus, the burden of production of evidence to refute the presumption of exposure-route equivalence should be placed on the defendant chemical marketer because of the inequality of resources between plaintiff and defense. *See* Richard A. Posner, *An Economic Approach to the Law of Evidence*, 51 STAN. L. REV., 1477, 1542 (1999), arguing that burdens of persuasion and production are economizing devices and should be placed on the party with the greatest access to resources.

98 *See, e.g., Glaser v. Thompson Medical Co.*, 32 F. 3d, 969, 975 (6th Cir. 1994); *Conde v. Velsicol Chem. Corp.*, 24 F. 3d, 809, 811 (6th Cir. 1994); *Grimes v. Hoffman-LaRoche Inc.*, 907 F. Supp. 33 (D. N.H. 1995); *Raynor v. Merrell Dow Pharms., Inc.*, 104 F. 3d 1371, 1374 (D.D.C. 1997), rejecting in vitro studies as unreliable. There is some reason for this reluctance: these tests have rarely been compared with outcomes in live animal studies. Nonetheless, if an in vitro test consistently and accurately measures toxicity and predicts outcomes on the same cells or organs as in live studies, the results should not be ignored.

Structure-activity relationship studies, which rarely make it into court, explore the structure of the chemical at issue and how its structure is related to biological effects by comparing it to chemicals with similar structure and known toxic effects. Structure-activity relationships are a standard part of toxicology. They too provide key insights into the ways chemicals affect the body.

In vitro studies and structure-activity relationship studies illuminate the mechanisms of a chemical at the cellular or organ level. They are not inferior studies because they present important information that needs to be accounted for in any valid hypothesis. What is important is understanding that each of these studies is a small piece of the assembled puzzle; all are needed to put the puzzle together. But, because all the puzzles are more or less incomplete, it is the judge's job to decide whether the pieces *could plausibly* fit together according to the expert's analysis or whether too many pieces are missing to tell. It is emphatically not the judge's job to decide whether the pieces *do* fit together; rather, it is up to the judge to decide only whether the studies relied on – the pieces of the puzzle – provide answers to questions within the purview of the factfinder, not whether they provide the "correct" answers.[99]

Science is a collaborative enterprise and scientific studies cannot be interpreted in isolation. Scientific studies integrate with and build on one another. Because they ignore this pivotal idea, courts frequently find the issue of "fit" a difficult determination to make.[100] Although the relevance of a single study may be a fairly straightforward determination, relevance becomes more complicated when a number of studies are involved – each of which is only marginally relevant – that together form the basis of an expert's conclusions. This is by far the most common situation, particularly in toxic tort cases. Only rarely will an expert rely on a single study. More often, many different studies need to be offered to cumulatively support the expert's conclusions, although no single study could do so on its own.

In *Joiner*, for example, the Eleventh Circuit reversed the district court's exclusion of the plaintiff's expert testimony on this basis, explaining that "[o]pinions of any kind are derived from individual pieces of evidence, each of which by itself might not be conclusive, but when viewed in their entirety are the building blocks of a perfectly reasonable conclusion."[101] The U. S. Supreme Court did not address this view of the evidence, except to note that the individual studies proffered as the bases of the expert testimony could not support the experts' conclusions and that Joiner

---

99 Thus, the court in *Hall* was mistaken when it excluded the expert testimony because the studies relied on only showed that silicone *could* have caused the plaintiff's diseases, not that it did. *Hall v. Baxter Healthcare Corp.*, 947 F. Supp. 1387, 1398 (D. Or. 1996). Deciding whether an expert's conclusion is relevant and otherwise admissible is not the same as deciding whether the conclusions are right; that is the province of the factfinder.

100 *See Habecker v. Clark Equipment Co.*, 36 F. 3d, 278 (3d Cir. 1994), excluding accident reconstruction evidence as irrelevant; *In re Hanford Nuclear Reservation Litig.*, 1998 WL 775340, *139–40 (E.D. Wash. 1998), finding too great an analytical gap between proffered animal studies and the causation issue for human plaintiffs.

101 *See Joiner*, 864 F. Supp., p. 532.

did not explain how to link the studies together to show their applicability to his claims.[102]

Scientists recognize that multiple confirmatory studies in different disciplines reinforce the results from a single study. Biologically based descriptions seek to describe critical events along the causal pathway between exposure and effect. In order to do so, all available information must be assessed. There is no scientifically justifiable basis for excluding information from any source that aids in this assessment, whether chemical, cellular, or animal.[103]

Conflating admissibility with sufficiency

In a toxic tort case, the plaintiff must prove causation by a preponderance of the evidence.[104] Preponderance is only one of the legal standards that come into play when assessing causation evidence. The proponent of scientific evidence must first persuade the judge that the proffered evidence is more likely than not scientifically valid. Then there is the *Daubert* standard, which requires only a scintilla of scientifically valid and relevant evidence to survive an admissibility determination. How these legal standards ought to be interpreted is far from clear and how to prove causation is a debate that predates *Daubert* by a considerable margin.[105] *Daubert* and *Joiner* have, however, further muddied the waters.

Traditionally, in tort cases, proving causation means the factfinder must conclude that, having heard both sides of the story – including the scientific evidence supporting each side – the defendant's action, inaction, or product caused the plaintiff's harm. What such proof of causation does not require – or permit – is that judges first decide as a matter of law whose evidence is most persuasive and then exclude evidence pointing the other way.[106] That is a decision of fact and is the function of the factfinder, whether the jury or the judge in a nonjury case. Nor should a court in an admissibility determination weigh the gravamen of the parties'

---

102 Joiner's brief to the U.S. Supreme Court merely argues that "[a]nalysis of the overall weight of the available data is the very methodology used by the EPA." "Brief for Respondents," 40, *General Elec. Co. v. Joiner*, 118 S. Ct. 512 (1997) (No. 96–188), available in 1997 WL 436250. It may be, as Justice Stevens remarked in his concurrence and dissent, that there existed sufficient studies to cumulatively support the plaintiff's position – the Court of Appeals pointed out that the plaintiffs' experts relied on thirteen studies as well as reports of the World Health Organization – but only one of the studies made it into the record, and the District Court discussed only the six studies referred to in the Supreme Court opinion. *See Joiner*, 118 S. Ct. 521. The majority also remarked on Joiner's failure to explain how and why the experts could have extrapolated their opinions from the proffered studies. *Id.* at 517.

103 *See Principles and Methods*, note 21, p. 309, observing that the ideal mix of information to provide a complete biological explanation "would include pharmocokinetics and pharmacodynamics of the effect and its relation to the level and duration of existing exposures as well as differences in susceptibility within the exposed population" but acknowledging that such information is rarely available.

104 *See* McCORMICK ON EVIDENCE § 337 (E. Cleary, 3d ed., 1984); Green, note 55, p. 680. "plaintiffs should be required to prove causation by a preponderance of the available evidence, not by some predetermined standard that may require nonexistent studies."

105 At least since Hart and Honore's critique of Hume's causal chain analysis, legal scholars have debated the meaning of causation in tort law. *See* H. L. A. HART AND A. M. HONORE, CAUSATION IN THE LAW 80 (1959).

106 *See, e.g., National Bank of Commerce v. Dow Chem. Co.,* 965 F. Supp. 1490 (E.D. Ark. 1996).

proffered evidence against each other to determine whether a reasonable jury could find for the nonmoving party. That is a question of sufficiency.[107] Yet, this conflation of sufficiency with admissibility, although mistaken, is widespread among the federal courts.[108]

The issue is rendered more confusing because, in *Daubert* hearings, the causation issue frequently surfaces in the context of a dual motion, challenging the admissibility of expert testimony and moving for summary judgment. If the expert affidavits submitted to defeat the motion for summary judgment are deemed inadmissible under *Daubert*, the motion will be granted and the case dismissed. Thus, the first gatekeeping inquiry must be whether the testimony is scientifically valid. Once this determination has been made, the remaining inquiry is whether the totality of a party's evidence is sufficient to establish causation. Courts, however, including the U.S. Supreme Court in *Joiner*, are conflating the inquiries, finding testimony inadmissible because it is deemed insufficient to support causation. Only if the "scintilla of evidence presented is insufficient to allow a reasonable juror to conclude that the position more likely than not is true" may the judge grant summary judgment or direct a verdict.[109] Nothing in the opinion warrants conflating the two inquiries.

In *Daubert*, "fit" is a relevancy, not a sufficiency, problem. In *Joiner*, however, Justice Rehnquist turned the question of "fit" into a sufficiency issue by sequentially excluding the studies relied on and then finding the resulting testimony insufficiently supported to withstand summary judgment.[110] This is at odds with both the *Daubert* articulation of "fit," which required only a minimal relevance (testimony about the phase of the moon could be admissible to show degree of darkness), and the minimal logical relevance the federal courts require in other contexts. It is also contrary to the explanation of the rule given in the Advisory Committee Note to Rule 401, which warns against conflating sufficiency with admissibility. Conflating the two standards is pernicious because it precludes a cumulative impact analysis, the very kind of analysis that is the most scientifically reliable. *Daubert* explicitly separated the two considerations.[111]

107 As the U.S. Supreme Court explained, "there is no issue for trial unless there is sufficient evidence favoring the nonmoving party for a jury to return a verdict for that party." *Anderson v. Liberty Lobby, Inc.*, 477 U.S. 242, 249–50 (1986). "Merely colorable" or "not significantly probative" evidence will not withstand summary judgment. *See id.* On the other hand, the court is not to weigh the evidence in making this determination but rather is to make all inferences in favor of the nonmoving party. *Id.*, p. 249. If, after all, there is an absence of evidence to support the nonmoving party's case, the court may grant summary judgment. *Celotex Corp. v. Catrett*, 477 U.S. 317, 325 (1986). If the plaintiff's theory of the case is so implausible that a jury could not rationally buy it, summary judgment may be proper. *See Matsushita Electric Industrial Co. v. Zenith Radio Corp.*, 475 U.S. 574, 587 (1986).

108 *See, e.g., Hall v. Baxter Healthcare, Inc.*, 947 F. Supp. 1387, 1397 (D. Ore., 1996); *Conde v. Velsicol Chemical Corp.*, 24 F. 3d, 809, 814 (6th Cir. 1994); *In re Hanford Nuclear Reservation Litig.*, 1998 WL 775340, *140–41 (E.D. Wash. 1998); *National Bank of Commerce v. Dow Chem. Co.*, 965 F. Supp. 1490 (E.D. Ark. 1996).

109 *Daubert*, 509 U.S. 579.

110 *Joiner*, 118 S. Ct. 517.

111 *See Daubert*, 509 U.S. 579.

The real question for admissibility is whether each of the proffered studies is methodologically sound and contributes toward a biologically plausible theory of causation. The question of sufficiency, on the other hand, is whether all the party's evidence taken together makes a plausible causation argument.[112] Sequentially excluding bits of evidence as unable individually to support the entirety of a causation argument is unjustified, both intellectually and procedurally. It is a travesty of intellectual due process.

Progeny of *Daubert* and *Joiner*

Although the U.S. Supreme Court's opinions in *Daubert* and *Joiner* introduced judges to some basic scientific concepts, they left a great many questions unanswered. How a judge is to determine whether a particular experimental method is good science or how a judge is to decide whether imperfect studies are sound enough to be admissible are open questions. The U.S. Supreme Court also failed to acknowledge that the scientific method is not the same for all scientific disciplines and that scientific reliability is not an all-or-nothing proposition but rather depends on the use to which the evidence will be put and the acceptable risk of error. Nor did the Court give any guidance on ways in which separate studies, each individually inadequate to support a given conclusion, may cumulatively provide a proper foundation for a scientifically valid expert opinion. Statistical analysis, although concededly important to a *Daubert* determination, was neither discussed nor explained. Probabilistic causation issues were ignored.

Illustrating the difficulty in leaving such questions hanging, in the toxic tort case, *Wright v. Willamette Industries, Inc.*,[113] the Eighth Circuit overturned a jury verdict for plaintiffs, who claimed their injuries were caused by formaldehyde-laced emissions of a fiberboard factory, because it decided the expert's testimony was not based on scientific knowledge.[114] *Willamette* has been widely cited by other judges as a rationale for excluding expert testimony in the Eighth Circuit and elsewhere.[115]

---

112 *See Matsuhita*, 475 U.S. 587. The question on summary judgment is whether, accepting the nonmoving party's inferences as true, a reasonable jury could find causation more probable than not.

113 91 F. 3d, 1105, 1108 (8th Cir. 1996).

114 *Id.*, 1108.

115 *See, e.g., Moore v. Ashland Chem., Inc.*, 126 F. 3d, 679, 709 (5th Cir. 1997) *rev'd* 151 F. 3d, 269 (5th Cir. 1998); *Allen v. Pennsylvania Eng'g Corp.*, 102 F. 3d, 194, 198 (5th Cir. 1996); *National Bank of Commerce v. Associated Milk Prod., Inc.* 22 F. Supp. 2d, 942 (E.D. Ark., 1998), excluding causation testimony for lack of exposure level data, *aff'd* 191 F. 3d,858 (8th, 1999); *Mancuso v. Consolidated Edison Co.*, 967 F. Supp. 592, 601 (D. Kan., 1997). The *Milk Products* case is instructive, having correctly excluded causation testimony, but for the wrong reasons. The plaintiff in *Milk Products* claimed his laryngeal cancer had been caused by exposure to aflatoxins in contaminated milk at his workplace. Citing *Willamette*, the court excluded the testimony because the plaintiff was unable to show level of exposure. Had the court used the default assumptions proposed in this book, however, it would have recognized that a linear dose-response default makes knowledge of exposure levels unnecessary. A linear default is strongly defensible for cancer, the ailment from which the plaintiff suffered. The judge was unconvinced, citing Paracelsus's maxim, and disregarded the expert's testimony regarding linearity. Using a linear dose response, the amount of contaminated milk to which the plaintiff was exposed would be irrelevant because exposure to

The plaintiffs were a family who lived a short distance from a fiberboard manufacturing plant and suffered from headaches, sore throats, respiratory ailments, and dizziness, which they claimed were caused by toxic emissions from the plant. It was undisputed that the plant emitted particles laced with formaldehyde, that the polluting emissions exceeded state maximum levels, and that the plaintiffs were exposed to these particles.

After a jury trial at which the plaintiffs prevailed, they were awarded $226,250 in compensatory damages. On appeal, the Eighth Circuit overturned the jury verdict, ruling that the plaintiffs were unable to meet their burden of proving proximate cause because their expert testimony should have been excluded as "speculation."[116] As far as the Eighth Circuit was concerned, the problem was that although the plaintiffs could demonstrate exposure to fiberboard particles emanating from the manufacturer and that these particles were found "in their house, their sputum, and their urine, they failed to produce evidence that they were exposed to a hazardous level of formaldehyde from the fibers emanating from Willamette's plant."[117] Had the Eighth Circuit applied the heuristic suggested in this book, the outcome would have been different.

Applying the heuristic

What's the theory?

In *Willamette*, the causation hypothesis was based on the uncontroversial theory that exposure to formaldehyde causes respiratory disease in humans.[118] More specifically, their hypothesis was that when the plaintiffs breathed the formaldehyde contained on the particles invading the plaintiffs' home, it caused their particular array of symptoms. This hypothesis – that formaldehyde attached to wood particles has similar effects to gaseous formaldehyde – was too great a leap for the Eighth Circuit. Thus, although the court could accept the theory that exposure to "gaseous formaldehyde" could cause human respiratory ailments, it found causation from formaldehyde attached to wood particles to be unsubstantiated.[119]

---

any amount would pose a small but not zero risk of genetic damage ultimately leading to cancer. But aflatoxin, even in its most virulent form – commonly associated with corn and peanut butter – causes liver cancer rather than laryngeal cancer. See *Milk Products*, 22 F. Supp. 2d, 962; Bruce N. Ames, "Ranking Possible Carcinogenic Hazards," 236 *Sci.* 271 (1987). The default criteria for target organs would preclude using evidence of liver-cancer causation to show causation for laryngeal cancer. Thus, the judge was correct in excluding the testimony but for the wrong reason.

116 *Willamette*, 91 F.3d at 1108. Although *Willamette* was decided before *Joiner*, which reiterated the traditional abuse-of-discretion standard of review, it is nonetheless remarkable that the Eighth Circuit felt no compunction about its lack of deference to the trial judge. The Eighth Circuit did acknowledge its burden in overturning a jury verdict. See *id.*, 1106.

117 *Id.*, 1107.

118 See Robert E. Gosselin et al., Clinical Toxicology of Commercial Products: Acute Poisoning, 166–7 (4th ed., 1976), noting common symptoms including dizziness, nausea, headaches, skin and eye irritation, nose and throat irritation, and difficulty in breathing).

119 See *Willamette*, 91 F. 3d, 1107.

What is the available evidence?

Although formaldehyde is ubiquitous in the civilized world,[120] the defendant plant's emissions far exceeded statutory permitting levels. The manufacturer had failed to install available equipment to control the emissions. Emissions from the plant fell "like snow" on plaintiffs' property. The manufacturer was the only source of formaldehyde-coated wood particles in the vicinity of the plaintiffs' home. Significant levels of the plant's toxic emissions were found in the plaintiffs' bodily fluids. In fact, the Wright plaintiffs were exposed to enough formaldehyde to cause metabolic by-products to appear in their bodily fluids.

The plaintiffs' testifying experts included a forensic pathologist, a toxicologist, and a specialist in medical particulate research. The toxicologist and forensic pathologist testified to general causation. The particle-science expert testified that the metabolic mechanism of chemicals attached to particles (e.g., the fiberboard emissions) in the human respiratory system is similar to chemicals in the gaseous state. The plaintiffs' treating physician made a differential diagnosis that their symptoms were more probably than not caused by formaldehyde exposure. Each of the experts relied on studies in his or her own area of expertise as well as studies from other fields. Among the studies they relied on were government studies showing formaldehyde to be a carcinogen and respiratory irritant and as causing symptoms similar to those the plaintiffs suffered. Material Safety Data Sheets showed formaldehyde to be a carcinogen in laboratory animals.

There is ample evidence (although the court did not discuss it) – and presumably the experts based their testimony on this evidence – that "[f]ormaldehyde can produce health effects ranging from acute nausea, eye irritation, and respiratory impairment to longer term effects, like cancer."[121] In 1979, the Chemical Industry Institute of Toxicology issued a report that inhalation of formaldehyde causes nasal cancer in rodents.[122] Formaldehyde is a well-known allergen, as well as a mucousmembrane irritant,[123] causing eye, nose, and throat irritation; wheezing; fatigue; and skin rash.[124] Exposure levels of 0.1 parts per million (ppm) may cause difficulty in breathing and asthma.[125] The Occupational Safety and Health Administration (OSHA)'s formaldehyde exposure standard is 0.75 ppm for an 8-hour period, with a

120 See Indoor Air Pollution: A Health Perspective, 224–5 (Jonathan M. Samet and John D. Spencer, eds., 1991).
121 Frank P. Grad, Treatise on Environmental Law § 4A.01[4] (1999).
122 See W. D. Kearns et al., *The Chronic Effects of Formaldehyde Inhalation in Rats and Mice: A Preliminary Report* in Formaldehyde Toxicity 111–31 (J. E. Gibson, ed., 1983).
123 See E. P. Horvath, Jr. et al., *Effects of Formaldehyde on the Mucous Membranes and Lungs: A Study of an Industrial Population*, 259 JAMA 701 (1988); T. J. Kulle et al., *Formaldehyde Dose-Response in Healthy Nonsmokers*, 37 Int'l J. Air Pollution Control & Hazardous Waste Mgmt. 919 (1987); L. R. Sauder, *Acute Pulmonary Response to Formaldehyde Exposure in Healthy Non-Smokers*, 28 J. Occup. Med., 420 (1986); E. N. Schachter et al., *A Study of Respiratory Effects from Exposure to 2 ppm Formaldehyde in Healthy Subjects*, 30 Arch. Envtl Health, 229 (1986).
124 See Marian C. Marbury and Robert A. Krieger, *Formaldehyde* in Indoor Air Pollution: A Health Perspective, 223–5 (Jonathan M. Samet and John D. Spencer, eds., 1991).
125 See Andrew N. Davis and Paul E. Schaffman, The Home Environmental Sourcebook, 89 (1996).

maximum of 2 ppm for a 15-minute short-term exposure limit.[126] Just having large amounts of particle board in the home is a risk factor for asthma, headache, and throat irritation.[127] Moreover, the absorption rate of inhaled or ingested formaldehyde is very high.[128] The EPA found that 95 percent of people respond to concentrations of 0.1 to 3 ppm.[129] Formaldehyde metabolites such as those found in the plaintiffs' urine are known to be toxic in animals and to cause cell-membrane disruption in humans.[130]

What valid assumptions can fill the gaps?

The appellate court found that the plaintiffs' inability to demonstrate their exposure levels was dispositive.[131] There is no question that the Wrights were exposed to formaldehyde and that the formaldehyde to which they were exposed came from the defendant's lumber mill. The data show a strong association between exposure to formaldehyde at low levels and symptoms such as the plaintiffs suffered. But the court concluded that because there was no exposure-level data, the rest of the testimony was irrelevant. In addition, the court was unconvinced that the absorption of gaseous formaldehyde would be similar to that of formaldehyde bonded to particles of fiberboard. The two information gaps the court was unable to fill were exposure level and absorption mechanisms.

Exposure level

The *Willamette* court insisted that "a plaintiff in a toxic tort case must prove the levels of exposure that are hazardous to human beings generally as well as the plaintiff's actual level of exposure to the defendant's toxic substance" in order to recover. There is ample data to show the level at which formaldehyde affects people.[132] The problem for the Wrights was that formaldehyde is ubiquitous and they could

---

126 *See Occupational Exposure to Formaldehyde*, 57 Fed. Reg. 22, 290 (1992), codified at 29 C.F.R. § 1910.1048(c) (1999).

127 *See* P. Daugbjerg, *Is Particleboard in the Home Detrimental to Health?*, 48 Envtl. Res., 154, 154–63 (1989).

128 *See* J. L. Egle, Jr., *Retention of Inhaled Formaldehyde, Propionaldehyde and Acrolein in the Dog*, 25 Arch. Envtl. Health 119 (1972); C. E. Dallas et al., *Effects of Subchronic Formaldehyde Inhalation on Minute Volume and Nasal Deposition in Sprague-Dawley Rats*, 16 J. Toxicol. Environ. Health 553 (1985).

129 *See* U.S. Environmental Protection Agency (Office of Pesticides and Toxic Substances), *Assessment of Health Risks to Garment Workers and Certain Home Residents from Exposure to Formaldehyde* (1987).

130 *See* Appellees' Brief at 26, *Willamette* (No. 95–4227), testimony of Dr. Valentine.

131 *See Willamette*, 91 F. 3d, 1106.

132 Whether the experts relied on this is another question; presumably, they did. If not, it was an expert, and ultimately a lawyering, failure, which is beyond the scope of this book. This kind of failure can be remedied by the judge asking for a supplemental briefing on which underlying studies the expert relied on. The point is that there is ample evidence available (and easily accessible) about formaldehyde and its effects. Indeed, it has been so well litigated and the subject of numerous reports and publicized proceedings, the court could have taken judicial notice of the harmful exposure levels. Moreover, the Wrights' expert pharmacologist proffered testimony about the levels of exposure that would cause symptoms like the plaintiffs'. *See Willamette*, 91 F. 3d 1107. He relied on research performed by OSHA, among others, although he did not go back and reexamine the underlying studies for their methodology.

not show exposure levels greater than background. This does not mean that they were not exposed to levels greater than background. A sample of emissions from the plant showed 18,000 to 20,000 ppm of formaldehyde, far in excess of state maximum levels. OSHA set maximum exposure limits at 0.75 ppm (with short-term exposure limits at 2 ppm). Although the Wright home was located at some distance from the lumber mill, it was close enough to receive particulate matter falling "like snow" on the premises,[133] and their bodily fluids had significant levels of formaldehyde and its metabolites. When the metabolite level is known, the dose can be calculated.

Because formaldehyde is known to have a nonlinear response (i.e., an exposure threshold), the lumber mill argued that the Wrights had to show exposure above this threshold level. This argument reflects a misunderstanding of the probabilistic nature of the threshold response. The Wrights were already showing symptoms consistent with exposure. In other words, whether or not most people would show symptoms at that level, their threshold had been reached.

The concept of a threshold is a probabilistic one that, in general, exposure must exceed a certain amount (e.g., OSHA's 0.75 ppm). But scientists understand that some individuals will be more sensitive and, for them, the level will be lower.[134] These plaintiffs demonstrated exposure and symptoms consistent with exposure.[135] There was testimony that distinguished the effects of dust and other nontoxic air pollutants from formaldehyde. After engaging in differential diagnosis to account for other possible causes, a medical doctor testified that the Wright family's symptoms were more probably than not caused by formaldehyde exposure. Requiring more shows a misunderstanding of the probabilistic nature of scientific evidence.[136]

Absorption

The *Willamette* court was unduly concerned about the difference between exposure to "pure" gaseous formaldehyde and formaldehyde attached to sawdust particles. Once formaldehyde gets into the lungs, it makes little difference whether it got there in pure form or along with a sawdust carrier; the metabolism of the internal dose will be the same. The quantitative relationships between administered and delivered doses of formaldehyde are known.[137] In this case, the formaldehyde metabolites were found in the Wrights' bodily fluids, showing that absorption did take place.

---

133 *See Willamette*, 91 F. 3d, 1109, Heaney, J., dissenting.

134 *See, e.g.,* Rees and Hattis, note 66, p. 277.

135 They were clearly exposed to enough of the emissions that particles of fiberboard laced with formaldehyde were found in the plaintiffs' bodily fluids. *Willamette*, 91 F. 3d, 1109, Heaney, J., dissenting. That is not a naturally occurring phenomenon. In addition, the testimony that formaldehyde was capable of causing the kinds of diseases from which the plaintiffs suffered was well supported. *Id.*

136 In addition, arguing in favor of a threshold response was the plaintiffs' statement that their symptoms improved when they left home and worsened when they returned. *See* Appellees' Brief at 24, *Willamette* (No. 95–4227). Such reversibility suggests traditional acute/chronic toxicity damage produced by processes reversible at low doses. *See* Rees and Hattis, note 67, 276–7.

137 *See* T. B. Starr and R. D. Buck, *The Importance of Delivered Dose in Estimating Low-Dose Cancer Risk from Inhalation Exposure to Formaldehyde*, 4 Fund. Appl. Toxicol. 740, 740–53 (1984).

The effect of this decision is drastic for victims of environmental torts.[138] Information about exposure levels is commonly absent in toxic tort actions.[139] Requiring that plaintiffs show the level of toxic chemical to which they were exposed is requiring them to achieve the impossible. The default assumptions proposed here would have closed both of these gaps in a scientifically sound manner.

Methodology

None of the experts' methodologies was contested. The court did not examine or discuss the methodology of the underlying reports. It was willing to accept the published literature as validly demonstrating causation at least with respect to gaseous formaldehyde. Because formaldehyde has been so widely studied and the studies have been subjected to critique, there may have been some arguable basis for the court's failure to examine the methodology. Moreover, in this civil case, discovery was available to the parties, the opponents had access to each others' experts during depositions, and the experts disclosed the underlying studies on which they relied. Because such access was available, one would expect severe methodological flaws to come to light had there been any.

Assessing the expert's conclusion

Establishing a valid basis for the experts' causation hypothesis that the lumber mill's emissions caused the Wright family's illnesses was the plaintiffs' burden. The data supporting the hypothesis include formaldehyde exposure (by a plant emitting far greater amounts of formaldehyde than permissible) and symptoms that are consistent with formaldehyde exposure. Do any of the data refute the hypothesis that formaldehyde caused the plaintiffs' symptoms?[140] Although the manufacturer

---

138 For cases requiring evidence of exposure level based on *Willamette, see Allen v. Pennsylvania Engineering Corp.*, 102 F. 3d, 194, 198 (5th Cir. 1996); *National Bank of Commerce v. Associated Milk Prod., Inc.*, 22 F. Supp. 2d, 942 (E. D. Ark., 1998), *aff'd* 191 F. 3d, 858 (8th Cir. 1999); *Mitchell v. Gencorp Inc.*, 165 F. 3d, 778, 781 (10th Cir. 1999); *National Bank of Commerce v. Dow Chemical Co.*, 965 F. Supp. 1490, 1502 (E.D. Ark., 1996).

139 *See, e.g., Conde v. Velsicol Chemical Corp.*, 24 F. 3d, 809, 810 (6th Cir. 1994), excluding expert testimony that chlordane, an acknowledged carcinogen, applied in a manner that violated federal criminal law, caused plaintiffs' injuries where testimony was based on animal studies that used high-dosage levels rather than the low-dose levels to which plaintiffs were exposed; *Chikovsky v. Ortho Pharmaceutical Corp.*, 832 F. Supp. 341, 345–6 (S. D. Fla., 1993), excluding testimony where the expert did not know how much Retin-A was absorbed by the plaintiff or the dosage level at which Retin-A becomes unsafe for pregnant women; *Schmaltz v. Norfolk & Western Ry. Co.*, 878 F. Supp. 1119, 1122 (E. D. Ill., 1995), excluding testimony where the expert did not know how much herbicide plaintiff had been exposed to; *Cavallo v. Star Enterprise*, 892 F. Supp. 756 (E. D. Va., 1995), finding testimony inadmissible because the expert could not identify plaintiff's exposure levels or a dose-response relationship with respect to the jet fuel at issue; *National Bank of Commerce v. Dow Chemical Co.*, 965 F. Supp. 1490, 1518, 1552 (E. D. Ark., 1996), discrediting the plaintiff's expert testimony because the defendants' expert proffered a single epidemiology study showing no effects, even though the plaintiff offered evidence to show the study's results were inconclusive because it involved only five subjects, who were exposed to unknown pesticides at unknown levels.

140 Contrast *Willamette* with *Rutigliano v. Valley Business Forms*, 929 F. Supp. 779 (D. N.J., 1996), where the plaintiff's expert causation testimony was excluded because the expert failed to account

argued that the symptoms were equally consistent with exposure to other naturally occurring agents (e.g., pollen), there were no data to support this.[141] A physician engaging in differential diagnosis disagreed. The competing hypotheses should have – and did – go to the jury for its factfinding determination. Only on appeal did the court exclude this testimony.

For general causation testimony to be admissible, several hypotheses had to be supported: first, that formaldehyde can cause human disease; second, that it can cause the kinds of diseases suffered by the plaintiffs; and third, that formaldehyde in the form and levels to which plaintiffs were exposed (i.e., formaldehyde carried on sawdust) can cause the kinds of illnesses the plaintiffs suffered. The first two prongs the court acknowledged to have been established. The third prong was the issue the Eighth Circuit found the plaintiffs unable to meet;[142] but, had it understood the probabilistic reasoning underlying the concept of threshold responses, it would have let the verdict stand.[143]

Specific causation has yet another underlying hypothesis: that the formaldehyde-impregnated sawdust particles emanating from the defendants' plant caused the plaintiffs' illness. In toxic tort cases, even if general causation is well enough established to achieve acceptability as a theory (i.e., formaldehyde exposure causes disease in humans), direct evidence of specific causation is nearly always problematic.[144]

for copious data that the plaintiff's symptoms predated her exposure to the formaldehyde in carbonless copy paper. In *Rutigliano*, it was not the plaintiff's inability to demonstrate the level of her exposure that was fatal to her case but rather her inability to account for the data that carbonless copy paper was not implicated in the kind of injuries from which the plaintiff suffered (she complained of "formaldehyde sensitization," and her symptoms consisted of headache, tight throat, skin rash, fatigue, depression, and rhinitis which, she claimed, made it impossible for her to work in an office, in a retail operation, or outdoors). See *Rutigliano*, 929 F. Supp., 782–3. Moreover, Rutigliano's expert did not perform differential diagnosis on her patient and was unable to account for Rutigliano's allergy testing (which came back negative for formaldehyde sensitivity), her predominantly normal lung-function tests, or why the plaintiff's Epstein Barr virus diagnosis did not account for her symptoms. *Id.*, 789–90. In addition, Rutigliano's expert failed to analyze her client's office environment, an analysis she usually undertook in detail. *Id.*, 791. Thus, because Rutigliano's expert's conclusions were untestable and because her expert failed to account for the contrary data, which indicated her conclusions might be incorrect, the court excluded the testimony. See *id.*

141 The symptoms were, the manufacturer argued, common allergic symptoms. Thus, the argument was that something else – unspecified – could have caused the plaintiffs' ailments. See Appellant's Brief, 18, *Willamette* (No. 95–4227).

142 Curiously, the Eighth Circuit court acknowledged that it should not require a "mathematically precise table equating levels of exposure with levels of harm." *Willamette*, 91 F. 3d, 1107. However, it nevertheless insisted on a showing of exposure level that few people exposed to environmental harms could demonstrate.

143 The court neither discussed nor does it appear to have applied the traditional deference standard for the trial court's admissibility determination. Instead, it reviewed the district court's "denial of a motion for judgment as a matter of law by applying the same standard that the district court applied originally." *Willamette*, 91 F. 3d, 1106. The deference standard for admissibility determinations was subsequently reaffirmed by the U.S. Supreme Court in *Joiner. General Electric Co., v. Joiner*, 522 U.S. 136, 139 (1997). Had the *Willamette* court applied the *Joiner* deference standard, it is unlikely that the Eighth Circuit would have reversed because it would have had to find an abuse of discretion.

144 See *Merrell Dow Pharmaceuticals, Inc. v. Havner*, 953 S.W. 2d, 706, 715 (Tex., 1997), acknowledging the difficulties in adducing "direct, scientifically reliable" proof of specific causation in toxic tort cases.

Specific causation is nearly always demonstrated by a physician who has engaged in differential diagnosis.[145] The Wrights proffered such testimony.[146] This testimony was supported by data that showed the presence of the lumber mill's product in the plaintiffs' home and bodies, a huge body of literature showing the effects of formaldehyde, symptoms consistent with formaldehyde exposure, and a temporal response that improved when the Wrights left the area.

The lumber mill argued that because the plaintiffs' medical expert initially testified only that the plaintiffs' symptoms were "consistent" with exposure to formaldehyde, his testimony was irrelevant and inadmissible.[147] The lumber mill contended that "testimony as to 'consistency' (as opposed to causation)" was inadmissible.[148] Eventually – "after a great deal of prodding" – the Wrights' physician phrased the causation hypothesis in the terms the court demanded, that the symptoms were "more probably than not related to exposure to formaldehyde."[149] Failing to understand the language of science and scientific conclusion-drawing, the Eighth Circuit concluded that the physician's testimony was "speculation."[150] Had it understood the language of scientific argument, it would have concluded otherwise.

Finally, the appellate court set aside the jury verdict because the causation testimony involved gaseous formaldehyde rather than formaldehyde inhaled on wood particles.[151] The court was unable to analogize from inhalation of gaseous formaldehyde to particulate inhalation and failed to understand that the metabolism of the internal dose would not differ. Although this case may illustrate an extreme example, it underscores courts' unwillingness to reason by analogy where it comes to scientific evidence.[152] Because the court had little understanding of the proffered

---

145 *See, e.g., Rutigliano*, 929 F. Supp., 791.
146 Compare *Willamette* where the expert's causation testimony was completely excluded with *Moore v. Ashland Chemical, Inc.*, 151 F. 3d, 269 (5th Cir. 1998), where the physician was permitted to testify about his examination of the plaintiff, the tests he conducted, and the diagnosis he reached. *Moore*, 151 F. 3d, 273. The treating physician was familiar with studies linking exposure to toluene with respiratory disease, giving the district court a sound basis for its validity determination. The problem for Moore was that the defendant's physician concluded that Moore's disease was caused by smoking and pneumonia rather than toluene, and the jury chose to believe him. *Id.*, 274. In contrast, in *Willamette*, no medical diagnostic testimony was found admissible, although the court did not point to any errors in the diagnosis and there was no evidence presented of other causes.
147 *See* Appellants' Brief, 40, *Willamette* (No. 95–4227).
148 *See id.*
149 *See Willamette*, 91 F. 3d, 1108.
150 The Eighth Circuit was apparently unfamiliar with the writings of David Hume, who pointed out that "observers cannot perceive causal connections, but only a series of events." Kenneth J. Rothman, *Causal Inference – Habit, Faith or Logic?*, in Causal Inference, 5 (Kenneth J. Rothman, ed., 1988).
151 *See Willamette*, 91 F. 3d, pp. 1107–1108.
152 For other cases exhibiting this failure, *see Moore v. Ashland Chemical, Inc.* 126 F. 3d, 679, 709 (5th Cir. 1997); *Sutera v. Perrier Group of America, Inc.*, 986 F. Supp. 655, 664 (D. Mass., 1997); *In re Potash Antitrust Litig.*, 954 F. Supp. 1334, 1353 (D. Minn., 1997); *Mascarenas v. Miles, Inc.* 986 F. Supp. 582, 587 (W.D. Mo., 1997); *Mancuso v. Consolidated Edison*, 967 F. Supp. 1437, 1445 (S.D.N.Y., 1997). The Third Circuit's Judge Becker, in contrast, clearly understood the importance of scientific analogy. *In re Paoli RR Yard Litig.*, like *Joiner*, involved plaintiffs exposed to PCBs. As Judge Becker explained, the judge not only must assess the investigative process used by the expert, the judge must also make an independent assessment of the reliability of the expert's

evidence and because it had no framework for analysis, it reached a decision that is scientifically – and, from a policy standpoint – indefensible. Had it used the heuristic provided in Chapter 3, together with the precepts outlined in this chapter, it could have done far better.

Resolving the courts' causation conundrum

The courts' contortions over causal attribution reflect uncertainty not primarily about the validity of research results but about the inferences that can be properly drawn from these results.[153] What they need to understand is that causal inference is a matter of explanation.[154] The operative question is not only what data can establish causation but also what theories can explain the data. The procedural language of scientific argument should not blind judges and lawyers to the fact that it is nonetheless argument. The common preconception that the scientific method consists of "systematic controlled observation or experiment whose results lead to hypotheses, which are found valid or invalid through further work, leading to theories that are reliable because they were arrived at with initial open mindedness and continual critical skepticism" turns the process of science on its head.[155] As Jerome Frank remarked, the notion that "science is a charter of certainty" is an unsophisticated and unscientific view of science, which any intelligent scientist would recognize as fiction "made simply to aid in getting work done, made with complete recognition of its unreality."[156]

Science, no less than law, literature, or philosophy, seeks to make sense of the world. Both lawyers and scientists are concerned with the presentation of evidence and argue about the meaning of perceived facts.[157] Although law also seeks to explain

data and understand which inferences justifiably may be drawn from it. Under this part of the analysis, the judge is making a Rule 703 analysis, using the same standards as those used in Rule 702's reliability determination. *In re Paoli Railroad Yard Litig.*, 35 F. 3d, 717, 747 (3d Cir. 1994).

153 *See* Stephan F. Lanes, *The Logic of Causal Inference in Medicine* in CAUSAL INFERENCE 65 (Kenneth J. Rothman, ed., 1988).

154 *See id.*, 66.

155 HENRY H. BAUER, SCIENTIFIC LITERACY AND THE MYTH OF THE SCIENTIFIC METHOD, 19 (1992).

156 JEROME FRANK, LAW AND THE MODERN MIND, 307–11 (1970).

157 "[T]he practice of the scientific method is the persistent critique of arguments in the light of tried canons for judging the reliability of the procedures by which evidential data are obtained, and for assessing the probative force of the evidence on which conclusions are based." Ernest Nagel, *The Structure of Science*, 13 (1961). In legal argument, also, canons of construction are often used as focal points for argument, although their indeterminacy is well acknowledged. *See, e.g.*, KARL N. LLEWELLYN, THE COMMON LAW TRADITION, 62–120, 522–35 (1960), setting out the thrust and parry of statutory canons and the leeways of precedent. The point of the "science as process" movement in science, as with the legal realism movement in law, is that while the canons themselves are indeterminate, there are evolved "steadying factors" that make for continuity and predictability. For an explanation of this point in the legal context, *see id.*, p. 5, setting out fourteen clusters of factors providing predictability in the courts and explaining that "the most vital element in reckonability and stability is the courts' constant use, in application of doctrine, and also in choosing among the branching doctrinal possibilities, of the best sense and wisdom it can muster – but always in terms of those same traditions of the work that we have seen as "steadying factors." For readings in "science as process," *see*, generally, SHEILA JASANOFF ET AL., HANDBOOK OF SCIENCE AND TECHNOLOGY STUDIES, 507 (1994).

its outcomes as a search for truth,[158] observation and experiment are not normally considered part of the legal repertoire. However, this apparent divergence over "genuine testability" is misleading. In both science and law, what counts as factual proof is a mixture of inductive and deductive reasoning hung on a theoretical framework. Scientific reasoning, like legal reasoning, involves the use of analogy and precedent and depends for its coherence on the ability to discern patterns and draw on relationships of the observed phenomena.[159] Careful construction of the hypothesis identifies, defines, and clarifies the parameters of the experiment. Analytically, both science and law rely on subjective judgments or assumptions at every step on the way to reaching a conclusion. Science and legal analysis are also alike in that both function in relation to the social and cultural conditions from which they emerge, and both have reasonably consensual standards for testing claims within a given paradigm.

Rather than focusing on "positive" and "negative" studies, interpretation should concentrate on the theory and the methodology: what alternative explanations were and were not examined. For example, concerning the association between cigarette smoking and lung cancer, the claim of a causal relation can only be justified by examining the studies and refuting the noncausal explanations. In the absence of a competing causal theory, the theory that cigarette smoking causes lung cancer is the best available explanation of the data. In sum, the studies concerning causal theories should be interpreted by describing testable competing hypotheses.

Practically, this ought to mean that even studies that cannot entirely support a causation hypothesis may be used in conjunction with other studies to explain the hypothesis. The critical issue for general causation is whether, based on all the evidence presented, an agent is more likely than not to cause disease in humans. Certainly, that is the way scientists themselves assess the studies.[160] Yet, courts – including the U.S. Supreme Court[161] – are excluding evidence simply because a single study cannot support the entire causation hypothesis. Such an exclusion makes little sense from a scientific or legal viewpoint.

---

158 *See* WILLIAM TWINING, THEORIES OF EVIDENCE: BENTHAM & WIGMORE, 12–18 (1985), discussing the rationalist tradition in evidence scholarship and its main epistemological assumption that the purpose of adjudication is to discover an objectively knowable truth.

159 "The practice of normal science depends on the ability, acquired from exemplars, to group objects and situations into similarity sets." THOMAS KUHN, THE THEORY OF SCIENTIFIC REVOLUTIONS, 200 (2d ed., 1970).

160 For example, an epidemiologist reviewing seventy-one epidemiological studies, none of which showed statistically significant effects, nonetheless concluded that the studies "were consistent with a moderate or strong effect of the treatment under investigation." Frieman, note 37, p. 690.

161 The U.S. Supreme Court in *Joiner* examined the proffered studies seriatim to find that because alone each was incapable of supporting the causation hypothesis, none was admissible. *See Joiner*, 118 S. Ct., 519. The plaintiff – and the dissent – on the other hand, argued that the studies should be assessed together. *See Joiner*, 118 S. Ct., 522, Stevens, J., concurring in part and dissenting in part.

5

Criminal identification evidence

In stark contrast to the toxic tort context, judges in criminal cases overwhelmingly permit experts to testify with little or no examination of the scientific basis for their testimony – and this is true in the Commonwealth countries, the United States, and in civil law systems as well.[1] The problem in criminal evidence is that microscopic hair analysis, bitemark identification, voice spectrography, handwriting analysis, and even such time-honored prosecutorial tools of identification as fingerprinting have crept into court with virtually no demonstration of their scientific bases. Each of these identification techniques is based on the theory that fingerprints, voice patterns, bitemarks, and other identifying evidence are uniquely personal.[2] This is a theory based on faith (and – in the case of fingerprints, at least – some experience)[3],

---

1 In English courts (and those that have adopted English procedure), expert witnesses may testify or submit a written report with leave of the court. *See* PAUL ROBERTS AND ADRIAN ZUCKERMAN, CRIMINAL EVIDENCE, 290 (2004), citing Criminal Justice Act 1988. English law has a "liberal approach to the admissibility of expert evidence." *Id.*, 318. The current standard *seems* to be a two-pronged test of whether the subject is beyond the knowledge of the judge or jury and whether the witness is skilled and has adequate knowledge. *See R. v. Dallagher*, [2003] 1 Cr. App. R. 12, ∗204. In New South Wales, Evidence Act 1995 §79 sets out an admissibility standard similarly based on specialized knowledge. Curiously, Professors Roberts and Zuckerman do not believe that "English criminal litigation [is] awash with 'junk science' – as the American tort system, for example, is said to be." *Id.*, 297. Nonetheless, even the English courts have had their share of experts testifying to dubious evidence without any examination into its scientific basis. *See, e.g., R. v. Dallagher* (2003) 1 Cr. App. R. 12, ear prints; *R. v. Singleton* (1995) 1 Cr. App. R. 431, bitemarks; *R. v. Clarke* (1995), 2 Cr. App. R. 425, facial mapping; *R. v. Robb* (1991) 93 Cr. App. R. 161, 165–66, voice identification; although voice identification testimony was excluded by the Northern Ireland Court of Appeal in *R. v. O'Doherty* (2003) 1 Cr. App. R. 5.

2 As Professor Twining points out, identification is not really a single issue but rather "a flow of decisions and events" covering "a complex range of mental processes and actions" requiring a "quite elaborate conceptual framework." WILLIAM TWINING, RETHINKING EVIDENCE: EXPLORATORY ESSAYS, 167–9 (1990). Thus, the identification of a suspect by "matching" his fingerprints, for example, with some fragments of fingerprints left at the scene of the crime requires a whole range of assumptions, from the degree of similarity required to call a "match" to the meaning of the presence of the suspect of the crime scene. The fingerprint may be offered as evidence of opportunity or it may be offered as evidence bearing on a material fact (*e.g.*, "whodunnit"). For an enlightening discussion of the complexities involved in the concept of identification, *see* Twining, 153–77.

3 Note, however, that although it is popular belief that no two fingerprints are alike, there have been no systematic controlled studies to prove it. Moreover, fingerprint identification techniques are far from infallible. *See, e.g., State v. Caldwell*, 322 N.W. 2d, 574, 587 (Minn., 1982), mandating a new

not on the rigorous testing expected of scientific disciplines or required to meet the *Daubert* standards of admissibility.[4]

A number of reasons have been proposed for this lackadaisical gatekeeping, but tradition undoubtedly has a strong influence here. Many of the stalwart techniques of criminal forensics crept into the courtroom nearly a century ago under the guise of science, although most had little rigorous study to support them. Judges undoubtedly fear that if rigorous gatekeeping standards were imposed now, after decades of use – and these techniques were found wanting – there would be drastic consequences for criminal justice. That begs the question, of course: What good is a high threshold for conviction (beyond a reasonable doubt, rather than the preponderance standard of civil justice) if a prosecution expert can testify to any claptrap?

In numerous jurisdictions, courts are circumventing rigorous analysis and admitting expert forensic testimony that is shockingly unscientific. Many common law courts circumvent their gatekeeping duties in criminal cases by simply citing to past precedent, grandfathering in the evidence. Some courts take judicial notice of the validity of these forensic techniques. Others categorically state that scientific standards have been met, without analysis. Still others perform (and are affirmed in) a cursory analysis in which forensic "sciences" are exempted from rigorous analysis. Burden shifting is not uncommon.[5]

As a result, convictions continue to be based on evidence for which the scientific foundation is highly suspect.[6] Continued admissibility in some jurisdictions

---

trial because the fingerprint expert's testimony later was discovered to be wrong; George Bonebreak, *Fabricating Fingerprint Evidence*, Identification News, October 1976, p. 3, describing fifteen cases of fabricated fingerprint evidence.

4 *See Suggs v. State*, 907 S.W. 2d, 124, 126 (Ark., 1995), finding hair sample admissible although the expert admitted on cross-examination that "the scientific field cannot prove the hair came from a certain individual to the exclusion of any other person."

5 It is the proponent's burden to demonstrate the scientific validity of the proffered expert testimony. Nonetheless, in numerous cases, the court has required the defense to show that the prosecution's proffered evidence is flawed. *See, e.g., U.S. v. Crisp*, 324 F. 3d, 261 (4th Cir. 2003), cert. denied, 540 U.S. 888 (2003), shifting burden to the defense to disprove the "consensus of the experts and judicial communities" regarding the scientific validity of fingerprints; *U.S. v. Havvard*, 260 F. 3d, 597 (7th Cir. 2001), upholding trial court's admissibility of fingerprint testimony because the "defense has presented no evidence of error rates or even of any errors"; *U.S. v. Mitchell*, 365 F. 3d 215 (3d Cir. 2004), shifting the burden to the defense to demonstrate error rate.

6 Not only convictions but also every step of the criminal process can be tainted by unscientific evidence, from police identification of the suspect, the decision to close the investigation (and stop searching for the real perpetrator, who may go on to cause more harm), to whether to prosecute, to the charges that are brought, and to whether the accused enters into a plea bargain or goes to trial. *See* William Twining, Rethinking Evidence: Exploratory Essays, 153–77 (1990), discussing the problem of mis-identification as having severe repercussions beyond the courtroom. At each of these steps, misidentification can have severe repercussions, not only on the accused but also on the accused's family, friends, job, and society. In England, the Crown Prosecution Service Charging Standards explicitly recognize that "prosecution has serious implications for all involved" and require the prosecutor to independently assess the evidence for its reliability and the likelihood that it will be admissible in court. *See* Crown Prosecution Service, Charging Standards, ¶¶1.1, 5.1, 5.4 (2005).

of bitemark analysis,[7] microscopic hair analysis,[8] voiceprint evidence,[9] and hand-writing analysis can be accounted for only as gatekeeping avoidance because there is virtually no theoretical basis, no population databases, no standardized method-ology, nor empirical data on error rates for this kind of evidence, and what data we have suggest that the so-called experts are wrong at least as often as they are right.[10] This egregious miscarriage of justice is a dereliction of the judge's job to distinguish between useful and misleading testimony. Failure to examine the logi-cal underpinnings – and, in particular, the error rates – for forensic identification techniques undermines the presumption of innocence to which the criminal courts give lip service. Why is this happening in the criminal courts?

Tension between perceived needs to protect society from criminals and to pro-vide a fair trial appears to animate these circumventing gambits. The dilemma for the criminal courts is that much criminal identification evidence in its cur-rent state of development cannot possibly meet the *Daubert* standards, and the only way it met the *Frye* general acceptance standards was by narrowly defining the professional group whose acceptance was necessary (e.g., handwriting experts rather than all scientists). Often, there is little theoretical or empirical support

---

7 Bitemark evidence has been admitted in more than fifty cases post-*Daubert*, usually by courts that take judicial notice of its reliability. *See, e.g., Howard v. State*, 853 So. 2d, 781, 788 (Miss., 2003), upholding over strenuous dissent trial court's admitting forensic odontologist's bitemark identification testimony; *Carter v. State*, 766 N.E. 2d, 377, 380 (Ind., 2002), upholding bitemark testimony because "[i]n 1977 this Court could find no reason why bitemark evidence should be rejected as unreliable" and declining to require a *Daubert* hearing; *State v. Blamer*, 2001 WL 109130 (Ohio App. 5 Dist.), upholding bitemark testimony as scientific, citing *Daubert* without analysis, and noting that "bitemark identification testimony has been presented by forensic odontologists in other cases" and finding the testimony, even if admitted erroneously, redundant; *Seivewright v. State*, 7 P. 3d, 24, 29 (Wyo., 2000), holding that it was unnecessary for trial court to hold a *Daubert* hearing on the admissibility of bitemark testimony because of its "wide acceptance"; *Brooks v. State*, 748 So. 2d, 736, 739 (Miss., 1999), stating categorically that "bite-mark identification evidence is admissible in Mississippi" without any discussion of the scientific basis of such evidence. It has also been admitted in the United Kingdom. *See, e.g., R. v. Singleton*, (1995) 1 Cr. App. R. 431, bitemark testimony was admissible, without discussion; *R. v. Ewing*, (1992) 95 Cr. App. R. 278, bitemark testimony.

8 *See, e.g., State v. West*, 877 A. 2d 787 (Conn., 2005), taking judicial notice of the validity of microscopic hair analysis because the technique "had been admitted in Connecticut courts for many years."

9 Voiceprint evidence was widely discredited in the 1970s, and many courts found it inadmissible under the *Frye* standard. *See, e.g., People v. Kelly*, 549 P. 2d, 1240 (1976), rejecting voiceprint testimony as not generally accepted in the scientific community. Nonetheless, in the only published case so far to analyze voiceprint testimony under *Daubert*, the Alaska court found it admissible. *State v. Coon*, 974 P. 2d, 386 (Alaska, 1999), finding voiceprint testimony met scientific validity standards despite the FBI's rejection of such evidence as unreliable.

10 *See, e.g.,* D. K. Whittaker, 25 Int'l J. Forensic Dentistry, 166, noting a 76 percent error rate in experienced bitemark experts who were tested (cited by C. Michael Bowers, *Identification from Bitemarks: The Scientific Status of Bitemark Comparisons* §24-2.1.1 in 2 Modern Scientific Evidence: The Law and Science Of Expert Testimony (David L. Faigman, et. al. eds., Supp. 2000)), Bruce E. Koenig, *Selected Topics in Forensic Voice Identification*, 20 FBI Crime Lab. Digest, 78, 80 (1993), explaining that the FBI no longer relies on voiceprint technology because of the high error rate and lack of standard methodology; D. Michael Risinger et al., *Exorcism of Ignorance as a Proxy for Rational Knowledge: The Lessons of Handwriting Identification 'Expertise,'* 137 U. Pa. L. Rev. 731, 744–51 (1994), detailing the unpublished results of tests given to handwriting analysts by the Forensic Science Foundation over several years, for which the most generous reading of the results was an accuracy rate of only 57 percent.

for the evidence. Appropriate scientific standards are widely ignored in forensic laboratories.[11] Perjury of experts and pervasively bad laboratory practices have bedeviled even the FBI laboratories, forcing a number of retrials and overturned convictions.[12]

Not that the various forensic techniques present themselves in court as standard-less. On the contrary, each of these forensic disciplines has elaborate membership requirements and fancy-sounding methods. But these rituals are devoid of scientific content and lack even the most elementary safeguards that would protect against biasing of results. For example, forensic odontologists (i.e., bitemark experts) have their own accreditation, a theory loosely based on the possibility of identifying a person from dental records, and a journal in which they publish articles about their field. However, they have little theoretical or empirical support for the idea that they can identify a perpetrator by comparing casts taken of an accused's teeth with marks found on a victim's body (or, in one case, a piece of cheese[13]). It is an entirely sub-jective procedure; there are no controls and there is no blind testing of these experts.

Nor is this a problem limited to the United States. In Australia[14] and the United Kingdom[15] as well, public outcry over miscarriages of justice resulting

---

11 In 1992, the National Research Council issued a report recommending stricter standards for certifying and testing forensic laboratories. National Research Council, "DNA Typing in Forensic Science" (April 14, 1992). To date, only New York State and (after an appalling series of forensic frauds was publicized) Texas have mandatory accreditation for their forensic laboratories.

12 *See* U.S. Department of Justice Office of Inspector General, FBI Labs Report 9 (May 30, 1997) (hereinafter FBI Labs Report), acknowledging significant impact of *Daubert* on the way forensic evidence must be analyzed and presented. Although the immediate cause of the Department of Justice investigation of the FBI laboratories was the whistleblowing of Frederic Whitehurst, the thoroughness of the investigation and the resulting recommended overhaul of the laboratories was, in large part, a response to what the department perceived as the mandate of *Daubert* to justify the scientific validity of forensic laboratory results.

13 *Sievewright v. State*, 7 P.3d 24 (Wyo. 2000), holding that no Daubert hearing was necessary to admit expert testimony identifying the marks left on a hunk of cheese as the bite mark of the robbery defendant.

14 In Australia, public outcry about the scientific evidence underlying the conviction of Alyce Chamberlain for the murder of her baby (whom she had claimed was carried off by a wild dingo while the family was camping) resulted in the establishment of a Royal Commission, which issued a report highly critical of the scientific basis of the blood evidence proffered in the case and resulted in the release of the imprisoned defendant. For an account of this case and its aftermath, and an analysis of the Royal Commission's report, *see* Ian R. Freckelton, *Of Blood, Babies and Bathwater*, 17 ALTERNATIVE L.J., 10, 11 (1992).

15 The most recent outcry in the United Kingdom about expert testimony involved the expert Roy Meadow, whose statistical testimony in the Sally Clark case, although not technically the basis for quashing her conviction (which was due to prosecutorial withholding of an expert report), ultimately resulted in reopening hundreds of cases in which he had previously testified. *See* C. P. Walker and Carole McCartney, *Evidence: Expert Witnesses Seriously Disagreeing as to Whether Cause of Death of Infants Natural or Unnatural*, CRIM. L. REV. February 2005, 126–30. Previous scandals involving expert testimony in the United Kingdom concerning the convictions of "the Birmingham Six" for an IRA bombing of two pubs, based on expert testimony that there was a 99 percent probability that residues on the defendants' hands had been nitroglycerine, were overturned following the public's outcry when it learned that the test used was unreliable and the residue could as easily have come from playing cards, adhesive tape, or soap. *See R. v. McIlkenny*, 93 Crim. App. 287 (1991). Another widely publicized case, the "Maguire Seven," also resulted in a public outcry about the one-sided scientific testimony about nitroglycerine on which the conviction had been based, and the eventual release of the accuseds. *See R. v. Maguire*, 1992, Q.B.

from misleading scientific testimony has resulted in overturned convictions and government inquiries. For example, controversy about expert testimony regarding the inferences permissible from multiple unexplained infant deaths have plagued the courts.[16] Rather than meet these problems head on, however, and risk being unable to admit key evidence, courts continue to avoid analysis that would reveal the absence of validity in much of the expert testimony proffered by the prosecution and of systemic inadequacies in forensic laboratories.[17] Were judges to insist on scientific validity as a precondition to admissibility, however, not only would the criminal trial process become more just, it is also likely that criminal forensics would improve, as they have in response to controversies about DNA testimony.[18] As things stand, forensic experts have little incentive to demonstrate a sound scientific basis for their assertions.

Forensic science is almost entirely the province of the state, and its only application is in the courtroom. Experts appear for the defense in only a small percentage of criminal cases.[19] All too often, the defense fails to challenge prosecution experts,

936. The public outcry in these cases caused the formation of a task force that issued a report recommending improved screening of scientific evidence. CHRISTOPHER ODDIE, SCIENCE AND THE ADMINISTRATION OF JUSTICE, 15 (1991).

16 Following the Sally Clark case, Professor Meadow was permitted to testify in *R. v. Cannings* (2004) 2 Cr. App. R.7 (Eng.). There, as in *Clark*, the only evidence of a crime came from expert testimony. Three of the accused's children had died as infants, without any apparent medical reason. Although Meadows did not offer mathematical probabilities (as he had in *Clark*), he opined that because of the extreme rarity of three unexplained infant deaths in a family, the deaths must have been caused by smothering. Although the defense experts vigorously opposed this testimony, the accused was convicted. The Court of Appeal held that where there is "serious disagreement between reputable experts about the cause of death . . . unless there is additional cogent evidence, extraneous to the expert evidence," the conviction cannot be safe. *Id.*, 110. The problem of multiple unexplained infant deaths has also troubled the U.S. courts. *See, e.g., State v. Ward*, 138 S.W. 3d, 245 (Tenn., 2004), reversing the conviction based on expert testimony on "the rule of three," that is, if the first death is attributed to SIDS, the cause of the second death is changed to "uncertain," and the third to homicide, where two or more children die without explanation; *Buchanan v. State*, 69 P. 3d, 694 (Nev., 2003), sustaining the homicide conviction where the expert testified to the "rule of three" because there had been expert disagreement, and the jury could accept or reject any of these opinions; *Wilson v. State*, 803 A. 2d, 1034 (Md. Ct. App., 2002), finding it an abuse of discretion to admit statistical data and a product-rule computation to prove the improbability of two SIDS deaths in a single family. In New South Wales, expert testimony on multiple unexplained deaths was admitted as relevant under Evidence Act 1995 (NSW). *See R. v. Folbigg*, 152 A. Crim. R. 35 (2005), finding no reason to exclude expert testimony that it was extremely unlikely that four children would die successively from unknown natural causes.

17 A classic case is *Llera Plaza*, in which Judge Pollack initially decided that although he could take judicial notice of the uniqueness and permanence of fingerprints, but that fingerprinting methodology could not meet *Daubert* standards, then reversed himself based on the British courts' willingness to abandon their previous methodological standards in favor of the subjective methodology used by American and Canadian laboratories. *See United States v. Llera Plaza*, 179 F. Supp. 2d, 492 (E.D. Penn., 2002), withdrawn and superseded on reconsideration, 2002 WL 839163.

18 *See, e.g.,* Michael J. Saks and Jonathan J. Koehler, *The Coming Paradigm Shift in Forensic Identification Science*, 309 SCI. 892 (2005), asserting that the courts' insistence on standards in the early DNA cases resulted in widespread interdisciplinary debates and that, as a result, the most unscientific practices were rooted out, to be replaced by scientifically defensible propositions.

19 For a discussion of this problem in the United Kingdom., *see* Peter Alldridge, *Forensic Science and Expert Evidence*, 21 J. L. & SOC'Y 136, 139 (1994).

even where the testimony is highly controversial.[20] As an example of this problem, the now-discredited technique of voiceprint analysis was once a widely used identification method that was never empirically tested.[21] Yet, in an overwhelming 80 percent of the cases in which such evidence was admitted, no opposing expert testified for the defense.[22] Less extensive discovery rights and fewer resources add to the defendants' handicap. These factors add another layer of unfairness to the lack of rigorous empirical testing from which so many widely used identification techniques suffer. The result is a weighting of the evidence in the prosecution's favor.[23]

Permitting experts to testify beyond the bounds of their expertise – a frequent occurrence in criminal trials – only makes matters worse.[24] Examples abound of forensic pathologists who have been allowed to testify about how guns work and the caliber of deformed bullets and of ballistics experts permitted to testify about the character of wounds – in both instances, fields that are obviously outside their area of expertise. Forensic dentists identifying scratch marks and forensic anthropologists claiming to identify the wearer from shoe prints are egregious examples of untested pseudo-science admitted into courts.[25] This problem too is not limited to the United States. The Australian report on the investigation into the Chamberlain case, in which a mother was convicted of murdering her child – whom she claimed had been carried off by a wild dingo – reported that the experts had relied on an antiserum that the manufacturer specified not be used for diagnosis but rather for research

---

20 For example, Jimmy Ray Bromgard was exonerated of rape by DNA evidence after serving more than fifteen years in a Montana prison on the basis of testimony that hairs found in the victim's bedsheet matched his. Although there was little else linking the defendant to the crime, the defense counsel failed to hire an expert to challenge the prosecution's expert. www.innocenceproject.org/case/display_profile.php?id=111 (last visited September 9, 2005). DNA identification testimony has been widely admitted in Australia, often without any objection by the defense. *See* Judy Bourke, *Misapplied Science: Unreliability in Scientific Test Evidence* (Part 1), 10 AUSTRL. B. REV., 123, 143, note 119 (1993).

21 *See* Bert Black, *Science and the Law in the Wake of Daubert: A New Search for Scientific Knowledge*, 72 TEX. L. REV. 715, 739, and note159 (1994), stating that "the assumption that no two persons produce the same sound spectrogram had never been verified; nor had anyone ever tested whether a person can intentionally change his voice to alter his spectrogram or to produce the same spectrogram as someone else."

22 National Research Council, "On the Theory and Practice of Voice Identification," 49 (1979).

23 Both the Australian and the U.K. Royal Commissions noted this endemic problem in their reports.

24 *See* Freckelton, note 14, 10–11, discussing the findings of the Australian Royal Commission. The U.K. Royal Commission also noted that experts fail to acknowledge the limitations of their methods and conclusions.

25 *See In re Investigation of the W. Va. State Police Crime Lab*, Serology Div., 438 S.E. 2d, 501, 511–17 (W.Va., 1993), noting systemic deficiencies in the state crime lab including failure to require written protocol, failure to follow generally recognized testing standards, and absence of quality control or proficiency testing; Marcia Coyle, *Expert Under Fire in Capital Cases*, NAT'L L.J., July 11, 1994, p. A1, reporting on bogus testimony of forensic dentist testifying about tool marks, shoeprints, fingernail comparisons, and knife-wound comparisons in which he used an unfounded and unreproducible lighting technique to make identifications; Mark Hansen, *Believe It or Not*, A.B.A. J., June 1993, 64–7, debunking the work of forensic anthropologist Louise Robbins, who claimed ability to identify a person who made a particular footprint by examining any other shoes belonging to that individual – a scientifically unexplained feat no one else could reproduce.

purposes only. As a result of this misuse, the experts mistook iron residues in the soil for blood. The report noted that, in *Chamberlain*, the experts' willingness to testify beyond their areas of expertise as well as their readiness to speculate on the evidence rather than be confined to the available data were the source of injustice. A court willing to question the scientific basis of the proffered testimony could have avoided this travesty.

Ironically, the one identification technique developed outside the adversarial setting, DNA typing, has proved a boon for the defense as well as the prosecution and has demonstrated the pitiful inadequacy of the other forensic techniques. Not infrequently, DNA typing has exonerated defendants previously convicted on the basis of faulty identification evidence.[26] DNA typing explicitly recognizes the probabilistic nature of "matching" DNA sequences. Population genetics theory derives probabilities of randomly matching DNA sequences across different reference populations; no such statistical databases have been developed for the other forensic sciences. With the exception of DNA typing, forensic identification techniques have problems at every level of inquiry: the theoretical basis is questionable, the assumptions have little support, and what evidence there is was developed for litigation purposes – there are no double-blind studies performed for the sake of hypothesis testing.

At the theory level, it should be clear at this point that living creatures share many attributes. What then of claims made by forensic scientists that they can achieve "absolute specificity and absolute identification" of individuals? Underlying the forensic sciences is the idea that people have unique physical attributes, such as fingerprints, handwriting, and bitemarks,. Such a claim is based on an assertion that "nature never repeats."[27] This is a wholly untested theory and, even if true for the entire genome, for example, it is certainly not true for the fragments used in DNA typing. With respect to fingerprints, even if one were to accept the premise of uniqueness based on the embryological formation of friction ridges (subject to so many variables that duplication is highly improbable),[28] that says nothing about the likelihood of two fragments of fingerprints matching. In the absence of information, is uniqueness a preferable theory to its alternative, that unique characteristics are unlikely, and that people will share at least some attributes?

When we do have empirical data, such data support only qualified possibilities of individualization. DNA testing explicitly relies on the presence of a database drawn from the general population for its ability to identify an individual, and it

---

26 As of 2005, 162 people have been exonerated of the crimes for which they were convicted through the Innocence Project. *See* www.innocenceproject.org. The Innocence Project, run by Barry Scheck and Peter Neufeld out of Cardozo Law School, estimates that of eighty-six DNA exoneration cases, 63 percent involved forensic science testing errors and 27 percent involved false or misleading testimony by forensic scientists. *See* Saks and Koehler, note 18, advocating an overhaul of forensic sciences based on the example of DNA typing, and including such basics as the "data-based, probabilistic assessments of the meaning of evidentiary 'matches.'"

27 HAROLD CUMMINS AND CHARLES MIDLO, FINGER PRINTS, PALMS AND SOLES: AN INTRODUCTION TO DERMATOGLYPHICS, 150 (1943).

28 *See* Kasey Wertheim and Alice Maceo, *The Critical Stage of Friction Ridge and Pattern Formation*, 52 J. FORENSIC IDENTIFICATION, 35 (2002), surveying the literature on fingerprint formation.

recognizes the implausibility of making an absolute identification statement. Thus, the theory that "nature never repeats" is not grounded on valid science. It should not be accepted by the courts without empirical support. Rather, the alternative hypothesis, that individuals share many characteristics, is more scientifically sound in the absence of data to the contrary.

Methodological problems in forensic laboratories appear to be universal, despite attempts to ameliorate the situation.[29] The absence of objective standards (again, with the exception of DNA testing) is characteristic of each of these techniques. Moreover, even with DNA typing, serious testing errors have plagued forensic laboratories and (when discovered) required reexamination of results. For example, the Virginia State Crime Laboratory committed serious errors in performing the standardized protocols for DNA typing in the case of Earl Washington, Jr., who had spent years on death row.[30] Not only did the laboratory make serious mistakes, the laboratory monitoring system also failed. Once an independent audit revealed these failures, the DNA results of more than 160 cases had to be reexamined. This highlights the need for requiring experts to provide information on protocols, controls, and error rates for given procedures as a pre-condition for admissibility.

A further example of the courts' undue deference to forensic experts is their failure to demand that forensic laboratories submit their findings and procedures to independent testing. Independent testing is necessary because even where there is some empirical justification for a given methodology, its use in a forensic laboratory may be problematic. Errors such as sample switching and contamination invalidate

29 In the United States, the FBI has attempted to respond to criticisms by revamping practices and procedures. In Australia, forensic services are provided to both prosecution and defense, either through independent laboratories or through state-run laboratories that recognize a nonpartisan role (although there is still some controversy about whether this is possible in state-run labs). *See* Malcolm Brown and Paul Wilson, Justice & Nightmares: Successes and Failures of Forensic Science, 16–17 (1992), noting that the State Forensic Service Centre in South Australia is an independent agency that provides services to both prosecution and defense; in Victoria, the State Forensic Science Laboratory is part of the police department, but is avowedly nonpartisan; and in New South Wales, the Institute of Forensic Medicine stresses the importance of independence. In the United Kingdom, changes in the Forensic Science Service and Metropolitan Police Forensic Science Laboratory have been made to upgrade practices and procedures. *See* Royal Comm'n on Crim. Just., *The Role of Forensic Science in Criminal Proceedings,* 145 (1993).

30 *See* ASCLD/Lab Interim Inspection Report, Commonwealth of Virginia Division of Forensic Science Central Laboratory, April 9, 2005, detailing the shortcomings of the laboratory analyses, especially deviations in protocol and failure of quality assurance checks (found at www.innocenceproject.org). Although Washington had been convicted and sentenced to death in 1985, DNA typing tests were performed in 1993 and 1994 that were somewhat equivocal, resulting in the commutation of Washington's death sentence but not his pardon. *Id.,* p. 6. In 2000, newly discovered smears were submitted to DNA analysis, along with previously examined evidence. The results of that analysis caused the governor to grant Washington a full pardon. *See Washington v. Buraker,* 322 F. Supp. 2d, 692 (W.D. Va., 2004), indicating that the pardon was granted on September 7, 2004. Washington then sued the state law-enforcement officers and prosecutor for violations of his civil rights and, in conjunction with that suit, filed for discovery of the DNA evidence. *See Washington v. Buraker,* 322 F. Supp. 2d, 702 (W.D. Va., 2004). It was as a result of that discovery that the flawed analysis of the DNA samples in his case came to light. In response to requests from the Innocence Project, the governor ordered an independent audit of the laboratory protocols and adopted the recommendations of the auditors.

results. These pervasive problems with forensic evidence were acknowledged, at least with respect to DNA evidence, in the passage of the 1994 DNA Identification Act,[31] which requires that laboratories receiving federal funding submit to proficiency testing. Proficiency testing and the maintenance of high laboratory standards are prerequisites for scientific validity, a factor recognized by the U.S. Supreme Court when it included the error rate as a reliability guideline under *Daubert*. However, this recognition that proper testing procedures are critical to the accuracy of laboratory results has not been followed in forensic areas such as bitemark analysis, microscopic hair identification, and fingerprinting.

Despite the significant role forensic evidence plays in criminal trials, there is no mandatory federal regulation of forensic laboratories.[32] As a result, questionable evidence resulting from slipshod practices and substandard procedures has been presented by the prosecution in hundreds of cases, all too frequently with consequent convictions.[33] For example, a pre-*Daubert* survey conducted under the auspices of the American Academy of Forensic Sciences identified competency as the most significant ethical problem in the field, together with the failure of forensic scientists to express the strengths and weaknesses of their data, giving opinions exceeding the limits of their data, and failure to remain objective in evaluating evidence and giving testimony.[34] A post-*Daubert* investigation into the FBI forensic laboratories revealed significant instances of substandard work, inadequate laboratory training, deficient knowledge, tailoring testimony in favor of the prosecution, and failures to present objective reports.[35]

These problems remain of great concern today. The U.S. Department of Justice directed major changes to take place in the FBI laboratories, including the development of written protocols, increased training, improved standards, quality control, and increased supervision of expert testimony. The report further recognized that "for the . . . Laboratory to have wide-ranging credibility in courts and in the forensic community, examiners must strictly adhere to established protocols for the analysis

---

31 Pub. L. No. 103–302, 108 Stat. 1796 (1994). The DNA Identification Act also authorized the FBI to collect and maintain a national database of DNA profiles for law-enforcement purposes, a database now known as the Combined DNA Index System (CODIS).

32 The National Academy of Science recognized the problem in its report on DNA testing, acknowledging that "[p]roficiency testing and audits are key assessment mechanisms in any program for critical self-evaluation of laboratory performance." National Research Council, *The Evaluation of Forensic DNA Evidence*, 78 (1996).

33 *See In re Investigation of the W. Va. State Police Crime Lab, Serology Div.*, 438 S.E. 2d, 501, 511–17 (W.Va., 1993), noting systemic deficiencies in the state crime lab including failure to require written protocols, failure to follow generally recognized testing standards, absence of quality control, and absence of proficiency testing; Marcia Coyle, *Expert Under Fire in Capital Cases*, NAT'L L.J., July 11, 1994, p. A1, reporting on bogus testimony of forensic dentist testifying about tool marks, shoeprints, fingernail comparisons, and knife-wound comparisons in which he used an unfounded and irreproducible lighting technique to make identifications; Hausen, *supra* note 25, pp. 64–67, debunking the work of forensic anthropologist Louise Robbins.

34 Joseph L. Peterson and John E. Murdock, *Forensic Sciences Ethics: Developing an Integrated System of Support and Enforcement*, 34 J. FORENSIC SCI. 749, 751 (1989).

35 FBI Labs Report, note 10, pp. 1, 2, 13.

of evidence or document the reasons for departing from them. The same is true for the handling of evidence and the adoption of measures to prevent and detect contamination."[36] Testifying forensic scientists are often reluctant to admit the possibility (and implications) of false-positive tests, although technical errors such as – in the case of DNA testing – enzyme failures, abnormal salt concentrations, and dirt, as well as human error, can all produce misleading DNA banding patterns, which may cause false-positive testing. In addition, scientific evidence at criminal trials nearly always involves a proffered probability statement, yet few judges have attempted to understand the statistical basis of these statements and their underlying assumptions. Statistical errors are committed routinely even by defense attorneys, suggesting that lawyers as well as judges could benefit from increased training in statistics.

In the U.K. as well, statistical testimony is problematic. In the Sally Clark case, for example, a woman was convicted of murdering her two infant sons based primarily on the testimony of a pediatrician about the statistical unlikelihood of two SIDS deaths in a family. Not only was this evidence unchallenged at the trial, but the expert testifying was not a statistician, and the statistics were fundamentally flawed, as statistician Philip Dawid and others have pointed out.[37] First, in reaching his unlikelihood figures (1 in 73 million for two SIDs deaths in one family) the pediatrician made the wholly unsupported assumption that the two deaths were independent events; second, the pediatrician fell into the prosecutor's fallacy by conflating the rarity of the event with the probability that the event has happened in this case. Rather, the competing probabilities–assuming the only choices are two murders vs. two SIDS deaths – should have been compared – giving the relative odds. None of this was raised at trial, however.

The remainder of this chapter explores three areas of forensic science: DNA typing, which most commentators consider the gold standard for forensic sciences; fingerprinting, which, although it is the granddaddy of the identification techniques and has been in use for nearly a century, illustrates many of their common failings; and bitemark identification, a much newer technique that did not find its way into court until the late 1970s but has never demonstrated its scientific basis and exemplifies the courts' struggles with scientific validity in the criminal arena. This is followed by a discussion of the work of some exemplary judges who have taken their gatekeeping duties seriously and have carefully examined the scientific basis for forensic science testimony. The last part of this chapter then demonstrates how using the heuristic outlined in Chapter 3 would help judges approach a novel identification technology – in this case, mitochondrial DNA (mtDNA) analysis.

36 FBI Labs Report, note 10, p. 1.
37 For a comprehensive discussion of the Sally Clark case, *see* A. Philip Dawid, *Statistics and the Law*, in EVIDENCE (John Swenson-Wright, et al., eds. 2006) (forthcoming Cambridge University Press).

DNA typing: why is it the gold standard?

The origin of DNA typing was in the fields of molecular biology and population genetics; at its most elementary, the theory is that although people share 99.9 percent of the base-pair sequences, there are regions in which short segments of base pairs are repeated. These variable numbers of tandem repeats (VNTR) or short tandem repeats (STR) vary greatly among individuals. If enough sites where there is variation are examined, in theory, one should be able to determine whether two samples came from the same person.[38] The FBI uses thirteen STR loci (sites) for testing;[39] the British system uses ten loci, of which eight are included in the FBI's set.[40] Using the thirteen loci, the most common profile has an estimated frequency of less than 1 in 10 billion, assuming each STR locus is independent of the other.

The technique depends on knowing the frequency of a given STR pattern within the population. The FBI created a system for indexing these STR loci in the Combined DNA Index System (CODIS). A technique widely used in molecular biology, polymerase chain reaction (PCR) amplifies the segment so that even tiny amounts of DNA at a crime scene can be tested. Numerous scientific debates about the adequacy of DNA databases,[41] probabilities of DNA matches,[42] laboratory standards, and error rates[43] have driven the technology to what is now a defensible position. Although the debates are far from over, most of the controversy now centers on how well the technique has been employed rather than the underlying scientific basis for DNA typing. Because the technology has improved its standards as a result of these debates, it is the technology that commentators generally refer to as the "gold standard" for forensic science.

Fingerprinting: is it "old reliable"?

DNA typing was originally called DNA "fingerprinting" to convey a sense of reliability; indeed, fingerprinting has been used by courts to identify criminal perpetrators

---

38 If only one area is examined, however, the chances that two individuals will share the same profile can be nearly 20 percent. *See* National Institute of Justice, *A Report from the National Commission on the Future of DNA Evidence, The Future of Forensic DNA Testing: Predictions of the Research and Development Working Group,* 39 (U.S. Dep't of Justice, Washington, D.C., November 2000), available at http://www.ncjrs.org/pdffiles1/nij/183697.pdf.

39 As a practical matter, this is because two commercial kits are available, one testing nine STR loci plus gender and one testing six plus gender; together STRs plus gender are amplified and run through electrophoresis, giving a total of thirteen loci with some overlap serving as quality control. *See State v. Grant,* 2002 Conn. Super. Lexis 1127, pp. 7–8, testimony of Dr. Carll Ladd, supervisor of the Connecticut State Forensic Science Laboratory.

40 U.S. Dep't. of Justice, The National Commission on the Future of DNA Evidence, *The Future of Forensic DNA Testing: Predictions of the Research and Development Working Group,* 13–20, 46–61 (2000). These STRs are not genes, and twelve of the thirteen are noncoding segments.

41 Committee on DNA Technology in Forensic Science, DNA Technology in Forensic Science (National Research Council, 1992).

42 Richard C. Lewontin and D. L. Hartl, *Population Genetics in Forensic DNA Typing,* 254 Sci. 1745 (1991).

43 *See* Richard Lempert, *After the DNA Wars: Skirmishing with NRC II,* 37 Jurimetrics J. 439, 448 (1997), noting that some proficiency tests have found a 2 percent rate of false positives.

since the early part of the twentieth century, with little judicial inquiry into its scientific basis. One of the earliest U.S. cases, *People v. Jennings*,[44] took judicial notice of the technique's validity, citing the *Encyclopedia Britannica* and the British courts' acceptance of the technique. Not much more in the way of analysis took place in the courts in the ensuing century, even after *Daubert*.[45] One court, in deciding (without serious analysis) that fingerprint technology was valid science, remarked that its decision was "comparable to a breathless announcement that the sky is blue and the sun rose in the east yesterday."[46] Not until 2002 did a court take a rigorous look at the scientific validity of fingerprint technology; that judge, having first found that the technique could not meet scientific standards, simply reversed himself on reconsideration.[47]

So what's the brouhaha about? First, the underlying theory of unique ridge patterns comes from embryology, where ridge patterns begin to form during the third month of gestation and are influenced by genetics as well as random environmental factors.[48] The idea is that these factors are so highly variable that no two patterns repeat. This assertion has never been tested, and – unlike DNA typing – no frequency data exist.

Although it is a popular belief that no two fingerprints are alike, there have been no systematic controlled studies to prove it. In response to the first *Daubert* challenge to fingerprints, the FBI did attempt to demonstrate the probability of two fingerprints being identical, using a database of fifty thousand prints, and comparing each print with itself and other prints in the database.[49] Each print in the database was then converted into a fragment (i.e., to simulate a latent print

---

44 96 N.E., 1077, 1081 (Ill., 1911).

45 The first post-*Daubert* fingerprint challenge occurred in *U.S. v. Mitchell*, 145 F. 3d, 572, 575 (3d Cir. 1998), finding fingerprint technology admissible under *Daubert*.

46 *United States v. Havvard*, 117 F. Supp. 2d, 848, 849 (S.D. Ind., 2000).

47 *United States v. Llera Plaza*, Nos. CR. 98–362–10, CR. 98–362–11, CR. 98–362–12, 2002 WL 27305 (E.D. Pa., January 7, 2002, *Llera Plaza I*), vacated and withdrawn by 188 F. Supp. 2d, 549 (E.D. Pa., 2002, *Llera Plaza II, Llera Plaza I* was redacted from the Federal Supplement. In reversing himself, Judge Pollack made his decision not on the basis of any new information about the science behind fingerprinting, but because a fingerprint "regime that is sufficiently reliable for an English court . . . should . . . be regarded by the federal courts of the United States as satisfying the requirements of Rule 702. . . ." *Llera Plaza II,* 575. A more recent case casting doubt on fingerprint testimony excluded the latent fingerprint evidence of simultaneous prints as unreliable. *See Commonwealth v. Patterson*, 840 N.E. 2d, 12, 33 (Mass., 2005). In *Patterson*, the judge acknowledged that ACE-V fingerprinting techniques had been upheld as reliable (and opined that testimony about a single fingerprint impression would have been admissible) but held that the application of the technique to simultaneous impressions could not meet the *Daubert* standard (and its state equivalent). The expert had proffered testimony that four latent impressions left on the murder victim's car were subjected to "analysis, comparison, evaluation and verification," and although no single latent impression lifted from the car could "match" any of the accused's full fingerprint impressions, collectively there was a "match." *Patterson*, 840 N.E. 2d, 18. Because no studies had validated this use of the technique, lack of evidence pertaining to error rate, the absence of standards, and failure of professional organizations to adopt professional guidelines regarding its use, the court vacated denial of the accused's motion to exclude and remanded.

48 *See* Sarah B. Holt, The Genetics of Dermal Ridges, 6 (1968), noting that "[t]he detailed structures of individual ridges are extremely variable."

49 Record 81, *U.S. v. Mitchell* (E.D. Pa., February 2000) (No. 96-407), testimony of Donald Zeisig, July 9, 1999.

found at a crime scene), which was then compared to the entire print. The scores generated by the computer program for these comparisons were converted into probability measures, yielding a number of 10 to the 97th power (i.e., 1 followed by 97 zeros), taken from the lowest scores that the program generated when comparing each finger with itself.

The problem with this reasoning, however, is that even two complete rolled (i.e., inked) prints of the same finger will not be identical because of distortions in the inking process.[50] Three different examples of multiple prints from the same finger were found in the database. The scores generated by the program when comparing two prints from the same finger were lower than when each fingerprint was compared with itself, and some fell within the range of scores generated when comparing prints of different fingers. Thus, two fingerprints of the same finger would not meet the definition of identical.[51] As one prominent fingerprint examiner explained, this test was "worthless for documenting the individuality of fingerprints."[52] Nonetheless, this "experiment" continues to be introduced by the prosecution as validation for fingerprint uniqueness during *Daubert* hearings.[53]

Although large fingerprint databases do exist, these are databases consisting of complete, rolled prints.[54] The question for criminal identification purposes is whether there are common repeat patterns within the complete fingerprint so that we would know the probabilities of a random match from the kind of partial fingerprint fragments commonly found at crime scenes. No tested probability models exist for fingerprint pattern comparison. As Henry Faulds, one of the early fingerprint proponents cautioned, "Repeat patterns in single fingers are often found which come so near, the one to the other, that the least smudginess in the printing of them might easily veil important divergences in one or two lineations, with appalling results."[55] How frequent these repeat patterns are no one has bothered to discover.

Nor have the statistical models used to generate probability estimates for matching two complete friction-ridge patterns from two different fingers been tested, although the first model was developed by Francis Galton in 1892.[56] Indeed, the

50 *Id.*, 86–7.
51 *Id.*, 92, 94–5.
52 David A. Stoney, *Measurement of Fingerprint Individuality*, in ADVANCES IN FINGERPRINT TECH-NOLOGY, 381, 383 (Henry C. Lee and Robert E. Gaensslen, eds., 2d ed., 2001).
53 *See, e.g., Llera Plaza*, note 17.
54 This database, known as the Automated Fingerprint Identification System (AFIS), contains thousands of prints, but it does not make matches. Rather, it generates a number of possibilities (scored by the program depending on the degree of similarity) that an examiner will then compare manually to the fragment at issue (i.e., the latent print). The number of possible matches generated is set by the operator. *See* Frank G. Woods, *Automated Fingerprint Identification System*, in ADVANCES IN FINGERPRINT TECHNOLOGY (Henry C. Lee and Robert E. Gaensslen, eds., 2001), noting that the program's accuracy rates range from 50 to 80 percent).
55 HENRY FAULDS, GUIDE TO FINGERPRINT IDENTIFICATION, 51 (1905).
56 *See*, generally, FRANCIS GALTON, FINGERPRINTS (1892). For a discussion of the flaws in each of the statistical models, *see* David A. Stoney, *Measurement of Fingerprint Individuality*, in ADVANCES IN FINGERPRINT TECHNOLOGY, 370–83 (Henry C. Lee and R. E. Gaensslen, eds., 2d ed., 2001).

National Institute of Justice identified the absence of empirical support for fingerprinting as a problem and solicited research proposals. Subsequently, however, it retreated from any interpretation of its solicitation that would imply a lack of validation.[57] In any event, the studies were never funded.

The real difficulty with fingerprint identification appears to lie more with the accuracy of the matching process – which is based on a subjective determination – than the underlying theory that each person has unique ridges (although that theory remains untested). Not only is the theory questionable and the statistical modeling flawed, but, in addition, the methodology is explicitly subjective, eschewing the use of any particular standards for determining a match, such as the number of points in common.[58] Although British fingerprint experts once required a sixteen-point minimum similarity in the prints being compared, they abandoned this system in favor of the U.S. and Canadian subjective standard after three documented misidentifications.[59] Now, the analyst determines a match as a matter of judgment.

Fingerprint experts claim that having a second analyst concur in the judgment provides a validity check; however, this is nonsense because there are no requirements of blind analysis and no controls.[60] Nothing prevents the second analyst from knowing the judgment of the first. In defense of this system, the expert in *Llera Plaza I* pointed to the self-administered proficiency tests of FBI examiners in which a set of ten prints is provided to the examiner together with a series of unknowns, and the examiner is required to determine whether there are any matches.[61] The examiners did extremely well in these tests, but as the British examiner for the *Llera Plaza*

---

57 National Institute of Justice, U.S. Dep't. of Justice, solicitation: *Forensic Friction Ridge (Fingerprint) Examination Validation Studies* (2000), available at http://www.ncjrs.org/pdffiles1/nij/s1000386.pdf (last visited June 2, 2004); Julie Samuels, "Letter from National Institute of Justice Regarding the Solicitation of Forensic Friction Ridge (Fingerprint) Examination Validation Studies," *Forensic Sci. Comm.*, July 2000 at http://www.fbi.gov/hq/lab/fsc/backiss/july 2000/index.htm.

58 *See* DAVID R. ASHBAUGH, QUANTITATIVE-QUALITATIVE FRICTION RIDGE ANALYSIS: AN INTRODUCTION TO BASIC AND ADVANCED RIDGEOLOGY, 146 (1999), describing the commonly used ACE-V system, an acronym for analysis, comparison, evaluation, and verification.

59 *See* Simon A. Cole, *Grandfathering Evidence: Fingerprint Admissibility Rulings from Jennings to Llera Plaza and Back Again*, 41 AM. CRIM. L. REV. 1189, 1208 (2004), documenting the switch to the U.S. system.

60 In explaining the misidentification of the Madrid bomber (in which the FBI misidentified the prints of a West Coast lawyer as those found at the crime scene), for example, the FBI reporter ascribed the misidentification to undue deference to the initial examiner's results. Robert B. Stacey, *A Report on the Erroneous Fingerprint Individualization in the Madrid Train Bombing Case*, 54 J. FORENSIC IDENTIFICATION, 706 (2004). It is precisely to avoid such human bias that scientific laboratories insist on blind and double-blind testing.

61 *Llera Plaza I,* note 17, p. 18, testimony of Stephen Meagher, FBI fingerprint specialist. In response to the *Mitchell* challenge, the FBI attempted to demonstrate the validity of its methodology by sending out the defendant's fingerprints along with the two latent print fragments found at the crime scene to fifty-three agencies. Of the thirty-four that responded, nine reported that they had not identified either one or both of the prints as the defendant's. Record 203–08, *U.S. v. Mitchell* (E.D. Pa., February 2000, No. 96–407). testimony of Stephen Meager, July 18, 1999. Appalled at how this would look to a jury, the FBI sent them out again, enlarged this time, and asked for reevaluation, which the participating laboratories did, this time finding the requested matches.

defense pointed out, the tests were absurdly easy.[62] When proficiency testing was administered by outside agencies, the results of these tests demonstrated an alarming error rate: only 44 percent of the practitioners in one 1995 test correctly matched the prints in the test, a result that improved to 58 percent in 1998.[63] Indeed, a proficiency test run by two British researchers for Scotland Yard had such appalling results that it may have resulted in Britain's abandonment of its sixteen-point standard.[64]

All of these problems are exacerbated by the examiners' claims to certainty in their conclusions of absolute identification – a requirement of their professional association, which prohibits testimony in probabilistic terms.[65] Typically, experts claim that the error rate for the method is zero.[66] If pressed, they will admit that an individual examiner may err, but they refuse to acknowledge that the (highly subjective) methodology can be flawed.

These claims are absurd because fingerprint identification techniques are far from infallible.[67] The techniques have come under scrutiny but only once have they been excluded – only to have the judge overrule himself on a motion for reconsideration.[68] The DNA evidence exoneration of Stephen Cowans, who served six years in prison on a conviction based on fingerprint identification, ought to have brought the reliability of fingerprint identification techniques into question.[69]

---

62 They were too clear and unrepresentative of the kinds of prints found at crime scenes, lacking background noise and distortion. *Llera Plaza II, supra* note 17, 557–8, citing the testimony of Alan Bayle: "If I gave my experts these tests, they'd fall about laughing."

63 *See* Robert Epstein, *Fingerprints Meet Daubert: The Myth of Fingerprint Science Revealed*, 75 S. CAL. L. REV. 605, 633 (2002), citing Collaborative Testing Service, Inc., *Forensic Testing Program: Latent Prints Examination* 2, Rep. No. 99–516, 1999. This proficiency test consisted of "seven latents and four suspects," which the head examiner for the Illinois State Police Forensic Sciences considered "neither overly demanding nor unrealistic." David L. Grieve, *Possession of Truth*, 46 J. FORENSIC IDENTIFICATION 521, 524 (1996).

64 *See* Ian Everett and R. L. Williams, *A Review of the Sixteen-Point Fingerprint Standard in England and Wales*, 46 J. FORENSIC IDENTIFICATION 49 (1996), describing the study in which ten pairs of latent and rolled fingerprints were sent to British forensic laboratories, in which the participants reached widely varying judgments.

65 Resolution VII, Identification News, International Ass'n. for Identification, August 1979, 1, prohibiting testimony in probabilistic terms.

66 *See, e.g., United States v. Havvard*, 117 F.Supp. 848, 854 (S.D. Ind., 2000), aff'd 260 F. 3d, 597 (7th Cir. 2001), describing the testimony of Stephen Meagher, who claimed that the error rate for the methodology was zero, while conceding that individual examiners could make errors.

67 *See, e.g., State v. Caldwell*, 322 N.W. 2d, 574, 587 (Minn., 1982), mandating a new trial because the fingerprint expert's testimony later was discovered to be wrong; George Bonebreak, *Fabricating Fingerprint Evidence*, IDENTIFICATION NEWS, October 1976, 3, describing fifteen cases of fabricated fingerprint evidence.

68 *See U.S. v. Llera Plaza*, 2002 WL 27305 (E.D. Pa., 2002), *Llera Plaza I*, vacated on motion for reconsideration, 118 F. Supp. 2d, 549 (E.D. Pa., 2002) (*Llera Plaza II*). In the first instance, Judge Becker found that fingerprint identification testimony failed all but the general acceptance prong of *Daubert*. On the government's motion for reconsideration, however, he reversed himself with scarcely any discussion of scientific validity. In *U.S. v. Mitchell*, 365 F. 3d, 215 (3d Cir. 2004), the court upheld the district court's admissibility determination, finding that the testimony about whether fingerprint identification was a science was immaterial and that the court's taking judicial notice of the uniqueness of fingerprints was harmless error.

69 *See Commonwealth v. Cowans*, 756 N.E. 2d, 622 (Mass. App. Ct., 2001).

Moreover, the FBI's misidentification of Oregon attorney Brandon Mayfield as the source of fingerprints in the Madrid train bombing on March 31, 2004, should – at the very least – cause some increased future scrutiny of government claims of zero error rate.[70]

Unfortunately, although the FBI participated in an international investigation of the cause of the Madrid bombing mix-up, the findings of the commission were published only as a synopsis written by an FBI laboratories employee rather than as a report from the commission.[71] That report identified several causes of error: the pressure of working on a high-profile case, confirmation bias (i.e., the tendency to see what one expects to see), and undue deference by subsequent examiners to the initial examiner, as well as a failure to document the procedures followed. The scientific method, with its insistence on blind testing, standardized protocols with the use of controls, and proficiency testing, is designed to avoid (or at least minimize) just those errors, which is precisely why the courts should be insisting that forensic laboratories meet scientific standards.

Bitemark identification

Identifying the source of marks found on the victim of a crime as being bitemarks of a particular person is the province of experts known as forensic odontologists. The underlying theory, arising from the use of dental records to identify corpses, is that people have unique bitemarks, which remain after death on the soft tissue of the victim (or, in some instances, on food). Although there is little controversy about the ability of a dentist to identify a person from a complete set of dental records, especially if there are anomalies in the teeth, there is a great deal of controversy about the ability of forensic odontologists to identify marks left on a victim's body as bitemarks at all, far less being able to identify the source of those marks as the teeth of a particular individual. In the first bitemark case, *People v. Marx*,[72] the testifying expert conceded that "there is no established science of identifying persons from bite marks as distinguished from, say, dental records and X-rays."[73] But, in that case, the defendant had distinctive irregularities in his teeth, and the mark on the victim's nose was "one of the most definitive and distinct and deepest bite marks on record in human skin."[74] These conditions are rarely met, yet courts continue to routinely admit bitemark testimony.

The controversies about bitemark evidence once more center on the absence of a sound underlying theory; failure to gather available evidence (i.e., there are no

---

70 *See* Sara Kershaw, *Spain and U.S. at Odds on Mistaken Terror Arrest*, N.Y. TIMES, June 5, 2005, A1, noting that the Spanish authorities had cleared Mayfield and identified an Algerian suspect instead.

71 Robert B. Stacey, *A Report on the Erroneous Fingerprint Individualization in the Madrid Train Bombing Case*, 54 J. FORENSIC IDENTIFICATION, 706 (2004).

72 126 *Cal. Rptr.*, 350 (Cal. Ct. App., 1975).

73 *Id.*, 355.

74 *Id.*, 354, explaining that most bitemarks are on softer tissue and not very deep.

databases establishing the frequency of bitemark patterns); the complete avoidance of probabilistic models; the absence of blind, external proficiency testing using realistic models; and unknown error rates. In at least one case, DNA evidence has later exonerated a man convicted on the basis of bitemark testimony. In *State v. Krone*,[75] the forensic odontologist testified that the defendant was the source of a bitemark found on the victim's body. Although Krone was convicted and sentenced to death, he was later exonerated through DNA analysis.[76]

There have been surprisingly few challenges to bitemark testimony.[77] In the few challenges to bitemark evidence post-*Daubert*, the courts have simply cited to precedent and let the evidence in without analysis of its validity.[78] Nor can the federal courts be counted on to mop up the mistakes of the state courts in habeas relief by finding trials fundamentally unfair. In a typical example, *Kunco v. Commonwealth*,[79] in which the petitioner claimed that admitting bitemark testimony employing an ultraviolet-light technique that other odontologists had castigated as unreliable, unethical, and incredible, the court held that was not enough to show the necessary violation of due process.

---

75 182 Ariz. 319 (1995).

76 Saks and Koehler, note 18, p. 893, fig. 2, showing the bitemark evidence exhibit from *Kone*. In another DNA exoneration case involving bitemark testimony, *Brewer v. State*, 819 So. 2d, 1169 (Miss., 2002), the court ordered a new trial, but refused to vacate the defendant's capital conviction.

77 The failure of defense counsel to object to bitemark evidence is astounding, considering the shaky basis of such testimony. In at least one case, habeas has been granted on the basis of the defense counsel's deficient performance in failing to object. *See Ege v. Yukins*, 380 F. Supp. 2d 852 (E.D., Mich. 2005), defendant was deprived of a fundamentally fair trial where the only evidence linking the defendant to the crime was the improperly admitted testimony of a forensic odontologist that a mark on the victim's cheek was a human bite that matched the defendant's dentition, and that of 3.5 million people residing in the Detroit metropolitan area, the defendant was the only one whose dentition could match the mark. In two cases involving the notorious Dr. Michael West (who claimed to be able to identify marks by shining a blue light on them, a technique no one else could replicate, and which caused his suspension from the American Board of Forensic Odontology and resignation from the International Association of Identification), the challenges were not to the scientific validity of the testimony but to the expert's qualifications. *See, e.g., Brooks v. State*, 748 So. 2d, 736, 738 (Miss., 1999), where, although the defense made no objection to the bitemark testimony at trial, "because of the controversial nature of bite-mark evidence," the court took the opportunity to announce – without analysis – "that bite-mark identification evidence is admissible in Mississippi"; *Brewer v. State*, 725 So. 2d, 106 (Miss., 1998), noting that although the defense challenged the expert's qualifications, the defense and prosecution "stipulated that there is a body of scientific knowledge which allows for the identification of individuals based upon bite mark examination on soft tissue."

78 *See, e.g., Carter v. State*, 766 N.E. 2d, 377 (Ind., 2002), admitting bitemark testimony because "defendant does not argue that it has become less reliable" than it was in 1977 when Indiana first admitted bitemark testimony; *State v. Blamer*, 2001 WL 109130 (Ohio App. 5 Dist.), holding, without analysis, that the challenged testimony was admissible; *Sievert v. State*, 7 P. 3d, 24, 30 (Wyo., 2000), holding it was no abuse of discretion for trial court to refuse to hold a *Daubert* hearing, "[g]iven the wide acceptance of bite mark identification testimony and [defendant's] failure to present evidence challenging the methodology"; *State v. Timmendequas*, 737 A. 2d, 55, 114 (N.J., 1999), finding bitemark testimony in a capital case reliable because "thirty states considering such evidence have found it reliable"; *Verdict v. State*, 868 S.W. 2d, 443, 447 (Ark., 1993), no error in admitting bitemark testimony of Dr. West because "evidence on human bite marks is widely accepted by the courts."

79 85 *Fed. Appx.* 819 (3d Cir. 2003).

Courts can do it

Circumventing the *Daubert* mandate to examine the underlying validity of proposed expert testimony is all the more shocking because performing these gatekeeping duties is not difficult. There are judges who apply *Daubert* routinely and well and whose rigorous standards should serve as a model to those overwhelmed by their gatekeeping responsibilities. *Williamson v. Reynolds*[80] involved an assessment of hair-analysis claims by the government and exemplifies a court's understanding of scientific issues. The government presented an expert who testified that of the hundreds of hairs found at the murder scene and submitted to the laboratory for analysis, two scalp hairs and two pubic hairs were "consistent microscopically" with the defendant's. But, because the expert failed to explain which of the twenty-five characteristics he examined were consistent – due to the absence of standards for determining whether the samples were consistent – and because the expert could not explain how many other people might be expected to share the same combination of characteristics, the court disallowed the testimony. The court noted that although hair analysis "has become a familiar and common component of criminal prosecutions," it has been criticized as being too subjective and having a high error rate. Judge Seay explained that independent studies showed that the method used by the expert in this case was especially subject to erroneous conclusions because the expert knew which hair samples came from the crime scene and which came from the crime suspect. In checking its conclusion that the proffered hair analysis was unscientific, the court found no general acceptance because the only consensus about such evidence was among hair experts, "who are generally technicians testifying for the prosecution, not scientists who can objectively evaluate such evidence." Thus, although the expert may have followed procedures accepted by other hair experts, the results were scientifically unreliable, despite a long history of admissibility.[81]

Another court, in *United States v. Lowe*,[82] facing even more impressive technology – a new twist in DNA methodology – also admirably analyzed the technique in light of *Daubert,* this time finding the new technology to be admissible. At issue in *Lowe* was the use of chemiluminescence in place of autoradiography in the detection

---

80 904 F. Supp. 1529 (E. D. Okla., 1995).

81 Judge Seay's analysis is borne out by subsequent cases such as the Central Park jogger case, in which the critical physical evidence came from hair comparison testimony that the hairs found on one of the defendants belonged to the victim, a claim that was shown to be false through subsequent DNA tests. Jim Dwyer, *Some Officials Shaken by New Central Park Jogger Inquiry*, N.Y. Times, September 28, 2002, B1, B3. *See* also Adam Liptak, *2 States to Review Lab Work of Expert who Erred on ID*, N.Y. Times, December 19, 2002, A24, reporting on Jimmy Ray Bromgard, who was convicted on the basis of hair identification and exonerated by DNA testing. Unfortunately, Judge Seay's analysis is far from the majority, and courts continue to accept microscopic hair analysis without analysis. *See, e.g., State v. West*, 877 A. 2d 787 (Conn., 2005), upholding the denial of any inquiry into the scientific basis for microscopic hair analysis because "the cases in which courts have excluded hair evidence are so rare that they literally amount to only a handful of precedents."

82 954 F. Supp. 401 (D. Mass., 1996).

phase of restriction fragment length polymorphism (RFLP) DNA analysis in order
to produce a clearer image. First, the court reviewed the RFLP methodology in
general, as well as its application to the evidence in the case. The court noted that
although RFLP analysis was widely accepted as scientifically valid, the change in
protocol to chemiluminescence technique required the court to review its testing,
error rate, peer review, and general acceptance. Two validation studies, which the
court discussed in detail, showed that the new techniques gave substantially similar
but crisper detection results in population frequencies as had the older autoradiography technique. The court heard detailed testimony with respect to the causes
of any variations between the methods and was able to conclude that there was no
significant impact on the reliability of the RFLP testing methodology.

Although error rate is an important factor in determining admissibility, the
FBI in *Lowe* had conducted no such studies. Neither laboratory error rate nor blind
proficiency tests were available. This might have posed a problem had the defendant
not had an opportunity to test the evidence himself. According to the court (citing
a report of the National Resource Council), the "wrongly accused person's best
insurance against the possibility of being falsely incriminated is the opportunity to
have the testing repeated." Split samples had been presented to the defendant for
analysis, and no contrary results were urged on the court.

Judge Pollack in *Llera Plaza I* also did an admirable analysis of fingerprint technology before losing his nerve and reversing himself. Although he took judicial
notice of the permanence and uniqueness of fingerprints, Judge Pollack analyzed
whether latent prints can be accurately matched to complete rolled fingerprints
obtained from an identified person with respect to each of the *Daubert* factors.[83]
He pointed out that testability was not established by the government's assertion
that the "process and the experts' conclusions have been tested empirically over
a period of 100 years and . . . examination of the evidence by another expert"
because "adversarial testing in court" does not qualify as scientific testing, and the
concurrence of a second expert – whom, the court pointed out, often knew the
first expert's conclusions – sheds no light on the validity of the theory underlying
the technique.[84] Moreover, the subjectivity of the examiner's identification, lack of
"uniformity and systemization" with respect to standards, " the failure to carry out
controlled empirical . . . experimentation, a failure to recognize the value of . . . the
error rate" caused the technique to fail the testability prong of the inquiry. The
government's claims that fingerprinting techniques had been published and peer
reviewed for more than 100 years fared no better because, as the court pointed
out, it is a fallacy to equate the narrow community of fingerprint examiners with
the scientific community at large.[85] Citing the FBI's survey in *Mitchell* (in which
nine of thirty-four responding agencies did not make an identification of the crime
scene prints with the defendants'), the 1995 study (in which only 44 percent of the

83 *Llera Plaza* I, 2.
84 *Id.*, 10.
85 *Id.*, 15.

respondents correctly identified all five latent prints, while 31 percent made erroneous identifications) and the 1998 test (in which only 58 percent of the examiners correctly identified all the matching prints and did not make incorrect identificaitons), Judge Pollack also failed the technique on error rate. The only factor passing the *Daubert* test, the court held, was general acceptance within the fingerprint-examiner community.

However, although he found that the technique could not meet the standards for scientific validity, Judge Pollack did not exclude the fingerprint evidence entirely. Instead, following the lead of other courts that had grappled with handwriting analysis testimony, the judge would have permitted testimony describing how any latent and rolled prints were obtained; identifying the prints together with any necessary magnification and giving them to the jury; and pointing out any similarities and differences between the latent and rolled prints alleged to belong to the same person. The expert, however, was not permitted to opine that a particular print matches or does not match the rolled fingerprint of a person and is or is not that person's fingerprint.[86] Although this compromise solution to the questionable basis of expert opinion would have prevented expert over-reaching without depriving the jury of information, Judge Pollack repudiated his own insights in *Llera Plaza II*, simply announcing that he had changed his mind. Thus, his clever compromise has not been utilized outside of the handwriting-analysis context.

These cases are merely a few of the many examples of courts adhering to the spirit if not the letter of the U.S. Supreme Court's mandate. What all these courts have in common is their willingness to use a critical approach when dealing with questions of scientific validity. In applying the *Daubert* guidelines, these courts examine the explanatory power of the proffered evidence, its logical consistency, its testability, the precision and objectivity of the testing method, and its consistency with accepted theories. To check their own analysis, the courts then turn to peer review and general acceptance. These examples demonstrate that trial courts can do the required analysis routinely and well.

What's a court to do?

A good example of the problems faced by the courts in determining admissibility standards in criminal cases is the state murder case of *State v. Council*,[87] in which the judge employed a *Daubert*-like standard to determine admissibility of mitochondrial deoxyribonucleic acid mtDNA testimony. *Council* was the second U.S. case in which an expert proffered mtDNA testimony, and it illustrates a number of the systemic problems endemic to criminal expert identification testimony.[88] Despite the novelty of mtDNA testimony, the court found no defense

---

86 *Id.*, 23.
87 515 S.E. 2d, 508 (S.C., 1999).
88 By 2001, mtDNA evidence had been found admissible in twenty-six states. *See* Constance L. Fisher, et al., Lab. Div., Fed. Bureau of Investigation, Publication No. 01–05, *Mitochondrial DNA: Today and Tomorrow*, 2 (2001), listing states.

expert to be necessary. Even without examining the expert's methodology or the basis for the expert's assertion of reliability, the court admitted the testimony in its entirety.

In this murder case, hairs found at the crime scene were subjected to both conventional hair analysis and mtDNA testing and compared with samples of the defendant's hair.[89] The testifying expert proffering the mtDNA analysis was an FBI laboratory technician who based his testimony on numerous publications about the methodology. The evidence was admitted over objection, despite the defendant's inability to procure an expert in his defense and despite a very curtailed opportunity to review the test data.[90] The court found the testimony admissible based on the opportunity to attack any "shaky but admissible evidence" on cross-examination.[91]

Of the hairs that could be sequenced, the expert testified that the "reliability of getting a correct sequence was 100%."[92] On this basis, the expert testified that "most probably" the hair recovered from the crime scene was the defendant's. The expert based his testimony on a microscopic hair analysis that he admitted was inconclusive and on comparing the sequence of mtDNA from the crime scene with that of the defendant. On-cross examination, the expert did admit that it was possible that the hair belonged to another individual.[93]

The heuristic outlined in Chapter 3 provides some useful guidelines for analyzing the judicial response to this particular criminal-expert testimony.

What's the theory?

The theory on which testimony about hair identification is proffered is that each individual has hair with unique characteristics. Is it a falsifiable theory? Perhaps, but there is little empirical support for a theory of uniqueness.[94] Probability theory is the

---

89 *Council*, 515 S.E. 2d, at 516.

90 *Id.*, 518. The mtDNA analysis was not released to the defense until the night before trial, leaving the defense no opportunity to seek an expert. *Id.* This highlights one of the major shortcomings of scientific testimony in criminal trials: the inability of the defense to procure an expert. *See* Paul C. Giannelli, *The Abuse of Scientific Evidence in Criminal Cases: The Need for Independent Crime Laboratories*, 4 VA. J. SOC. POL'Y & L., 439 (1997), detailing major abuses of scientific evidence by prosecution experts. Even after the U.S. Supreme Court recognized the right of the defense to expert assistance in *Ake v. Oklahoma*, 470 U.S. 68 (1985), access of indigent defendants to experts is frequently severely curtailed, as it was in *Council*. *See, e.g.,* Paul C. Giannelli, *The DNA Story: An Alternative View*, 88 J. CRIM. L. & CRIMINOLOGY, 380, 414–21 (1997), noting the difficulties defendants often face in obtaining access to experts and test data.

91 *See Council*, 515 S.E. 2d, 519.

92 *Id.* What can this statement mean? A judge with an understanding of statistics and probability theory would have to view this statement with skepticism, as no test can be 100 percent reliable.

93 *Id.*

94 *See* Michael J. Saks, *Merlin and Solomon: Lessons from the Law's Formative Encounters with Forensic Identification Science*, 49 HASTINGS L.J. 1069, 1082 (1998), observing the "almost complete lack of factual and statistical data pertaining to the problem of establishing identity" in the forensic sciences and explaining that (in the context of finger print identification) the absence of frequent fingerprint matches does not establish their uniqueness any more than the statement "all swans are white" establishes that all swans really are white just because no one has yet seen a black one.

antithesis of absolute statements about uniqueness.[95] How unlikely a coincidence of particular features might be is a question that must be based on the collection of data and the use of statistical analysis – which has been startlingly absent from this branch of courtroom science.

In *Council*, the prosecution theory was that the microscopic characteristics of hair differ among people, and that, in addition, each person has unique genetic characteristics that can be determined by sequencing the mtDNA in a hair follicle. Hair identification, which generally has been admissible in criminal prosecutions, continues to be admissible despite numerous studies showing the inadequacy of the currently available microscopic techniques. The subjectivity and statistical unbeliev-ability of the number of asserted comparisons appear to be the principal problems with the methodology. Indeed, even the progenitor of hair analysis techniques, B. D. Gaudette, expressed doubts about its objectivity.[96] The FBI's "whitepaper commentary" on microscopic hair analysis asserts that the "microscopic characteristics of hair can assist the examiner in determining the racial origin, body area, and whether disease damage or artificial treatment is present."[97] Although these characteristics may be "useful," the FBI recognizes that hair comparisons do not constitute a basis for personal identification and requires that microscopic hair comparisons be used in conjunction with mtDNA analysis.

The theory behind DNA analysis in general is that genetic differences exist between people and that DNA analysis can uncover those differences.[98] This theory is well accepted.[99] In brief, the human genome[100] is made up of approximately four billion organic base pairs[101] in a particular sequence, most of which is common to all human beings. At some locations on the genome, there are distinctive sequences

---

95 Probability theory cannot prove absolutes such as "no two are alike"; moreover, the assumption that the variables scrutinized are independent may be questionable, and the system of measure-ment and classification must itself be tested. *See* Michael J. Saks and Jonathan J. Koehler, *What DNA "Fingerprinting" Can Teach the Law About the Rest of Forensic Science*, 13 CARDOZO L. REV. 361 (1991), advocating the probabilistic analysis of DNA typing as a model for other forensic sciences.

96 B. D. Gaudette, *Some Further Thoughts on Probabilities and Human Hair Comparisons*, 23 J. FORENSIC SCI., 758, 759 (1978), noting that hair comparison is somewhat subjective. Firearms identification is a similar example of an essentially subjective technique, which – although based on apparently objective criteria such as striation marks on a bullet – depends on the subjective judgment of the technician, making the individual technician's error rate an important issue in the testimony's validity.

97 *See FBI Responds to Questions Raised About Hair Comparison Analysis*, 32 PROSECUTOR 27 (November/December 1998).

98 For an introduction to the forensic use of DNA evidence, *see*, generally, William C. Thompson, *Guide to Forensic DNA Evidence* in EXPERT EVIDENCE: A PRACTITIONER'S GUIDE TO LAW, SCIENCE, AND THE FJC MANUAL, 195 (Bert Black and Patrick W. Lee, eds., 1997).

99 *See* C.G.G. AITKEN, STATISTICS AND THE EVALUATION OF EVIDENCE FOR FORENSIC SCIENTISM, 10 (1995), discussing DNA profiling.

100 The "genome" is the full complement of human DNA.

101 These four base pairs consist of adenosine (A), thymine (T), cytosine (C), and guanine (G), A pairing with T and C with G on the two complementary strands of DNA. *See* Aitken, note 99, p. 10.

of base pairs, known as *alleles*.[102] Typically, two alleles are found at each location, one inherited from the mother and one from the father.

MtDNA analysis is different from nuclear DNA analysis, however, because in mtDNA all the DNA comes from the mother, whereas in nuclear DNA analysis, half comes from each parent. MtDNA differs from the nuclear DNA conventionally used in suspect identification in that mtDNA comes from the mitochondria of the cell rather than from the cell nucleus. Mitochondria are cellular structures with their own DNA. Because there is only one nucleus per cell but many mitochondria, the DNA can be obtained in much larger quantities. Moreover, mtDNA is more stable than nuclear DNA and, although nuclear DNA is found only in the living cells at the base of a hair follicle, mtDNA can be found in the hair shaft (as well as in bone fragments). The mitochondrial genome is made up of some sixteen thousand base pairs, although mtDNA sequencing is performed only within two highly variable regions consisting of 610 base pairs.[103] Nuclear testing is performed on thirteen sequence areas. All offspring from the same mother have the same mtDNA (unless there have been genetic mutations).[104] Thus, unlike nuclear DNA, mitochondrial DNA varies only moderately among different individuals, although some areas of the mitochondrial genome are more variable than others.

The mtDNA is obtained from the hair sample by a procedure called polymerase chain reaction (PCR), which allows a small amount of DNA extracted from the hair follicle to be amplified in a test tube, the same process now predominantly used for nuclear DNA testing. The amplified DNA is then examined to determine the sequence of base pairs. Proper procedures are critical because contamination from other biological material through handling or from previously performed

---

102 Forensic DNA testing examines these alleles. To estimate the relative frequency of a particular genotype by counting its occurrence in the population, a huge database of samples would be needed. *See* George Sensabaugh and David H. Kaye, *Non-Human DNA Evidence*, 39 JURIMETRICS J. 1, 11–12 (1998), explaining the statistical basis for DNA identification techniques. Therefore, instead of the complete genotype, what is ordinarily used are alleles, a grouping of distinct DNA characteristics at particular locations on the genome. *Id.* By comparing the groupings of the alleles of two samples at a number of different locations, the analyst can either exclude the two samples as being from the same source or conclude that they cannot be excluded as being from the same source. This is referred to as a "match," but what it really means is that the null hypothesis cannot be substantiated. Then the analyst performs statistical analysis to determine the probability that the nonexclusion would occur by chance in the population. This frequency is estimated through the use of a database. Combining the allele frequencies into the final profile frequency (i.e., the random match probability) is a mathematical function of the genetic diversity at each location on the genome and the number of the locations tested. *See* National Research Council, *The Evaluation of Forensic DNA Evidence*, 146–47 (1996). The method used by the expert in *Council* differed in that the sequences of base pairs in the defendant's and crime-scene samples were directly compared with each other and the population frequency of such sequences assessed through the database.
103 National Comm'n. on the Future of DNA Evidence, *The Future of DNA Testing: Predictions of the Research and Development Working Group*, 19 (Nat'l. Inst. Justice, 2000).
104 This is an important qualification because at least two studies have found that the mutation rates for mitochondrial DNA are higher than for nuclear DNA. *See* Ann Gibbons, *Calibrating the Mitochondrial Clock (DNA Mutations and Evolutionary Dating)*, 279 SCI. 28 (1998).

amplifications will cause the contaminating DNA to be amplified along with the sample.[105]

What evidence was available?

In *Council*, samples of the suspect's hair were analyzed and compared with samples of hair taken from the crime scene.[106] Microscopic hair analysis was offered in conjunction with the mtDNA analysis. The prosecution expert opined that the defendant's hair was the same as that found at the crime scene. The expert explained that he (or his lab) extracted DNA from the mitochondria of the hair cells, amplified, and examined it to determine its allele sequences. The sequence was compared with the sequence of a sample obtained from the defendant and then to the database of known mtDNA sequences, which contained 742 known sequences. Of the database that the expert used, 319 sequences were from African Americans (based on the fact that the defendant was an African American). The expert had found matching sequences between unrelated Caucasians in the database but not African Americans. Only two regions were analyzed and, according to the expert, they were the "most variable [regions] in African Americans."

The prosecution expert testified that mtDNA analysis has been used for research since 1981 and that it is currently used to identify bodies in disasters. He testified that six hundred papers had been published on mtDNA (although it was not clear from the testimony whether these papers focused on identification, evolution, or some other use of the technique). Presumably, these studies formed the basis of the expert's testimony (although he did not say so). MtDNA analysis has been used to identify the remains of people massacred in humans rights violations in Haiti, the Balkans, and Latin America, as well as in airline disasters.[107] It is also widely used for inferring evolutionary relationships among species and populations because the sequence of alleles stays the same from generation to generation.[108] Scientists have examined animal hairs for genetic information for more than a decade.[109] Thus, there appears to be some support for the use of this technique in identifying individuals.

Use valid assumptions to fill the gaps

The assumption that mtDNA testing can be used to identify the source of crime-scene hairs appears warranted. The theory is that each person's complete genome

---

105 *See* National Research Council, *DNA Technology in Forensic Science,* 65–66 (1992).
106 *See Council,* 515 S.E. 2d, 516.
107 *See* Ana Marusic, *DNA Lab Helps Identify Missing Persons in Croatia and Bosnia and Herzegovina,* 358 LANCET, 1243 (2001), reporting on the use of mtDNA testing for identification purposes; Eliot Marshall, *International Experts Probe Haiti's Bloody Past,* 269 SCI., 1812 (1995).
108 *See* Patricia Kahn and Ann Gibbons, *DNA from an Extinct Human (Analysis of DNA from a Neanderthal Bone),* 277 SCI. 176 (1997).
109 *See* Russell Higuchi et al., *DNA Typing from Single Hairs,* 332 NATURE 543, 545 (1988), noting hair offers many advantages in wildlife studies because it is more easily found, transported, and stored than blood.

is unique, and that although there are many common areas, some locations on the genome are more variable than others.[110] MtDNA is not quite as strong an identifying technique as nuclear DNA because all offspring of the same mother will share the same sequences of mtDNA (absent mutations). Although the assumption that DNA analysis is capable of identifying individual characteristics has strong empirical support, methodological flaws may severely undermine its application.

Examine the methodology

The technique used to analyze mtDNA is known as PCR, which takes a small amount of DNA and amplifies it in a test tube.[111] This process makes it extraordinarily sensitive to contamination.[112] Contamination in mtDNA testing increases the chances that sequences will be incorrect and may increase the chance of declaring a false match. Ordinarily, controls are run with the test sample to ensure than contamination does not occur.

The FBI expert testified that DNA extracted from the mitochondria in the crime-scene hair was extracted, amplified, and examined to determine its base-pair sequences.[113] He made no mention of controls. Two samples, one from the suspect and the other from the murder scene, were compared.[114] The expert did not discuss laboratory protocols, standards, or proficiency testing. On finding that the two sequences matched, the examiner then compared the sequence with 742 known sequences in the database.[115] The expert did not discuss the frequency of the examined sequences in the population. No error rate was proffered, although the court asserted that the FBI laboratories had "process and evaluated its [own] error rate."[116]

The National Research Council, which has issued two reports on DNA evidence, calls for the observation of high-quality laboratory standards, proficiency testing, and sample splitting for independent testing.[117] The court in *Council* did not question the expert on these issues or examine any of the expert's laboratory notes before ruling on admissibility, nor was this information available to the defense. Rather, the court relied on cross-examination to raise any problems relating to methodology. Releasing the test results the night before trial, however, effectively denied

---

110 *See* David H. Kaye, *DNA, NAS, NRC, DAB, RFLP, PCR, and More*, 37 JURIMETRICS J., 395, 399 (1997), explaining that the expected frequency of a DNA profile consisting of characteristics at several "loci" – the characteristics at each locus is called an *allele* – is the product of the frequencies of the alleles.

111 The process involves breaking the double-stranded DNA fragments into single strands and then inducing each single strand to bind with complementary base pairs floating in solution.

112 *See* National Research Council, note 105, pp. 65–66.

113 *See Council*, 515 S.E. 2d, p. 517.

114 A third sample from another suspect was also compared, but the results excluded the other suspect as a possibility.

115 Note that the expert referred to "known sequences" rather than the number of people in the database. This may indicate a problem with database size.

116 *See Council*, 515 S.E. 2d, p. 518.

117 *See* National Research Council, note 105, p. 4.

the defendant meaningful access to the expert's methodology and made a mockery of the judge's faith in cross-examination. Moreover, access to the test results alone were simply not enough to reveal the potential weaknesses of the testimony.[118] For example, control samples containing no DNA are normally processed at the time of the amplification and the entire test is discarded if DNA is found in the controls. Criminal-expert reports rarely indicate the details of methodology, although courts should insist on this information before permitting the expert to testify.

In terms of error rate, the expert also testified that of the hairs that could be sequenced, "the reliability of getting a correct sequence was 100%." Presumably, the expert meant that if the sequence were really ATA[119] (for example), it would always appear as ATA in the test results. The expert offered no support for his statement, however, nor was any demanded by the court. Without access to the methodology, the testimony is inherently untrustworthy.

Assess the expert's conclusion

The failure to give a defense expert access to the underlying laboratory notes is critical here. Failure to follow protocols is fundamental to the validity of DNA analysis.[120] Because the mtDNA technique's weakest aspect is its sensitivity to contamination, it is crucial to know whether the testing observed adequate controls. No meaningful results can be drawn from a test run without adequate controls. The court never sought that information.

The expert in *Council* concluded that "most probably" the hair recovered from the crime scene was that of the defendant.[121] This testimony was allowed despite the expert's concession that in other cases he had found matches in mtDNA analyses between unrelated people.[122] Although nuclear DNA identification techniques are supported by a coherent explanation and strong empirical support, and mtDNA methodology has been applied successfully in contexts other than litigation,[123] admissibility of this particular mtDNA testimony was ill advised. Mitochondrial

---

118 Defendant's counsel argued – correctly, in my opinion – that the admissibility determination could not be made without providing the defense with an expert to examine the testimony. *See Council*, 515 S.E. 2d, 518, note 16.

119 *See supra* note 101, for an explanation of base pairing.

120 *See United States v. Martinez*, 3 F. 3d, 1191, 1198 (8th Cir. 1993), *cert. denied*, 510 U.S. 1062 (1994), acknowledging that courts must determine whether the expert failed to follow protocols and, if so, whether the error made the results unreliable.

121 *See Council*, 515 S.E. 2d, p. 517.

122 *Id.*, 518. The expert qualified this statement, however, by saying that he had never found matches between unrelated African Americans, a statement that – because the defendant was African American – was highly misleading because it implies that there may be more similarities between the mtDNA of Caucasians than African Americans (an unsupported assumption) rather than the more likely cause, which was the small database of African Americans (consisting of only 319 sequences). *See* Jon Cohen, *Genes and Behavior Make an Appearance in the O.J. Trial*, 268 SCI. 22 (1995), observing that there have been cases of matching mtDNA for more than two hundred base pairs in the absence of a maternal link, and that the most frequent mtDNA sequence appears in 3 percent of the population.

123 *See, e.g.*, Gibbons, *supra* note 104, p. 28, using mtDNA testing to identify soldiers' remains and the remains of nine Russians exhumed from a Siberian grave thought to be Tsar Nicholas II

DNA testing is not as powerful a tool as nuclear DNA because people with no maternal link may have significant numbers of base-pair matching. Indeed, the expert conceded as much.

Moreover, the expert's assertion that mtDNA testing is extremely reliable is correct only if the test is correctly performed and interpreted – and the PCR method used in mtDNA testing is extraordinarily difficult to perform without error from contamination.[124] The error rate of false-positive "matches" is a serious concern in DNA evidence.[125] The real question the expert should have been responding to was how likely it was that the sequence would be reported the same in the two hair samples if the mtDNA was not the defendant's.[126]

Another problem is the database used for hair comparison in *Council*, which consisted of only 742 known sequences. Larger samples give more precise estimates of allele frequencies than small ones.[127] Moreover, a proper method of constructing a database would be to construct a local database of DNA samples with representative genotype frequencies from the geographical area of the crime. We do not have information about how the database was constructed. Neither was there any explanation offered – at least, none was noted by the court – of the extent of statistical error.

Instead, the court accepted at face value the expert's assertion that the "FBI laboratory validated the process and determined its rate of error" without any inquiry into whether any proficiency testing had been done.[128] Proficiency testing is important because it demonstrates that a technique is valid not only in theory but also in practice.[129] In summary, *Council* is an instance where the court's failure

and his family; Eliot Marshall, "International Experts Probe Haiti's Bloody Past," 269 Sci., 1812 (1995), identifying remains of the victims of mass killings.

124 *See* Kahn and Gibbons, *supra* note 108, p. 177, noting the difficulty in avoiding contamination in mtDNA testing and explaining that prior false claims to have sequenced Neanderthal bones were the product of contamination. *See also* Paul C. Giannelli, *Criminal Discovery, Scientific Evidence, and DNA*, 44 Vand. L. Rev., 791, 796 (1991), noting false identification problems in proficiency tests.

125 *See, e.g.,* William C. Thompson, *Accepting Lower Standards: The National Research Council's Second Report on Forensic DNA Evidence*, 37 Jurimetrics J. 405, 417 (1997), noting that "the probability of an erroneous match is difficult to estimate"; Jonathan J. Koehler, *Error and Exaggeration in the Presentation of DNA Evidence at Trial*, 34 Jurimetrics J., 21, 26 (1993), estimating false-positive matches.

126 *See* Lempert, *supra* note 43, p. 442, observing that "[a] scientist who testifies that false positive error never happens does not address the question the jury needs answered – namely, how likely is it that a match would be *reported* if the evidence DNA was not the suspect's?"

127 *See* National Research Council, *supra* note 103, p. 114, observing the need for confidence intervals with respect to the estimates if the database is small. But *see* Ranajit Chakraborty, *Sample Size Requirements for Addressing the Population Genetic Issues of Forensic Use of DNA Typing*, 64 Human Biology, 141, 156–57 (1992), suggesting that relatively small databases may allow statistically acceptable frequency estimation for the common alleles.

128 *See Council*, 515 S.E. 2d, 517. The National Research Council explained that "there is no substitute for rigorous proficiency testing, via blind trials." National Research Council, note 103, p. 55.

129 *See* National Research Council, note 105, p. 55, noting that "proficiency testing constitutes scientific confirmation that a laboratory's implementation of a method is valid not only in theory, but also in practice."

to conduct a meaningful inquiry into expert methodology may have significantly undermined its validity analysis.

This is by no means uncommon, and many courts attribute methodological problems to weight rather than validity. This is mistaken, however, because it undermines the very heart of the scientific method. A test run without controls, without proper standards, and without error-rate analysis is worthless; it is irrelevant and cannot possibly be helpful to the jury. Whereas controversies about expert interpretation of results (e.g., band-shifting in DNA typing) should not make such studies inadmissible, some flaws in performing these tests (e.g., contamination, switched samples, or lack of controls in DNA typing) render the results meaningless. Meaningless results cannot possibly be relevant to the issue of whether the defendant is the perpetrator of the crime; they cannot as a matter of logic make that fact at issue more or less probable.[130] By calling the problem one of weight rather than admissibility, the courts let in evidence that has no scientific basis, and can – at best – confuse the jury. A related gambit, taking judicial notice of a forensic technique without examining how it has been used in the particular instance at issue,[131] is similarly pernicious.

Conclusion

Until purportedly scientific evidence can justify itself on scientific grounds, it ought to be excluded. The inability of many identification techniques to meet these tests should preclude admissibility. Indeed, by insisting that evidence used in criminal trials have a scientifically valid basis before it may be admitted, courts can play a major role in advancing the quality and reliability of the fact-finding process. In this regard, *Daubert* presents a great opportunity to improve the quality of criminal jurisprudence. Courts that continue to admit forensic evidence that cannot justify itself on scientific grounds are not only misreading *Daubert*, they are also impeding much-needed reforms in forensic laboratories.

---

130 In the United States, the Federal Rules of Evidence define relevance as "evidence having any tendency to make the existence of any fact that is of consequence to the determination of the action more probable or less probable than it would be without the evidence." FED. R. EVID. 401.

131 *See, e.g., United States v. Coleman,* 202 F. Supp. 2d, 962, 968 (E.D. Mo., 2002), noting that the Eighth Circuit takes judicial notice of DNA testing; *United States v. Beasley,* 102 F. 3d, 1440, 1445 (8th Cir. 1996), taking judicial notice of DNA PCR techniques.

6

Future dangerousness testimony: The epistemology of prediction

The struggle over what counts as science is in dire straits when it comes to capital sentencing proceedings, where the judiciary has flung wide the gates to wholly unscientific expert testimony. For a democratic system, where the rule of law is foundational in asserting that the solution to the problems of power and freedom is to make the law apply to everyone and to provide rational criteria for distinguishing legitimate from illegitimate uses of power, this lack of rationality has consequences. Judicial failure to scrutinize expert testimony relating to future dangerousness results in a massive failure of intellectual due process.

As discussed in Chapter 2, evidentiary rules are based on the truth-seeking rationality goal of the rule of law. One consequence of this idea is that the methodologies of the justice system should have truth-generating capacity – a notion of due process. A second consequence is a concern for accurate evidentiary input: in order to reach a justifiable decision, reasoning must be based on trustworthy information.[1] A third consequence of the aspiration to rationality is that even trustworthy facts must have some logical tendency to prove or disprove an issue in the case.[2] This framework for justice is the inspiration for the rules of evidence, and a fundamental tenet is that only facts having relevance – rational probative value – should be admissible in the search for truth.[3]

---

1 The belief that decisions based on correct information come closer to the truth is the basis of normative epistemology, including "norms governing how individuals should acquire and weigh evidence as well as, ultimately, form beliefs." Ronald J. Allen & Brian Leiter, *Naturalized Epistemology and the Law of Evidence*, 87 Va. L. Rev. 1491, 1498 (2001) (contending that the rules of evidence "structure the epistemic process by which jurors arrive at beliefs" about disputed matters of fact at trials).

2 Sometimes this concept is called "materiality," and it is considered to be one of the generative principles of the law of evidence. *See* Robert P. Burns, *Notes on the Future of Evidence Law*, 74 Temp. L. Rev. 69, 70 (2001) (noting that the generative principle of materiality, now subsumed under the relevance requirement, permits into evidence only that evidence that is "of consequence" to the "legitimate determination of the action").

3 A corollary is that all facts that have rational probative value should be admissible unless forbidden under a competing concern of the justice system (such as, for example, the improper uses of state power implicated in the exclusionary rule). *See* William L. Twining, Rethinking Evidence 152

In one important category of proceedings, however, this framework is tossed to the winds. Sentencing hearings have become an evidentiary free-for-all.[4] Particularly in capital sentencing proceedings, where death is supposed to be different, juries are permitted to hear expert testimony that even the most optimistic could only characterize as not "always wrong."[5] This is a far cry from the truth-generating methodologies supposedly fundamental to due process, and the opposite end of the spectrum from what is happening in civil trials, where experts must demonstrate the reliability of their testimony.[6]

(1990). The doctrines of relevance and probativity are expressed as follows under the Federal Rules of Evidence:

> "Relevant evidence" means evidence having any tendency to make the existence of any fact that is of consequence to the determination of the action more probable or less probable than it would be without the evidence.

FED. R. EVID. 402. And:

> Although relevant, evidence may be excluded if its probative value is substantially outweighed by the danger of unfair prejudice, confusion of the issues, or misleading the jury, or by considerations of undue delay, waste of time, or needless presentation of cumulative evidence.

FED. R. EVID. 403.

4 Evidentiary rules do not necessarily apply at sentencing hearings. Federal Rule of Evidence 1101(d)(3) states that the rules do not apply to sentencing proceedings, so federal courts do not apply them. The states are divided about their application. *See, e.g.,* Robert A. Kelly, *Applicability of the Rules of Evidence to the Capital Sentencing Proceeding: Theoretical & Practical Support for Open Admission of Mitigating Information,* 60 UMKC L. REV. 411, 457 (1992) (analyzing capital sentencing statutes and concluding that nineteen states do not apply the rules of evidence, seventeen states use evidentiary rules for at least part of their sentencing proceedings; however, all thirty-eight states with capital punishment require that any evidence admitted be relevant and probative). *See also, U.S. Sentencing Guidelines Manual* § 6A1.3 ("In resolving any dispute concerning a factor important to the sentencing determination, the court may consider relevant information without regard to its admissibility under the rules of evidence applicable at trial"). Among the various types of evidence that are excluded from trials under rules of evidence, but constitutionally permitted at sentencing are victim impact statements, acquitted conduct, and unadjudicated conduct. *See, e.g., Payne v. Tennessee,* 501 U.S. 808 (1991) (victim impact evidence constitutionally admissible); *Romano v. Oklahoma,* 512 U.S. 1, 11 (1994) (prior death sentence admissible in capital sentencing). Hearsay is the most prevalent category of evidence that is widely admitted at sentencing, although proscribed during the guilt phase of the trial. *See, e.g., Williams v. New York,* 337 U.S. 241 (1949) (finding it constitutionally permissible to rely on a presentence report for sentencing because of the need for a broad spectrum of information). In recent years, the Supreme Court has cut back somewhat on the evidentiary free-for-all, with regard to judicial post-verdict factfinding in sentencing proceedings, ruling it unconstitutional to increase the sentence based on unadjudicated facts. *See Blakely v. Washington,* 542 U.S. 296 (2004) (the maximum sentence a judge may impose must be based on facts reflected in the jury verdict or admitted by the defendant); *Ring v. Arizona,* 536 U.S. 584 (2002) (jury must determine aggravating factors in death penalty sentencing proceedings); *Apprendi v. New Jersey,* 530 U.S. 446 (2000) (any fact that increases the penalty beyond the statutory maximum must be submitted to the jury and proved beyond a reasonable doubt, with the exception of prior convictions). It has not, however, revisited *Barefoot.*

5 *Barefoot v. Estelle,* 463 U.S. 880, 900 (1983) (refusing to exclude future dangerousness testimony because the defense could not show that "psychiatrists are always wrong with respect to future dangerousness, only most of the time").

6 *See, e.g.,* Julie G. Shoop, *Judges are Gaining Confidence in Assessing Expert Evidence, Study Finds,* 38 TRIAL 92 (2002) (discussing a report by the Rand Institute for Civil Justice, which found that *Daubert* has had a significant impact on admissibility of expert testimony in civil trials, so that judges are closely scrutinizing relevance and reliability, resulting in a dramatic increase in the percentage

This is a result due, in large part, to the Supreme Court's decision in *Barefoot v. Estelle*.[7] In this chapter, I argue that *Barefoot* was wrongly decided, both as a matter of evidentiary due process and because it was empirically wrong about the ability of the adversary system to sort out the reliable from the unreliable expert testimony. Moreover, I argue that *Barefoot* is egregiously wrong-headed by current standards for relevance, and that *Barefoot*'s effect on capital sentencing proceedings has been pernicious and pervasive, undermining basic rule-of-law precepts. Notably, no one persuasively argues that the testimony at issue in *Barefoot* could meet *Daubert* standards.[8] Perhaps it is true, as Justices Blackmun and Powell argued, that the death penalty cannot be administered in a way that meets constitutional requirements.[9]

If, as I contend, the test by which an evidentiary practice should be judged is whether it increases the likelihood that the truth – defined as correspondence to the real world – will be attained, expert future dangerousness testimony fails to make the grade. While there may be valid reasons for abandoning strict adherence to the rules of evidence when it comes to sentencing proceedings – and I am skeptical about this proposition – at a very minimum, expert testimony should be admissible only if it is scientifically valid.[10]

The rule this chapter proposes is a constitutionalization of *Daubert*, at least with respect to death penalty proceedings. The reason we need gatekeepers is to ensure that the statements offered into evidence comport with permissible legal theories, embedded as they are in cultural systems of belief, assumptions, and claims about the world. It is the judge whose role it is to manage coherence by reference to what is relevant to the legal determination. And *Daubert* is unequivocal that relevance in the context of expert testimony means scientific validity.

---

of excluded expert testimony in products liability trials, and a surge in summary judgments against the plaintiffs). As noted in Chapter 5, this increased scrutiny of scientific evidence has not affected criminal trials nearly so dramatically.

7 463 U.S. 880 (1983) (permitting experts to testify about future dangerousness as a constitutional matter).

8 The Texas courts require a scientific validity determination before admitting expert testimony, but the few courts that have actually conducted such an inquiry have made a mockery of it. *See, e.g., Nenno v. State*, 970 S.W. 2d 549 (Tex. 1998).

9 *See Callins v. Collins*, 510 U.S. 1141, 1145–46 (1994) (Blackmun, J., dissenting) (observing that "the inevitability of factual, legal, and moral error gives us a system that we know must wrongly kill some defendants, a system that fails to deliver the fair, consistent, and reliable sentences of death required by the Constitution"); Jeffrey L. Kirchmeier, *Aggravating and Mitigating Factors: The Paradox of Today's Arbitrary and Mandatory Capital Punishment Scheme*, 6 Wm. & Mary Bill Rts. J. 345, 347 (1998) (noting that "Justice Powell came to a similar conclusion after his retirement"). Notably, two states, Illinois and Maryland, reached similar conclusions, and placed a moratorium on death penalty prosecutions because of due process concerns. *See* Dirk Johnson, *Illinois, Citing Verdict Errors, Bars Executions*, New York Times, Feb. 1, 2000. While Maryland has since lifted its moratorium, Illinois's remains. *See Uncertain Justice*, Houston Chronicle Jan. 24, 2006 at B8.

10 Notably, as discussed in Chapter 5, one-third of the prisoners exonerated by the Actual Innocence Project had been convicted on the basis of "tainted or fraudulent science." Barry Scheck, et al., Actual Innocence 246 (2000).

Expert future dangerousness testimony in capital sentencing proceedings

Expert testimony about future dangerousness currently takes two forms: clinical and actuarial predictions. By far the most common form of testimony is the clinical prediction. In this testimony, the expert, usually a psychiatrist, sometimes a psychologist, proffers an opinion based on a courtroom hypothetical, with or without a prior examination of the defendant. Even under the best circumstances, where clinicians have the opportunity for an extensive examination, however, studies show that clinical predictions are highly inaccurate.[11]

There are a number of reasons for this inaccuracy. Clinical decisionmakers tend to assume the representativeness of events erroneously by ignoring sample sizes and base rates.[12] Ignoring base rates is a particular problem in predicting violence where the base rate of violent behavior is low overall and varies among different population sub-groups.[13] In addition, these studies show that clinicians tend to think they have more information than they really do.[14] Clinicians, like most of us, are poor at making extreme judgments.[15] Despite the well-known difficulty in

---

11 *See, e.g.,* Caroline M. Mee & Harold V. Hall, *Risky Business: Assessing Danger in Hawaii,* 24 U. HAW. L. REV. 63, (2001) (noting that "dangerousness prediction has heretofore been rudimentary and inaccurate, relying on clinical judgment rather than objective measures").

12 Daniel Kahneman & Amos Tversky, *Subjective Probability: A Judgment of Representativeness,* 3 COGNITIVE PSYCHOL. 430 (1972). These shortcuts are not consciously employed, but operate on a subliminal level to affect decision. The base rate is the frequency of a given subject in the population. For example, if a sample of 100 people consists of 70 lawyers and 30 engineers, the base rate of lawyers is 70 percent, and of engineers, 30 percent. Knowing only that, if you were asked the occupation of any given person, you would be wise to answer "lawyer." Interestingly, most people do not. In a study in which subjects were divided into two groups, both of which were told that 100 people were either lawyers or engineers, one subject group was told there were 70 lawyers and 30 engineers, the other group that there were 30 lawyers and 70 engineers, and both groups were given thumbnail descriptions of the people written by psychologists, designed to be nondiagnostic with respect to occupation. *See* Richard E. Nisbett et al., *Teaching Reasoning,* 238 SCI. 625 (Oct. 30, 1987). In both groups, the subjects based their answers on stereotypes rather than population base rates. *Id. But see* Jonathan J. Koehler, *The Base Rate Fallacy Reconsidered: Descriptive, Normative and Methodological Challenges,* 19 BEHAV. & BRAIN SCI. 1, 3 (arguing that it is not so much that base rates are ignored as that "subjects attach relatively less weight to base rate information than to descriptive, individuating information"). Regardless of whether base rates are ignored or given insufficient weight, however, when the goal is accuracy in judgment, structuring a decision process to minimize errors would appear advantageous. As Koehler explains, avoiding the base rate fallacy can best be accomplished by explicitly structuring the task to sensitize decisionmakers to the base rate, presenting the information in relative frequentist terms and giving the decisionmaker cues to base rate diagnosticity, as well as invoking heuristics that focus attention on the base rate. That is precisely what this chapter advocates in requiring judicial gatekeeping that limits expert prediction testimony to that which explicitly refers to population base rates. For further discussion of this research, see Chapter 9.

13 *See* Kahneman & Tversky, *supra* note 12 at 223 (explaining how the statistical base-rate problem affects predictions of dangerousness); VERNON L. QUINSEY ET AL., VIOLENT OFFENDERS: APPRAISING AND MANAGING RISK 60, 62 (1998).

14 Quinsey et al., *supra* note 13 at 56.

15 *See* Hillel J. Einhorn & Robin M. Hogarth, *Confidence in Judgment: Persistence of the Illusion of Validity,* 85 PSYCHOL. REV. 395 (1978) (noting that clinicians tend to have more confidence in predictive variables with extreme values than is warranted).

predicting statistically rare events (like violence), clinical judgments tend to ignore that difficulty.[16] Stereotypes and prejudices are just as likely to taint the decisions of clinicians as those of lay people.[17] As a result, clinicians are no better than lay people in making these predictions.[18]

Moreover, there is no information available about the individual error rate of the particular expert proffering a future dangerousness opinion.[19] Although some experts are undoubtedly better at diagnosis and prediction than others, there is no way to know how many times the expert has opined someone was dangerous when he was not (or vice-versa). Clinical judgment is thus virtually untestable.

Actuarial instruments attempt to correct these deficiencies by relying on statistically analyzed data rather than personal experience.[20] These instruments attempt to counter human cognitive error by taking into account the interrelationship of various risk factors, population base rates, and by assigning weights to the individual risk factors. Repeated studies of actuarial methods have demonstrated them to be superior to clinical judgment standing alone.[21] Even the best of these instruments is not particularly predictive, however.[22] Using structured analysis offers many advantages in human decisionmaking, particularly in light of the difficulty people have in synthesizing differently weighted likelihoods of varying significance (such as risk

---

16 *See* John W. Parry et al., ABA Comm'n on Mental Health and Physical Disability Law, *National Benchbook on Psychiatric and Psychological Evidence and Testimony* 20 (1998) [hereinafter *Benchbook*] (noting that "it is difficult to predict with certainty statistically rare events").

17 *See* Christopher Webster, et al., The Violence Prediction Scheme: Assessing Dangerousness in High Risk Men 28 & n.5 (1994) (quoting Judge Bazelon).

18 *See* Daniel W. Shuman & Bruce D. Sales, *The Admissibility of Expert Testimony Based Upon Clinical Judgment and Scientific Research*, 4 Psychol. Pub. Pol'y & L. 1226, 1228 (1998) (noting that "expert judgments that are clinically derived, as opposed to actuarially derived, are as susceptible to error as lay judgements"); Quinsey et al., *supra* note 14 at 62 (in a study assessing predictions of violence, "lay persons and the clinicians had few differences of opinion").

19 *See* Webster, et al., *supra* note 17 at 25 (noting the problem of illusory correlations when assessors – who usually have no information about the accuracy of their predictions – learn of a violent action by a previously assessed patient, making that instance stand out and giving the clinicians a mistakenly optimistic view of their own prowess).

20 Although there is some evidence that a multi-disciplinary team may be able to rival the accuracy of actuarial instruments, such teams are unlikely to be employed in capital sentencing determinations. *See* J. Fuller & J. Cowan, *Risk Assessment in a Multidisciplinary Forensic Setting: Clinical Judgement Revisited*, 10 J. Forensic Psych. 276 (1999) (acknowledging that a multidisciplinary team may provide increased accuracy approaching that of actuarial instruments).

21 *See* Mark. D. Cunningham & Thomas J. Reidy, *Don't Confuse Me With the Facts: Common Errors in Violence Risk Assessment at Capital Sentencing*, 26 Crim. Justice & Behav. 20, 28 (1999) (citing studies); Mark Dolan & Mary Doyle, *Violence Risk Prediction: Clinical and Actuarial Measures and the Role of the Psychopathy Checklist*, 177 Brit. J. Psych. 303, 303 (2000) (listing assessment instruments used for parole determinations) (citing studies).

22 *See, e.g.,* Neil M. Malamuth et al., *Risk Assessment*, 998 Ann. N.Y. Acad. Sci. 236, 237 (2003) (explaining that at best, current actuarial instruments are only "moderately predictive," having Rieciever Operating Characteristic curve statistics of about 0.70, or correlations of 0.30). Even with the best assessment instrument, the VRAG, only 55% of the individuals scoring as high risks recidivated, compared with 19% recidivism in the low-scoring group. *See* John Monahan, *Violence Risk Assessment: Scientific Validity and Evidentiary Admissibility*, 57 Wash. & Lee L. Rev. 901, 906 (2000).

factors for violent behavior).[23] In any event, however, actuarial instruments are only beginning to find their way into capital sentencing proceedings, and then only in conjunction with the vastly inferior clinical predictions.[24]

Evidentiary contradictions: *Barefoot* and *Daubert*

Barefoot and the regime of evidentiary federalism

The failure of courts to address issues of scientific validity at sentencing can be traced directly to *Barefoot v. Estelle*.[25] There, despite its previously articulated concern for providing the jury with accurate information with which to make its decision,[26] the Supreme Court upheld expert testimony about future dangerousness for which even the majority could not find any scientific support.[27] At issue was the constitutionality of permitting psychiatrists to testify about the defendant's future behavior, given that such predictions are wrong two out of three times.[28]

23 J. RICHARD EISER & JOOP VAN DER PLIGT, ATTITUDES AND DECISIONS 100 (1988) (observing that human decision "accuracy declines considerably when the number of features or the number or alternatives increases . . . [and] reliability with which choice rules are used tends to decrease as the decision-maker's information load increases"). J. Fuller & J. Cowan, *Risk Assessment in a Multi-disciplinary Forensic Setting: Clinical Judgement Revisited*, 10 J. FORENSIC PSYCH. 276 (1999) (empirical data demonstrates that such structured analysis improves decisionmaking considerably). Even actuarial instruments do not obviate all the problems of human judgment, however. For example, the risk factor descriptions may be vague, decreasing their reliability. *See* David Carson, *A Risk-Management Approach to Legal Decision-Making About 'Dangerous' People*, in LAW AND UNCERTAINTY: RISKS AND LEGAL PROCESS 258 (Robert Baldwin ed. 1997) (noting the problem of reliability). And even trained clinicians may differ on what exactly is meant by "glibness" (a factor on the PCL-R, an actuarial instrument) or "lack of insight" (a factor on the VRAG and HCR-20, two other actuarial instruments). Moreover, sometimes the factors used are not independent, as for example, anger and the inability to sustain relationships.
24 In *Barnette*, for example, the court held that the expert's opinion on future dangerousness was admissible under *Daubert*, but only because the expert relied on his clinical judgment as well as an actuarial instrument. *United States v. Barnette*, 211 F.3d 803 (4th Cir. 2000). In *Barnette*, the prosecution expert used an actuarial instrument (the PCL-R) to substantiate his opinion that the defendant posed a future danger. The court upheld the admissibility of this testimony under *Daubert* (although it declined to decide whether a *Daubert* analysis was required). *Id.* at 815. The court found that because the prosecution expert had based his opinion on "observations of Barnette's behavior; the actuarial approach; and the research on predicting future dangerousness" his testimony met *Daubert's* reliability standard. The court did not, however, analyze the scientific validity of the actuarial approach. Thus, although the court invoked *Daubert*, it circumvented *Daubert's* analysis requirements.
25 463 U.S. 880 (1983).
26 *Gregg v. Georgia*, 428 U.S. 153 (1976) (plurality opinion).
27 After acknowledging the opposition to future dangerousness testimony set out in the amicus brief of the American Psychiatric Association, stating that the unreliability of clinical predictions of dangerousness was an "established fact," the only support the majority could find for such testimony was a statement by a researcher (relied on by the state experts) that although "the best clinical research currently in existence indicates that psychiatrists and psychologists are accurate in no more than one out of three predictions of violent behavior . . . there *may be* circumstances in which prediction is both empirically possible and ethically appropriate" (emphasis added) and hoping that future research would clarify the issues; and one study showing "some predictive validity." *See Barefoot v. Estelle*, 463 U.S. 880, 901 (1983). Because the majority found that it was "not persuaded that such testimony is almost entirely unreliable," *id.* at 899, it would be up to the jury to "separate the wheat from the chaff." *Id.* at 901.
28 *Barefoot*, 463 U.S. at 901 ("Neither the petitioner nor the Association suggests that psychiatrists are always wrong with respect to future dangerousness, only most of the time").

The Court based its reasoning not only on precedent, but also on the rules of evidence, "generally extant at the federal and state levels," which, according to the Court, "anticipate that relevant, unprivileged evidence should be admitted and its weight left to the fact finder, who would have the benefit of cross examination and contrary evidence by the opposing party."[29] The Court thus reasoned that the testimony was admissible because it was admissible under the rules of evidence, and emphasized the ability of the adversary system to weed out inaccurate information. At stake were federalism notions that unless the state practice offended constitutional minimums, the Court would not interfere. The rules of evidence at the time did not require expert testimony to undergo any scrutiny for scientific validity.

Two psychiatrists testified in *Barefoot* that the defendant "would probably commit future acts of violence and represent a continuing threat to society."[30] They did not base their opinions on any personal examination of the defendant, nor upon any history of past violent behavior (the defendant had prior convictions for drug offenses and unlawful possession of firearms, but had no history of violent crime[31]). Instead, the experts based their testimony on a hypothetical question based on the crime and the defendant's conduct.[32] The Supreme Court upheld the admissibility of such testimony, remarking that disallowing it would be like "disinvent[ing] the wheel."[33] Because courts had traditionally admitted such testimony, the Court refused to overturn its precedent. The Court acknowledged the American Psychiatric Association's opposition to future dangerousness testimony because of its extreme unreliability. Although the American Psychiatric Association explained that no one, including psychiatrists, can predict with any degree of reliability whether an individual will commit other crimes in the future,[34] the Court found that because the Association did not claim that psychiatrists were *always* wrong with respect to future dangerousness predictions – only that they were wrong more often than not – it would not exclude such testimony, because it comported with the state's rules of evidence.

State rules of evidence have changed since *Barefoot*, thanks to the Supreme Court's ruling in *Daubert*. Even states that elected not to follow *Daubert*, but to retain their general consensus standard, have modified their approach to expert testimony to incorporate some inquiry into scientific validity.[35] What has not changed, and what

---

29 *Id.* at 898.
30 *Id.* at 884.
31 *Id.* at 916 (Blackmun, J. dissenting).
32 The prosecutor's hypothetical asked the psychiatrists to assume a number of facts (taken from the testimony at trial): conviction for five nonviolent criminal offenses, arrests for sexual offenses against children; a bad reputation in the eight communities the defendant had lived in over ten years; unemployment during the two months preceding the crime; drug use; boasting of plans to commit crimes to acquaintances; shooting a police officer without provocation from a distance of six inches; acting as though there were nothing unusual after the crime. Brief of the American Psychiatric Association as Amicus Curiae at 5, *Barefoot v. Estelle*, 463 U.S. 880 (1983).
33 *Barefoot*, 463. U.S. at 896.
34 *See Barefoot*, 463 U.S. at 899.
35 E.g., *United States v. Norwood*, 939 F. Supp. 1132 (D.N.J. 1996).

the Supreme Court did not mention, is that the rules of evidence do not generally apply to sentencing hearings. Thus, if *Daubert* requires rethinking expert testimony at capital sentencing, it must be because *Daubert*'s foundation is a constitutional one.

Daubert, its progeny, and the federal rules of evidence

Justice Blackmun, who wrote the dissenting opinion in *Barefoot*, wrote the majority opinion in *Daubert v. Merril Dow Pharmaceuticals, Inc.*,[36] and, as discussed in Chapter 1, transformed the jurisprudence of expert testimony by requiring judges to examine the empirical basis of statements made by experts in federal courts. *Daubert* held that scientific validity and "fit" of expert testimony to the facts in the case are questions of reliability and relevance.[37] The rationale for a gatekeeping requirement is based on relevance.[38] Scientifically invalid testimony is not relevant because it cannot assist the jury, and assisting the jury is the only reason for admitting expert testimony. In two subsequent cases, *General Electric Co. v. Joiner*,[39] and *Kumho Tire v. Carmichael*,[40] the Court reiterated the *Daubert* standards, expounded on its notion of "fit," and explained that not only do judges have to evaluate the scientific validity of testimony based on the traditional "hard" sciences, but that they must also evaluate the validity of expert testimony based on what are often referred to as the "soft" sciences, such as psychology.[41] Thus, *Daubert*'s general principles apply to all expert testimony.

Future dangerousness testimony based on clinical judgment alone has been overwhelmingly castigated by the profession (and so fails peer review, publication and the general acceptance prongs of *Daubert*). Because such predictions are wrong more often than they are right, they cannot meet the error rate inquiry.[42] Thus, it is plain that the future dangerousness testimony in *Barefoot*, which was based neither on scientific study, nor on personal medical diagnosis, and did not even purport to be based on the scientific method, cannot meet criteria for valid science.

---

36 509 U.S. 579 (1993).

37 Although the argument has been made that *Daubert* is not technically inconsistent with *Barefoot* because *Daubert* involved interpretation of the Federal Rules of Evidence while *Barefoot* involved interpretation of the Due Process Clause of the Constitution, nearly everyone acknowledges the tension between the two decisions. *See, e.g.,* Craig J. Albert, *Challenging Deterrence: New Insights on Capital Punishment Derived from Panel Data*, 60 U. Pitt. L. Rev. 321 (1999) (asserting that "it goes too far to say simply that *Daubert* impliedly overruled *Barefoot*," but acknowledging that "they cannot co-exist as a matter of common sense"); Paul C. Gianelli, *Daubert: Interpreting the Federal Rules of Evidence*, 15 Cardozo L. Rev. 1999 (1994) (observing that "*Daubert* required a higher standard for money damages than *Barefoot* required for the death penalty").

38 *Kumho Tire*, 526 U.S. at 147.

39 522 U.S. 136 (1997).

40 526 U.S. 137 (1999).

41 Engineering testimony was at issue in *Kumho Tire*. *Id.* at 137. Congress subsequently amended the Federal Rules of Evidence to codify these cases. *Fed. R. Evid.* 702.

42 Although they made bald assertions that they were invariably accurate, the experts in *Barefoot* offered no substantiation for their claims. *Barefoot v. Estelle,* 463 U.S. 880, 896–97 (1983).

Indeed, the basis for the Supreme Court's finding future dangerousness testimony admissible was that in Texas even a lay person could testify to future dangerousness. Unlike the laypersons involved, however, these experts had no personal knowledge of the defendant. The *Barefoot* experts, as most such experts still do in Texas, based their testimony entirely on the defendant's conduct at trial and the facts of the crime. This was enough, according to one of the experts, to demonstrate future dangerousness with "one hundred percent accuracy."[43] Such a statement alone ought to alert the court to the unreliability of his testimony.[44]

One of the reasons for permitting all relevant evidence into a sentencing hearing (providing it is sufficiently reliable), is to assist the jury in making an individualized determination of whether the death penalty is appropriate under the particular circumstances of this defendant. That is similar to the issue of "fit," which the *Daubert* court explained concerns whether otherwise valid testimony will actually assist the factfinder.[45] The Court pointed out in *Joiner* that conclusions and methodology must have a valid connection between them.[46] Thus, unless an expert can demonstrate sound methodology and scientific reasoning, as well as pertinence to an issue in the case, no opinion testimony is admissible.

But the most fundamental reason courts should exclude clinical future dangerousness testimony is that relevance is not "merely" a matter of evidentiary rules, it is a constitutional minimum, a requirement of due process and a fundamental fairness requirement of the rule of law. The relevancy requirement functions as the primary control of the court over what information will be presented. As Professor Damaska explains, "Anglo-American criteria of relevancy make the factual basis of a decision closer to social reality, where fact and value are intertwined."[47] In an adversarial system, truth is understood to be more a matter of perspective than in the inquisitorial system, and the court controls the flow of information presented by the parties as a way of controlling social conflict. Contrary to the Court's contention in *Barefoot*,[48] the adversary process cannot be trusted "to sort out the reliable from the unreliable evidence and opinion about future dangerousness." Rather, as the Supreme Court explained in *Daubert*, the requirement that expert testimony be helpful to the jury, "supported by appropriate validation – i.e., 'good grounds,' based upon what is known," is a condition of relevance.[49] If testimony is without

---

43 *Id.* at 919 (J. Blackmun, dissenting).

44 No one can testify with "one hundred percent accuracy." Nor had this expert any empirical data to support his – highly improbable – statement. Such expert hyperbole is by no means uncommon. A Texas psychiatrist, who by 1992 had participated in 144 capital cases, testified in each of them that, with medical and scientific certainty, he was sure the defendant would kill again. *See* Joseph T. McCann, "Standards for Expert Testimony in New York Death Penalty Cases," *N.Y. St. Bar J. Jul.-Aug.1996*, at 30, 31 (outlining the prevalence of improper assessments of future dangerousness). One of those condemned was later found to be innocent of the crime. *Id.* at 32.

45 *Daubert v. Merrell Dow Pharms., Inc*, 509 U.S. 579, 591 (1993).

46 *See Gen. Elec. Co. v. Joiner*, 522 U.S. 136, 146–47 (1997).

47 Mirjan Damaska, *Presentation of Evidence and Fact Finding Precision*, 123 U. Pa. L. Rev. 1083, 1105 (1975) (contrasting the adversary and inquisitorial systems of adjudication).

48 *Barefoot*, 463 U.S. at 900.

49 *Daubert*, 509 U.S. at 590–91.

foundation – that is, if testimony purporting to be scientific is based on the expert's *ipse dixit* – it cannot meet due process requirements of relevance and reliability.[50]

Gatekeeping and capital sentencing

The excuse for the courts' refusal to scrutinize expert testimony at sentencing is that the rules of evidence do not generally apply.[51] The reason for this is that sentencing proceedings historically have been nonadversarial. In the pre-sentencing guidelines era, the judge had access to a wide variety of information and had discretion in imposing sentences within statutory prescriptions. Although the federal and states' guideline regimes have narrowed judicial discretion somewhat, the norm remains of judicial access to a wide variety of background material.

This makes ordinary sentencing similar to the European inquisitorial system of adjudication, in which the judge has access to the defendant's file, both parties may present their views, but only the judge directs the investigation and questions the

50 Nonetheless, the argument that future dangerousness testimony is inherently unreliable has been remarkably unsuccessful. See Webster et al., *supra* note 18 at 17 (observing that the political and legal pressures on experts to predict violence in the United States and Canada are overwhelming) (citing cases). The overwhelming majority of courts that have addressed the issue since *Barefoot* have simply found its constitutionality beyond question. The Texas Court of Criminal Appeals, for example, found future dangerousness testimony to be reliable enough. *Nenno v. State,* 970 S.W. 2d 549 (Tex. 1998) (finding future dangerousness testimony reliable under the Texas equivalent to *Daubert*). There have been, however, a few muted stirrings of unease. For example, the Fifth Circuit acknowledged the issue of whether *Daubert* implicitly overruled *Barefoot*, although it declined to reach that issue, in *Tigner v. Cockrell*, 264 F.3d 521 (5th Cir. 2001) (dismissing because a decision on collateral review would have violated the non-retroactivity principle). In addition, concurring in the Fifth Circuit's per curiam opinion in *Flores v. Johnson*, 210 F.3d 456 (5th Cir. 2000) (per curiam), Judge Garza excoriated the Texas courts' use of expert future dangerousness testimony (but found himself bound nonetheless by *Barefoot*). Judge Garza noted that the expert who testified in *Flores*, Dr. Griffith, was "frequently the state's star witness" and had never once testified that any defendant did not pose a future danger. *Flores*, 210 F.3d at 462. Judge Garza observed that "neither the Court nor the state of Texas has cited a single reputable scientific source contradicting the unanimous conclusion of professionals in this field that psychiatric predictions of long-term future violence are wrong more often than they are right." Moreover, Judge Garza noted, when considered in juxtaposition with the strict admissibility requirements for most expert testimony – especially in civil trials, where the stakes are much lower – Dr. Griffith's testimony became strikingly inadequate. Judge Garza opined that admitting a psychiatric prediction of dangerousness was akin to permitting a phrenologist – the example Justice Stevens used in *Joiner* of junk science – that the bumps on a defendant's skull could predict dangerousness. Although he acknowledged the jury's right to impose death as an appropriate punishment for a vicious crime, Judge Garza concluded that "the legitimacy of our legal process is threatened" by allowing such testimony without any scientific validity into evidence. *Id.* at 466. Nonetheless, he concurred in Flores' death sentence.

51 The Federal Rules of Evidence – which include the *Daubert* standard for expert witnesses – do not apply at federal capital sentencing proceedings under 18 U.S.C. § 3593 (c) ("information is admissible regardless of its admissibility under the rules governing admission of evidence at criminal trials"), despite the Supreme Court's recognition that capital sentencing requires a "heightened reliability" standard. 21 U.S. C. § 848 (j). See *Ford v. Wainwright*, 477 U.S. 399, 411 (1986) (setting a "heightened reliability" standard for capital sentencing). Nonetheless, this testimony must have "indicia of reliability" and relevance to be admissible even at sentencing hearings. See *Dawson v. Delaware*, 503 U.S. 159 (1992) (finding evidence presented at sentencing hearing that convicted murderer was a member of the Aryan Brotherhood irrelevant and thus unconstitutional); *United States v. Huckins*, 53 F.3d 276 (9th Cir. 1995) (to be admissible at sentencing, hearsay must have some other corroboration).

witnesses.[52] Under such a regime, there is little concern for rules of evidence – the judge is presumed to rely only on relevant information. The idea of gatekeeping is therefore unnecessary, and the continental view of relevance is very technical and precise.[53] On the other hand, in the adversarial mode, it is the parties who control – initially, at least – what information will be available to decisionmaking, and judicial gatekeeping ensures that the proceedings do not degenerate into a show that will mislead the jury from its mission, by ensuring that proffered testimony has some propensity to bring out the truth.

Capital sentencing is different from other criminal sentencing. Following a constitutionally mandated bifurcated trial,[54] capital sentencing is by a jury.[55] Because of the severity of the sanction, the imposition of death must be handled in a way that permits a defendant to present whatever facts might impel a jury to mercy.[56] A common justification for declining to apply the rules of evidence strictly at sentencing is that such proceedings have become a search for justice rather than truth.[57] Justice, however, ought to include the search for truth and the importance of accuracy, in the context of what is an unabashedly adversarial proceeding, demands that there be some control over what count as facts in the proceeding. The importance of a structured reasoning process for rationality argues for judicial screening of expert testimony.

Thus, the jury's "reasoned moral response" to the evidence and arguments at sentencing, according to the Supreme Court, must be supported with information sufficient and relevant for reliable rational decisionmaking.[58] At capital sentencing hearings, both prosecution and defense present testimony and argument. Expert

---

52 See Damaska, *supra* note 47, at 1083–1106 (contrasting the adversary and inquisitorial systems of adjudication). In an inquisitorial system, prosecution and defense do not have separate witnesses, and it is the judge's responsibility to question the witnesses and inquire into the record. Of course, in practice, there are no purely inquisitorial or purely adversarial systems; both borrow from each other. *See* Mirjan Damaska, The Faces of Justice and State Authority: A Comparative Approach to the Legal Process 44 (1986) (acknowledging that although the continental inquisitorial system is ideally to be regulated by "an internally consistent network of unbending rules" in reality "some matters have to be unregulated").

53 Damaska, *supra* note 47 at 1105.

54 *Lockett v. Ohio*, 438 U.S. 586, 605 (1978) (mandating bifurcated trials to accommodate the need for both "guided discretion" and "individualized consideration" in capital sentencing).

55 In *Ring v. Arizona*, 536 U.S. 584 (2002) the U.S. Supreme Court ruled that the capital sentencing decision must be made by a jury.

56 *See Lockett v. Ohio*, 438 U.S. 586, 605 (1978) ("Given that the imposition of death by public authority is so profoundly different from all other penalties, we cannot avoid the conclusion that an individualized decision is essential in capital cases. . . . [and that] treating each defendant in a capital case with that degree of respect due the uniqueness of the individual is far more important than in noncapital cases.").

57 As the U.S. Supreme Court held in *Lockett v. Ohio*, the evidentiary standards in the sentencing phase are fairly open because "any aspect [of the defendant's] character or record and any of the circumstances of the offense ought to be available to support a sentence less than death. *Lockett v. Ohio*, 438 U.S. at 604.

58 *Penry v. Lynaugh*, 492 U.S. 302, 319 (1989) (explaining that "the sentence imposed at the penalty stage should reflect a reasoned moral response to the defendant's background, character, and crime").

testimony is prevalent.[59] With or without formal requirements for evidentiary rules, however, there is virtually no structured examination of the scientific basis for such testimony actually taking place.[60]

Both state and federal courts are lackadaisical about gatekeeping when it comes to capital sentencing.[61] This tension between heightened reliability for death sentencing proceedings and the inapplicability of evidentiary rules is only occasionally recognized by the courts, and only rarely is a scientific validity inquiry referred to.[62]

Why *Daubert* should be a constitutional minimum

Questions of evidence law in state courts are state law questions, and habeas relief is not usually granted for failure to follow the state evidentiary rules.[63] This means that

59 Expert testimony is frequently proffered at capital sentencing proceedings. For example, in the Capital Jury Project, funded by the National Science Foundation, the California portion of the study examined thirty-six death penalty cases, and found that the prosecution called an expert in 81 percent of the cases, and the defense called an expert in 90 percent. Scott E. Sundby, *The Jury as Critic: An Empirical Look at How Capital Juries Perceive Expert and Lay Testimony*, 83 VA. L. REV. 1109, 1119 (1997) (noting that "conventional practice at the penalty phase involves presenting an expert to the jury at some point – sometimes more than one – who will testify based upon an expertise gained through training and study").

60 Although Texas requires a modified *Daubert* assessment of admissibility for expert testimony at sentencing, the Texas courts have failed to seriously inquire into the scientific validity of such testimony, and have cursorily held that clinical future dangerousness predictions meet this standard. *See Nenno v. State*, 970 S.W.2d 549 (Tex. Crim. App. 1998) (holding clinical predictions meet scientific validity standards).

61 The Federal Death Penalty Act of 1994 significantly expanded the scope of federal capital crimes. Federal Death Penalty Act of 1994 (Pub. L. No. 103–322, 108 Stat. 1796, 1959 (scattered in various sections of 18 U.S.C.). Even in federal cases, however, *Daubert* is generally not invoked at sentencing, because the rules of evidence do not apply. *See, e.g., U.S. Sentencing Guidelines Manual* § 6A1.3 ("In resolving any dispute concerning a factor important to the sentencing determination, the court may consider relevant information without regard to its admissibility under the rules of evidence applicable at trial. . . . "). Many states similarly permit expansive criteria for admissibility at sentencing. *See, e.g.,* Ala. Code § 13A-5–45 (Repl. 1994) (providing that "[a]ny evidence which has probative value and is relevant to sentence shall be received at the sentence hearing regardless of its admissibility under the exclusionary rules of evidence").

62 For example, in *Barnette*, 211 F.3d at 816, the court disposed of prosecution arguments that the federal rules do not apply at sentencing and found that the contested future dangerousness evidence met *Daubert* standards. The defense argued that prosecution psychiatric testimony predicting dangerousness based on an actuarial instrument (the Hare Psychopathy Checklist-Revised, or "PCL-R"), did not meet *Daubert* standards of reliable scientific evidence, and that three of the PCL-R checklist factors were impermissible: race, poverty, and age. The Fourth Circuit noted that the defense did not contest relevancy, and although the court acknowledged that the PCL-R did use the three impermissible factors, the court found that the expert had not relied on them exclusively, but also on seventeen other factors, the DIAGNOSTIC AND STATISTICAL MANUAL, FOURTH EDITION (DSM-IV), personal observations and research on predicting future dangerousness.

63 *See Spencer v. Texas*, 385 U.S. 554, 563–64 (1967) ("The Due Process Clause guarantees the fundamental elements of the fairness in a criminal trial . . . [b]ut it has never been thought that such Cases establish this Court as a rulemaking organ for the promulgation of state rules of criminal procedure"). All states invoking the death penalty, however, provide that any evidence admitted be both relevant and material. *See* Kelly, *supra* note 4 at 457 (for evidence to be relevant and probative, as all death penalty states require, evidence must be "logically relevant, legally relevant, and offered for the purpose of proving or supporting a material proposition"). The floor of relevance and materiality, in the context of science is that the testimony reflect valid science. Although the

even if admitting clinical predictions into testimony violates state rules of evidence, federal courts will not hear such claims unless the state law violations amount to violations of the federal constitution.[64] The flip side, however, is that the failure to meet threshold standards of relevance and reliability in expert testimony is no mere state law failure, but a constitutional error. The issue of expert future dangerousness testimony poses a relevance issue at a threshold due process level. That is, if the expert testimony about future dangerousness were scientifically valid, it would unquestionably be relevant to the reasoned moral inquiry about retribution for this defendant. Any weaknesses could be exposed by cross-examination. But when the expert testimony has no basis in reality, when it is not grounded in science, it is wholly irrelevant to the jury's task, making its admission arbitrary.

At a minimum, imposing the ultimate sentence ought not to be arbitrary.[65] Throughout its death penalty jurisprudence, the Court has maintained that "there is a significant constitutional difference between the death penalty and lesser punishments."[66] In its later cases, the Supreme Court has defined two important Eighth

---

U.S. Supreme Court, in *Daubert v. Merrill Dow Pharmaceuticals, Inc*, 509 U.S. 579 (1993), was addressing the admissibility of scientific evidence under the Federal Rules of Evidence, its reasoning was based on concepts of relevance and probative value, which it linked to the requirement that the evidence assist the jury. *See id.* at 591 (assisting the trier of fact "goes primarily to relevance").

64 *Estelle v. McGuire*, 502 U.S. 62, 67–68 (1991) (holding that "it is not the province of a federal habeas court to reexamine state court determinations of state law questions"). In *Estelle v. McGuire*, the Supreme Court found that it had been error to grant habeas relief for the admission into evidence of battered child syndrome evidence to prove intent in the second degree murder trial of a father for his six-month old daughter. *Id.* at 66. The Ninth Circuit granted habeas based on its holding that this evidence was "incorrectly admitted . . . pursuant to California law." Because the evidence was proffered to show that the injuries were not accidental, but were a product of child abuse, the Supreme Court held that the evidence of prior injuries was relevant to show intent, even if it did not purport to show who caused those injuries. The Court noted that "nothing in the Due Process Clause of the Fourteenth Amendment requires the State to refrain from introducing relevant evidence simply because the defense chooses not to contest the point" (the defense had not contested that the baby had been abused). *Id.* at 70. The only evidentiary question the habeas court may review is whether the evidence "so infected" the proceeding that it resulted in the violation of a constitutional right. *Id.* at 72. The Court held that neither the battered child syndrome evidence nor the instruction as to its use amounted to such a violation because the evidence was relevant to intent, served to narrow the possible perpetrators, was consistent with "the familiar use of evidence of prior acts for the purpose of showing intent, identity, motive or plan." *Id.* at 75 (citing *Fed. R. Evid.* 404(b)). Thus, the framework that the Court established is that a mere violation of state evidentiary rules will not be sufficient for federal relief; there must be some constitutional violation. *See Marshall v. Lonberger*, 459 U.S. 422, 438 n.6 (1983) ("the Due Process Clause does not permit the federal courts to engage in a finely tuned review of the wisdom of state evidentiary rules"). Notably, no one contested the scientific validity of the testimony in *McGuire*. Rather, the dispute was over its relevance for proving intent, and the Supreme Court found it to be relevant to that issue.

65 As the Gregg Court explained, "discretion must be suitably directed and limited so as to minimize the risk of wholly arbitrary and capricious action." *Gregg*, 428 U.S. at 189. *See also Jurek v. Texas*, 428 U. S. 262 (1976).

66 *Beck v. Alabama*, 447 U.S. 625, 637 (1980) (Stevens, J., plurality opinion).In *Furman v. Georgia*, 408 U.S. 238 (1972), the Supreme Court found that the imposition of the death penalty in three cases violated the Eighth and Fourteenth Amendments as "cruel and unusual punishment." In a subsequent series of cases, the death penalty was reinstated, as long as the authorizing legislation provided guided discretion in its imposition. *Gregg v. Georgia*, 428 U.S. 153 (1976); *Jurek*, 428 U.S. at 262; *Proffitt v. Florida*, 428 U.S. 242 (1976).

Amendment principles in its death penalty jurisprudence: eliminating arbitrariness through channeled discretion; and individualized sentencing.[67] The "evenhanded, rational, and consistent imposition of death sentences under law" was the goal.[68] In making its decision, the sentencing body must reach "a reasoned moral response" free of impediments to relevant sentencing considerations.[69] Expert testimony that purports to do what it cannot do would appear to be precisely such an impediment.

Not only the Eighth Amendment but also the Due Process Clause of the Fourteenth Amendment mandates that sentencing determinations not be made in an "arbitrary and capricious" manner.[70] Because many of the rights given at trial do not apply at sentencing, due process is the primary source of regulation. The Due Process Clause of the Fourteenth Amendment provides a right to fundamentally fair proceedings, and a relevance requirement is an integral part of a fair and rational proceeding.[71] Due process, for example, governs the right to accurate information.[72] In *Gregg v. Georgia*, the Court warned that "accurate sentencing information is an indispensable prerequisite to a reasoned determination of whether a defendant shall live or die by a jury of people who may never before have made a sentencing decision."[73] Information from a source that is wrong as often as it is right can hardly be described as "accurate."

Fundamental fairness, the freestanding content of the Fourteenth Amendment, demands that the procedure preclude subjecting the defendant to an unacceptably high risk of erroneous decisions.[74] Due process is limited, however, to proscribing

---

67 *Lockett v. Ohio*, 438 U.S. 586, 604 (1978) (prohibiting the preclusion of "any mitigating factor, any aspect of a defendant's character or record and any of the circumstances of the offense that the defendant proffers as a basis for a sentence less than death").

68 *Jurek v. Texas*, 428 U.S. 262 (1976).

69 *California v. Brown*, 479 U.S. 538, 545 (1987).

70 *See Gregg v. Georgia*, 428 U.S. 153, 189 (1976) ("where discretion is afforded a sentencing body on a matter so grave as the determination of whether a human life should be taken or spared, that discretion must be suitably directed and limited so as to minimize the risk of wholly arbitrary and capricious action"). This due process right, sometimes called "free-standing due process" because it stands apart from the Bill of Rights, is to procedure "necessary to an Anglo-American regime of ordered liberty." *Duncan v. Louisiana*, 391 U.S. 145, 159 n.14 (1968). For a discussion of the jurisprudence of free-standing due process in the Supreme Court, *see* Jerold H. Israel, *Free-Standing Due Process and Criminal Procedure: The Supreme Court's Search for Interpretive Guidelines*, 45 St. Louis U.L.J. 303 (2001).

71 *See Payne v. Tennessee*, 501 U.S. 808, 825 (1991) (the Due Process Clause provides a right to relief when a proceeding is "fundamentally unfair"); *Lankford v. Idaho*, 500 U.S. 110, 121 (1991) (the clause represents a profound attitude of fairness between the individual and the government).

72 *Williams v. New York*, 337 U.S. 241, 245–52 (1949).

73 *Gregg v. Georgia*, 428 U.S. 153, 190 (1976) (plurality opinion). Along with its two companion cases, *Proffitt v. Florida*, 428 U.S. 242 (1976) (plurality opinion) and *Jurek v. Texas*, 428 U.S. 262 (1976) (plurality opinion), the Supreme Court authorized the states to return to capital punishment in *Gregg*.

74 *See, e.g., Napue v. Illinois*, 360 U.S. 264 (1959)(due process prohibits prosecution knowing use of perjured testimony*); Rideau v. Louisiana*, 373 U.S. 723 (1963) (constitutional due process right to a change in venue to protect the defendant from local prejudice); *Foster v. United States*, 394 U.S. 440 (1969) (excluding suggestive lineup on due process grounds); *United States v. Bagley*,

only those state procedures that "offend some principle of justice so rooted in the traditions and conscience of our people as to be ranked as fundamental."[75] Thus, in determining whether a fundamental right is implicated, the Court has looked to principles having "deep roots" in our heritage.[76]

While this might appear to require a historical inquiry, a requirement of "deep roots" extends beyond historical practices and requires adherence to basic rule of law principles.[77] Relevance of the information that is put before the jury for its decision making is one such principle. The requirement of fundamental fairness encompasses a requirement of rationality, so that the state may not present the jury with inaccurate or misleading evidence.[78] Expert testimony that is without scientific foundation cannot be relevant, because it cannot make a fact at issue in the case – future dangerousness in sentencing proceedings – more or less likely to be true. Meritless testimony cannot assist the jury in making its determination, and permitting experts to testify without scientific basis for their assertions is thus inimical to due process standards. The unresolved – and possibly unresolvable – problem for clinical predictions of future dangerousness is that they have no scientific basis.

The Supreme Court set the minimal standard for imposing the death penalty as "the evenhanded, rational, and consistent imposition of death sentences under the law."[79] Admitting expert testimony that has no scientific basis is misleading to the jury and thus precludes rational decisionmaking. If reliable, rational decision making has been precluded by the introduction of junk science in the form of clinical predictions, due process is violated.[80] Further, because testimony

473 U.S. 667 (1985) (disclosure of exculpatory evidence required under due process); *Crane v. Kentucky*, 476 U.S. 683 (1986) (admission of reliable exculpatory defense evidence required under due process and compulsory process analysis); *Ake v. Oklahoma*, 470 U.S. 68 (1985) (due process requires state to provide expert for defense under certain circumstances).

75 *Medina v. California*, 505 U.S. 437, 445 (quoting *Patterson v. New Jersey*).

76 *Medina*, 505 U.S. at 446.

77 *Stovall v. Denno*, 388 U.S. 293 (1967) (rejecting the state position putting lineup reliability to the jury, to hold that a substantial likelihood of misidentification precluded the admission of lineup identification evidence as a violation of due process, even without reference to common law traditions or contemporary consensus). *See* also Israel, *supra* note 70 at 417 (noting a number of Supreme Court free-standing due process decisions that addressed neither historical practice nor contemporary consensus).

78 *See Caldwell v. Mississippi*, 472 U.S. 320 (1985) (prosecution argument at sentencing that juror's decision was reviewable was unconstitutional because it was both inaccurate and misleading); *Washington v. Texas*, 388 U.S. 14, 22(1967) (addressing the defendant's right to present witnesses and finding a rule of exclusion arbitrary if it had no rational basis); *Chambers v. Mississippi*, 410 U.S. 284 (1973) (holding hearsay evidence admissible because the statements had "considerable assurance of reliability"); *United States v. Scheffer*, 523 U.S. 303 (1998) (upholding military rule excluding polygraph evidence as a rational interest in eliminating unreliable evidence).

79 *Jurek v. Texas*, 428 U.S. 262, 276 (1976).

80 Notably, the Supreme Court announced a three-part balancing test in *Mathews v. Eldridge*, 404 U.S. 319 (1976): consideration of the private interest that would be affected by state action; risk of erroneously depriving someone of that interest through the procedures used; and the government's interest (including fiscal and administrative burdens imposed). Mathews, 404 U.S. at 334–35. In *Medina*, however, it declined to apply such a balancing test to state procedural rules that are part of criminal procedure, because it considered any expansion of explicit

that is without scientific merit is inimical to rational decisionmaking, a state process permitting such testimony undermines the fundamental fairness of the proceeding.[81]

Gatekeeping, epistemic norms, and jury decisionmaking

From an epistemic vantage point, the question of whether we need judges to act as gatekeepers is whether gatekeeping actually promotes the acquisition of knowledge in the context of a particular social practice, here the capital sentencing hearing. The dynamics of jury decisionmaking in the context of capital sentencing decisions help to explain why the relevance requirement is a constitutional concern of fundamental fairness, and how that requirement plays out with respect to expert testimony on future dangerousness. The capital jury is charged with making reasoned moral judgments about the fate of the defendant – a policy decision.[82] Policy makers as well as fact finders require relevant and reliable information for their task.

In order to reach a just decision, jurors are supposed to be provided with "information relevant to the imposition of the sentence and provided with standards to guide its use of the information."[83] The purpose of testifying experts – witnesses without personal knowledge of the defendant or incident – is the same in capital sentencing as it is at trial: to inform the jury about matters outside their common experience in order to assist the jury make an accurate and just determination. The question is therefore whether initial screening by the judge for scientific validity aids in this task.

---

constitutional guarantees "invites undue interference with both considered legislation and the the careful balance the Constitution strikes between liberty and order." *Medina*, 505 U.S. at 443. However, as Jerold Israel explains, Mathews' concept of free-standing due process has purchase not so much in balancing, but in looking at the "logical implications of a basic principle of fairness." Israel, *supra* note 70, at 423. Permitting expert testimony that borders on the fraudulent can do little other than undermine these basic principles. Israel suggests that the Court's fundamental fairness jurisprudence can be interpreted in four ways: 1) insistence on "a few basic elements of trial-type adjudication" with the addition of "a wide variety of rational procedures;" 2) assuring that the process does not convict the innocent; 3) giving the specific guarantees of the Bill of Rights preemptive influence; 4) giving basic procedural protection of the common law with the addition of a cost-benefit analysis. Israel, *supra* note 70, at 425.

81 Fundamental fairness is infrequently invoked by the Supreme Court, and when it is, it is generally without explanation. *See, e.g., Payne v. Tennessee*, 501 U.S. 808, 825 (1991) (noting that the Due Process Clause provides relief when the introduction of evidence – there, victim impact evidence – makes the trial "fundamentally unfair"); *Lassiter v. Dept. of Soc. Servs.*, 452 U.S. 18, 24 (1981) (fundamental fairness is "a requirement whose meaning can be as opaque as its importance is lofty").

82 *California v. Ramos*, 463 U.S. 992, 1007 (1983) (at the penalty phase, the jury no longer acts strictly as fact finder; rather the jury's mission involves "a myriad of factors"); *Ford v. Strickland*, 696 F.2d 804, 831 n. 17 (11th Cir. 1983) ("The sentencer, therefore, acts not as fact finder, but as policy maker.").

83 *Gregg v. Georgia*, 428 U.S. 153, 195 (1976).

There are a number of reasons that judicial gatekeeping – screening for accuracy before permitting expert testimony – makes for more accurate judgments.[84] The three-part story model of Pennington and Hastie described in Chapter 7 has implications for death sentencing juries. First, the idea that juries' preconceptions are woven into the evidence they hear at trial has resonance with the Capital Juror Project findings that a shared perception that violent recidivism is common makes the jurors more likely to opt for the death sentence.[85] In addition, because the jury has recently heard in graphic detail how the defendant committed one atrociously violent act (on the basis of which they convicted), they may construct a story about the defendant's personality and propensities that correlates with this story.

Complexity theory and the inherent limits of prediction

The precise prediction of future behavior is impossible. At best, predictions in complex systems are highly contingent, and human behavior is a paradigmatic complex system.[86] Complexity theory explains that human individuals are interacting parts of a complex world, interacting with our environment, and other creatures and that each brain (originating behavior) is itself a complex organ.[87] The most successful predictions about complex systems are of weather phenomena and even there,

---

84 As discussed earlier in this book, to call something an "accurate" judgment is a normative statement that raises complex issues about what we know, how we know it and what our goals are. In the context of the goals of a capital juror, the jury appears to focus on the goal of determining whether this defendant would kill again if released. Interviews with capital jurors reflect this overwhelming concern. *See* William J. Bowers & Benjamin D. Steiner, *Death by Default: An Empirical Demonstration of False and Forced Choices in Capital Sentencing*, 77 TEX. L. REV. 605 (1999) (discussing the Capital Juror Project). The arguments of lawyers and legal scholars that the question ought to be whether the defendant will pose a threat to other inmates or prison personnel are thus beside the point. In light of the jury's goal, the presentation of irrelevant – unscientific – expert testimony makes their determination less accurate.

85 Interviews with capital jurors, for example, found that jurors overwhelmingly underestimated the amount of time a defendant would have to serve before becoming eligible for parole, relying primarily on memory of vivid media accounts of violent recidivism. *See* William J. Bowers & Benjamin D. Steiner, *Death by Default: An Empirical Demonstration of False and Forced Choices in Capital Sentencing*, 77 TEX. L. REV. 605, 671–72 (1999) (discussing the interviews of 916 capital jurors in the Capital Juror Project).

86 "A complex adaptive system is a collection of individual agents with freedom to act in ways that are not always totally predictable, and whose actions are interconnected so that one agent's actions changes the context for other agents." Paul E. Plsek & Trisha Greenhalgh, *The Challenge of Complexity in Health Care*, 323 BRIT. J. MED. 625, 625 (2001)(giving as examples the immune system, a colony of termites, the financial market and "just about any collection of humans").

87 *See* ILYA PRIGOGINE, THE END OF CERTAINTY: TIME, CHAOS AND THE NEW LAWS OF NATURE 4–5 (1997) (explaining that while "[c]lassical science emphasized order and stability; now, in contrast, we *see* fluctuations, instability, multiple choices, and limited predictability at all levels of observation.... [so that] we are now able to include probabilities in the formulation of the basic laws of physics"); Mark D. Albertson, *Can Violence Be Predicted? Future Dangerousness: The Testimony of Experts in Capital Cases*, 3 CRIM. JUST. 18, 21 (1989) (explaining that a "person-focused assessment ... is extremely inaccurate because people do not live in vacuums" and research emphasizes "the importance of situational and environmental influences on behavior").

small changes in underlying conditions can have a huge impact on result.[88] This is because small errors in determining the initial conditions (i.e. the predictors) may yield large errors in calculating expected outcomes; and, even when the properties of the individual components are understood, the behavior of a system with many interacting components is inherently unpredictable. Weather patterns display both order and chaos, so that weather predictions are fairly accurate for the next day, but fall off rapidly for three-day forecasts, and become highly chaotic after six days.[89] This has implications for predicting human behavior, especially over a lifetime.

Measuring initial conditions is crucial in making predictions about complex systems such as the weather and human behavior. In weather prediction, for example, "more than 10,000 land-based stations and hundreds of ships collect weather information daily at six-hour intervals."[90] Human behavior is simply not monitored in such detail. We often do not know the relevant factors about a defendant's environment (internal or external), and even what factors are relevant is hotly debated.

Moreover, making accurate predictions requires expertise, that is, accountability, feedback, and opportunities for repeat performance. Weather experts, for example, make their predictions based on information from weather stations, satellites, balloons, aircraft and human spotters making daily observations, all of which information is funneled to one of several meteorological centers. These centers generate regional reports, which are then adapted to local conditions. This means that a huge amount of information is generated, and analyzed at frequent intervals, and predictions compared with actual results, something unlikely to be achieved in human behavior.

Further, even using all available data, there are limits to prediction. There are three reasons for these limits. First, the human brain is the premier example of nonlinearity: that is, there is no predictable relationship between cause and effect; and the brain itself is composed of multiple interacting and self-regulating physiological systems including biochemical and neuroendocrine feedback loops, which influence human behavior partly through an internal set of responses and partly through adaptive responses to new stimuli from the environment, forming a web of interacting systems, that are dynamic and fluid.[91] Second, an individual's conduct results

---

88 We cannot predict the weather because it is a "classic case of chaotic behavior." Sole & Goodwin, Signs of Life 9 (2000). That is because "small errors in initial conditions give rise to very large errors in calculating expected outcomes." Id. at 12. Complexity theory, the study of nonlinear systems (like the weather), involves both the study of chaos, with sensitivity to initial conditions that makes dynamics unpredictable, and emergent properties, in which the general inability of observers to predict the behavior of nonlinear systems from their parts and interactions. Id. at 20.

89 R. Kerr, *Official Forecasts Pushed Out to a Year Ahead*, 266 Sci. 1940, 1940 (1994) (weather predictions are "swamped by chaos beyond six days or so").

90 See John Monahan & Henry Steadman, *Violent Storms and Violent People: How Meteorology Can Inform Risk Communication in Mental Health Law*, Sept. Am. Psychol., 931, 933 (1996).

91 Sole & Goodwin, supra note 88, at 1. As an article in a noted scientific journal explained:

The human body is composed of multiple interacting and self regulating physiological systems including biochemical and neuroendocrine feedback loops. The behavior of any individual is determined partly by an internal set of rules based on past experience and partly by unique

from both internal stimuli and from stimuli from the environment, including a web of relationships affecting beliefs, expectations, and behavior.[92] Third, individuals and their immediate social relationships are further embedded within wider social, political, and cultural systems that are continuously interacting; nature, nurture, and notions of free will all interact in a way that can only be considered probabilistic. The equilibrium of each of these systems can be radically altered by seemingly inconsequential stimuli.

Actuarial instruments: admissible under a best evidence theory?

Because of the inherent limits of predictability in complex systems, the most that can be said is that actuarial instruments may improve on the woeful inadequacy of clinical predictions.[93] Is that enough to get them through the gate of scientific validity analysis? My answer is a highly tentative yes, based on the Popperian notion that what makes a theory scientifically valid is its explanatory power. Explanatory power is the ability of a theory, model, or hypothesis to take into account all the observed data and make a persuasive scientific argument. Unlike clinical diagnostic predictions, the explanatory power of actuarial instruments rests on the idea of risk analysis, a statistical methodology commonly used by epidemiologists, toxicologists, the Environmental Protection Agency, and the insurance industry, among others.

The theory underlying actuarial instruments is that structured reasoning processes improve accuracy of judgment. Human judgment is not abandoned in actuarial instruments, it is simply structured into a formal reasoning process.[94] Using structured analysis offers many advantages in human decisionmaking, particularly in light of the difficulty people have in synthesizing differently weighted likelihoods

and adaptive responses to new stimuli from the environment. The web of relationships in which individuals exist contains many varied and powerful determinants of their beliefs, expectations, and behavior. Individuals and their immediate social relationships are further embedded within wider social, political, and cultural systems which can influence outcomes in entirely novel and unpredictable ways. All these interacting systems are dynamic and fluid. A small change to one part of this web of interacting systems may lead to a much larger change in another part through amplification effects. For all these reasons, neither illness nor human behavior is predictable and neither can safely be "modeled" in a simple cause and effect system. The human body is not a machine and its malfunctioning cannot be adequately analysed by breaking the system down into its component parts and considering each in isolation.

Tim Wilson & Tim Holt, *Complexity and Clinical Care*, 323 BRIT. J. MED. 685 (2001).

92 *See generally*, ANTONIO R. DAMASIO, DESCARTES' ERROR: EMOTION, REASON, AND THE HUMAN BRAIN (2000 ed.) (discussing the neural underpinnings of reason, emotion and the complex, interactive systems of the brain, which in turn interact with systems in the rest of the body, the environment, other individuals, and culture).

93 *See* Webster et al., *supra* note 17, at 20 (noting that courts and legislatures continue to demand these predictions, although "three decades of research has failed to produce an accurate scheme for predicting violence" and outlining a "scheme for prediction which we hope will offer better accuracy").

94 Quinsey et al., *supra* note 13, at 65; Dolan & Doyle, *supra* note 21, at 304 (observing that "[s]tructured clinical judgment represents a composit of emperical knowledge and clinical/professional expertise").

of varying significance (such as risk factors for violent behavior).[95] Thus, actuarial instruments may offer a distinct advantage in assessing risk of violent behavior.

Risk analysis is based on statistical concepts of correlation. Statistical analysis provides an important tool for examining whether theories correspond with observation. One should not, however, permit statistical analyses to generate hypotheses about causation. Statistical measurements must be understood within the context of the system being studied.[96] Here, the context is human behavior, a quintessentially complex phenomenon. And while actuarial instruments measure observed statistical correlations of violent behavior with factors such as past patterns of violence, age, and ability to form lasting relationships (among others) there is little linking these factors to a theory of human violence. Moreover, one cannot expect statistics to provide an answer about any particular individual.[97] The most that can be said from even the best statistical analyses is that someone falls within a group that has a certain statistical propensity for violence.

A further complication is that rare events – and recurring violence is statistically rare, even among violent offenders – are inherently difficult to predict. The most that can be said for any actuarial risk assessment instrument is that it can give a probabilistic estimate of the level of risk for people that share characteristics with the person who is being assessed.[98] And the estimate is subject to a great deal of error.[99]

It is important to bear in mind that risk is a social construct. Although it uses probabilistic analysis and quantification, it is not an exact science.[100] Indeed, all science is value-laden, and risk assessment is not different in that regard. The ultimate question of whether a particular individual ought to be sentenced to death or to life in prison can be informed by, but cannot be answered through, a risk appraisal.[101]

---

95 J. Richard Eiser & Joop Van der Pligt, Attitudes and Decisions 100 (1988) (observing that human decision "accuracy declines considerably when the number of features or the number or alternatives increases . . . [and] reliability with which choice rules are used tends to decrease as the decision-maker's information load increases").

96 See Theodore Colton, Statistics in Medicine 117, 304 (1974) (explaining that although a result may be statistically significant, it may still be medically meaningless, and cautioning against permitting statistical analyses to generate hypotheses).

97 As epidemiologists studying the statistical incidence of disease have discovered, one simply cannot predict the probability of disease in any given case. See Sander Greenland & Jerome Robins, Epidemiology, Justice, and the Probability of Causation, 40 Jurimetrics J. 321, 328 (2000) (explaining that "when an exposure is known to be harmful in some cases, available data from epidemiology and biology are simply incapable of telling us whether a given case was 'more probably than not' harmed by exposure"). The most that can be said is that exposure caused a certain statistical increase of disease over background levels.

98 See Webster, supra note 17, at 33 (discussing probabilistic estimates of dangerousness).

99 As the VRAG authors explain, "there is a predictive sound barrier" of some unknown dimension, although they assert it is greater than 40 percent accuracy, they do not have the data to substantiate the assertion. Quinsey et al., supra note 13, at 168.

100 See Royal Society, Risk: Analysis, Perception and Management 7 (1992) (explaining that some subjectivity is always a part of risk assessment).

101 See Quinsey, et al., supra note 13, at 152–53 (explaining that the question about how to apply the information gleaned from an actuarial instrument is a matter of policy and depends on the relative costs of false positives and false negatives).

It is something the jury must weigh, assessing the relative costs of imprisoning a person that may ultimately prove to be violent despite a mistaken prediction of nonviolence, versus sentencing to death a person who was mistakenly predicted to be violent.

Finally, a caveat. Even if actuarial testimony is demonstrably more accurate than clinical testimony, not all actuarial testimony will meet standards of scientific validity. First, not all actuarial instruments have the same empirical foundation. Second, experts may conclude more from the instruments than they warrant, and testify outside the scope of valid inferences. This is a particular problem when experts use a categorical rather than a statistical articulation of their results: dangerous/not dangerous rather than "this defendant falls within a group that has a (blank) probability of recurring violence." Third, when experts rely on factors in addition to the actuarial instruments, each of those factors must have a demonstrable empirical basis. For example, in *Barnette*, not only did the expert testify that he relied on the PCL-R for his opinion that the defendant posed a future danger to society, but he also testified that psychopaths are like "fake fruit" in that they may look normal, but they are not – a statement wholly unsupported by any scientific studies.[102]

Assisting the jury

Gatekeeping standards require that even scientifically valid expert testimony be capable of assisting the jury in its deliberations. Future dangerousness testimony is the major means of persuading the sentencing jury that a convicted defendant poses a threat to society and thus merits the death penalty. Instead of using clinical testimony, because actuarial predictions provide the best information available, they should be admitted to help guide decision makers in their determinations.[103]

The most hotly debated topic in juror sentencing deliberations – next to the crime itself – is the issue of the defendant's dangerousness on return to society.[104] Future dangerousness takes precedence in jury deliberations over any mitigating evidence, such as remorse, mental illness, intelligence, or drug/alcohol addiction, and any concern about the defendant's behavior in prison. In fact, dangerousness determinations are part of the explicitly authorized grounds for imposing death in

---

102 *See* John Eden, et al., *Psychopathy and the Death Penalty: Can the Psychopathy Checklist-Revised Identify Offenders Who Represent "a Continuing Threat to Society?"* J. Psych. & L. (citing and quoting *U.S. v. Barnette*, Transcript, Sentencing Phase, File No. 3:97CR23-P, Feb. 5, 1998). The expert also testified that he based his opinion on the defendant's callousness, as demonstrated by the defendant's eating lunch during his discussion with the expert, and his inability to define compassion on an intelligence test; both similarly unscientific bases.

103 The American Bar Association, for example, notes that even though future dangerousness testimony is highly subjective, courts are reluctant to exclude such evidence because it is the "best evidence available." *See Benchbook, supra* note 16, at 49.

104 *See* John H. Blume et al., *Future Dangerousness in Capital Cases: Always "At Issue,"* 86 Cornell L. Rev. 397, 398 (2001) (observing, on the basis of interviews with over a hundred capital jurors, that "future dangerousness is in the minds of most capital jurors, and is thus 'at issue' in virtually all capital trials, no matter what the prosecution says or does not say").

a number of states and are required in Texas and Oregon.[105] But whether or not future dangerousness is permitted or required by statute, and whether or not it is even mentioned by prosecutors, or presented as evidence in the penalty phase of the case, it remains the major focus of the factfinders.[106] This is true regardless of the presence or absence of expert testimony about future dangerousness in the hearing.[107]

Jurors often believe – incorrectly – that the law requires a death sentence upon a showing of the defendant's future dangerousness.[108] Most people do not believe that defendants sentenced to life will actually be required to spend the rest of their lives in prison.[109] They fear that a dangerous person will be released into the community; and that is a highly motivating factor in choosing between death and a life sentence.[110]

There are a number of factors about jury deliberations that increase the likelihood that jurors will overestimate the threat of future violence. The most important of these is lack of objective information about such predictions.[111] Base rate errors plague human decisionmaking in general, so there is no reason to suppose capital jurors are any different. Moreover, jurors are seldom informed of the true rate of violent recidivism among murderers released from prison.[112] Interviews with

---

105 Tex. Code Crime. Proc. Ann. Ant. 37-071(b)(1) (Vernon 2005); Or. Rev. Stat. §163.150 (1)(b) (8) (2003).

106 *See, e.g.,* Stephen P. Garvey, *Aggravation and Mitigation in Capital Cases: What Do Jurors Think?* 98 COLUM. L. REV. 1538, 1559 (1998) (citing studies emphasizing the "pervasive role future dangerousness testimony plays in and on the minds of capital sentencing jurors").

107 *See* Blume et al., *supra* note 104, at 404 (reporting that "even in cases in which the prosecution's evidence and argument at the penalty phase did 'not at all' emphasize the defendant's future dangerousness, jurors who believed the defendant would be released in under twenty years if not sentenced to death were still more likely to cast their final vote for death than were jurors who thought the alternative to death was twenty years or more"). Indeed, it was the explicit recognition of the importance the jury gives to future dangerousness that motivated the Supreme Court to rule that defendants have a constitutional right to be informed of a death penalty alternative if the prosecution alleged future danger as an aggravating circumstance and the alternative is life in prison without parole in *Simmons v. South Carolina,* 512 U.S. 154 (1994). *See also Kelley v. South Carolina,* 534 U.S. 246 (2002) (reiterating the Court's earlier holding in Simmons; *cf.* Garvey, *supra* note 107, at 1559 (observing that future dangerousness "appears to be one of the primary determinants of capital-sentencing juries").

108 *See* James Liginbuhl & Julie Howe, *Discretion in Capital Sentencing Instructions: Guided or Misguided?,* 70 IND. L.J. 1161, 1174 (1995) (43% of surveyed jurors believed the law required a death sentence upon a showing of future dangerousness).

109 *See Simmons,* 512 U.S. at 159 (citing South Carolina survey showing that 92.9% of all jury-eligible adults surveyed believed that a life sentence meant the defendant would be out of prison within 30 years).

110 *See, e.g., id.* at 159 (noting survey in which 75% of those surveyed said that the amount of time actually spent in prison was either "extremely" or "very important" in choosing between life and death).

111 *See* Jonathan R. Sorensen & Rocky L. Pilgrim, *Actuarial Risk Assessment of Violence Posed by Capital Murder Defendants,* 90 J. CRIM. L. & CRIMINOL. 1251, 1254 (2000) (noting that lack of objective information about future dangerousness predictions is one of the prime reasons jurors overestimate the defendant's threat of future violence).

112 *Id.* at 1254–55 (noting studies showing that jurors are unaware of the base rates of violent recidivism among murderers).

capital jurors revealed that jurors who sentenced the defendant to death had median estimates of future violence of 85 percent, with a 50 percent median estimate that the defendant would commit another murder.[113] Yet, empirical studies demonstrate a counter-intuitive decreased base rate for violence among capital commutees in prison.[114] In one study of 188 death-sentenced prisoners whose sentences were commuted after *Furman*, for example, over the more than five years after their release, only one killed again, and only six committed violent offenses.[115] In studies of capital commutees paroled into the community, 20 percent returned to prison, but only 8 to 10 percent committed new felonies.[116] Unless jurors are informed about population base rates and how they should use them in making their decision, risk estimates amount to little more than speculation.

In addition, jurors consistently underestimate the number of years that must be served for a term of "life in prison," which means that the prisoner will be much older and have less opportunity in terms of potential risk period than jurors believe. Decreasing violence and criminal activity with age is a well-established principle of criminology. Base rates of violence are far lower after the age of sixty (when most life prisoners would be eligible for parole) than in the twenties.

Thus, there is ample reason to believe that probabilistic estimates would be helpful to the jury. Violence risk assessment is not a yes/no dichotomy, and should not be presented in such an unscientific way. Rather, risk estimates are uncertain and the base rate of serious violence among capital offenders is quite low. In order to be helpful, the expert needs to educate the jury in a scientifically sound manner, and this includes explicitly stating the statistical basis for the opinion. Because of the centrality of the dangerousness determination to juror deliberations, it would be helpful to the jury to have information relating to it. It should, however, be the best information available. Currently, actuarial instruments offer the most accurate way of making such predictions, but care must be taken that the expert carefully explain the limits of such testimony.[117]

Conclusion

Limiting testimony to what is relevant is a basic notion of procedural fairness. Even expert testimony must abide by this stricture, which means that it must have a sound scientific basis. Gatekeeping for scientific validity of expert testimony in

---

113 *Id.* at 1269.
114 Cunningham & Reidy, *supra* note 21, at 23 (citing studies).
115 Sorensen & Pilgrim, *supra* note 111, at 1254–55.
116 Cunningham & Reidy, *supra* note 21, at 25 (citing studies and noting that there are now longer minimum sentences that must be served before parole, making the defendants in the studies much younger than current defendants will be when parole eligible).
117 *See, e.g.*, Monahan & Steadman, *supra* note 90 at 935–36 (explaining that predictions of the risk of future violence should be modeled explicitly on weather predictions, with all their qualifiers and uncertainties).

capital sentencing proceedings is therefore basic to the rule of law, with its goal of rational truth-seeking.

A decision as important as a death sentence simply cannot be based on bunkum. Permitting expert witnesses to confuse the jury with wholly unscientific assertions should not be tolerated in any civilized country, much less one that prides itself on constitutional principles of due process. So, in addition to being sound cognitive practice, and mandated by the rule of law, judicial gatekeeping to prevent jury confusion is a minimum for fundamental fairness. Clinical predictions of future dangerousness cannot meet these standards. Actuarial testimony can barely squeak through. Predicting violence, like predicting the weather, is – at best – subject to a large margin of error. In a system that strives for justice, the least that can be expected is that judges will evaluate expert testimony that may result in a determination of death with as much care as they routinely scrutinize expert civil testimony.

7

Barefoot or *Daubert*? A cognitive perspective on vetting future dangerousness testimony

Despite the well-known shakiness of its scientific credentials, expert testimony continues to be prevalent at capital-sentencing hearings. It is difficult to imagine a more critical setting for accurate expert testimony. Yet, because the rules of evidence do not generally apply (and, even where they supposedly apply, they are ignored in practice), future-dangerousness testimony goes unexamined. The reason often given for admitting evidence without regard to evidentiary rules is that the capital jury is charged with making reasoned moral judgments about the fate of the defendant – a policy decision rather than a factual finding.[1] Policy makers as well as factfinders, however, require relevant and reliable information for their task. The dynamics of jury decision making in the context of capital-sentencing decisions demonstrate the importance of recognizing that the relevance requirement is a constitutional concern of fundamental fairness and how that requirement plays out with respect to expert testimony on future dangerousness.

To reach a just decision, jurors are supposed to be provided with "information relevant to the imposition of the sentence and provided with standards to guide its use of the information."[2] The purpose of testifying experts – that is, witnesses without personal knowledge of the defendant or incident – is the same in capital sentencing as it is at trial: to inform the jury about matters outside their common experience in order to assist the jury in making an accurate and just determination. The question is, therefore, whether initial screening by the judge for scientific validity aids in this task.

The U.S. Supreme Court in *Barefoot* thought the adversary system could be relied on to present enough information to jurors so that they could sort reliable from unreliable expert testimony. The *Daubert* Court thought expert testimony needed to be screened for relevance and reliability first. Which was correct? Two lines of research about juror decision making suggest a framework for analysis.

---

1 *California v. Ramos*, 463 U.S. 992, 1007 (1983) (at the penalty phase, the jury no longer acts strictly as fact finder; rather the jury's mission involves "a myriad of factors"); *Ford v. Strickland*, 696 F.2d 804, 831 n. 17 (11th Cir. 1983) ("The sentencer, therefore, acts not as fact finder, but as policy maker").
2 *Gregg v. Georgia*, 428 U.S. 153, 195 (1976).

The story model

A model of juror decision making proposed by Pennington and Hastie is the story model, in which the juror's decision depends on how well the expert's testimony fits with the juror's preexisting views.[3] Although Pennington and Hastie did not directly apply their framework to expert testimony, they posited a model consisting of three parts: first, the jurors use their own preconceptions to weave a story from the evidence they heard at trial; second, they take the jury instructions and create verdict alternatives; and third, they attempt to find the best correlation between the story they constructed and the verdict alternatives.[4] This model has a number of consequences regarding jury processing of expert future-dangerousness testimony.

Interviews with death-penalty jurors demonstrate that connecting the facts of the case to the proffered expert opinion increases the influence of the opinion on the jury.[5] Thus, when an expert opines with certainty in response to the prosecutor's hypothetical reiterating the facts of the case, this is very persuasive storytelling, even though it is the most inaccurate form of prediction. Not only is the opinion persuasive because of the storytelling aspect of the hypothetical, but its credibility also increases with the strength of expert certainty. A number of surveys have shown that jurors rated experts who conveyed low confidence in their opinions as a cause for concern.[6] Thus, the confidence with which an expert opinion is offered bears a direct relationship to its credibility with the jury. Evidence that corresponds to strongly held beliefs is particularly persuasive.[7] For juries already predisposed to believe a defendant poses a danger to society through lurid media accounts of

---

3 *See* REID HASTIE, ET AL. INSIDE THE JURY (1983); Nancy Pennington & Reid Hastie, *Evidence Evaluation in Complex Decision Making*, 51 J. PERSONALITY & SOC. PSYCHOL. 242, 243–45 (1986).

4 See Pennington & Hastie, *supra* note 3 at 243–45. The story model is similar to the idea of schemata in psychology. See, *e.g.,* David E. Rumelhart, *Schemata and the Cognitive System*, in 2 HANDBOOK OF SOCIAL COGNITION 163 (1984). A schema is an "informal, private, unarticulated theory about the nature of the events, objects, or situations we face. The total set of schemata we have available for interpreting our world in a sense constitutes our private theory of the nature of reality." Rumelhart at 163.

5 Steven Sundby, *The Jury as Critic: An Empirical Look at How Capital Juries Perceive Expert and Lay Testimony*, 83 VA. L. REV. 1109 (1996) (finding that jurors rated as more influential those experts who connected the facts of the case to their opinion).

6 See D. Shuman, E. Whitker & A. Champagne, *Empirical Examination of the Use of Expert Witnesses in the Courts–Part II: A Three-Part Study*, 34 JURIMETRICS J. 193 (1994).

7 Certainty in witness testimony is especially persuasive when it correlates with strongly held beliefs such as, for example, in eyewitness testimony where eyewitnesses who testify with certainty are likely to be believed and expert testimony that there is inverse correlation between certainty and correctness is likely to be disbelieved because jurors who strongly believe that witness confidence in identification is correlated to accuracy tend to discount or ignore the expert. See Daniel A. Krauss & Bruce D. Sales, *The Effects of Clinical and Scientific Expert Testimony on Juror Decision Making in Capital Sentencing*, 7 PSYCHOL. PUB. POL'Y & L. 267, 270, 276 (2001) (citing studies). *See also* Sundby, *supra* note 5 at 1133 (citing interviews with capital jurors who found expert eyewitness experts incredible because it contradicted their preconceptions).

violence in society, a tendency to overvalue predictions that confirm such beliefs is a likely outcome.[8]

The adversary process exacerbates these problems. First, in experimental settings, expert clinical testimony was more persuasive to jurors than actuarial testimony, even after adversarial manipulations, such as effective cross-examination and the testimony of a competing expert.[9] In addition, although effective cross examination caused these jurors to reevaluate the expert testimony, it had far less effect on clinical opinion testimony than on actuarial testimony.[10] This may be because of juror familiarity (and trust) with medical diagnoses for common diseases. These clinical predictions of violence differ from medical diagnoses, however. The best medical diagnosis of current condition requires personal examination and patient history, analyzed against a background of empirical data about the etiology of the disease being diagnosed. These factors are notably absent from clinical predictions of violence.[11]

Persuasion theory and the impact of cognitive quirks on capital sentencing

The persuasion theory posits that when an argument is complex or difficult to understand, people rely on cognitive shortcuts to evaluate the argument and that expert qualifications then become a surrogate for trustworthiness. Studies have shown that juror reliance on expert credentials are directly proportional to the complexity of the information presented.[12] Moreover, there is some evidence that

---

8 See C. Walter Showalter & Richard J. Bonnie, *Psychiatrists and Capital Sentencing: Risks and Responsibilities in a Unique Legal Setting*, 12 BULL. AM. ACAD. PSYCH. L. 159, 165 (1984) (jurors tend to overvalue predictions that confirm their beliefs).

9 See Krauss & Sales, *supra* note 7 at 291 (discussing the experiment and its results).

10 *Id.* at 302, 305 (observing that "[a]dversary procedures failed to return mock jurors who received clinical opinion expert testimony to their initial dangerousness rating levels" and concluding that jurors have a "predilection for less accurate clinical opinion testimony").

11 Even the most scientific predictions based on thorough examination, diagnosis of mental symptoms, past patterns of behavior, and probabilistic assessment are wrong nearly as often as they are right. See, e.g., Charles W. Lidz, et al., *The Accuracy of Predictions of Violence to Others*, 269 JAMA 1007 (1993) (concluding that "clinicians are relatively inaccurate predictors of violence"). In this study, when clinicians divided institutionalized men into two groups, "violent" and "nonviolent," and examined their behavior more than three years later, 53 percent of the "violent" group had committed acts of violence, as opposed to 36 percent of the "nonviolent" group. *Id.* Random predictions would have a sensitivity and specificity of 50 percent. *Id.* at 1009. Thus, while the results are better than chance, the low sensitivity and specificity of the predictions show "substantial room for improvement." Sensitivity is the percentage of times that a test correctly gives a positive result when the individual tested actually has the characteristic in question. Specificity is the percentage of times a test correctly reports that a person does not have the characteristic under investigation. Actuarial studies, though more accurate than clinical predictions, still predict with less than stellar accuracy: when scores on the most accurate of the actuarial instruments, the VRAG, "were dichotomized into "high" and "low" risk groups, the results indicated that at most, 55% of the 'high scoring' subjects committed violent recidivism, compared with 19% of the 'low scoring' group." John Monahan, *Violence Risk Assessment: Scientific Validity and Evidentiary Admissibility*, 57 WASH. & LEE L. REV. 901, 907 (2000).

12 James Cooper, et al., *Complex Scientific Testimony: How do Jurors Make Decisions?* 20 LAW & HUM. BEHAV. 379–95 (1996).

jurors tend to rank medical expertise higher than "merely" scientific expertise, so that even when the information is identical, jurors listening to two experts – one a medical doctor and one a psychologist – found the medical expert more persuasive even though the testimony was identical.[13] There is no reason to suppose that judges are any different from jurors in this respect, but the kind of structured analysis required under *Daubert* counters this tendency by requiring the judge to actually evaluate the information presented, focusing on four important factors.[14]

Without such a structured examination, the jury has little hope of accurately assessing the alternatives or of making an optimal decision. Irrelevant information may result in poor decisions from the dilution effect. As discussed in Chapter 2, the dilution effect is a cognitive bias that occurs when people are presented with complex information, some of which is relevant to the decision task and some of which is irrelevant. Because irrelevant information obscures what is relevant, the dilution effect explains the harmful consequences of simply throwing expert testimony (even cross-examined expert testimony) at the jury for evaluation.

In addition to the dilution effect, the dynamics of group decision making also bear on why the *Barefoot* court was mistaken that the jury deliberation is the right phase of the proceeding to sort out good science from bad. Group polarization may skew the jury's decision in the direction of any initial tendency. The jury's sentencing determination is unanimous, a group decision reached after deliberation, based on ideals of deliberative democracy that argument and reflection among competing views will lead to better – more accurate – outcomes. At the same time, however, a single dissenter can shift the result to a hung jury. Thus, the process has aspects of both group consensus reaching and interactive individual decision making.

Although both individual and group decision making are subject to biases – that is, decisions about what and how information is relevant[15] – there are some characteristics of group decision making that make it crucial to protect the jury from irrelevant information that exacerbates biases and to provide instructions that can guide the group's reasoning process.[16] The capital jury faces a judgment task that is essentially predictive, without a shared framework for defining right or

13 J. Greenberg & A. Wursten, *The Psychologist and the Psychiatrist as Expert Witnesses: Perceived Credibility and Influence*, 19 Prof. Psychol. Res. & Prac. 373–78 (simulated insanity trial).

14 As discussed in Chapter 1, the *Daubert* factors are testability; methodology and error rate; peer review and publication; and general consensus.

15 *See* Norbert L. Kerr, et al., *Bias in Judgment: Comparing Individuals and Groups*, 103 Psychol. Rev. 687, 714–15 (1996) (defining bias as reflecting "decisions about whether and how to use information" and demonstrating that "groups will amplify bias under some conditions but attenuate it under others"); Chip Heath & Rich Gonzalez, *Interaction with Others Increases Decision Confidence but not Decision Quality: Evidence Against Information Collection Views of Interactive Decision Making*, 61 Org. Behav. & Hum. Dec. Proc. 305, 323 (1995) (concluding that individual interactive decisionmaking exhibits similar characteristics to group consensus decisionmaking).

16 See William J. Bowers & Benjamin D. Steiner, *Death by Default: An Empirical Demonstration of False and Forced Choices in Capital Sentencing*, 77 Tex. L. Rev. 605, 609 (1999) (arguing that keeping jurors uninformed about sentencing alternatives skews the decision in favor of death). Jurors' release estimates are strongly correlated with their final punishment vote. *Id.* at 665 (noting that jurors who estimate release in 20 or more years are consistently and substantially less likely to vote for death than those who thought release would come in 0–9 years or 10–19 years).

wrong answers, which is precisely the kind of task in which polarization is likely to occur.[17] This confluence of systematic errors mandates careful judicial screening of information that the jury will use to make its collective decision, together with comprehensible jury instructions.

Systematic biases of concern in capital sentencing

The overconfidence heuristic may have unforeseen consequences in the context of capital sentencing. Not only do capital jurors, like all people, tend to believe that their judgment is correct[18] but also cognitive dissonance theory suggests that people tend to take further actions that justify and reinforce decisions that they have already made.[19] The jury has already decided that the defendant is a very dangerous person when it found the defendant guilty, and the overconfidence bias will tend to make jurors more confident in their prior decision – a guilty verdict – than the facts would suggest. Any information that supports their decision is likely to have a disproportionate impact on their sentencing decision, due to the related phenomenon of cognitive dissonance. This appears to be what happens in capital sentencing: capital jurors overwhelmingly focus on the question of guilt even after the verdict has been rendered and they are supposed to be focusing on the separate question of the appropriate punishment.[20] Overconfidence and cognitive dissonance suggest that jurors may be overconfident in their decision of guilt and subsequently overvalue the expert prediction that confirms their decision, giving disproportionate weight to any information that confirms their initial decision of guilt.[21] This is another reason to exclude testimony unsupported by data, such as when an expert testifies with more certainty than is warranted (e.g., the statement that the expert can be "one hundred percent certain" that the defendant will kill again).

17 See, e.g., Garold Stasser et al., *The Social Psychology of Jury Deliberations: Structure, Process and Product*, in The Psychology of the Courtroom 221–56 (Norbert L. Kerr & Robert Bray, eds. 1982) (jury studies).

18 See Hart Blanton, et al., *Overconfidence as Dissonance Reduction*, 37 J. Expt'l Soc. Psychol. 373, 373 (2001) (citing studies asking people to evaluate their ability in solving laboratory problems and showing that "people think that they can solve problems that they cannot, think that the have made progress toward correct solutions when they have not, and think that they have drawn correct conclusions when they have not").

19 Cognitive dissonance is a phenomenon in which people will adjust their attitudes and beliefs in order to justify a previously undertaken decision or course of action. *See* Leon Festinger, A Theory of Cognitive Dissonance (1957). Festinger's theory provoked a great deal of controversy, but the empirical basis for it appears to have survived the controversy. *See, e.g.*, Robyn M. Dawes, *Behavioral Decision Making and Judgment*, in Vol. 1, Handbook of Social Psychol. 497, 557–61 (Daniel T. Gilbert et al., eds. 4th ed. 1998) (detailing the controversy and concluding that "cognitive dissonance theory is resilient").

20 See Ursula Bentele & William J. Bowers, *How Jurors Decide on Death: Guilt Is Overwhelming; Aggravation Requires Death; and Mitigation Is No Excuse*, 66 Brook. L. Rev. 1011,1017–19 (2001) (describing the capital juror project and its findings that jurors continue to focus on guilt after the verdict and that they appear to ignore, discredit and devalue mitigating evidence even when it appears to be extensive and credible).

21 See, e.g., Ziva Kunda, *The Case for Motivated Reasoning*, 108 Psychol. Bull. 480–98 (1990) (observing that people will often construct theories and use evidence in ways that make their final inferences come out the way they want them to).

The representativeness and overconfidence heuristics are particularly troubling in this regard. For example, the representativeness heuristic may cause the individual jurors to base decisions on the extent to which a particular event (or person) resembles a certain category of events (or fits within their stereotypes of people).[22] If people share a particular bias, polarization may magnify this tendency. Thus, in assessing the probability of future violent behavior for a particular defendant, jurors are likely to think that one violent incident is representative of a pattern because they are unlikely to know, much less refer to, the probabilities of a recurring incident.[23] In addition, because people frequently overestimate the relevance of memorable incidents at the expense of statistical base rates and make judgments on the basis of what they remember, the jury may share a skewed perception of how common violent recidivism is.[24] A shared perception that violent recidivism is common may make the jurors more likely to opt for the death sentence.[25] Judges may be equally swayed by media reports, but group polarization may magnify this initial tendency of individual jurors.

In addition, because the jury has recently heard in graphic detail how the defendant committed one atrociously violent act, they are likely to believe that it is representative of the way the defendant will behave in the future. The representativeness heuristic suggests that jurors do not refer to base rates (of which they are usually ignorant in any event) in their decision-making process. Related to this bias is the availability heuristic, which is the tendency of people to confuse the facility with which they can recall an event with its likelihood of recurrence,[26] suggesting that the jurors' vivid recollection of a horrendous crime the defendant committed will be confused with future propensities for violence. The anchoring heuristic suggests

22 See Daniel Kahneman & Amos Tversky, *Subjective Probability: A Judgment of Representativeness*, 3 COGNITIVE PSYCHOL. 430, 431 (1972) (defining the representativeness heuristic as evaluating "the probability of an uncertain event, or a sample, by the degree to which it is (i) similar in essential properties to its parent population and (ii) reflects the salient features of the process by which it is generated" so that a characteristic is matched to a category and the probability evaluated in terms of the closeness of the match). The classic study on this bias was that of Meehl and Rosen, who documented the degree that psychiatric diagnoses made in staff meetings ignored population base rates. See P. E. Meehl & A. Rosen, *Antecedent Probability in the Efficiency of Psychometric Signs, Patterns, or Cutting Scores*, 52 PSYCHOL. BULL. 194–216 (1955). A simple example is that "a politician of erect bearing walking briskly to the podium is likely to be seen as strong and decisive; this is an example of judgment by representativeness." Daniel Kahneman & Amos Tversky, *On the Reality of Cognitive Illusions*, 103 PSYCHOL. REV. 582, 582 (1996).
23 *See* Dawes, *supra* note 19, at 532 (explaining the fallacy of "considering the probability of the evidence given the hypothesis . . . without looking at . . . the prior odds").
24 The number of dramatic deaths, for example, were greatly overestimated by medical student and physician participants in a study that asked participants to estimate the number of deaths due to each of forty-two diseases. Christensen-Szalanski et al., *Effects of Expertise and Experience on Risk Judgments*, 68 J. APP. PSYCHOL. 278–84 (1983).
25 Interviews with capital jurors, for example, found that jurors overwhelmingly underestimated the amount of time a defendant would have to serve before becoming eligible for parole, relying primarily on memory of vivid media accounts of violent recidivism. *See* William J. Bowers & Benjamin D. Steiner, *Death by Default: An Empirical Demonstration of False and Forced Choices in Capital Sentencing*, 77 TEX. L. REV. 605, 671–72 (1999) (discussing the interviews of 916 capital jurors in the Capital Juror Project).
26 *See* Tversky & Kahneman *infra* note 27, at 1163 (describing the availability heuristic and the cognitive biases that may result).

that because the jurors first learned about the defendant in the context of a graphically violent crime, they are likely to persist in thinking of the defendant as violent, even in the face of contrary evidence.[27] People frequently arrive at a decision that varies according to their starting point. The overconfidence bias similarly may have unforeseen consequences in the context of capital sentencing.

Moreover, pressures for uniformity and group loyalty can build up in collective-decision processes to the point where they can adversely affect both cognitive efficiency and moral judgment.[28] Irving Janis analyzed a number of political decisions and concluded that group dynamics could lead to policies that "deserved to be fiascoes."[29] Janis found that in these "fiascoes," group members were so motivated to maintain each other's respect that critical thought and dissenting opinions were inhibited. Groups isolated from outside influences and lacking systematic procedures for evaluating evidence were especially prone to this kind of cognitive error. Stressful conditions further magnified these effects. As a result, in the fiasco situations, decision makers began to experience excessive optimism about the correctness of their judgment, silencing deviant opinions to reestablish consensus.[30] These conditions closely parallel those in the jury room.

The situation is not irremediable for group decision making, however. Janis contrasted the "groupthink" conditions with conditions (he called these "vigilance conditions") that led to more rational outcomes. Critical appraisal and open discussion of options made for more careful analysis. Group final judgment depends on both where the individual members begin deliberation and the processes where the group combines preferences to define a group decision.[31] The importance of

---

27 Anchoring is the tendency for arbitrary starting points to influence decisions. Amos Tversky and Daniel Kahneman, *Availability: A Heuristic for Judging Frequency and Probability*, in JUDGMENT UNDER UNCERTAINTY: HEURISTICS AND BIASES 1124, 1128–29 (Daniel Kahneman et al., eds. 1982). For example, when asked to estimate percentages of United Nations countries that are African after being exposed to the result of a roulette wheel – an obviously random and irrelevant value – people responded with marked differences according to the value spun on the wheel (the median answer of people for whom the value on the wheel was 10 was considerably lower than that for people exposed to a wheel value of 65). This seemingly irrational behavior is explained by cognitive psychologists as the anchoring effect, in which decisions are made according to some (perhaps irrelevant) starting value. *Id.*

28 Philip E. Tetlock, et al., *Assessing Political Group Dynamics: A Test of the Groupthink Model*, 63 J. PERSONALITY AND SOCIAL PSYCHOL. 403, 403 (1992) (performing multiple regression analysis of various collective decision processes and concluding that there was ample support for the groupthink hypothesis first advanced by Irving Janis).

29 IRVING JANIS, VICTIMS OF GROUPTHINK 9 (2d ed. 1982).

30 The kinds of cognitive errors from this kind of group pressure include:

(a) truncated consideration of alternatives and objectives (often, the group discussed only the option initially favored by group members), (b) a failure to examine the risks of the initially preferred choice, (c) a failure to reappraise initially rejected alternatives, (d) poor search for relevant information, (e) biased processing of information and (f) a failure to work out contingency plans in the event known risks materialized.

Tetlock, *supra* note 28, at 404 (citing Janis).

31 Kerr, et al., *supra* note 15, at 694.

screening expert testimony for relevance and reliability has to do with focusing the starting point of deliberations.

Gatekeeping is an important first step, but clear jury instructions are also a factor. The importance of clear jury instructions is emphasized by the findings that if the individual members recognize the normative use of particular information, the group is more likely to use that information properly.[32] Studies demonstrate that jurors lack understanding of how to weigh the evidence presented in death-penalty proceedings.[33] Jurors simply do not know how to assess the expert testimony.[34] These misunderstandings play a pivotal role because jurors use them as persuasive devices. Frequently, jurors think that the instructions require them to impose death unless they can conceive of a reason not to do so. Thus, not only do judges need to exercise their gatekeeping powers, they also need to clarify the instructions they give to the jury.

In sum, the dilution effect together with the dynamics of group decision making bear on why the *Barefoot* court[35] was mistaken that the jury deliberation is the right phase of the proceeding to sort out good science from bad. The jury's unanimous sentencing decision, reached after group deliberation, needs both initial gatekeeping to screen out irrelevant information and subsequent clear instructions to guide the deliberative process. Without this, the decision process may get hopelessly mired by irrelevant information, skewed by initial tendencies (e.g., toward overweighting medical at the expense of other scientific expertise or, in death penalty juries, toward the expert who agrees with death-qualified juries' preconceptions), and stymied by the exertion of an unfamiliar cognitive task (i.e., evaluating scientific testimony) for which they have no training and no guidance.

Judicial gatekeeping

Judges are the relevance gatekeepers for good reason. They have training in critical thinking, they are accountable to superior courts and to legal commentators, and they get regular feedback about how well they have followed their procedures. Jurors, like most people, expect that the information they are being presented is relevant to their task, especially because they have heard lawyers make objections to evidence

---

32 *See* Kerr, *supra* note 15 at 715 (arguing that guidance in principles of rational judgment improves collective decisionmaking).

33 *See* James Luginbuhl and Julie Howe, *Discretion in Capital Sentencing: Guided or Misguided*, 70 IND. L. J., 1161, 1177, demonstrating how confusing jury instructions systematically predispose jurors toward a sentence of death.

34 *See* Joseph L. Hoffman, *Where's the Buck? – Juror Misperception of Sentencing Responsibility in Death Penalty Cases*, 70 IND. L. J. 1137, 1150 (1995), citing Capital Juror Project interviews of jurors who found death-penalty instructions confusing, particularly with regard to how they were supposed to evaluate aggravating and mitigating factors.

35 *Barefoot v. Estelle*, 463 U.S. 880, 900 (1983) (refusing to exclude future dangerousness testimony as a constitutional matter because the defense could not show that "psychiatrists are always wrong with respect to future dangerousness, only most of the time").

at trial. Judges, on the other hand, are explicitly aware that they must be vigilant in this regard.

Moreover, judges have at least rudimentary guidelines for the factors they should be examining in making their evaluation. Because they are supposed to engage in a structured evaluation process, and write up the process in an opinion, they have the opportunity to reach more accurate determinations. Further, judges are accountable for their evaluation processes to the appellate courts, and their decisions are scrutinized by the bar, the media, and the legal academy. They have ongoing training in making scientific-validity evaluations in the form of continuing judicial education, workshops, and scholarly critique. Together, these factors give them at least "a leg up" on the jury for the evaluation process.

These biasing heuristics are not insoluble problems. The jury can be helped to make more rational (i.e., less biased) decisions by judicial insistence that the expert testimony they hear be grounded in fact rather than guesswork and be presented in a way that is comprehensible. Making the probabilistic nature of the evaluation task explicit tends to reduce the frequency of these errors.[36]

Further, the judge can insist on having the expert testify in a comprehensible manner. People making decisions, whether jurors or judges, make better decisions when presented with frequentist probabilities rather than subjective probabilities.[37] People, for example, who are asked how many times out of ten they are likely to choose the wrong answer are more likely to be accurate (and pick eight out of ten, say), even when they assess their accuracy at 95 percent. Presenting probabilistic evidence in frequentist terms makes it more comprehensible, and the judge can insist on such presentation. Actuarial testimony presented as a frequency determination is apt to be less skewed than a subjective clinical determination, and judges could requires this kind of testimony.

People are capable of sound reasoning if the information is presented to them correctly.[38] Thus, if judges were to demand that experts testify in such a way as to make the probabilistic nature of their assessment task both explicit and frequentist, neither of which they currently do, the jury would be aided in its task of making an accurate decision. Judges should not abdicate their important gatekeeping responsibility when it comes to expert testimony. If the goal of a justice system is accurate determinations, limiting evidence to relevant information is sound cognitive practice.

---

36 *See* Gerd Gigerenzer, *From Tools to Theories: A Heuristic of Discovery* in Cognitive Psychology, 98 Psychol. Rev. 254–67 (1991).

37 *See* Gerd Gigerenzer, Calculated Risk, 7 and *passim* (2002), urging communication of risk in frequentist terms.

38 *See* Jonathan J. Koehler, *The Base Rate Fallacy Reconsidered: Descriptive, Normative and Methodological Challenges*, 19 Behav. & Brain Sci. 1, 15 (citing studies demonstrating that when information is presented in certain ways people are capable of sound probabilistic reasoning).

8

Future dangerousness and sexual offenders

When it comes to gruesome murders and violent sex offenses, basic rule-of-law precepts appear to be tossed out with the bathwater.[1] Predictions of future dangerousness are not only prevalent in capital sentencing, they also are rampant in post-conviction commitment of sexual offenders. Sexually violent predator acts, enacted in at least sixteen states, uniformly require predictions about the likelihood of reoffending.[2] Predictions of future dangerousness have become routine in the

---

1 Not only are people deemed to be at risk for sexually violent recidivism singled out for involuntary post-sentence commitment, community registration, or lifetime parole, but even the determination of guilt for sexual offenses is based on evidence of past crimes that is impermissible "character evidence" for other felony defendants. *See* Fed. R. Evid. 413 (Evidence of Similar Crimes in Sexual Assault Cases) and Fed. R. Evid. 414 (Evidence of Similar Crimes in Child Molestation Cases), enacted by Congress as part of the Violent Crime Control and Law Enforcement Act of 1994; effective July 9, 1995. The justification for this disparate treatment is that sex crimes are different from other crimes of violence and that sex offenders are more incorrigible and less likely to be deterred by the threat of incarceration. There is, however, little evidence for this, and Congress cited none in passing the Violent Crime Control and Law Enforcement Act of 1994. In the United Kingdom also, new legislation has made evidence of a defendant's bad character more readily admissible than previously. *See* Roderick Munday, *Bad Character Rules and Riddles: 'Explanatory Notes' and True Meanings of S.103(1) of the Criminal Justice Act 2003*, Cr. L. Rev., May 2005, 337. Community notification statutes, of which Megan's Law was the first in the United States, are also based on predicting the dangerousness of sex offenders. The New Jersey legislature in 1994 adopted a series of measures under the name "Megan's Law," including extending prison terms, involuntary civil commitment, lifetime parole supervision, and mandatory DNA sampling for identification. *N.J. Stat. Ann.* 2C §§ 7–1–7–11 (West 1994). The registration provisions require sex-offender registration with law enforcement and community notification. Selective community notification is now commonplace for released sex offenders. In New Jersey (and most other states), offenders are scaled on a risk assessment instrument and are entitled to a hearing on their dangerousness. *In re* G.B., 685 A. 2d 1252, 1260–1261 (N.J., 1996). If the offenders are deemed to be a danger to the community, they must register, with dire effects on their ability to obtain housing, employment, and other resources.

2 These states include Arizona, *Ariz. Rev. Stat.* §§ 36–3701–3717 (2003) effective July 1, 1996; California, *Cal. Welf. & Inst. Code* §§ 6600–09.3 (West 1998 & Supp. 2004); Florida, *Fla. Stat. Ann.* §§ 394.910–.931 (West 2002 & Supp. 2004) effective January 1, 1999; Illinois, 725 *Ill. Comp. Stat.* 207/1–99 (2002 & Supp. 2004), effective January 1, 1998; Iowa, *Iowa Code Ann.* §§ 229A.1–.16 (West Supp. 2004), effective May 6, 1998; Kansas, *Kan. Stat. Ann.* §59–29a02 (West 2005); Massachusetts, *Mass. Gen. L. Ann. Ch.* 123A (West Supp. 1998); Minnesota, *Minn. Stat. Ann.* § 253B.02 (West 2002); Missouri, *Mo. Stat. Ann.* §632.480 (West Supp. 1999); New Jersey, *N.J. Stat. Ann.* § 30:4–27.24 (West Supp.1999); Oregon, *Or. Rev. Stat.* § 426.005 (1998); South Carolina, *S.C. Code Ann.* §§ 44–48–10 (West Supp. 1998); Texas, *Tex. Stat. Ann.* §841.002 (West 2005); Virginia, *Va.Code*

United Kingdom also.[3] These predictions are frequently based on actuarial instruments, but rarely – either in the United States or the United Kingdom – is there any inquiry into their scientific soundness. That these predictions are admitted without serious judicial inquiry into their scientific validity is astonishing in a system that has as a fundamental tenet that only facts having rational probative value should be admissible in the search for truth.

Public pressure for strengthened crime control measures is fed by stories of sexual murders, especially the sexual murders and rapes of children, which occupy the national and international media. Violent recidivism is perceived to be a horrifying reality.[4] The response in the United States as well as the United Kingdom has been an increased emphasis on preventive detention, magnifying the role of future-dangerousness predictions.[5]

Sexually violent predator statutes rely on predictions of dangerousness to commit people who have already served their prison sentences to indefinite terms of confinement. A common definition of a sexual predator is someone who has committed a crime of sexual violence and has a mental or personality disorder that makes future acts of sexual violence likely. Although definitions of sexual predator may vary by statute, they all require findings that future acts of sexual violence are likely. Clinical predictions alone, or in combination with actuarial risk assessment instruments, have been widely accepted as adequately reliable for the severe deprivations of liberty authorized by the violent sexual predator statutes.[6]

Future dangerousness predictions under *Hendricks* and *Crane*

In *Kansas v. Hendricks*,[7] the U.S. Supreme Court examined the constitutionality of the Kansas Sexually Violent Predator Act ("Kansas Act"),[8] which provided for

---

Ann. §§37.1–70.1(2005); Washington, *Wash. Rev. Code Wash. Ann.* § 71.09 (West 2005); Wisconsin, *Wisc. Stat. Ann.* §980.01 (West 1998).

3　*See* Stephen Shute, *The Sexual Offences Act 2003: (4) New Civil Preventative Orders – Sexual Offences Prevention Orders; Foreign Travel Orders; Risk of Sexual Harm Orders*, Cr. L. Rev. June 2004, 417, 434–5 discussing the role of experts in the new risk-based regime for sexual offenders.

4　The base rate of violent recidivism is actually quite low. "Overall, the observed rates [of sexual recidivism] are between 10% and 15% after 5 years and approximately 20% after 10 years." R. Karl Hanson et al., *Sex Offender Recidivism: What We Know and What We Need to Know*, in Sexually Coercive Behavior: Understanding and Management 163 (Robert A. Prentky et al., eds., 2003).

5　*See* D. A. Thomas, *Sentencing: Rape – Forcible Oral Sex*, Cr. L. Rev. June 2005, 491, 491–92, discussing the increase in maximum sentence under new legislation for the same conduct from ten years to life imprisonment; Paul H. Robinson, *Preventing Dangerousness: Cloaking Preventive Detention as Criminal Justice*, 114 Harv. L. Rev. 1429 (2001) noting that the focus of criminal justice has shifted from punishment to deterrence through incarceration, indefinite civil commitment, or death.

6　*See, e.g., In recommitment of R.S.*, 773 A. 2d 72 (N.J. Super. Ct. App. Div., 2001), upholding use of actuarial instruments to assess future dangerousness; *Johnson v. Missouri*, 2001 WL 527494 (Mo. Ct. App. May 18, 2001) finding that expert testimony was necessary to determine that a defendant incarcerated since his teens had a mental abnormality that made him likely to commit sexual violence; *State v. Post*, 541 N.W. 2d, 115, 132 (Wis., 1995), rejecting a challenge based on impossibility of prediction; *In re Blodgett*, 510 N.W. 2d 910, 917, n.15 (Minn., 1994), broad deference to expert predictions of future dangerousness.

7　521 U.S. 346 (1997).

8　*Kan. Stat. Ann.* § 59–29a01 et seq. (1994).

the indefinite civil commitment of people who were likely to engage in future "predatory acts of sexual violence" due to a "mental abnormality or personality disorder." Because it requires a finding of likely future violence, the statute appears to provide for an expert future-dangerousness prediction. In *Hendricks*, both the state's expert and the defense expert testified about future dangerousness.

The defendant, Leroy Hendricks, had been convicted of "taking indecent liberties with two thirteen-year-old boys."[9] He served a ten-year sentence for his crime. Shortly before he was due to be released to a halfway house, the state sought civil commitment under the Kansas Act. During his commitment jury trial, Hendricks testified that he had five prior convictions for sexually molesting children and had been treated (and discharged) from a state psychiatric institution, after which he continued to abuse children, including his own stepchildren. He testified that when he was under stress he could not "control the urge," and that the only way he could keep from sexually molesting children in the future was "to die."[10]

The state's experts, a clinical social worker and a psychologist, both opined that Hendricks was a pedophile. In addition, the psychologist testified that, unless confined, Hendricks was likely to commit sexual offenses in the future. To counter this testimony, Hendricks' expert, a psychiatrist, testified that "it was not possible to predict with any degree of accuracy the future dangerousness of a sex offender."[11] The jury nonetheless was persuaded beyond a reasonable doubt that Hendricks was likely to commit a future crime, the judge determined that pedophilia qualifies as a mental abnormality under the statute, and Hendricks was committed.

The issues on appeal included due process, double jeopardy, and ex-post facto clause claims. The Kansas Supreme Court accepted Hendricks's due-process claim, holding that substantive due process requires a showing, by clear and convincing evidence, that the person to be committed is both mentally ill and poses a danger to self or others.[12] The U.S. Supreme Court disagreed, holding that the Kansas Act's definition of mental abnormality satisfied due-process requirements. Although it acknowledged the need for a showing of "more than a mere predisposition to violence," the Court determined that the Kansas Act's twin requirements of evidence of past sexual offenses and present mental abnormality making recidivism likely were sufficient.[13]

Crucially, however, despite acknowledging that involuntary commitment statutes must adhere to "proper procedures and evidentiary standards," the Court did not discuss those evidentiary standards. The Court made no mention of *Barefoot*, *Daubert*, the need for reliability, or any scientific basis for the expert testimony on dangerousness. The Court did cite to a 1984 (pre-*Daubert*) case for the proposition

---

9 *Hendricks*, 521 U.S. 353.

10 *Id.*

11 *Id.*

12 *Id.* at 356.

13 *Id.* The Court acknowledged that dangerousness alone was not enough for commitment but held that as long as there was a showing that the offender had inadequate control over his behavior, that would suffice. *Id.* at 358, 364.

that "there is nothing inherently unattainable about a prediction of future criminal conduct."[14] However, it did not elaborate. Nowhere in its opinion does the court grapple with the scientific basis for a prediction of future dangerousness.

In *Kansas v. Crane*,[15] the U.S. Supreme Court revisited the Kansas Act to determine the application of *Hendricks* to the indefinite civil commitment of a convicted flasher.[16] Michael Crane was convicted and served time for lewd and lascivious behavior, after which the state sought civil commitment under the Kansas Act. Crane argued that the state had not proved that he completely lacked control over his behavior and that *Hendricks* required such a showing.

The U.S. Supreme Court held that the state need not prove a complete lack of control under the Kansas Act, although the Constitution does require some "proof of serious difficulty in controlling behavior."[17] On this basis, the Court vacated and remanded for such a determination. Once more, however, the Court avoided any discussion of the reliability of predictions of dangerousness or what such predictions could mean in the context of an exhibitionist.

Expert testimony in sexual offender proceedings

In seeking post-conviction commitment of sexual offenders, actuarial instruments are being used with some frequency. Many of the same researchers who developed the violence risk instruments began to study ways to improve the accuracy of predictions about future sexual violence.[18] Their goal was to develop an empirically based actuarial instrument that would reflect a state of the art understanding of the factors correlated with sexual violence and their interrelationships.[19] Several instruments resulted from this research. In each of the instruments, these risk factors are combined to take into account their interrelationship and population base rates, and weights were assigned to the individual risk factors. Each instrument then yields an overall "score" that ranks levels of risk.[20]

---

14 *Hendricks*, 521 U.S. at 358 (citing *Schall v. Martin*, 467 U.S. 253 (1984)).

15 534 U.S. 407 (2002).

16 Crane was convicted of lewd and lascivious behavior for exposing himself to a tanning-salon attendant. *In re Crane*, 7 P. 3d 285, 286 (Kan. 2000). The prior conduct required for commitment under the Kansas Act consisted of an aggravated sexual battery conviction that was overturned on appeal. *Id.* The event giving rise to the sexual battery charges actually occurred thirty minutes *after* Crane left the tanning salon. He entered a video store, grabbed a clerk, exposed himself, and threatened to rape her. He suddenly stopped and ran out of the store. Crane pled guilty to aggravated sexual battery, which met the requirement for prior sexual-offense history.

17 *Crane*, 534 U.S. at 413.

18 Christopher Webster et al., The Violence Prediction Scheme: Assessing Dangerousness in High Risk Men, xi, xii (1994) describing the genesis and goals of the violence risk assessment guide.

19 *See* Vernon L. Quinsey et al., Violent Offenders: Appraising and Managing Risk, 190 (1998).

20 John Monahan, *Violence Risk Assessment: Scientific Validity and Evidentiary Admissibility*, 57 Wash. & Lee L. Rev. 901, 903 (2000) evaluating risk assessment instruments. The concept of risk encompasses not only the presence of danger but also its probability of occurrence. *See* Eric S. Janus and Robert A. Prentky, *Forensic Use of Actuarial Risk Assessment with Sex Offenders: Accuracy,*

The predominant instruments used in assessing sexual violence are the Violence Risk Assessment Guide (VRAG),[21] the Sexual Offender Risk Assessment Guide (SORAG),[22] and the Rapid Risk Assessment for Sexual Offense Recidivism (RRASOR).[23] Of these, the VRAG is "the best currently available method to predict future violence," including sexual violence.[24] Its close cousin, the SORAG, is not quite as predictively accurate.[25]

What is the underlying theory?

Risk assessment is supposed to objectively quantify the probabilities and consequences of adverse events.[26] Risk encompasses notions of statistical probability, factor analysis, and the likelihood of event occurrence. Risk shifts the focus from a yes/no dangerousness analysis to a probabilistic statement.[27] The key variables in risk assessment of any stripe are the outcomes, their probabilities of occurrence, the uncertainty about the outcomes, and time.[28]

Although, as noted in Chapter 6, risk analysis is a statistical methodology commonly used by epidemiologists, toxicologists, the EPA, and the insurance industry, among others, the question here is whether it is scientifically valid for predicting human behavior rather than natural events or disease. The answer to that question requires an evaluation not only of the mathematical logic but also of the underlying theory. Statistical analysis provides an important tool for examining whether theories correspond with observation.[29] However, one cannot expect statistics to provide an answer about any particular individual.[30] The most that can be said from

---

Admissibility and Accountability, 40 Am. Crim L. Rev. J. 1443, 1449 (2003), addressing the concept of risk in predictions.

21 Quinsey et al., *supra* note 19, at 141.

22 *Id.* at 155–9, proposing SORAG as an enhancement to VRAG.

23 RRASOR is based on four factors: prior sexual offenses, age at release (young is worse), gender of the victim (male is worse), and relationship to the victim (related is better). Caroline M. Mee and Harold V. Hall, *Risky Business: Assessing Danger in Hawaii*, 24 U. Haw. L. Rev. 63, 102 (2001). Although the Minnesota Sex Offender Screening Test-Revised (MnSOST-R) is often used as a sex-offender instrument, Barbaree's study found that it "failed to meet conventional levels of statistical significance in the prediction of serious and sexual recidivism" and so it has been omitted here. *See* Howard E. Barbaree et al., *Evaluating the Predictive Accuracy of Six Risk Assessment Instruments for Adult Sex Offenders*, 28 Crim. J. & Behav., 490, 512 (2001).

24 Mee and Hall, *supra* note 23, at 102.

25 *See id.* at n. 227 citing interview with Quinsey, developer of both the VRAG and the SORAG.

26 *See* Paul Slovic, *Trust, Emotion, Sex, Politics, and Science: Surveying the Risk Assessment Battlefield*, 1997 U. Chi. Legal F., 59, 63, discussing risk analysis and differences among population groups in risk assessment.

27 *See* David Carson, *A Risk-Management Approach to Legal Decision-Making About 'Dangerous' People*, in Law and Uncertainty: Risks and Legal Process, 20 (Robert Baldwin, ed., 1997) discussing the paradigm shift from dangerousness to risk.

28 *See* K. R. McCrimmon and D. A. Wehrung, Taking Risks: The Management of Uncertainty (1988).

29 *See* Kenneth J. Rothman, *Significance Questing*, 105 Annals Internal Med., 445, 445 (1986), editorial.

30 As epidemiologists studying the statistical incidence of disease have discovered, one simply cannot predict the probability of disease in any given case. *See* Sander Greenland and Jerome Robins,

even the best statistical analyses is that someone falls within a group that has a certain statistical propensity for sexual violence. Moreover, the context here is human behavior, a quintessentially complex phenomenon, in which there is continuous interaction of individuals with each other and the whole system of which they are a part, responding to both random events and dynamic phenomena.

Statistical theory is based on the idea that there is an underlying structure in large matrices of data. The problem with this theory is that, although the mathematics are unimpeachable, "the fact and strength of the correlation rarely specifies the nature of the cause."[31] For example, the positive statistical correlation[32] between poverty and violence does not show anything about which one may be a cause of the other or what the causal nature might be.[33] For example, if a propensity for sexual violence correlates with socioeconomic situation, is that because poverty breeds despair or because poverty causes poor childhood nutrition, which affects the growing brain (and, therefore, decisionmaking), or because there is a high level of lead paint (linked to neural deficits) in poor neighborhoods? Or is it because violent people have trouble relating to others and so become poor through an inability to hold a job? Or is the correlation due to something else entirely? Thus, the question underlying the choice of factors used in each of the instruments must be: Why this factor and not others?

Notably, none of the actuarial instruments claims a causal connection. The underlying theory of any actuarial violence-risk instrument is that if you combine a critical number of risk factors, each of which has been demonstrated to have a statistically significant correlation with a recurrence of violent behavior, as long

---

Epidemiology, Justice, and the Probability of Causation, 40 JURIMETRICS J. 321, 328 (2000), explaining in the context of tort causation that "when an exposure is known to be harmful in some cases, available data from epidemiology and biology are simply incapable of telling us whether a given case was 'more probably than not' harmed by exposure."

31 STEPHEN J. GOULD, THE MISMEASURE OF MAN, 268, 273 (2d ed., 1981).

32 Correlation is the statistical degree of relationship between two variables. CHRIS SPATZ, BASIC STATISTICS: TALES OF DISTRIBUTIONS, 77, 81 (5th ed., 1993) defining correlation and explaining that the symbol for correlation – the correlation coefficient – is r. A variable is something that can be quantified and that exists in more than one amount. *Id.*, 6. In simple terms, when there is a perfect correlation between two variables, $r = 1.00$; when there is no correlation, $r = 0$. *Id.*, 81. As Gould explains, "[c]orrelation assesses the tendency of one measure to vary in concert with another." Gould, *supra* note 33, at 269. The way correlation is measured – for linear relationships – is by Pearson's product moment correlation coefficient, which ranges from $+1$ for perfect positive correlation, to 0 for no correlation, to -1 for perfect negative correlation. *Id.*, 270.

33 *See*, e.g., Eric Silver, et al., *Assessing Violence Risk Among Discharged Psychiatric Patients: Toward an Ecological Approach*, 23 LAW & HUMAN BEHAVIOR, 237, 250 (1999), observing that "concentrated poverty in the neighborhoods where patients resided after discharge was significantly related to the overall amount of violence they committed." This correlation says nothing about cause. Similarly, just because war has been an enduring fact of human history does not mean that violence is an innate trait of human beings; rather, the potential for aggression may be an expression of some other underlying biological principles that anticipate peaceful interactions in other environments. *See* Gould, *supra* note 31 at 360 critiquing the assertions of E. O. Wilson that aggression is innate in human beings. In other words, there is a wide range of human behaviors that are different expressions of biological potentials in various environments.

as you choose the factors carefully (i.e., by controlling for interrelationships among the various factors – such as previous criminal charges and prior convictions),[34] you can predict the probability of recurring violent conduct. The theory underlying the creation of such an instrument is that patterns of behavior in populations can predict the probability that an individual's behavior will fall within that range. Is this assertion falsifiable? At least in theory, it is, although in practice (because of the large sample sizes needed and the length of time necessary to assess recurrence), it may be difficult. A more fundamental problem is whether precise prediction is ever possible in biological systems.

What data support (or undermine) the theory?

The variables considered for the instruments were drawn from empirical studies showing a statistical association with sexually violent behavior.[35] No one of these factors, however, standing alone, has predictive power; they must be analyzed in concert.[36] In each of these instruments, violent behavior (i.e., violent sexual behavior in the SORAG and RRASOR) is statistically correlated with specific factors either in the person's past behavior (e.g., a pattern of past violence), circumstances (e.g., poverty), attitudes toward others (e.g., failure to marry or form equivalent relationship); medical and psychiatric history (e.g., age when problems began and any injuries to the brain); and substance abuse (e.g., alcohol or drugs).[37] The sexual violence instruments tend to include phallometric studies.[38] They also include factors such as whether the victim was a stranger and whether the victim was male.[39] These factors are then used in combination to probabilistically assess a level of risk for the future.

---

34 These factors are not "causes" of violence. They are factors that are associated with violence. *See* Stephen F. Lanes, *Error and Uncertainty in Causal Inference*, in CAUSAL INFERENCE 173, 182 (Kenneth J. Rothman, ed., 1988). "The uncertainty in causal inference is attributable to the fact that we cannot establish that an association is valid." *Id.*, 185. An unidentifiable error may exist and it may cause the observation. The most that can be expected of strength of association and the level of statistical significance is that they affect subjective beliefs.

35 Association means that there is a statistically significant correlation of a particular factor with violent behavior. Recall that statistical significance is set by convention at a level of significance, or p-value, of 0.05 (which corresponds to a confidence level of 95 percent).

36 *See* John Monahan, *Clinical and Actuarial Predictions of Violence*, in 1 DAVID L. FAIGMAN ET AL., MODERN SCIENTIFIC EVIDENCE: THE LAW AND SCIENCE OF EXPERT TESTIMONY (1997) § 7–2.1.1 (Supp. 2000), noting that "it is crucial for future studies to use multiple measures of violence rather than the single measures that have characterized most prior research."

37 *See* Hanson et al., *supra* note 4, at 157, discussing factors.

38 "Phallometry is a diagnostic method to assess sexual arousal by measuring blood flow (tumescence) to the penis during the presentation of potentially erotic stimuli in the laboratory." Center for Sex Offender Management, *Understanding Juvenile Sexual Offending Behavior: Emerging Research, Treatment Approaches, and Management Practices* (1999), noting that this is a controversial practice and explaining the pitfalls, especially with juvenile offenders.

39 *See* Hanson et al., *supra* note 4, at 157, discussing factors.

What assumptions are being made?

Although structured analysis offers many advantages in light of the difficulty people have in synthesizing differently weighted likelihoods of varying significance (e.g., risk factors for violent behavior),[40] the actuarial instrument is only as effective as the risk factors used in it and the weight that is given them, making accurate prediction elusive in all but the highest of the risk categories.[41] Vagueness and independence of factors may be a problem, as well as some of the assessment techniques used. Penile plethysmographs (used in phallometric studies), for example, are highly questionable for many of the same reasons as lie detectors.

Moreover, all future-dangerousness predictions rely heavily on prior criminal record as an important factor, which is both under- and over-inclusive. It is under-inclusive because it misses the highest percentage of violence: that between intimates. Many people with violently aggressive behaviors and a high likelihood of repeating violent behavior, such as chronic spouse abusers and stalkers, do not have criminal records. Using criminal record as an important factor is also over-inclusive because it does not allow for the changes that occur with aging or other dynamic factors.[42]

Probabilistic assessments inevitably employ assumptions, and the actuarial instruments used in predicting dangerousness are no different in this respect. As the authors of the VRAG acknowledge, the more assumptions that are made about the data, the less predictive is the resulting instrument.[43] One major assumption of all the instruments is that the population that was the subject of the underlying studies can be generalized to the people on whom the instrument will be used to predict future dangerousness. Each instrument was developed based on studies of men incarcerated in psychiatric hospitals or prisons. That does not seem too great

---

40 J. Richard Eiser and Joop Van der Pligt, Attitudes and Decisions 100 (1988), observing that human decision "accuracy declines considerably when the number of features or the number or alternatives increases ... [and] reliability with which choice rules are used tends to decrease as the decision-maker's information load increases."

41 See Stephen J. Morse, Preventive Confinement of Dangerous Offenders, 32 J. L. Med. & Ethics, 56, 59 (2004), noting that "it is a truism of behavioral science that statistical 'cookbook' predictions based on empirically validated risk factors is more accurate than clinical prediction, but despite advances in the database that have improved the cookbook, highly accurate prediction by any method eludes us in all but the most obvious cases."

42 Three-strike rules, for example, are premised on the notion that repeated bad behavior escalates in violence and overlook the natural decrease in aggression after adolescence. Thus, while offending rates drop after the twenties, three-strike rules are often triggered just when "the natural forces of aging would rein in the offenders." Robinson, note 5, p. 1451. Moreover, with treatment, most adolescent brains can be retrained. The abnormal stress responses in violent offenders can be normalized with medication. See Debra Niehoff, The Biology of Violence, 238, 265 (1998), advocating the "selective and thoughtful use of medications that normalize stress responses, delay impulsive reactions, block the craving for drugs, or suppress nonlethal paraphilias." Moreover, the time period that the risk assessment is to cover, the circumstances under which it will be implemented (i.e., confinement or release), and the individual's motivation to refrain from violence (including motivation to comply with treatment) must all be considered in assessing risk. Niehoff, at 261. Yet, none of these are factored into the actuarial instrument.

43 Quinsey et al., supra note 19, at 146.

a stretch because the patients studied had all been admitted for crimes of violence, a population similar to convicted defendants facing sexual-offender commitment proceedings.

The necessary assumptions for the regression analysis used in creating actuarial instruments include the assumption that the model has been correctly specified; that any measurement errors are random and independent; that measurement errors are independent of the corresponding observations for each of the model's explanatory variables; and that no explanatory variable is perfectly correlated with a combination of other variables.[44] The methodology for the individual instruments must be examined to be sure that these assumptions hold true. Moreover, the assumption of nonlinearity and interactive models would improve accuracy.[45] Other methods, such as neural networks and entropy minimax, which include these assumptions, have been used to discover predictive relationships and might be useful models to consider in developing future instruments, although they are not used in any of the instruments currently being used in sexual offender (or violence) risk assessment.[46]

Methodology and error rate

The hypothesis underlying the VRAG – which, although designed to analyze the risk of violent recidivism, is the most predictive instrument for sexual offending as well – was tested through a retrospective study of a population of 618 released offenders over a period of seven years, the effect of each factor on overall risk was scored, and the percentage of people who had reoffended after the release was correlated with the score.[47] The higher the score, the more violence was committed by that particular group. The VRAG study's definitions of violent conduct appear to be the kinds of behavior judges and jurors might worry about: killing, attempted killing, rape, sexual assaults involving robbery, kidnapping, forcible confinement, wounding, assault causing bodily harm, and pointing a firearm. This definition probably corresponds to the kinds of behaviors a jury would be concerned about in deciding whether someone would be likely to reoffend. The particular statistical tool used by the actuarial instruments is multiple regression, a method for probing the relationship of two or more variables. Multiple regression takes a variable that must

44 Daniel L. Rubinfeld, *Reference Guide on Multiple Regression*, in Reference Manual on Scientific Evidence, 181 (Federal Judicial Center, 2d ed., 2000) at 213.
45 An example of nonlinearity is the correlation of arousal and performance where, although there is a strong correlation the relationship is a curved line (nonlinear), showing low performance at both high and low arousal and optimal performance in the mid-range. *See* Spatz, *supra* note 32, at 96 graphing the relationship between arousal and efficiency of performance. But *see* Quinsey, *supra* note 20, at 146 arguing that these improvements would make little difference, given the possibility of measurement error and the level of accuracy already achieved.
46 *See* Quinsey et al., *supra* note 19, at 146, 168 citing studies and acknowledging that other kinds of studies might be an improvement, but arguing that the VRAG's accuracy rivals that for predicting violent storms.
47 *See* Quinsey et al., *supra* note 19, at 141–51.

be explained (recurring violence, in this instance) and examines its association with other variables (e.g., poverty).[48] Multiple regression is a way of relating one variable to the values of other explanatory variables to predict the value of one variable using the values of others. Multiple regression is a technique frequently employed by experts outside the context of sexual offender litigation, such as in antitrust litigation, antidiscrimination class actions, and market-manipulation cases.[49]

If any variables (selected on the basis of having a significant correlation with recurring violence) were highly correlated with each other, the one with the lowest correlation with recurring violence was dropped.[50] Least-squares stepwise multiple regression analysis was employed "to select variables that added independently[51] to the prediction of violent recidivism." Least-squares is a well-regarded technique for estimating the underlying parameters[52] and a method of reducing error when making predictions from a linear relationship.[53]

To construct the VRAG, separate regression analyses were run on different sets of variables, such as childhood history, adult adjustment, the characteristics of the original offense, and results of various tests (e.g., IQ tests).[54] The resulting variables selected in a majority of subgroups then underwent a final regression analysis. The researchers selected twelve variables for the instrument, based on the results of the regression analysis, and each was weighted with reference to the overall base rate

---

48 Daniel L. Rubinfeld, *Reference Guide on Multiple Regression*, in REFERENCE MANUAL ON SCIENTIFIC EVIDENCE, 181 (Federal Judicial Center, 2d ed., 2000), explaining that multiple regression "involves a variable to be explained – called the dependent variable – and additional explanatory variables that are thought to produce or be associated with changes in the dependent variable."

49 *See* MICHAEL O. FINKELSTEIN AND BRUCE D. LEVIN, STATISTICS FOR LAWYERS, 350 (2d ed., 2001) giving examples of regression models in law.

50 Quinsey, *supra* note 19, at 146.

51 Independence is when "two variables are not correlated with each other in the population." Rubinfeld, *supra* note 48 at 179. Two events, A and B, are independent when $P(A/B) = P(A)$. As Suppes explains, "the concept of independence is one of the most profound and fundamental ideas, not only of probability theory but of science in general." PATRICK SUPPES, A PROBABILISTIC THEORY OF CAUSALITY, 8 (1970). The concept of independence asserts that discrete biological or physical events, like coin tosses, have no memory of time and place. *See* Lynn A. Steen, *The Science of Patterns*, 240 SCI. 611 (1988). In other words, knowing whether a coin toss yielded heads or tails last time will not help predict what the next coin toss will yield. *See* FREDERICK MOSTELLER ET AL., PROBABILITY WITH STATISTICAL APPLICATIONS 8 (2d ed., 1970).

52 *See* Rubinfeld, *supra* note 48 at 213, 224 noting that the desirable properties of the least-squares technique include unbiased estimators – so that if the regression were calculated with different samples, the average of the estimates for each coefficient would be the true parameters; consistent estimators – so that if the sample were very large, the estimates would come close to the true parameters; and efficiency, in that the least-squares estimators have the smallest variance among all linear unbiased estimators. "Least-squares minimize the sum of the squared differences between the actual values of the dependent variable and the values predicted by the regression equation." *Id.*, 224.

53 *See* Spatz, *supra* note 32 at 101–102 explaining that when you have many data points that vary in relationship to each other, drawing a line that best represents the data depends on which points are chosen for the equation, and that least-squares is a method to minimize error in drawing a regression line, so that it best fits the data scores when the scores vary together.

54 Quinsey et al., *supra* note 19, at 146.

in the population and given a score.[55] The distribution of offenders' scores was a normal curve.[56] This means that roughly as many people fell within the lowest possible risk category (where the probability of recurring violence was close to 0) as fell into the highest risk category (where the probability of recidivism was close to 1.0).[57]

The authors of the VRAG attribute its accuracy to having measured the variables with reference to "detailed and complete psychosocial histories" gleaned from collateral sources (i.e., family members) and descriptions of actual behavior rather than self-reporting and "reliance on hypothetical internal states" as its basis.[58] The authors acknowledge that the accuracy of the instrument depends on the base rate of violent recidivism in the population being studied so that at very low base rates, predictions would not be worthwhile.[59] Although they acknowledge that the instrument is not nearly as accurate as concurrent diagnostic tests[60] or short-term weather predictions,[61] the authors contend that the instrument at least rivals the accuracy of predicting violent storms.[62]

55 *Id.* at 147. Each of the twelve variables was assigned a weight of +1 or −1 for every + or − 5 percent difference from the violence recidivism base rate of 31 percent. *See* Webster et al. *supra* note 18, 33, using the example of the "ever married" factor, where the recidivism rate for subjects who had ever been married was 21 percent, yielding a 10 percent difference from the mean recidivism rate of 31 percent, giving a weight of −2; and comparing this with the "never married" recidivism rate of 38 percent, which − yielding a 5 percent increase over the 31 percent base rate − was given a score of +1. The highest weight was given to the PCL-R score because, of all the variables, it had the strongest correlation with recurring violence. Webster et al. *Supra* note 18, 33. Scores ranged from −28 to +33. Quinsey et al., supra note 19, at 147. The mean VRAG score for the population tested was close to zero, with a standard deviation of 12.9. *Id.* The standard deviation is the amount that the typical measurement differs from the average. David H. Kaye and David A. Freedman, *Reference Guide on Statistics*, Federal Judicial Center Manual on Scientific Evidence (2d ed., 2000), noting that "Deviations from the average that exceed three or four SDs are extremely unusual." This high standard deviation remains unexplained. *See* Kroner and Mills, 486, noting that this may be due to "inadequacies in conceptualization and, of even more importance, instrumentalization."

56 *Id.* at 148. A normal curve, or bell-shaped distribution, means that 95 percent of the distribution lies within two standard deviations of the mean. Rubinfeld, *supra* note 47, at 224. The standard deviation indicates how far two particular data points deviate from the mean. *See, e.g.,* Statistics and the Law, 409 (Morris H. DeGroot et al., eds., 1986), explaining the importance of statistics to scientific data, using the example of environmental data.

57 Webster et al. *supra* note 18, at 34.

58 *Id.* at 165 observing that one reason for this may be that "the defining properties of psychopathy (lying, conning, and glib speech) may increase measurement error during personal interviews).

59 Quinsey et al., *supra* note 19, at 152 noting that "when the base rate is low enough, the optimal decision is to release everyone."

60 The accuracy of concurrent diagnostic tests achieves an ROC of over 0.90, as compared with the VRAG's 0.73. *Id.* at 168.

61 The authors insist that "the prediction of weather phenomena (where there is essentially zero outcome measurement error) probably cannot be accomplished in the prediction of violent recidivism." *Id.* at 168. John Monahan and Henry Steadman similarly draw an explicit analogy to weather reports in advocating the use of actuarial instruments and probabilistic communication for predicting violence.

62 Quinsey et al., *supra* note 19, at 168.

Assessing the links between theory and conclusion

Violence risk assessments are probabilistic risk estimates that should be acknowledged as uncertain.[63] Although testimony based on actuarial instruments is more accurate than clinical predictions[64] and thus is preferable to clinical testimony, these predictions are still tenuous bases for making such important decisions as death and indefinite confinement. At best, these actuarial instruments correlate only moderately with violent (and violent sexual) recidivism.[65] Thus, if they are to meet standards for scientific validity, the expert must carefully explain the limits of such testimony.[66] To be helpful, the expert needs to educate the jury in a scientifically sound manner, which includes explicitly stating the statistical basis for the opinion.[67]

Moreover, what is missing from any of the actuarial instruments is causal theory; recognition of the biology of violence; and explicit discussion of the interrelatedness of genes, organisms, and their environment. Thus, the instruments do little to advance our understanding about violent behavior and do not give us any insight into prevention (other than removal from society). This is curious, in light of the explosion of knowledge about how biological factors, combined with

63 It is important that juries be informed that even the most accurate of the actuarial instruments made predictions of dangerousness for people that did not, in fact, later commit acts of violence. Of people who were placed in the "high risk" category under the VRAG, for example, only 55 percent actually committed violent acts upon release; that means 45 percent did not. Had the "high risk" prediction been the basis for indefinite incarceration, nearly half the people sentenced would not, in fact, go on to commit any more acts of violence.

64 There is some evidence that a multidisciplinary team may be able to rival the accuracy of actuarial instruments. *See* J. Fuller and J. Cowan, *Risk Assessment in a Multidisciplinary Forensic Setting: Clinical Judgement Revisited*, 10 J. FORENSIC PSYCH., 276 (1999), acknowledging that a multidisciplinary team may provide increased accuracy approaching that of actuarial instruments. However, such teams are unlikely to be employed in capital-sentencing or sexual-predator determinations.

65 *See* Barbaree et al., *supra* note 23 at 492–5, noting VRAG correlations of 0.44 with violent recidivism; RRASOR correlations of 0.27 with sexual recidivism; Janus and Prentky, *supra* note 20, at 1471, noting the efficacy of VRAG, SORAG, and RRASOR and explaining that the "correlation between the SORAG and violent recidivism was 0.38." As these authors observed, "all [actuarial] instruments have shortcomings, and these shortcomings detract from the reliability of the instruments." Another measure of accuracy is a statistical analysis known as the Relative Operating Characteristic (ROC). Mark Binderman, *Understanding VRAG: The Violence Risk Assessment Guide*, in FORENSIC EXAMINER, Jan.–Feb. 2001, at 29. A test that is no better than chance would have an ROC of 0.50; the VRAG ROC was 0.76, which means that "if an offender were drawn randomly from each of the recidivist and nonrecidivist groups, there was a probability of 0.76 that the recidivist had the higher score on the VRAG." Quinsey et al., *supra* note 19, at 148. This is a statistically significant result, comparable to ROC scores for predictions in meteorology and medical imaging. Binderman, *supra* at 29.

66 *See, e.g.*, John Monahan and Henry Steadman, *Violent Storms and Violent People: How Meteorology Can Inform Risk Communication in Mental Health Law*, AM. PSYCHOLOGIST, Sept. 1996, 935–6, explaining that predictions of the risk of future violence should be modeled explicitly on weather predictions, with all their qualifiers and uncertainties.

67 *See* Mark. D. Cunningham and Thomas J. Reidy, *Don't Confuse Me With the Facts: Common Errors in Violence Risk Assessment at Capital Sentencing*, 26 CRIM. JUSTICE & BEHAV. 20, 36–8 (1999), advocating that experts limit their testimony to predominantly statistical analyses to avoid going beyond the limits of their scientific expertise.

environmental factors – such as stress, including drug and alcohol abuse – can increase the chances that a particular individual will become violent.[68] Indeed, many of the risk factors measured by actuarial assessments of violence risk may be tied to an underlying biological function. But no testable theoretical basis is advanced for why the chosen risk factors correlate with violence. Thus, a major problem with each of the risk instruments is a failure to correlate the risk factors with the biology of violence and to articulate a hypothesis for the mechanisms of violence. Until we have an understanding of how violence occurs, we will have little ability to control or predict it.

In sum, despite an ocean of literature explaining the flaws of expert behavioral predictions, legislatures continue to demand future-dangerousness predictions in the statutes they write as a politically expedient solution to the problem of sexual violence. Long aware that these predictions are tenuous at best, courts ignore their gatekeeping duties and admit future-dangerousness predictions into evidence. Experts, whose training and professional literature excoriate such testimony, continue to make future-dangerousness predictions.

While legislatures and judges are under enormous public pressure to "solve" the problem of sexually violent crime, admitting the dubious testimony of experts willing to testify that an individual poses a future danger to society is an easy – but disingenuous – answer. Whether one justifies the enforcement of social norms through a utilitarian calculus or by retributivist principles, or by some hybrid combination of the two, science ought to inform the debates both about what violence is preventable and about what controls are likely to be effective.

Law's moral authority is based on the accuracy of its assumptions and predictions. Admitting scientifically baseless expert testimony on future dangerousness into evidence is not only cynical, it also undermines law's moral authority. The very least we can do in a system that aspires to do justice is to be sure that the scientific testimony admitted in our courts has been tested, scrutinized, and properly limited. If what we seek is justice, and if justice depends on the willingness to seek the truth, the current charade undermines the rule of law.

---

68 Alcohol consumption, for example, which can effectively shut down the activity of small brain cells responsible for cortical function, figures into two of every three violent crimes. J. Roizen, *Issues of Epidemiology of Alcohol and Violence*, in ALCOHOL AND INTERPERSONAL VIOLENCE: FOSTERING MULTIDISCIPLINARY PERSPECTIVES (Susan E. Martin, ed., 1993).

9

Models of rationality: evaluating social psychology

Social psychology[1] is suddenly an important argument in law. Increasingly, references to framing effects, hindsight bias, overconfidence, and optimism bias, to name just a few, are pervading the legal literature.[2] Occasionally, such references even creep into court opinions.[3] Jury studies and eyewitness unreliability studies are the subject of admissibility disputes.[4] Behavioral studies are cited as support for everything from antitrust reform[5] and environmental reform[6] to failures in the securities markets.[7] In large measure, this use of social psychology is intended to counter the pervasive influence on legal scholarship (and jurisprudence) of the law and economics movement.

The use of social science for legal argument is by no means a bad thing because it reflects a growing awareness that law can become more effective by using scientific

---

1 I use the term interchangeably with cognitive psychology.
2 *See* Donald C. Langevoort, *Behavioral Theories of Judgment and Decision Making in Legal Scholarship: A Literature Review*, 51 Vand. L. Rev. 1499, 1501–1502 (1998), noting the existence of "heuristics, biases, and other departures from rational decision-making processes that are systematic and predictable"; Behavioral Law & Economics, 221–3 (Cass R. Sunstein, ed., 2000); Jeffrey L. Rachlinski, *Heuristics and Biases in the Courts: Ignorance or Adaptation*, 79 Or. L. Rev. 61 (2000), explaining that the brain's limited ability to process information leads people to rely on mental shortcuts, which "leaves people susceptible to all manner of illusions: visual, mnemonic, and judgmental."
3 See, e.g., *United States v. Shonubi*, 895 F. Supp. 460, 462 (E.D.N.Y., 1995), noting that "the sentencing judge may take note of the possibility of heuristic pitfalls, including 'availability,' which would suggest to the trier that every trip [as a drug courier] involved the amount known from the one trip that is familiar, and 'anchoring,' which would lead to the persistence of early decisions", vacated, 103 F. 3d, 1085 (2d Cir., 1997), on other grounds.
4 See, e.g., *People v. Smith*, 2004 WL 960321, slip op., N.Y. Sup. Ct., March 26, 2004, excluding expert testimony on the unreliability of eyewitness testimony based, in part, on the research being conducted on mock juries and noting "serious issues as to whether [mock jury] studies reflect the tasks set before an actual jury."
5 *See, e.g.,* Troy A. Paredes, *Blinded by the Light: Information Overload and Its Consequences for Securities Regulation*, 18 Wash. U. L. Q. 417, 419 (2003).
6 See, e.g., Cass R. Sunstein, *Lives, Life-Years, and Willingness to Pay*, 104 Colum. L. Rev. 205 (2004).
7 See John C. Coffee, *What Caused Enron? A Capsule Social and Economic History of the 1990s*, 89 Cornell L. Rev., 269, 295 (2003), noting "the 'availability heuristic' that has special relevance to the context of securities markets"; Stephen J. Choi and A.C. Pritchard, *Behavioral Economics and the SEC*, 56 Stan. L. Rev., 1 (2003), discussing a number of heuristics in the context of market regulation.

insights into human behavior. However, to properly apply these insights, legal actors (i.e., scholars, judges, and lawyers) need to be intellectually careful to minimize the risk of abuse. With little analysis of the research on which it is based, thousands of legal articles have cited to various aspects of social psychology as though it were accepted dogma, like the laws of thermodynamics. Worse, these legal scholars occasionally attempt to replicate psychological experiments in their own classrooms (and cite such findings as support for their arguments) without any of the benefits of scientific process.[8] Partly because the social psychology research on which they relied was not well integrated with biological knowledge, legal use of social psychology has been woefully unsophisticated.

Although there are many facets to social and cognitive psychology, the research strategies are similar, as is the criticism of these strategies. Because it is achieving widespread notoriety in legal scholarship (including arguments made in this book) and because it purports to counter the highly successful law and economics movement, this chapter focuses on evaluating the use of social psychology in legal argument. The advocates of behavioral economics need a more sophisticated approach to scientific research. No viable framework for interdisciplinary evaluation has yet emerged, however. This chapter's goal is to provide such a framework, contending that with a more nuanced appreciation of the strengths and weaknesses of social psychology, it has much to offer legal theory.

Behavioral economics versus law and economics: a tale of two theories

Behavioral economics evolved from social psychology as a challenge to economists' assertions that rational choice involves maximizing utility.[9] As Gary Becker explained the principle of maximizing expected utility, "All human behavior can be viewed as involving participants who maximize their utility from a stable set of preferences and accumulate an optimal amount of information and other inputs from

---

8 For example, one empirical demonstration of the endowment effect is the mugs experiment performed by Jolls et al., designed to test the Coasian prediction that (absent transaction costs) initial assignment of legal entitlement is irrelevant. *See* Christine Jolls, et al., *Theories and Tropes: A Reply to Posner and Kelman*, 50 Stan. L. Rev. 1593, 1601 (1998), describing the impact of the mugs study. In this experiment, students who were given mugs refused to part with them for less than twice the cost of the same mugs in the school bookstore. *See* Behavioral Law & Economics, 221–3 (Cass R. Sunnstein, ed., 2000), describing experiment. Although providing interesting anecdotes, this kind of "experimentation" is performed without any of the benefits of scientific process, such as controls, detailed analysis, statistical modeling, examination of other explanations for the data, or peer review, to name a few.

9 *See* Gerd Gigerenzer and Reinhard Selten, *Rethinking Rationality*, in Bounded Rationality: The Adaptive Toolbox (G. Gigerenzer and R. Selten, eds., 2002), explaining that "bounded rationality, as we understand it, dispenses with optimization" and discussing biases research; Thomas Gilovich and Dale Griffen, *Introduction – Heuristics and Biases: Then and Now*, in Heuristics and Biases: The Psychology of Intuitive Judgment, 1 (Thomas Gilovich et al., eds., 2002), noting that "the modern history of research on everyday judgment must take note of the large shadow cast by the classical model of rational choice."

a variety of markets."[10] But social psychologists observed that human beings do not act optimally in a large number of situations.[11] Social psychologists contend that where people make judgments under conditions of uncertainty (i.e., where there are no clear answers), they are particularly likely to use shortcuts.[12] They claim that people use these common heuristics unconsciously and automatically.[13]

Using the rational-actor model as the null hypothesis that must be falsified has resulted in a large body of research demonstrating a number of ways in which people do not behave as that model would predict.[14] This is both the strength and the weakness of behavioral economics. It is the strength because virtually no one believes anymore that rational-choice models of human decision making reflect reality.[15] Although some scholars contend that some of these heuristics and biases may be artifacts of the experimental setting, virtually no one thinks systematic biases are illusory.

The weakness of the theory, however, is that by equating the null hypothesis with the rational-actor theory, social psychologists have failed to propose an alternative unifying theory. As interesting as the perceived anomalies may be, data without an underlying theory of behavior are fairly useless.[16] Moreover, what has been

---

10 GARY BECKER, THE ECONOMIC APPROACH TO HUMAN BEHAVIOR, 14 (1976).

11 See, e.g., Amos Tversky and Daniel Kahneman, *Rational Choice and the Framing of Decisions*, in RATIONAL CHOICE: THE CONTRAST BETWEEN ECONOMICS AND PSYCHOLOGY, 91 (R. M. Hogarth and M. W. Reder, eds., 1987), concluding that the "normative and descriptive analyses of choice should be viewed as separate enterprises."

12 These "quirks" are often called heuristics and biases but, whatever they are called, the idea is that people take cognitive shortcuts as a strategy for processing information. *See* JOHN W. PAYNE, ET AL., THE ADAPTIVE DECISION MAKER, 34 (1993), noting that "as decisions become more complex, people will tend to use simplifying heuristics." These are not irrational responses, although the resulting decision may be less than optimal.

13 See Richard Selton, *What Is Bounded Rationality?*, in BOUNDED RATIONALITY: THE ADAPTIVE TOOLBOX, 16 (G. Gigerenzer and R. Selten, eds., 2002), explaining that "[m]uch of human behavior is automatized" and that "[e]ven thinking is based on automatized routine"; Daniel Kahneman and Shane Frederick, *Representativeness Revisited: Attribute Substitution in Intuitive Judgment*, in HEURISTICS AND BIASES: THE PSYCHOLOGY OF INTUITIVE JUDGMENT 49, 58 (Thomas Gilovich et al., eds., 2002), describing "judgment by heuristic as an intuitive and unintentional process" but acknowledging that it is "highly plausible" that some heuristics are a "deliberate strategy."

14 See, e.g., Joachim Krueger, *The Bet on Bias: A Foregone Conclusion?* 9 PSYCHOLOQUY 46 (1999) observing the ease with which the rationality assumption is shown to be false. Even before the social psychologists began their heuristics and biases research program, Popper remarked that falsifying the rationality assumption was a foregone conclusion. Popper noted that anyone seeing drivers at a traffic circle could observe that most people did not act rationally. KARL R. POPPER, THE POVERTY OF HISTORICISM 95 (1961).

15 See, e.g., Bernard Grofman, *On the Gentle Art of Rational Choice Bashing*, in INFORMATION, PARTICIPATION, AND CHOICE, 239, 240 (Bernard Grofman, ed., 1993), "Only an idiot (or an economist) would claim that rational choice models can explain all of human behavior." Even critics of behavioral economics, such as Professor Mitchell, acknowledge that "there is indisputable empirical proof that humans often fail to achieve perfect rationality in their judgment and decision-making behavior." Gregory Mitchell, *Mapping Evidence Law*, 2003 MICHIGAN ST. L. REV., 1065, note 23.

16 See, e.g., Mark Klock, *Finding Random Coincidences While Searching for the Holy Writ of Truth: Specification Searches in Law and Public Policy or Cum Hoc Ergo Propter Hoc*, 2001 WISC. L. REV.,

notably absent until recently (from law and economics as well as social psychology) is interdisciplinary cross-pollination. Neither law and economics nor social psychology have drawn on the explosion of information that has been occurring in neuroscience.

This is especially a problem for social psychologists because, for a number of biases, moderating factors make it difficult to predict which bias will predominate. To remedy this, researchers have been attempting to formulate more precise theories about the processes underlying sound reasoning, and cross-references to developments in related fields are becoming more common.[17] Gerd Gigerenzer, for example, acknowledges that any viable theory of decision making must incorporate human biology as well as the structure of the evolutionary environment in which these processes evolved.[18] Reid Hastie and Robyn Dawes similarly claim that any analysis of the decision-making process ought to take into account biological and evolutionary processes as well as the context of the decision making.[19] Increasingly, even economists recognize that because the world is uncertain, efficient solutions must encompass the notions of probability theory, and they admit that economic formulations are merely the starting point for analysis.[20]

This makes sense because decision making is an inherently biological process, involving the connections among perception, brain, and behavior, interactive with other people and with the outside world.[21] Social psychologists increasingly

1007, 1038, explaining that "random data creates patterns" and that in the absence of a particular hypothesis that is being tested, given a sufficiently large search, spurious patterns can result in spurious theories of relationship. Just because the theoretical underpinnings of social psychology research are still contentious, however, does not denigrate its finding that rational utility theory is demonstrably false in numerous instances.

17 *See, e.g.*, Steven A. Sloman, *Two Systems of Reasoning*, in HEURISTICS & BIASES, note 12, 379, 384, noting "a dual process neuropsychological theory of category learning that parallels the associative/rule-based dichotomy," citing Ashby, et al., *A New Psychological Theory of Multiple Systems in Category Learning*, 105 PSYCHOL. REV., 442–8 (1998).

18 *See* Gigerenzer and Selten, note 9, p. 6, explaining the theory of bounded rationality and describing its genesis from Simon's theory of the interaction of biology and the evolutionary environment. Recently, there have been attempts to put behavioral-decision theory in a wider context of biological interactive systems. See, e.g., REID HASTIE & ROBYN DAWES, RATIONAL CHOICE IN AN UNCERTAIN WORLD xi–xiv; 1–19 (2001), discussing decision making in the context of biology, evolutionary biology, and social context.

19 *See* Hastie and Dawes, *supra* p. 2, claiming that "[m]ost of the conclusions in this book follow from research conducted by psychologists, economists, and biologists."

20 *See* PAUL W. GLIMCHER, DECISIONS, UNCERTAINTY, AND THE BRAIN 208 (2003). In David Stephens' and John Krebs' bird-foraging experiments, for example, although they predicted birds encountering both large and small worms at a certain frequency would maximize efficiency by going after only large and ignoring small worms, they did so only 85 percent of the time rather than the 100 percent predicted by theory. Id., 208–23 (describing these experiments and concluding that in an uncertain world, "the birds occasionally select a small worm in order to update an internal estimate of the relative profitability of the two prey types . . . the birds probably are behaving optimally; it is the mathematical model that is in error.")

21 Evolutionary biologists have started from the premise that "animals must generate efficient solutions to the problems their environments present in order to maximize the rate at which their genes are propagated." Glimcher, *supra* p. 207. For a discussion of the evolution of sexual signals

recognize that the way human beings think is a product of evolutionary history and depends not only on brain structure but also on adaptive responses to the environment (including other human beings).[22] The nervous system – including the brain – evolved to connect sensation and action.[23] In animals, behavioral strategies that promote survival and reproductive success tend to become genetically programmed.[24] In humans also, genes for behavior are subject to natural selection just as are genes for toes and strong thumbs.[25]

Social psychologists recognize that natural selection does not mean, however, that the existing status quo – such as our current pattern of behavior, including decision making – is necessarily the optimal solution to problems facing a species. Random events play a role in natural selection[26] as do cooperation and competition.[27] Interactions of individuals with each other, with other creatures, and with their environment are reciprocal affairs and mutually interdependent.[28]

in primate species as a function of social competition for attention, see Jared Diamond, Why Is Sex Fun?, 140–41 (1997).

22 The view of natural selection as "survival of the fittest" is often characterized as Darwinian, but Darwin's view was far more subtle. See Charles Darwin, On the Origin of Species (1859; 1964 facsimile of 1st ed.), describing natural selection as the evolutionary "preservation of favorable variations and the rejection of injurious variations" and recognizing that these variations would occur randomly. Strongly influenced by Malthus, Darwin understood the complex interactions of living creatures and explained natural selection as favoring increasing divergence of new species that are able to adapt to the varying aspects of their environment. See Richard Sole and Brian Goodwin, Signs of Life: How Complexity Pervades Biology, 247–8 (2000).

23 Glimcher, note 20, p. 112, discussing the connections between brain, mind, and behavior.

24 See Jared Diamond, The Third Chimpanzee 18 (1999), noting that although animals do not make conscious choices about behavioral strategies, it is "choice" in the sense of pursuing one of several alternatives through differences in anatomy, physiology, or instinct.

25 Id. at 16, explaining that parenting "choices" are genetically programmed. Genes, however, do not mandate life outcomes; genes, environment, and social context interact with opportunity for each individual. See Richard J. Rose, Genes and Human Behavior, 46 Ann. Rev. Psychol. 625 (1995), explaining that although obesity is heritable, even identical twins often show different weight changes in response to uniform diet or standardized exercise. Moreover, genes for instinctive behavior frequently do not become active until they are triggered by an environmental cue. See, e.g., Matt Ridley, Nature via Nurture, 48–9 (2003), using as an example the fighting behavior of the male stickleback fish, which is triggered in the presence of a red belly on even a crudely designed model, but not in its absence, citing N. Tinbergen, The Study of Instinct (1951). In mice bred with the same genotype for aggressiveness, the aggressive behavior only manifested if the mice were handled by humans as babies. People, too, appear to have genetic components of aggression that are triggered by environmental influences. See id. pp. 267–8, discussing studies of the expression of the monamine oxidase A gene – MAOA – in which men with highly active MAOA genes rarely exhibited behavioral aggression, whether they were mistreated as children or not, but men with low-activity MAOA genes were more sensitive to both mistreatment (producing adults with antisocial behavioral problems) and good treatment (producing well-adapted adults). Ridley notes that this low-activity MAOA gene is found in about 37 percent of men. Id., p. 268.

26 See Stephen J. Gould, Wonderful Life: The Burgess Shale and the Nature of History (1989), explaining the explosion of new species at the beginning of the Cambrian Age and the relatively slow pace of evolution since.

27 See Stuart Kauffman, At Home in the Universe: The Search for the Laws of Self-Organization and Complexity, 215 (1995), describing evolution as "coupled dancing landscapes" in which all creatures evolve together and in response to each other.

28 See Kauffman supra at 217, observing that humans are not the only creatures that cooperate; flowers and the insects pollinating them "cooperate" in the sense that they coevolve.

Natural selection does not occur in a vacuum.[29] Creatures evolve new traits – including behavior – in response to their environment and to each other.[30] Sometimes cooperation will leave more genetic copies than competition.[31] For this (unconscious) reason, individuals often act against self-interest, the interest of their families, and the interests of their group, as long as their acts benefit their genes in the long run.[32] And, sometimes it takes a crisis for the genes that eventually predominate to become successful.[33] All of these facets of evolution have important implications for a theory of human decision making, and social psychologists now explicitly recognize this.[34]

Social psychologists, however, have yet to incorporate evolutionary biology into solving the problem of context. Context, or "moderating factors," affects the heuristic chosen. For example, depending on the context, people produce apparently

29 Complexity theory recognizes the continuous interaction of individuals with the whole system of which they are a part, responding to both random events and dynamic phenomena. *See* RICHARD SOLE AND BRIAN GOODWIN, SIGNS OF LIFE: HOW COMPLEXITY PERVADES BIOLOGY 20 (2000), noting the "continuous conversation between parts and wholes."

30 *See* Diamond, note 24, pp. 10–11, explaining that by natural selection, "Darwin meant that plants and animals vary in their anatomical adaptations, that certain adaptations enable individuals bearing them to survive and reproduce more successfully than other individuals, and that those particular adaptations therefore increase in frequency in a population from generation to generation."

31 As Randolph Nesse explained, "tendencies to altruism are shaped by benefits to genes. . . . " Commentary in D.S. Wilson and E. Sober, *Reintroducing Group Selection to the Human and Behavioral Sciences*, 17 BEHAVIORAL AND BRAIN SCIENCES, 585–684 (1994). An example of this behavior is found in bees defending the hive at their own peril, not because they are concerned about the hive's survival, but in order to assure survival of the genes the bees share with their sisters in the hive. See E. Szathmary and J. Maynard Smith, *The Major Evolutionary Transitions*, 374 NATURE 227–32 (1995).

32 *See* W. D. Hamilton, *The Genetical Evolution of Social Behavior*, 7 J. THEORETICAL BIOLOGY, 1–52 (1964), interpreting the selfless behavior of ants in caring for their sisters' offspring as the behavior motivated by the selfish genes of the ants, because chances of genetic survival are greater by acting selflessly than by procreating individually. Conversely, even relationships that have always been assumed to be altruistic, such as the mother's nurture of her child in utero, have an element of competition. *See* D. Haig, *Genetic Conflicts in Human Pregnancy*, 68 QUARTERLY REVIEW OF BIOLOGY, 495–531 (1993), describing the hormonal conflicts between mother and child over blood-sugar levels as an example of diverging genetic interests. This paradox of how harmony prevails over selfishness in biological terms is resolved by understanding that for each self-interested gene that would be only too happy to individually self-maximize (e.g., in the form of cancer, the paradigmatic mutiny of selfish cells), there are many others that will combine to suppress it. *See* EGBERT LEIGH, ADAPTATION AND DIVERSITY (1971), "It is as if we had to do with a parliament of genes: each acts in its own self-interest, but if its acts hurt others, they will combine together to suppress it."

33 *See* Gould (*Wonderful Life*), note 26, p. 51, presenting the punctuated equilibrium theory of evolution. The punctuated equilibrium theory of evolution claims that once creatures reach a plateau of evolution, their genetic characteristics are relatively stable until there is a crisis – great climate change, for example – when most of the species will die off, except for a few with advantageous mutations. Id. This is a controversial theory that has yet to be resolved. *See* RICHARD DAWKINS, RIVER OUT OF EDEN: A DARWINIAN VIEW OF LIFE, 11, 83 (1995), articulating a gradual view of evolution.

34 See, e.g., Hastie and Dawes, note 18, p. 95, explaining the use of heuristics as an evolutionary adaptation; Gilovich and Griffen, note 11, p. 10, claiming that the heuristics and biases approach is an evolutionary account; Gigerenzer and Selten, note 9, pp. 8–9, explaining the concept of heuristics as an evolutionary adaptive toolbox.

opposite biases to the same decision problem. One scenario that produces apparently opposite biases has to do with base-rate neglect. When people who have estimated the contents of a jar of red- and blue-colored marbles are asked what a sample of colored marbles tells them about the contents of a jar of marbles, they typically respond conservatively; that is, they underestimate the importance of information given by the sample. Krueger explains that "judgments are conservative [in the sense of failing to update information] when they refer to the population and when sample information is pallid."[35] On the other hand, when the test involves vivid examples of particular instances, people tend to overestimate the importance of the sample in relation to the population to which these samples belong (as, for example, capital juries, who overestimate the incidence of violent recidivism because of vivid media accounts of rare events).

Similarly, people tend to go in opposite directions with respect to perceptions of randomness. In the "hot hand fallacy," for example, people misperceive a process of chance as one of skill.[36] In the gambler's fallacy, people tend to incorrectly believe that random processes will self-correct in the short run.[37] Thus, although peoples' intuitions about chance appear to depart systematically from the laws of probability, they do so in opposite directions.[38] In the hot hand fallacy, they expect wins in a random sequence to continue to produce wins, while in the gambler's fallacy, on the other hand, they expect even short sequences to reflect the probability distribution. No evolutionary or biological explanation has yet been incorporated into an explanation for these observations.

Research on self-perception similarly points in two directions, depending on the context. In studies of overconfidence, in what is often called the hard/easy effect, task difficulty appears to be a moderator. If the test subjects are asked to assess their ability to get along with others, they typically overestimate their peers' assessment (presumably because most people think getting along with others is easy). On the other hand, subjects underestimate their peers' assessment of their acting ability (presumably considered difficult). Neglect of base rates can thus lead to both overconfidence and underconfidence.[39] Apparently, "people are prone to

---

35 See Joachim Krueger, *Three Ways to Get Two Biases by Rejecting One Null*, 11 Psycholoquy, 51 (2000), http://www.cogsci.ecs.soton.ac.uk/cgi/psyc/newpsy?11.051, discussing the importance of moderator variables and the studies that demonstrate that importance.

36 For a discussion of the "hot hand fallacy," see Thomas Gilovich, et al., *The Hot Hand in Basketball: On the Misperception of Random Sequences*, in Heuristics & Biases, note 13, p. 601, describing studies.

37 The reason these are "misperceptions" is explained by the law of large numbers. As Suppes explains, "the concept of independence is one of the most profound and fundamental ideas, not only of probability theory but of science in general." Patrick Suppes, A Probabilistic Theory of Causality, 109 (1970). Two events, A and B, are independent when $P(A/B) = P(A)$. David A. Schum, The Evidential Foundations of Probabilistic Reasoning, 150–1 (1994). The concept of independence asserts that discrete biological or physical events, like coin tosses, have no memory of time and place. Lynn A. Steen, *The Science of Patterns*, 240 Sci., 611 (1988).

38 *See* Gilovich, et al., *supra* note 36, at 601, noting that the "conception of chance based on representativeness ... produces two related biases."

39 *See* Dale Griffen and Amos Tversky, *The Weighting of Evidence and the Determinants of Confidence*, in Heuristics & Biases, *supra* note 13, pp. 230, 236, observing that base-rate "neglect can lead to

overconfidence when the base rate is low and to underconfidence when the base rate is high."[40] The explanation for this is that "the judged probability of an event depends on the explicitness of its description."[41]

The open question for decision theorists at this stage is delineating the circumstances in which once-adaptive behaviors are now counterproductive, how prevalent the use of shortcuts is in real-world situations, and how to identify which of the multiple heuristics that could be drawn on for decision making will come into play in a given situation. Not all evolutionary solutions are optimal,[42] but at least some of the specialized cognitive mechanisms humans evolved to deal with decision making in a complex world must have been adaptive.[43] How well they remain so, and under what modern circumstances they become active, remains to be elucidated.[44]

To what extent our human choices are the result of natural selection and to what extent we make counterevolutionary choices are similarly mysterious. As evolutionary biologist Jared Diamond remarked, "Most of us choose to renounce murder, rape and genocide, despite their advantages as a means for transmitting our genes, and despite their widespread occurrence among other animal species and earlier human societies."[45] To what extent heuristics and biases are the result of "instinct," programmed into us by natural selection, is still highly controversial. Whether a particular bias is the result of the failure to consciously use (or know) a normative

either underconfidence or overconfidence" and discussing studies of this effect that "contradict the claim . . . that explicit random sampling eliminates base-rate neglect." Overconfidence may be something of a misnomer; what is meant is a miscalibration between information people have available and their confidence. *See, e.g.*, Baruch Fischoff, *Heuristics and Biases in Application*, Heuristics and Biases, note 13, pp. 730, 733, explaining that overconfidence is "a mismatch between how confident people are and how confident they should be (given how much they know)."

40 Griffen and Tversky, *supra* note 39, at 237.

41 Amos Tversky and Derek J. Koehler, *Support Theory: A Nonextensional Representation of Subjective Probability*, in Heuristics & Biases, note 13, pp. 441, 443, explaining the basis for support theory, which asserts that "failures of extensionality . . . represent an essential feature of human judgment." Extensionality is defined as the idea that "events with the same extension are assigned the same probability." *Id.*, at 442. In other words, support theory challenges the idea that probability theory even applies to analysis of belief or that subjective degrees of belief can be quantified. The explanation for these opposite judgment strategies is provided by support theory, which describes judgment as an assessment of competing hypotheses, the more explicit of which will prevail. Lyle A. Brenner, et al., *Remarks on Support Theory: Recent Advances and Future Directions*, in Heuristics & Biases, note 13, at 489. For example, support theory explains the above-average effect (where most people rate themselves as happier, better drivers, and less likely to suffer a heart attack than their peers) as a consequence of having a more vivid description of oneself than anonymous peers.

42 See, e.g., Gilovich and Griffen, *supra* note 9, pp. 9–10, noting the presence of evolutionary anomalies in the animal kingdom, such as warblers raising cuckoo chicks and lions stalking prey upwind.

43 These decision-making strategies must on the whole have been advantageous, at least in terms of survival and reproduction, because as Quine remarked, "Creatures inveterately wrong in their inductions have a pathetic but praiseworthy tendency to die before reproducing their kind." Willard V. Quine, *Natural Kinds*, in Ontological Relativity and Other Essays, 114, 126 (1969).

44 See Gerd Gigerenzer, et al., Simple Heuristics that Make Us Smart (1999), proposing the analogy of an "adaptive toolbox" of multiple heuristics that can be drawn on for particular circumstances.

45 Diamond, *supra* note 24, at 62.

rule or the result of automatic processes is also far from clear.[46] Thus, whereas the social psychologists' program of research has succeeded well in showing that the rational-actor model of decision making is violated in many contexts and has identified particular ways in which this model is violated, a theory for which of multiple heuristics might be used in any given circumstance is still under construction.

What assumptions underlie the theory?

The debate about the scientific validity of social psychology research has three primary components and mimics the debate about the methodology of other social science evidence. These are primarily debates about methodology, and involve the use of laboratory settings rather than real-world contexts for hypothesis testing; the use of college students as test subjects; and averaging experimental results across groups of test subjects.

Decision theorists claim that the heuristics and biases they have discovered are employed across the spectrum of decision makers, at least under certain conditions. They claim that these patterns of thinking are widespread in the population – everyone is subject to them, although not in the same degree and not uniformly. They also claim that statistical techniques can address the problem of individual variance. The next section on methodology will address each of these concerns.

Methodology: experimental design in social psychology research

The role of statistics in social psychologists' experimental design

One of the common critiques of decision research is that it is done on small groups of people. Recall from Chapter 3 that the conventional wisdom in experimental design is that large samples (on a large number of subjects) are better than small ones. Small sample size may present a problem because when the sample (study) is small, using few individual measurements, the variance[47] and standard deviation[48] increase, and the confidence intervals widen.[49] This decreases the power (or sensitivity) of the test to detect changes.[50] If either standard deviation or confidence intervals are large, the

---

46 See, e.g., H. R. Arkes, *Costs and Benefits of Judgment Errors: Implications for Debiasing*, 110 Psychol. Bull. 486–98 (1991), discussing the two possible bases for biased reasoning; Walter C. Sa and Keith E. Stanovich, *The Domain Specificity and Generality of Mental Contamination: Accuracy and Projection in Judgments of Mental Content*, Brit. J. Psychol., May 1, 2001, 2001 WL 19139214, discussing biases as a result of mental contamination from automatic processes.

47 Variance is the square of the standard deviation. Theodore Colton, Statistics in Medicine 412 (1974)Id.

48 Recall that the standard deviation indicates how far two particular data points deviate from the mean. With some variability, researchers expect the data to cluster around the mean in a characteristic manner. *See* discussion in Chapters 3 and 4.

49 The confidence interval is an estimate for a quantity in a population. *Id.* Thus, when only a few data points are used, there may be statistical significance for rejecting the null hypothesis, but confidence intervals detract from the study's conclusions.

50 Stephen E. Fienberg et al., *Understanding and Evaluating Statistical Evidence in Litigation*, 36 Jurimetrics J. 1, 22 (1995).

study included too small a number of observations (or data points) or the method used to measure the data was imprecise.[51]

The problem of small sample sizes is by no means unique to social psychology. It is a common problem in epidemiology and toxicology, for example. One way to counter the problem of small sample sizes is to repeat the study.[52] Increases in power can also be accomplished by adjusting significance levels and reducing error variance.[53] For example, in toxicology, the availability of a variety of studies in different disciplines showing association of agent and disease permits scientists to make valid causal inferences even in the absence of statistical significance. Statistical significance, however, does not appear to be the focus of the legal critics of social psychology, as is so often the case in epidemiology and toxicology.

Using college students as subjects

Rather, these critics are concerned about the widespread use of convenience samples in social psychology. The prevalent use of college students as experimental subjects is frequently criticized.[54] Although statistical analyses rely on the assumption that errors are independently and randomly sampled from a single normally distributed population, social psychology research rarely meets this standard.[55] Random sampling from a well-specified population to test hypotheses is not used; instead, randomization is limited to the process of obtaining equivalent sample groups.[56]

---

51 *See* Colton, note 47 at 194, noting common statistical errors.
52 *See* IAN HACKING, THE EMERGENCE OF PROBABILITY 148 (1975), quoting Heisenberg as solving the problem by "repeating the experiment many times."
53 *See* Charles M. Judd, et al., *Data Analysis: Continuing Issues in the Everyday Analysis of Psychological Data*, 1995 ANN. REV. PSYCHOL. 433, explaining that "there is nothing sacred about an alpha level arbitrarily set at .05" and that "power can be increased by standard methods of improving the reliability of the dependent variable, such as the use of better measures and of multiple measures."
54 *See* Eliot Aronson et al., *Experimentation in Social Psychology*, in HANDBOOK OF SOCIAL PSYCHOLOGY, 99, 130 (Daniel T. Gilbert et al., eds., 4th ed., 1998), noting that "social psychology is criticized as being 'the psychology of the college sophomore'" and explaining that external validity – the generalizability of a study – depends on replicating the study in a variety of contexts.
55 *See* Robyn M. Dawes, *Behavioral Decision Making and Judgment*, in Vol. 1, HANDBOOK OF SOCIAL PSYCHOLOGY 503 (Daniel T. Gilbert et al., eds., 1998), noting that rather than random sampling, "in experiments in behavioral decision making, statistics are computed as if the subjects have been randomly selected from a well-specified population of "people" about whom we wish to generalize." Violations of randomness assumptions should be noted but may be solved with statistical transformations that correct for the violations. *See* MICHAEL O. FINKELSTEIN & BRUCE LEVIN, STATISTICS FOR LAWYERS, 339–40 (1990) (explaining that nonparametric tests, which "hold no matter what distribution may underlie the observations," and noting that because when parametric tests apply they are more powerful, the tradeoff for nonparametric tests is "power for robustness against departures from distributional assumptions"). Among these tests are the Wilcoxon signed-rank test and Wilcoxon rank-sum test, and these "have remarkably high efficiency relative to the best parametric tests – 90% or better – so that the loss of efficiency is of lesser concern." *Id.* at 341.
56 *See* JEANE W. ANASTAS, RESEARCH DESIGN FOR SOCIAL WORK AND THE HUMAN SERVICES 291 (2d ed. 1999) explaining that "experiments depend on their internal logic and often on their ability to achieve equivalent groups within the study sample at least as much as on how people were selected to participate in the study to begin with." The issue of random assignment is handled differently in within-subjects and between-subjects experimental designs. In within-subjects designs, the participants serve as their own controls by being exposed to a number of conditions. In

Limiting randomization to obtaining equivalent sample groups is not fatal to the research, however. For one thing, very little research on humans can meet these standards and in human research, generally, this assumption is routinely violated.

The point of random sampling is to obtain a sample most likely to be representative of the population of interest.[57] Random sampling is the ideal way to achieve a sample that represents the universe of people in which the variable being studied exists.[58] True random sampling is an ideal that is frequently unreachable, however, even in medical research, which often depends on volunteers who are in many ways uncharacteristic of the target population.[59]

Although college students – like most volunteers in medical research – may differ from the general population in many ways (e.g., intelligence, socioeconomic status, and age), the operative question is whether the ways in which the volunteers differ from the target population would bias the results. The default assumption of generalizability is made in most medical research. In the context of epidemiology testimony, courts have little difficulty with the presumption that humans are functionally equivalent.[60]

The assumption being made by social psychologists is that college students' brains function in more or less the same fashion as everyone else's. There are good reasons for employing the assumption that people think pretty much alike, despite variations in intelligence and temperament. First, people are biologically very similar.[61] Second, biologically speaking, people's thought processes develop as the brain does,

between-subjects experiments, the subjects are randomly assigned to different levels of the independent variable. *See* Aronson, *supra* note 54, at p. 113.

57 CHRIS SPATZ, BASIC STATISTICS: TALES OF DISTRIBUTIONS, 138 (5th ed., 1993); Colton, supra note 47, at 4, explaining that the "target population is that population about which the investigator wishes to draw a conclusion," whereas the "population sampled is that population from which the sample actually was drawn and about which a conclusion can be made."

58 As Anastas explains, p. 135:

> If the research interest is in describing a phenomenon ... then the sampling method should include a way to identify ... the entire population ... in which the phenomenon exists. Then, using some credibly random process, the subset of that population that will comprise the study sample can be identified and selected from that list. Provided that the random sample is also large, chances are very good that sample statistics will provide an acceptably accurate and stable basis for drawing inferences about how the phenomenon would be likely to look in other cases also from the population ....

59 See GLEN MCPHERSON, STATISTICS IN SCIENTIFIC INVESTIGATION, 39 (1990), noting that medical researchers must often rely on volunteers and that "there may be strong grounds for arguing that the method of sampling can reasonably be claimed to possess the properties of random sampling which underlie the preferred statistical methods."

60 See, e.g., Tyler, 19 F. Supp. 2d, at 1239; *Arnold v. Dow Chemical Co.,* 32 F. Supp. 2d, 584 (E.D.N.Y., 1999); *Sy v. United Parcel Service General Services Co.,* No. Civ. 94–1464-FR, 1999 WL 39550 (D. Or., January 22, 1999); *Hand v. Norfolk So. Ry. Co.,* No. 03A01–9704-CV00123, 1998 WL 281946 (Tenn. Ct. App., June 2, 1998).

61 *See* ANTONIO DAMASIO, THE FEELING OF WHAT HAPPENS: BODY AND EMOTION IN THE MAKING OF CONSCIOUSNESS, 85 explaining why it is valid to assume that "we as human beings, in spite of remarkable individual traits that make each of us unique, share similar biological characteristics, in terms of structure, organization, and function of our organism."

are based on brain activity, and brains as well as thought processes are remarkably consistent across cultures.[62] Although people unquestionably have different cultural experiences that influence their thinking to some degree, there are basic similarities in memory and learning that are pervasive and transcend language and culture.[63] In fact, from an evolutionary perspective, the processing of information in both humans and animals is remarkably similar.[64]

There is no *a priori* reason to think that college students would exhibit more biased reasoning than other segments of the population. The hypothesis being tested is whether college students – presumably as least as rational as the general population – violate rationality in predictable ways. If anything, it should be more difficult to demonstrate bias using college students than a random sample of the population because education theoretically trains students to think carefully. Moreover, using college students has an advantage because these subjects tend to be of similar age, socioeconomic background, education, and intelligence, and homogeneity increases the power of the study.[65] Furthermore, the automatic nature of heuristic thinking is believed to precede conscious thought (and, therefore, to be unaffected by education level).[66] For example, in a test of the perceptual matching bias (sometimes called the "not-heuristic"), researchers were able to demonstrate that neither task repetition nor logical training enabled subjects to change their strategy.[67]

---

62 *See, e.g.*, MERLIN DONALD, A MIND SO RARE: THE EVOLUTION OF HUMAN CONSCIOUSNESS, 112 (2001) explaining that, in the process of evolution, "we have not only kept our vestigial primate brain but also retained many of the underlying cognitive traits that go with it"; Baruch Fischoff, *Strategic Policy Preferences: A Behavioral Decision Theory Perspective*, 39 J. Soc. ISSUES 133 (1983), noting that "the thought processes of most uninstitutionalized adults are quite similar."

63 Memory, for example, is a dynamic systemic property of neurons in which the brain records how the body explores and reacts to the world. *See* ANTONIO DAMASIO, LOOKING FOR SPINOZA: JOY, SORROW, AND THE FEELING BRAIN, 15–19 (2003). For a discussion of the crosscultural use of metaphor, *generally* STEVEN WINTER, A CLEARING IN THE FOREST (2002).

64 *See* Leslie A. Real, *Animal Choice Behavior and the Evolution of Cognitive Architecture*, 253 SCI., 980, citing studies in animals and humans.

65 *See, e.g.*, Daniel B. Wright, *People, Materials, and Situations*, in LABORATORY PSYCHOLOGY: A BEGINNER'S GUIDE 97, 101 (Julia Nunn, ed., 1998), "If the sample from which the groups are randomly allocated is homogeneous, then this within-group variation is likely to be smaller and therefore if a difference is present, it is more likely to be detected with a homogeneous sample. In statistical terminology, the power is increased."

66 It may well be that covert biases assist the reasoning process in a cooperative manner. *See* Antoine Bechara, et al., *Deciding Advantageously Before Knowing the Advantageous Strategy*, 275 SCI. 1293 (1997), describing experiments involving a gambling task in which players were given four decks of cards, two of which contained penalties that led to overall losses and two of which led to an overall gain, in which normal participants began to generate autonomic skin conductance responses to the bad decks even before they were able to generate a "hunch" about the riskier decks; subjects who had amygdalar lesions did not generate anticipatory autonomic responses and continued to select cards from the riskier decks even after they were able to correctly identify the decks as risky, leading to the conclusion that nonconscious emotional pathways are engaged in the processing of knowledge and logic.

67 Olivier Houde, et al., *Shifting from the Perceptual Brain to the Logical Brain: The Neural Impact of Cognitive Inhibition Training*, 12 J. COGNITIVE NEUROSCIENCE 721 (2000), describing experiments in which people tend to prefer items mentioned in a rule (e.g., the rule "if there is not a red square on the left, then there is a yellow circle on the right") and neglect logically correct answers (e.g.,

In this respect also, the importance of a research program becomes apparent. In most of the well-studied heuristics and biases, such as framing effects, over-optimism, and the like, the heuristics have been tested in many settings and with people – experts and lay people, not just college students – from many cultures.[68] As with research programs that include studies on animals and humans, observational field studies, and laboratory experiments, studies using convenience samples become more trustworthy if the behavior is seen in studies of different types among different people.[69]

Individual studies may be the building blocks of scientific knowledge, but one can have little confidence in them unless there is converging evidence from many different kinds of studies.[70] The greater the evidence linking physiological, evolutionary, and psychological outcomes, the higher the value of this convergence.[71] Furthermore, meta-analyses,[72] which have been performed on nearly every group of heuristics,[73] make the use of convenience samples less troubling.[74] Indeed, a

placing a blue square on the left of a green diamond), because the word "not" directs attention to the proposition it denies (i.e., the red square).

68 *See* Dawes, *supra* note 55, p. 503, observing that "the consistency of the results across types of subjects and across samplings of tasks" is what makes a research program trustworthy.

69 David H. Kaye and David A. Freedman, *Reference Guide on Statistics*, in FEDERAL JUDICIAL CENTER, REFERENCE MANUAL ON SCIENTIFIC EVIDENCE 96 (2d ed., 2000).

70 See, e.g., Melvin M. Mark and Charles S. Reichart, *Quasi-Experimental and Correlational Designs*, in THE SAGE HANDBOOK OF METHODS IN SOCIAL PSYCHOLOGY 265, 281 (Carol Sansone, et al., eds., 2004), explaining the importance of a research program, lines of research, and research syntheses.

71 *See* John T. Cacioppo et al., *Social Neuroscience: Bridging Social and Biological Systems*, in THE SAGE HANDBOOK OF METHODS IN SOCIAL PSYCHOLOGY, 383, 387 (2004), explaining the significance, in reaction-time studies, of convergent evidence, in that "the greater the extant evidence linking the observed physiological event/profile to a specific psychological operation, the greater the value of the convergent evidence."

72 Meta-analysis is a technique that combines the results of many studies. It is widely used in epidemiology and toxicology and, when used appropriately, "can enhance understanding of associations between sources and their effects that may not be apparent from examination of . . . studies individually." "Proposed Guidelines for Carcinogen Risk Assessment," 61 FED. REG., 17,974 (October 31, 1996). For an explanation of the method, *see, generally*, D. M. EDDY, ET AL., META-ANALYSIS BY THE CONFIDENCE PROFILE METHOD: THE STATISTICAL SYNTHESIS OF EVIDENCE (1992).

73 See, e.g., Anton Kuhberger, *The Influence of Framing on Risky Decisions: A Meta-Analysis*, 75 ORGA-NIZATIONAL BEHAVIOR AND DECISION PROCESSES 23–55 (1998); C. A. Meissner and J. C. Brigham, *Thirty Years of Investigating the Own Race Bias in Memory for Faces: A Meta-Analytic Review*, 7 PSYCHOL., PUB. POL'Y, & LAW, 3–35 (2001), examining memory for other-race faces; Paul A. Mabe, III, and Stephen G. West, *Validity of Self-Evaluation of Ability: A Review and Meta-Analysis*, 67 J. APPLIED PSYCHOL., 280–94 (1982); Jerry M. Burger, *Motivational Biases in the Attribution of Responsibility for an Accident: A MetaAnalysis of the Defensive-Attribution Hypothesis*, 90 PSYCHOL. BULL., 486 (1981); William M. Grove, et al., *Comparative Efficiency of Informal (Subjective, Impressionistic) and Formal (Mechanical, Algorithmic) Prediction Procedures: The Clinical–Statistical Controversy*, 2 PSYCHOL. PUB. POL'Y & L., 293 (1996), clinicians ignore base rates; Daniel J. Isenberg, *Group Polarization and Meta-Analysis*, 50 J. OF PERSONALITY & SOCIAL PSYCHOLOGY, 1141 (1986); J. J. Christensen-Szalanski and C.F. Willham, *The Hindsight Bias: A Meta-Analysis*, 48 ORGANIZA-TIONAL BEHAVIOR & HUMAN DECISION PROCESSES, 147 (1991); S .J. Karau and K. D. Williams, *Social Loafing: A Meta-Analytic Review and Theoretical Integration*, 65 J. PERSONALITY & SOC. PSYCHOL., 681 (1993).

74 See, e.g., Thomas D. Cook and Carla Groom, *The Methodological Assumptions of Social Psychology*, in THE SAGE HANDBOOK OF METHODS IN SOCIAL PSYCHOLOGY, 19, 28 (2004), noting that

meta-analysis comparing cognitive studies using student subjects with nonstudent subjects found that there were no significant differences.[75]

The problem of individual differences

The problem of individual variation is also a focus of critique.[76] People who participate as subjects in social psychology research are individuals. They may vary in their genetic traits, intelligence, past experiences, anatomy, physiology, emotion, gender, motivation, and cognition. Even the same person may vary in emotional state and activity level from one time to another.[77] There is no such thing as an average person. Yet, the critics argue, responses to tests are averaged across the entire group of people taking the test. This argument, however, fails to recognize that individual variation is a general concern of research design, not only in the social sciences but also in biology and the medical sciences generally.[78]

There are, however, statistical solutions. Statistical methods for dealing with this problem include nonparametric tests, to resolve the problem of non-normal distribution, and logit regressions to stabilize variance.[79] Statistical techniques, such as analysis of variance,[80] reveal whether the groups differ on a basis other than random fluctuation.[81] The operative question is whether any of these individual variations is apt to influence the dependent variable being studied.[82] If these factors do not differentially affect the study – that is, if one can assume they are randomly distributed in the population being studied – random assignment of individuals to each study group should equalize the variations.[83]

meta-analysis is "the best developed form of multi-experimental design and analysis, and its use is common in social psychology."

75 *See* Kuhberger, *supra* note 73, pp. 204–31 (1998), reviewing studies of framing effects.

76 *See* Gregory Mitchell, *Why Law and Economics' Perfect Rationality Should Not Be Traded for Behavioral Law and Economics' Equal Incompetence*, 91 Georgetown L. J. 1, 75 (2002), explaining that there are "individual and situational differences in rational behavior" and noting that one should not "assume a uniformity in cognitive performance across persons and situations that is not supported by empirical data."

77 *See* Colton, *supra* note 47, p. 39, explaining that in medical research, laboratory experiments are subject to three types of variation: biological, temporal, and measurement.

78 *See* Jay E. Gould, Concise Handbook of Experimental Methods for the Behavioral and Biological Sciences, 177 (2002), noting the goals of good experimental design as including the three minimax principles: maximize the primary variance; make equivalent the secondary variance; and minimize the error variance.

79 *See* Judd et al., *supra* note 53 noting that "variance-stabilizing transformations (e.g., the arcsin and the logit for probabilities and proportions, Fisher's Z for correlations, and to a lesser extent the log for reaction times) have been well received by psychologists."

80 *See* Colton, *supra* note 47, p. 41, using studies on the insulin clearance rate for dogs as an example and describing the process for determining inter-subject variability, biologic variability, and intra-subject variability.

81 F.J. McGuigan, Experimental Psychology: Methods of Research 90 (7th ed. 1997).

82 *Id.*, pp. 79–80, explaining the problem of individual variation and how researchers attempt to control for it.

83 *See, e.g.* Thomas D. Cook & Carla Groom, *The Methodological Assumptions of Social Psychology*, in The Sage Handbook of Methods in Social Psychology 19, 29 (2004) remarking that the "overwhelming majority of social psychology studies are conducted in a laboratory setting, use

The debate about the consequences of individual variation surfaces in a controversy over experimental design.[84] Laboratory research in social psychology is divided into between-subjects design and within-subjects design.[85] Between-subjects designs consist of experiments in which different subjects are assigned (randomly) to different groups, and test results are compared to determine whether there is some difference between the two groups.[86] The within-subjects design is one in which the same subjects are tested in all conditions and their scores under the various conditions are compared.

Some critics charge that the use of between-subjects design means that social psychology cannot be widely generalized because the between-subjects design averages responses, whereas in real life people vary in their uses of heuristics.[87] These critics advocate greater use of the within-subjects experimental design, which measures the dependent variable (i.e., the response of interest) on the same individuals at different levels of an independent variable (i.e., the stimulus or condition that the researcher manipulates to determine its effect on the dependent variable).[88]

The major advantage of the within-subjects design is its reduced statistical error variance.[89] Each subject serves not only as the experimental subject but also as the control.[90] Fewer participants are needed, and every subject is run in every condition.[91] Masking (i.e., hiding the effects of extraneous variables) is decreased in within-subjects design by the reduction in statistical error variance

---

undergraduate participants, last no longer than an hour, and involve random assignment to two or more experimental conditions ... [and] 95% used analysis of variance ... one of the strongest frameworks" for research.

84 *See, e.g.*, Daniel Kahneman & Shane Frederick, *Representativeness Revisited: Attribute Substitution in Intuitive Judgment*, in HEURISTICS AND BIASES: THE PSYCHOLOGY OF INTUITIVE JUDGMENT 49, 58 (Thomas Gilovich et al, eds. 2002) (acknowledging that the "relative virtues of between-subjects and within-subjects designs in studies of judgment are a highly contentious issue" but concluding that "between-subjects designs are more appropriate for the study of heuristics").

85 Aronson et al., *supra* note 54, p. 113, explaining the two designs.

86 Elizabeth J. Hellier, *Within-Subjects Designs*, in LABORATORY PSYCHOLOGY, *supra* note 65, at 39, describing the between-subjects design and using as an example a test of whether glare on a computer screen affected reading comprehension, in which subjects were divided into two groups, one of which performed the task while there was glare on the screen and one of which performed the task in the absence of glare.

87 *See, e.g.* Gregory Mitchell, *Taking Behavioralism Too Seriously? The Unwarranted Pessimism of the New Behavioral Analysis of Law*, 43 WM. & MARY L. REV. 1907, 1953 (2002)., contending that the "lack of a uniform context paired with the averaging of results in between-subjects designs can lead to obvious contradictions that single individuals would not make if tested in all experimental conditions."

88 *See* JAY E. GOULD, CONCISE HANDBOOK OF EXPERIMENTAL METHODS FOR THE BEHAVIORAL AND BIOLOGICAL SCIENCES, 250 (2002), describing within-groups experimental design.

89 *See id.*, 267, explaining that "error variance associated with individual participant differences is reduced in proportion to twice the correlation of the participants' scores under the different conditions" and incorporated into the statistical equations, such as the t-test for related/correlated measures.

90 Aronson et al., *supra* note 54, p. 113.

91 Hellier, *supra* note 86, p. 45, noting that power is increased in within-subjects designs.

associated with differences among subjects, and power (i.e., sensitivity) is therefore increased.[92] Neither of these designs is perfect; each has advantages and disadvantages. Some kinds of experiments are better run as within-subjects designs. For example, experiments involving learning are typically designed as within-subjects experiments.[93]

All experimental design involves tradeoffs. The disadvantages of within-subjects design include the difficulty of controlling sequence effects. If the same subjects perform in all the experimental conditions, they must do them in a particular order, and that may influence their scores.[94] In other words, the sequence aspect of performance confounds the results if the experimental treatment is not the only thing influencing the score.[95] Another danger is that, on repeated exposure, the subjects may discover what they think the researcher is looking for, a problem because of the tendency of people to behave in ways they believe the investigator desires.[96] A third danger is that of range effects, in which the performance hits either a ceiling or a floor.[97] If any of these situations is likely, a between-subjects design must be used.

In between-subjects designs, people are randomly assigned to two groups, performing under different conditions.[98] The researcher then compares the group in an experimental condition with a group in a control condition, usually by comparing the group average, so that comparisons are made between subjects.[99] The researcher attempts to keep conditions in the two groups identical except for the variable being tested. If another factor varies systematically between the groups – a confounding factor, as it is called – the results of the experiment will be inconclusive.

Because people in between-subjects experiments are randomly assigned to each group, individual differences are averaged across condition, making it difficult to separate the effects of the independent variable from the noise of personality

92 See Gould, note 88 (*Handbook*), p. 267.

93 See Hellier, note 86, p. 45, noting that "some areas of investigation require the same subjects to recieve all of the experimental conditions, such as learning experiments, or instances where the experimenter is interested in how subjects judge the relative differences between levels of the independent variable."

94 *Id.*, p. 47, noting that sequence effects can be further categorized as either practice effects or carryover effects, both of which are confounding to the results.

95 *Id.*, using the example of the effect of glare on computer-screen reading tasks where, if subjects were given the same passage to read under all conditions, they improved their scores regardless of the effects of glare because they had read the passage before.

96 Gould, note 88 (*Handbook*), p. 268.

97 *See* James Hampton, *The Between-Subjects Experiment*, in LABORATORY PSYCHOLOGY: A BEGINNER'S GUIDE, 26 (Julia Nunn, ed., 1998). Using as an example an experiment testing memory performance, in which the researcher manipulates whether faces to be remembered are well known or unknown and presented in full-face or profile; if all faces are presented together, there is a risk of 100 percent memory of well-known faces and 0 percent memory of unknown faces, regardless of whether presented in full-face or profile.

98 *See id.* at 29.

99 Gould, *supra* note 88 (*Handbook*) p. 251.

differences.[100] Large sample sizes and random assignment average out the differences in individuals, such as personality, attitudes, ability, and experiences that might otherwise impact the response to the experimental conditions in between-subjects experiments (and must be treated as error variance). In addition to randomization, another solution to avoid the dangers of confounding variables is to obtain a baseline measure of performance for all participants (as in a preliminary pre-test).[101] Then a statistical analysis of covariance can adjust the individual scores for baseline differences.[102]

Although by no means trivial, the problem of individual differences is common to all laboratory science. For example, to minimize individual differences in toxicology studies, genetic differences in rats and mice are bred out of the laboratory animals. Even so, there are individual differences that persist. That is the reason for employing analysis of variance techniques.[103] For this reason also, to have confidence in the research regarding a particular heuristic or bias, there should be a robust research program in which a number of researchers have engaged in a series of experiments employing "a number of empirical techniques that differ in as many ways as possible, having in common only our basic conceptual variable."[104] If many techniques yield consistent results, there is less concern that the results are a fluke. When different experimental designs yield divergent results, the researcher must be able to explain why.[105] At a minimum, legal analysts should be aware of the significance of experimental design.

---

100 As Aronson explains, using a hypothetical study of the ability of people to detect lying in others:

> Suppose, for example, that one participant has a very suspicious view of the world and thinks that people are lying most of the time. Another participant is very trusting and thinks that people seldom lie. Suppose further that a between-subject design was used, and the distrustful and trustful people are randomly assigned to different conditions. In this design, it would be difficult to separate the effects of the independent variable (e.g., whether the person on the tape was lying or telling the truth) from how suspicious participants are in general. With random assignment, of course, individual differences are averaged across condition; the number of suspicious versus trusting people should be roughly the same in all conditions. Nonetheless the "noise " produced by personality differences makes it difficult to detect the "signal of the effects of the independent variable, and a large number of participants have to be run to detect the "signal." In a within-subject design this problem is solved by running every person in every condition. The suspicious person's responses to the lies are compared to his or her responses to the nonlies, thereby "subtracting out" his or her tendency to rate everyone as deceptive.

> Aronson, *supra* note 54, pp. 113–14.

101 Hampton, *supra* note 97, at 28, noting that a pre-test will "reduce the impact of individual differences on the experiment, and so greatly improve the power of the design."
102 *Id.*, 28, using the example of a reaction-time test, in which individuals' initial decision times are used as a baseline against which experimental reaction times are measured.
103 *See, e.g.*, Cook and Groom, *supra* note 74, p. 36, noting that "individual differences are not completely ignored; nor are statistical interactions ... when they occur, the focus is mostly on those individual difference factors that might moderate psychological mechanisms assumed to be universal."
104 Aronson, et al., *supra* note 54, p. 134, using as an example the cognitive dissonance studies, in which people were tested in a variety of field and laboratory studies using a variety of techniques.
105 *See, e.g.*, Kahneman and Frederick, *supra* note 84, pp. 72–3, explaining that between-subjects and within-subjects experiments "often yield different results in studies of intuitive judgment" and arguing that the between-subjects design better "mimics the haphazard encounters in which

One important aspect of social psychology experiments is that they lack the controls of medical science's randomized double-blind experiments.[106] For example, the kind of control-based rankings used in medical research – with clinical double-blind studies at the top,[107] cohort studies[108] next, case-control studies[109] fairly close behind, and case reports[110] bringing up the rear – may not even be contemplated.[111] On the other hand, an advantage of the social psychology studies is that they involve humans rather than animals so that the problems of animal-to-human extrapolation are avoided.

The downside is that human studies are subject to numerous imperfections: controls in human studies tend to be imperfect, they are notoriously poor at observing small effects, and the effects may differ among human populations. These difficulties plague all human studies.[112] The problem of control – internal validity – in experiments with human beings is a well-recognized problem in epidemiology. Again, there are statistical methods for attempting to ameliorate these problems, but they do not disappear.

Good experimental design focuses on balancing the two poles of control and generalizability, and this includes experimental design in the social sciences.[113] Using human beings as experimental subjects presents problems of control but

most judgments are made and is more likely to evoke the casually intuitive mode of judgment that governs much of mental life in routine situations."

106 *See* David H. Kaye and David A. Freedman, *Reference Guide on Statistics*, in FEDERAL JUDICIAL CENTER, REFERENCE MANUAL ON SCIENTIFIC EVIDENCE (2d ed., 2000), explaining that observational studies do not have the same kind of controls as randomized controlled experiments, even though the researchers may attempt to control for confounding variables.

107 The "gold standard" is the human clinical trial, used by the FDA in its approval process, in which participants are randomly separated into groups receiving either the drug being studied or a placebo, and neither the researchers nor the participants know who is in which group. See Michael D. Green, *Expert Witnesses and Sufficiency of Evidence in Toxic Substances Litigation: The Legacy of Agent Orange and Bendectin Litigation*, 86 Nw. U. L. REV., 643, 647 (1992).

108 In cohort studies, the researcher identifies two groups of individuals, exposed and unexposed; follows the groups for a length of time; and the number of individuals who develop the disease is statistically analyzed. *See* Linda A. Bailey et al., *Reference Guide on Epidemiology*, in FEDERAL JUDICIAL CTR., REFERENCE MANUAL ON SCIENTIFIC EVIDENCE 134 (2d ed. 2000).

109 Case-control studies compare a group of individuals with a particular disease with a control group that does not have the disease. *See* Bailey et al., *supra* p. 134.

110 Case reports are anecdotal filings describing "the temporal relation between an exposure and a disease." *See* Troyen A. Brennan, *Helping Courts with Toxic Torts: Some Proposals Regarding Alternative Methods for Presenting and Assessing Scientific Evidence in Common Law Courts*, 51 U. PITT. L. REV., 1, 46, note 192 (1989).

111 Instead, researchers attempt to randomly assign people to conditions and to control variations to make sure the stimuli under the experimental conditions are similar. Aronson, note 60, p. 103, using stereotyping studies as an example.

112 *See, e.g.*, Gary Taubes, *Epidemiology Faces Its Limits*, 269 SCI., 164 (1995), discussing the difficulty of distinguishing between no effects and small effects in epidemiology studies; Alvan R. Feinstein, *Scientific Standards in Epidemiologic Studies of the Menace of Daily Life*, 242 SCI., 1257 (1988), observing that conflicting results were obtained in fifty-six epidemiology studies and attributing this to the difficulty in conducting such studies.

113 Aronson, *supra* note 54, pp. 130–1, noting that the goal of experimental design is to create a study that is "well-controlled (high in internal validity), has independent and dependent variables that are good reflections of the conceptual variables of interest (high in construct validity), and is generalizable to other settings and people (high in external validity)."

improves the generalizability of the studies. Animal studies (e.g., often used in toxicology) offer more in the way of controls but have less generalizability. The question of generalizability is an important one, although it is "never completely answerable."[114] It is important to recognize that all hypothesis testing involves tradeoffs between controls and generalizability. Rather than seeking perfect studies, scientists' confidence in the strength of a research program increases as it includes a variety of studies on both humans and animals, in the laboratory, and in the field.

The laboratory research versus field research debate

It is curious that the problem of internal validity – controls – is not the primary focus of the legal critics. Rather, they complain that the experimental setting bears little resemblance to real-world decision making and that, therefore, the results are not generalizable. Their argument is that people respond in anomalous ways in the artificial setting of the laboratory (or, in most cases, the classroom) and that the subjects' decision making there bears little resemblance to the way people solve real-world problems. Although generalizability is a real concern, the question should be focused on whether the study evokes behavior like that in the real world rather than how closely the conditions mirror those of the real world.[115]

Although the idea of studying decision making in real-world environments is intuitively appealing, such studies are actually riddled with flaws. Because of the noisiness and irreproducibility of real-world conditions, they are of little use for testing hypotheses. Systematically observing and recording behavior in the real world has advantages for generating hypotheses about behavior, and these observational studies may uncover variables that are correlated with specific behaviors, but unless the conditions can be controlled, knowing that there is a relationship between the variables tells you little about what the relationship is.[116]

To learn more about the relationship among variables requires the researcher to attempt controlling all factors except the one being studied (i.e., the independent variable).[117] Otherwise, uncontrolled environmental conditions may swamp the

114 John Monahan and Laurens Walker, *Social Authority: Obtaining, Evaluating, and Establishing Social Science in Law*, 134 U. Pa. L. Rev., 477, 506–508 (1986), explaining how to evaluate "how far beyond the specific facts of the study validly-produced research findings remain valid."

115 *See* Jennifer K. Robbennolt, *Evaluating Empirical Research Methods: Using Empirical Research in Law and Policy*, 81 Neb. L. Rev., 777, 788 (2002), discussing the unfounded judicial disdain for mock-jury studies based on their lack of verisimilitude and explaining that such experimental research is valid if it evokes or predicts similar behavior to that exhibited in the real world.

116 *See, e.g.*, Peter Ayton, *Experimental Versus Correlational Methods*, in Laboratory Psychology: A Beginners Guide, 59, 62 (Julia Nunn, ed., 1998), describing correlational studies and explaining that "there will often be more than one possible explanation" for each observed correlation.

117 *See* Karl R. Popper, The Logic of Scientific Discovery, 42 (rev. ed., 1992), explaining that "what characterizes the empirical method is its manner of exposing to falsification, in every

effect the researcher desires to study. In addition, attempting to exert control in a field setting may introduce unexpected anomalies.[118] Moreover, randomization is problematic in field settings.

One particular critique involves the incentive structure of the experiments. The critics contend that there is so little at stake for the subjects of the experiment that the costs of making a careful decision may just not be worth it.[119] The argument is that people who seem to be irrational may just be bored and that in real life they would pay attention and make better decisions.[120] Although it is difficult to dispute the theory that people make better decisions when they are alert, it does not answer the question of why there should be evidence of systematic rather than random error.[121] In any event, this concern about motivating participants means that many experiments are now run with real monetary rewards in nontrivial amounts.

The controversy between experimental and field researchers can be resolved in a research program if studies have been performed in both laboratory and field settings, with convergent results. A point that I hope becomes increasingly clear throughout this chapter is that one study is not sufficient to explain any facet of human behavior. Ideally, a research program should include both human and animal studies; it should also include both laboratory and field research. Some of the best research programs move from laboratory to field several times as, for example, the research on the effect of feelings of control on stress responses, which began with experimental animal studies, extended to field studies of stress in humans,

conceivable way, the system to be tested." The importance of a null hypothesis is that it exposes the proposed hypothesis to the possibility of falsification: If data gathered with the proper controls do not refute the proposed hypothesis, it may be provisionally valid. Laboratory settings permit more control over the independent variable.

118 See Aronson, *supra* note 54, p. 129, noting the problems of obtrusive observation.

119 See S. Siegel, *Decision Making and Learning Under Varying Conditions of Reinforcement*, 89 ANN. N.Y. ACAD. SCI., 766–83 (1961), finding that prediction tasks improved when the monetary stakes were increased.

120 One facet of this argument is the controversy about whether monetary rewards matter. *See, e.g.,* Vernon L. Smith, *Rational Choice: The Contrast Between Economics and Psychology*, in BARGAINING AND MARKET BEHAVIOR: ESSAYS IN EXPERIMENTAL ECONOMICS (Vernon L. Smith, ed., 2000), observing that in seventeen studies, "one effect of increased payoffs is to reduce the standard error of the observations around the predicted or estimated optimal decision" and arguing that monetary rewards matter because there is a tradeoff between the benefits of detailed decision making and the costs of making them. As a result, many of the newer studies have incorporated rewards in the design. See, e.g. Peter Knetz, et al., *Individual Rationality, Market Rationality, and Value Estimation*, in BARGAINING, *supra* at 257, noting studies of framing effects "that have carefully introduced actual monetary payments and cash compensations and have not relied on hypothetical choices."

121 Indeed, some experiments are designed to explore what people do when in a state of reduced attention. *See, e.g.,* S. Chaiken, *The Heuristic Model of Persuasion*, in SOCIAL INFLUENCE: THE ONTARIO SYMPOSIUM, Vol. 5, 3–39 (M. P. Hanna, et al., eds., 1987), studying the heuristic processing of persuasive messages. To test processes occurring when people are fully alert, however, experiments must be designed to achieve maximum attention. *See* Aronson, *supra* note 54, p. 132, citing an example of cognitive dissonance and stereotyping studies.

returned to the laboratory for further refinement, and then were again tested in the field.

Effect size and practical significance

Another quarrel about the generalizability of social psychology research is that the effect sizes measured are small so that the results, although statistically significant, lack practical significance. Effect size, the magnitude of an observed effect, is an important concern of anyone attempting to evaluate consequences of experimental manipulations, including experiments to determine cognitive bias.[122] Although information about whether an effect exists usually is presented through statistical significance, meaningfulness of the effect is measured by effect size.[123] Effect size, power, sample size, and significance level are intimately related.[124] If too small a sample is used, even large effects may not be statistically significant.[125] Because most studies on humans (and all decision-making studies) are based on samples of less than one thousand, effect sizes will differ from the "true" effect size because of sampling error.[126]

Just because an effect size is small, however, does not mean that it is inconsequential.[127] Toxicology studies, for example, frequently have small effect sizes but large consequences.[128] Moreover, even when effect sizes are small, the comparison of effect sizes in a number of studies may help determine the impact of a cognitive bias. For example, in studying the hindsight bias, Bukszar and Connolly examined whether participation in group discussions after receiving potentially biasing information, but before making a probability assessment, affected the impact of

---

122 *See* Jay J. Christensen-Szalanski, *A Comment on Applying Experimental Findings of Cognitive Biases to Naturalistic Environments*, in DECISION MAKING IN ACTION: MODELS AND METHODS 252, 255 (Gary A. Klein et al., eds., 1993), noting that "researchers evaluating data on the harm of cognitive biases or the merit of debiasing techniques need information about the magnitude of the observed effect, that is, the effect size."

123 *Id.* at 256, observing that even if the researcher fails to provide effect-size figures, they are easy to calculate from the statistical information normally included in experimental studies.) Effect size is a concept similar to relative risk (or odds ratio) in epidemiological studies and describes the measured strength of association between a disease and a risk factor. *See* HAROLD A. KAHN, AN INTRODUCTION TO EPIDEMIOLOGIC METHODS, 38–55 (1983).

124 *See* Judd, et al., *supra* note 53, noting that "In any study, four factors are intimately related: the power of the study, the effect size, the sample size, and the a level."

125 *See* SHAYNE C. GAD, STATISTICS AND EXPERIMENTAL DESIGN FOR TOXICOLOGISTS (3rd ed., 1999), "The smaller the critical effect size, the larger the necessary sample size."

126 Christensen-Szalanski, *supra* note 122 at 260, noting that the "smaller the sample size, the more the observed effect size may depart from the true effect size, and the more likely an observed difference may reflect the impact of sampling error."

127 *See* David Clark-Carter, *The Account Taken of Statistical Power in Research Published in the British Journal of Psychology*, 88 BRIT. J. PSYCHOL. (1997), observing that "a small ES is important and worth detecting when life and death are involved."

128 *See*, e.g., Christensen-Szalanski, *supra* note 122, p. 260, observing that "even effect sizes as small as r = 0.05 can easily become meaningfully important when they are obtained from studies that examine changes in success rates, survival rates, or improvement rates."

the hindsight bias.[129] The authors concluded that group discussion had no effect because they observed a statistically significant effect under both conditions. However, on reanalysis, Christensen-Szalanski demonstrated that "group discussion did reduce the impact of the bias to as little as one-sixth of its original size."[130] Thus, comparison through meta-analysis helped illuminate the impact of hindsight bias.

Linking data and hypothesis: assessing particular heuristics and biases

Despite quibbles over methodology and analysis, virtually everyone agrees that sometimes systematic mental shortcuts can get in the way of optimal decision making.[131] Arguments about generalizability, variability, and rigor of design are best answered by a research program that includes multiple studies in different contexts, performed using different populations. A single study, no matter how perfectly executed, can reveal only so much. Multiple avenues of reasoning based on persuasive data are what lead to scientific acceptance of a theory.[132]

However, a major failing of decision-theory research has been its failure to incorporate biological information and, therefore, its failure to explain underlying mechanisms for the observed heuristics and biases. Although recent works have attempted an increased interdisciplinarity by explicitly endorsing an evolutionary biology perspective[133] and by incorporating some developments in neuroscience,[134] much remains to be accomplished. For example, not one of the recent major books on the topic of heuristics discusses the role of dopamine receptors, oxytocin, or the neural basis for memory, although these topics are highly relevant to understanding how heuristics may work.[135] Thus, in postulating a "dual-process model" of

129 E. Bukszar and T. Connolly, *Hindsight Bias and Strategic Choice: Some Problems in Learning from Experience*, 31 ACADEMY OF MANAGEMENT J. 628–41 (1988).
130 Christensen-Szalanski, *supra* note 122, p. 257.
131 *See, e.g.*, Colin F. Camerer, *Individual Decision Making*, in THE HANDBOOK OF EXPERIMENTAL ECONOMICS, 587 (J. H. Kagel and A.E. Roth, eds., 1995), noting that "[n]ot a single major recent (post-1970) anomaly has been 'destroyed' by hostile replication."
132 *See* Hacking, *supra* note 52, p. 14, examining the relationship between data, observation, and theory.
133 *See, e.g.*, Gilovich and Griffen, *supra* note 9, p. 10, "Kahneman and Tversky's frequent analogies between perceptual and cognitive processes...reflect an important recognition that cognition evolved after (and out of) perception"; Gigerenzer and Selten, *supra* note 9, p. 8, "the heuristics, available to a species at a given point in its evolution, is called its 'adaptive toolbox'"; Hastie and Dawes, *supra* note 18, p. 2, noting that heuristic "limitations are most obvious when we must make judgments and decisions that are not like those we were 'selected' to make in the ancestral environments where we evolved."
134 *See, e.g.*, Gigerenzer and Selten, *supra* note 9, p. 9, acknowledging a role for emotions in cognition; Hastie and Dawes, note 21, p. 209, discussing the work of neuroscientist Antonio Damasio on the role of emotions in cognition; Paul Slovic, et al., *The Affect Heuristic*, in HEURISTICS & BIASES, *supra* note 9, p. 397, 420, citing Damasio for the proposition that "rationality is not only a product of the analytic mind, but of the experiential mind as well."
135 In contrast, Lakoff and Johnson, who propose a metaphorical basis for reasoning, base their theory on neuroscience and pull together both psychology and biology in a coherent framework. *See, generally*, GEORGE LAKOFF AND MARK JOHNSON, PHILOSOPHY IN THE FLESH (1999), explaining

reasoning,[136] no description of neural architecture correlating with such a model is proffered. In postulating "support theory," as an overarching explanation for how heuristics work, Tversky and Koehler provide no biological explanation whatsoever.[137] Thus, although there is much to be learned from the decision-theory research, the explanations remain incomplete.

Framing effects, risk aversion, and regret

One of the earliest heuristics described was that of framing effects. Daniel Kahnemann and Amos Tversky proposed a formal model – prospect theory[138] – to explain a phenomenon that had puzzled mathematicians and economists for centuries: although people were thought to be naturally either risk-averse or risk-seeking, their attitude toward risk actually is relative, related to their circumstances.[139]

that prototypes are neurological phenomena, manifest in various cognitive functions such as memory and learning, transcending language and culture, and have multiple neurological bases, including neural networks and reentrant processing. For a lucid introduction to Lakoff's theories and an application to legal analysis, see STEVEN L. WINTER, A CLEARING IN THE FOREST: LAW, LIFE AND MIND (2001).

136 See Kahneman and Frederick, *supra* note 84, p. 51, describing "the role of two systems in determining stated judgments."

137 See Tversky and Kahnemann, *supra* note 11, 441–73. Curiously, although the work of neuroscientists (including that of Antonio Damasio on emotions) is cited throughout the latest compilation on heuristics and biases, no attempt is made to correlate support theory with this information. See *Heuristics & Biases*, note 12 *passim*. Although the importance of feelings of "goodness" and "badness" in decision making is recognized as an "affect heuristic" and evolution is mentioned briefly in passing, there is no attempt to tie any of these factors together with support theory. See Paul Slovic, et al., *The Affect Heuristic*, in HEURISTICS AND BIASES, *supra* note 12, p. 397. Thus, these explanations remain fundamentally incomplete.

138 Under prospect theory, a choice (or behavior) is made by a two-step process in which people first edit alternatives, through setting a reference point – most commonly the status quo, a security level, or an aspiration level – then combining or segregating outcomes and a second step of evaluating each alternative through a process of "weighting outcomes by their probabilities of occurrence or expectations." Hastie and Dawes, *supra* note 19, pp. 290–5, describing prospect theory. The three characteristics of this process are a view of consequences in terms of a particular reference level, diminishing returns, and a value function steeper for losses than for gains. Id. at 294. This scale is used to explain people's overreactions to small probability risks, willingness to pay huge amounts to eliminate low probability risks, and why people buy lottery tickets. Id. at 296–7. It is also used to explain why in many gambling situations, where the objective probability is about 0.20, "people are well calibrated in terms of their sense of 'objective' probabilities." Id. at 298. At the central portion of the curve, from about 0.25 to 0.75 on the objective probability scale, people become "superadditive for events associated with these objective probabilities." Id. at 298.

139 Early examinations of the concept of diminishing returns, which reflects risk aversion, include the St. Petersburg paradox, in which players ought to be willing to play for any finite amount, but no one has ever been observed to pay more than a few dollars to play the game once. Anatol Rapoport, *Spin-Offs of Game Theory to Social Psychology, Theoretical Biology and Philosophy*, in EVOLUTION AND PROGRESS IN DEMOCRACIES, 241, 244 (Johann Gotschl, ed., 2001). Bernoulli devised a mathematical formula to explain the paradox, demonstrating that the value of each increment of gain is inversely proportional to the player's accumulated wealth. Daniel Bernoulli, *Specimen theoriae novae de Mensura Sortis*, Comentarii Academiae Scientiarum Imperialis Petropolitanae 5, 175–92 (1738), translated by L. Sommer as "New Expositions on the Measurement of Risk," 22 ECONOMETRICA 23–6. Like these explanations, prospect theory is expressed as a mathematical formula. See Hastie and Dawes, *supra* note 18, p. 290, explaining

People appear to avoid risky actions only when they are experiencing relative wealth.[140] They favor risky actions when they are in a losing situation.[141] For example, when all options are undesirable, high-risk gambles are often preferred to fairly certain losses.[142] Thus, people tend to be risk-averse for moderate probabilities and risk-seeking for small probabilities of gain; they tend in the opposite direction for probabilities of loss.[143] Similarly, when the same problem is expressed in two different ways, the same people often make radically different choices.[144] For example, both patients and physicians reverse their decisions about treatment when the same information is presented as survival rates versus mortality rates.[145]

Framing effects also occur when, in playing social-dilemma games (like the prisoner's dilemma), the players are told at the outset of the game (either explicitly or implicitly) to cooperate or compete. The economic payoffs remain the same; nonetheless, players told to cooperate (or who are told they are playing a "community game") are more likely to cooperate, and players told that they are competing (or that they are playing a "Wall Street game") are more likely to defect.[146]

Since its original proposal, prospect theory has been tested extensively.[147] A meta-analysis of more than 100 framing-effect studies found only small to moderate effect sizes.[148] Nonetheless, the meta-analysis found these framing effects robust: in

the formula in algebraic terms expressing the idea that a "prospect is an alternative or course of action defined by one or more outcomes, which result in consequence values, which are weighted by decision weights, which are related to the objective probabilities for each outcome's occurrence."

140 *See* Amos Tversky and D. Kahnman, *Rational Choice and the Framing of Decisions*, 59 J. Bus. L. 251–94 (1986), studies showing that people treat risks concerning perceived gains differently from risks concerning perceived losses.

141 *See* T. S. Bateman and C.T. Zeithaml, *The Psychological Context of Strategic Decisions: A Model and Convergent Findings*, 10 J. Strategic Mgt., 59–74 (1989).

142 *See* Daniel Kahneman and Amos Tversky, *Prospect Theory: An Analysis of Decision Under Risk*, 47 Econometrica 263–90 (1979).

143 *Id.* at 263–91 (1979).

144 This phenomenon is known as preference reversal. *See, e.g.*, Hastie and Dawes, *supra* note 18, at 298–308, describing gain-loss framing effects; Wulf Albers, *Prominence Theory as a Tool to Model Boundedly Rational Decisions*, in Bounded Rationality, *supra* note 11, p. 308, describing framing effects as "modify[ing] the structure of the decision before the theory is applied"; Paul Slovic, et al., *Compatibility Effects in Judgment and Choice*, in Heuristics & Biases, *supra* note 13, p. 222, explaining preference reversals as "a pattern of choices in which normatively equivalent elicitation procedures give rise to inconsistent preferences."

145 *See* Hastie and Dawes, *supra* note 18, p. 302, describing a decision test in which people who were informed about treatment options in terms of mortality or survival rates reversed their treatment preferences depending on how the options were framed.

146 *See* David Sally, *Conversation and Cooperation in Social Dilemmas: A Meta-Analysis of Experiments from 1958 to 1992*, 7 Rationality & Soc. 58 (1995).

147 *See, e.g.*, George Wu, et al. *Decision Under Risk*, in Blackwell Handbook of Judgment and Decision Making (Nigel Harvey and Derek Koehler, eds., forthcoming), reviewing the literature and discussing the original prospect theory and its later refinements, evaluating their strengths and weaknesses.

148 Anton Kuhberger, *The Influence of Framing on Risky Decisions: A Meta-Analysis*, 75 Organizational Behav. & Hum. Decision Processes, 23, 42, 47 (1998), explaining that these meta-analyses showed small to moderate effect size of d= 0.31. In a further meta-analysis by the same researcher, 60 percent of all subjects were found to exhibit framing effects. *Id.*

60 percent of the studies, subjects chose the sure gain and in only 40 percent did subjects choose the risky gain when the problem was presented as gains, whereas when the problem was framed as losses, the results were reversed.[149] Moreover, framing effects are durable; they persist even after their inconsistencies are explained to people.[150]

Adding pertinent social-context information, however, can affect the way people respond to these effects.[151] In addition, there is some evidence that people in repeated markets may learn to approximate the utility-maximizing response.[152] At the very least, however, these studies indicate the importance of asking the same question in a variety of ways before making a decision.[153]

The explanation for such behavior has been the concept of regret, which posits a feeling of chagrin over lost opportunities.[154] There is some evidence from neuroscience about how this may work.[155] Emotion (or at least the mechanism for producing behavioral reactions to an object or event) lets an organism respond to circumstances that are bad or good for its life.[156]

149 Anton Kuhberger, et al., *The Effects of Framing, Reflection, Probability, and Payoff on Risk Preference in Choice Tasks*, 78 ORGANIZATIONAL BEHAV. & HUM. DECISION PROCESSES, 204, 209 (1999), meta-analysis. There have been a host of empirical studies of prospect theory, both in its original and in its modified version. Wu, *supra* note 147, p. 14, reviewing the literature and concluding that "a relatively clear picture of risky decision making and prospect theory has emerged" and proposing future research in mixed gambles, where there is some possibility of gain and some possibility of loss, and into the role of emotion in choice.

150 *See* Hastie and Dawes, note 18, at 306, explaining that people "stood by their original, contradictory choice" even after the inconsistency was explained to them.

151 James N. Druckman, *Using Credible Advice to Overcome Framing Effects*, 17 J. L. ECON. & ORG., 62, 77 (2001), concluding that the pervasiveness of framing effects may be overstated.

152 *See, e.g.*, Knetz, et al., *supra* note 120, pp. 258–9, although "not denying the reality of... farming effects" urging caution in applying these results uncritically to market behavior, which "show[s] some learning effects over time, with equilibrium behavior quite different from start-up behavior."

153 *See* Slovic, et al., *supra* note 134, at 229, advocating the use of "multiple procedures (e.g., choice, pricing, rating)" and comparison of results.

154 Anatol Rapoport, *Spin-Offs of Game Theory to Social Psychology, Theoretical Biology and Philosophy*, in EVOLUTION AND PROGRESS IN DEMOCRACIES, 241, 247 (Johann Gotschl, ed., 2001).

155 *See* ANTONIO DAMASIO, LOOKING FOR SPINOZA: JOY, SORROW, AND THE FEELING BRAIN, 51 (2003), noting that even organisms without a nervous system can react advantageously to a stimulus, by seeking good and avoiding harm to their organisms, without deciding to react and without feeling the reaction. Damasio explains that emotions (and their visible manifestations in behavior) are built from reactions that promote survival. *Id.* at 31.

156 *Id.* at 80. As Antonio Damasio explains the evolutionary process:

> The first device, emotion, enabled organisms to respond effectively but not creatively to a number of circumstances conducive or threatening to life – "good for life" or "bad for life" circumstances, "good for life" or "bad for life" outcomes. The second device, feeling, introduced a mental alert for the good or bad circumstances and prolonged the impact of emotions by affecting attention and memory lastingly. Eventually in a fruitful combination with past memories, imagination, and reasoning, feelings led to the emergence of foresight and the possibility of creating novel, nonstereotypical responses.

> *Id.* Feelings are defined as "the perception of a certain state of the body along with the perception of a certain mode of thinking and of thoughts with certain themes." *Id.* at 86. Damasio asserts that "we react to most, perhaps all, objects with emotions, however weak, and subsequent feelings,

The emotions consist of a complex collection of chemical and neural responses to an actual or remembered event, forming a distinct pattern in the brain. These are automatic responses that manifest in behavior, some of which are evolutionarily programmed and some of which are learned. The result of these responses is to temporarily change the state of the body and the brain structures that map the body and support feeling. Feelings (at an unconscious level) help mark the related neural maps as something important and, therefore, aid in the process of managing life.[157]

Framing effects, as well as other perceived anomalies, may occur when memory, imagination, and feeling interact to produce emotions and their seeking or avoidance behaviors. An emotion-stimulating event, object, or idea will arouse an emotion and then feelings, thoughts, and behaviors that go with it.[158] There is nothing random about emotions.[159] Memory promotes avoidance of events associated with negative feelings and seeking of events associated with positive feelings.[160] Thus, the vividness of a description may more strongly evoke a memory (or the imagination) and its feeling and incline people toward a particular behavior. Probably the more

however feeble." *Id.*, 93. Although preceding neuroscience, William James had a similar insight about the role of emotion, believing that when we feel emotions, we perceive body states. WILLIAM JAMES, THE PRINCIPLES OF PSYCHOLOGY (1890). Damasio further divides emotions into background emotions, reflecting our overall "state of being"; primary emotions, such as fear, anger, disgust, surprise, sadness, and happiness; and social emotions, such as sympathy, embarrassment, shame, guilt, indignation, pride, jealousy, envy, admiration, and contempt. Damasio, p. 45.

157 Damasio, *supra* p. 178, noting that "feelings are necessary because they are a mental-level expression of emotions and what lies beneath them" integrating present, past, and anticipated future. In studies of the midbrain dopamine neurons, alert monkeys presented with appetizing stimuli (usually by receiving fruit juice as a reward) showed activation of these neurons. Wolfram Schultz, et al., *A Neural Substrate of Prediction and Reward*, 275 SCI 1593 (1997). Dopamine neurons are correlated with incentive motivation and behavioral pursuit of a reward. *See, e.g.*, Randolph M. Nesse, *Psychoactive Drug Use in Evolutionary Perspective*, 278 SCI 63 (1997), discussing neural mechanisms regulating emotion and behavior and explaining that dopamine neurons activate a "wanting" system that anticipates rewards and motivates instrumental behavior. When exposed to aversive stimuli (e.g., air puffs to the hand or saline in the mouth), these same neurons show activation. *Id.* However, after repeated training that couples a reward with a stimulus, the monkey's dopamine neurons begin to react in a spike of activity when the cue (e.g., a light or sound) is received, the reward itself no longer generates the spike; if the reward is not given after the cue is received, the dopamine neurons are depressed below their normal firing rate. *Id.* In other words, the dopamine neurons encode expectations about the future: the dopamine neurons emit a positive signal if events turn out to be better than predicted, a negative signal if worse, and no signal if as predicted. *Id.* Dopamine neurons are thus closely linked to predicting the probability of future events, and "regret" (and the attempt to avoid it) may correlate with the negative signal.

158 Damasio, *supra* p. 73–77, noting instances where, if electrically stimulated by electrodes implanted in specific areas of the brain, people took on the demeanor of sadness (or mirth), cried (or laughed), talked about feelings of despair and exhaustion (or euphoria) until the electric current was switched off, when they resumed their normal demeanor. When individuals suffer damage in the areas of the brain responsible for certain kinds of emotions and feelings, their social behavior is often drastically altered. Damasio, at 140–1, noting that these patients have difficulty determining who is trustworthy and lack a sense of what is socially appropriate.

159 *Id.* at 205, explaining that drives and emotions "are highly specific and evolutionarily preserved repertoires of behaviors whose execution the brain faithfully calls into duty, in certain circumstances." As Damasio explains, "the mind is engaged in telling the story of the body's multifarious events, and uses that story to optimize the life of the organism." *Id.* at 206.

160 *Id.* at 178.

closely linked to survival or reproduction that a particular behavior/emotion was in evolutionary terms, the more difficult it will be to change. Stress responses (the fight or flight response), for example, are very difficult to moderate.[161]

But none of this is discussed in the heuristics and biases literature. No explicit link is made between support theory and the burgeoning work in the neuroscience of emotions. No direct analogy to evolution is brought to bear on framing effects or any other heuristic. This makes it difficult to explain why losses should loom larger than gains, or why people should become attached to mugs but not tokens in studies of the endowment effect. A more biological perspective, however, might provide the necessary insights.

Availability, representativeness, and base rate neglect

The availability heuristic, in which people decide how likely an event is based on how easily they can imagine it[162]; the representativeness heuristic, in which people tend to make decisions based on how alike something is to a prototype[163]; and base rate neglect, in which people ignore the frequency of a given subject in the population, are closely related to memory and imagination. Although this research is not new, "support theory" – the theory that people respond to detailed stories – is an attempt to "weave together the different heuristics into a unified account."[164] Under support theory, people make judgments based on how vivid a description of the event they can bring to mind.

Research on the availability heuristic has been plagued by confounding the ease of recall with the amount of recall.[165] Nonetheless, numerous studies show that when these confounding factors are separated, people still estimate the frequency, likelihood, and typicality according to the ease with which associations come to mind. Emotion, experience, vividness of description, and motivation are important factors. But, exactly how this happens or what makes something vivid is still unexplained in this research.

The representativeness heuristic was originally studied through word descriptions that asked people to choose the profession of a person described in a particular

---

161 *See* Erica Beecher-Monas and Edgar Garcia-Rill, *Law and the Brain*, J. App. Prac. & Proc., discussing the stress response.

162 *See* Steven J. Sherman, et al., *Imagining Can Heighten or Lower the Perceived Likelihood of Contracting a Disease: The Mediating Effect of Ease of Imagery*, in Heuristics & Biases, *supra* note 9, p. 98, noting that "the more available an outcome is, the more likely it is perceived to be."

163 *See* Thomas Gilovich and Kenneth Savitsky, *Like Goes with Like: The Role of Representativeness in Erroneous and Pseudo-Scientific Beliefs*, in Heuristics & Biases, *supra* note 9, p. 617, 618, defining representativeness as the "overarching rule: 'like goes with like.'"

164 Lyle A. Brenner, et al., Heuristics & Biases, *supra* note 9, p. 489, noting that memory is involved in each of these heurisitcs.

165 *See* Norbert Schwarz and Leigh Ann Vaugn, *The Availability Heuristic Revisited: Ease of Recall and Content of Recall as Distinct Sources of Information*, in Heuristics & Biases, *supra* note 9, pp. 103, 118, reviewing the literature and explaining that this "confound rendered many of the classic tests of the availability heuristic nondiagnostic."

way.[166] The results of these studies engendered much controversy about the choice of words and the method of administration.[167] A number of studies demonstrated instances in which base-rate information was used.[168] As a result of this controversy, further studies have separated prototype effects from base-rate information.[169]

The base-rate fallacy asserts that contrary to rational-choice predictions that people will consider the statistical probability that an event will occur and update it with particularized specific information, people actually tend to ignore base rates and overestimate the correlation between what something appears to be and what it is, adhering to stereotypes.[170] In other words, they are likely to base decisions on the extent to which a particular event (or person) resembles a certain category of events (or fits within their stereotypes of people).[171] For example, in assessing the career of a person described as overbearing, aggressive, rude, and skilled at rhetorical argument, people will refer mentally to known stereotypes rather than population base rates.[172] As noted previously, people think by association, and

166 In one of these, the "Tom W." description, people were asked to rank the degree to which the person described resembled a typical graduate student in each of nine fields of study and were also given information about the general base rates for each field. *See* Kahneman and Frederick, *supra* note 84, pp. 61, 65. In the "Linda problem," people were asked, on the basis of a short description, to rank the probability of each of eight choices, including "bank teller" and "feminist bank teller." *Id.*, 62. In each of these, people tended to find the particularized choice that fit stereotypical attributes more likely than the more general choice (i.e., feminist banker was chosen more often than banker). *Id.*

167 *Id.*, 65, noting the challenges to the findings as "artifacts of ambiguous language, confusing instructions, conversational norms, or inappropriate normative standards."

168 *See* Derek J. Koehler, *A Strength Model for Probability Judgments for Tournaments*, 66 Org. Behav. & Human Dec. Processes, 16–21 (1996), reviewing the literature.

169 *See* Kahneman and Frederick, *supra* note 84, p. 65.

170 *See* H. J. Einhorn and R.M. Hogarth, *Confidence in Judgment: Persistence of the Illusion of Validity*, 85 Psychol. Rev., 395–416 (1978), giving the example of a waiter who gives better service to well-dressed patrons because of a belief that well-dressed patrons leave better tips, which is validated when the patron leaves a good tip.

171 *See* Daniel Kahneman and Amos Tversky, *Subjective Probability: A Judgment of Representativeness*, 3 Cognitive Psychol., 430, 431 (1972), defining the representativeness heuristic as evaluating "the probability of an uncertain event, or a sample, by the degree to which it is (i) similar in essential properties to its parent population, and (ii) reflects the salient features of the process by which it is generated" so that a characteristic is matched to a category and the probability evaluated in terms of the closeness of the match. The classic study on this bias was that of Meehl and Rosen, who documented the degree that psychiatric diagnoses made in staff meetings ignored population base rates. *See* P.E. Meehl and A. Rosen, *Antecedent Probability in the Efficiency of Psychometric Signs, Patterns, or Cutting Scores*, 52 Psychol. Bull. 194–216 (1955).

172 Amos Tversky and Daniel Kahneman, *Availability: A Heuristic for Judging Frequency and Probability*, in Judgment Under Uncertainty: Heuristics and Biases, 1124 (Daniel Kahneman et al., eds., 1982). There is an ongoing debate between Kahneman/Tversky and Gigerenzer about whether this is a reasoning error or not, with the focus of the disagreement on interpretations of probability. *See, e.g.*, Gerd Gigerenzer, *The Bounded Rationality of Probabilistic Mental Modes*, in Rationality: Psychological and Philosophical Perspectives, 284, 291–7 (K. I. Manktelow and D. E. Over, eds., 1993), arguing that you cannot assign probabilities to unique events and that, therefore, there is no normative basis for assigning error to stereotyping and suggesting that errors are eliminated by asking questions in terms of frequencies rather than in terms of probabilities and increasing the use of random sampling; Daniel Kahneman and Amos Tversky, *On the Reality of Cognitive Illusions*, 103 Psych. Rev., 582, 582–3 (1996), acknowledging that representation in terms of absolute frequencies improves accuracy but citing

respond to patterns – even infants recognize shape patterns.[173] The more richly detailed a description is, the more likely it is to evoke stereotypical thinking and result in people ignoring base rates.[174] For example, people will predict that a specific event (e.g., a thousand people dying in an earthquake) is more likely than a more inclusive event (i.e., a thousand people dying from a natural disaster).[175]

One very strong heuristic is the stereotyping of outsiders.[176] This may have an emotional component.[177] It undoubtedly has unfortunate consequences, xenophobia and prejudice among them.[178] On the other hand, it may have been an essential component of civilization. Evolutionary biologist Jared Diamond remarks that "genocide has been part of our human and prehuman heritage for millions of years."[179] He details the genocidal patterns of chimpanzees, gorillas, and wolves, and suggests that, based on chimpanzee behavior, "a major reason for our human hallmark of group living was defense against other human groups, especially once we acquired weapons and a large enough brain to plan ambushes."[180] Obviously, even if this behavior may once have been adaptive, that is no excuse to perpetuate it.

Although stereotyping appears to be a characteristic of human thought and undoubtedly speeds up the thinking process, permitting people to react automatically and largely unconsciously to people that they perceive as belonging to a different group, one moderating effect is the anticipation of future dependency. For example, when subjects were divided into groups who were or were not anticipating having

> studies to demonstrate that people nonetheless perceive correlations that do not exist and that "some significant judgmental biases are not readily corrected by the observation of natural frequencies."
>
> 173 *See, e.g.*, Roger Lecuyer and Christine Cybula, *Categorization of Geometric Figures Composed of Three or Four Elements by 3-Month-Old Infants*, Current Psychol. Cognition 221, 221–44 (2000), noting studies showing that infants recognize geometric patterns; Dawes, note 66, p. 534, explaining the problems of representativeness and pseudodiagnosticity as probabilistic fallacies.
>
> 174 Amos Tverky and Derek J. Koehler, *Support Theory: A Nonextensional Representation of Subjective Probability*, in Heuristics & Biases, *supra* note 9, pp. 441, 443, outlining the basis for "support theory," in which belief in the likelihood of a particular proposition is based on the explicitness of its description rather than ascribing probabilities to events.
>
> 175 *See id.* at 474; Norbert Schwarz, *Feelings as Information*, Heuristics & Biases, *supra* note 9, pp. 534, 536, hypothesizing that "the impact of feelings on evaluative judgments is a function of the feelings' perceived informational value."
>
> 176 *See* Ridley, *supra* note 25, p. 264, discussing the idea of racial stereotyping as a proxy for information about coalitions. Ridley notes that like ape society, human society is riddled with factions and that there may have been an evolutionary advantage to being able to recognize outsiders. *Id.*, pp. 265–6, discussing the experiments of Robert Kurzban, in which stronger clues as to coalition membership made people ignore race.
>
> 177 *See, e.g.*, Antonio Damasio, Looking for Spinoza: Joy, Sorrow, and the Feeling Brain, 140, noting the "growing evidence that feelings, along with the appetites and emotions that most often cause them, play a decisive role in social behavior." Damasio postulates that heuristics and biases such as those observed by Kahneman and Tversky are probably due to the "covert activation of biases related to prior emotional experiences of comparable situations." *Id.*, 149.
>
> 178 *See* Jared Diamond, The Third Chimpanzee, 294 (1992), "Chimps also share xenophobia with us: they clearly recognize members of other bands as different from members of their own band, and treat them very differently."
>
> 179 *Id.* at 297.
>
> 180 *Id.* at 294.

to depend on another individual to win a twenty-dollar prize, those subjects that were anticipating being dependent paid closer attention to individual characteristics and relied less on stereotypes.[181] Moreover, racial stereotyping may be more about identifying rival factions than "race" because racial clues can be swamped by stronger clues to coalition membership.[182]

A problem that may be related to pattern recognition is the overestimation of the relevance of memorable incidents at the expense of statistical base rates. The problem appears to arise when people think that what they remember is representative of the population as a whole. Medical student and physician participants, for example, greatly overestimated the number of dramatic deaths in a study that asked participants to estimate the number of deaths due to each of forty-two diseases.[183]

Base-rate neglect has been a highly controversial subject.[184] Some of the strongest evidence of this effect comes not from studies of college students but from studies of psychology and medical clinicians.[185] In a meta-analysis of more than 100 comparative studies, an actuarial method outperformed the clinical diagnosis in all but eight.[186] Even when based on the same information, clinicians' diagnoses were less accurate than the Minnesota Multiphase Personality Inventory (MMPI), a commonly used psychological assessment instrument.[187] Actuarial instruments also diagnosed progressive brain dysfunction better than clinicians.[188] In numerous other studies, physicians' diagnoses and prognoses were similarly improved with actuarial instruments.[189] Even a layperson armed with a programmed calculator has a better chance of correct diagnosis than an unaided expert.[190]

---

181 *See* Thane S. Pittman, "Motivation," in *Handbook of Social Psychology, supra* note 55, at 554.

182 *See* Ridley, *supra* note 25, p. 266, noting that in sports, "white fans cheer a black player on 'their' team as he beats a white player on the opposing team."

183 Christensen-Szalanski et al., *Effects of Expertise and Experience on Risk Judgments*, 68 J. App. Psychol. 278–84 (1983).

184 *See* Kahneman and Frederick, note 84, p. 66, discussing "why the strong forms of base-rate neglect . . . sparked so much controversy."

185 *See* Robyn M. Dawes, et al., *Clinical versus Actuarial Judgment*, in Heuristics & Biases, *supra* note 9, pp. 716, 717, describing studies.

186 Grove, et al., *Clinical versus Mechanical Prediction: A Meta-Analysis*, 12 Psychol. Assessment, 19–30 (2000).

187 Dawes et al., *supra* note 185, p. 718, explaining that using a decision rule yielded a 70 percent accuracy rate, whereas the clinicians averaged only a 62 percent accuracy, and the most accurate clinician was only 67 percent correct, based on the same information. When the clinicians' own decision rules were used as models for actuarial instruments, the "models were more often accurate than the very judges on whom they were based" probably because of human variability in applying decision rules.

188 *See* D. A. Leli and S.B. Filskov, *Clinical Detection of Intellectual Deterioration Associated with Brain Damage*, 37 J. Clin. Psychol., 623–29 (1984), observing that clinicians could not match the actuarial instrument's accuracy.

189 *See* Dawes et al., *supra* note 185, p. 719.

190 This finding is one of the rationales for the evidence-based medicine movement, which advocates the use of statistical base-rates by physicians. *See, e.g.*, Lars Noah, *Medicine's Epistemology: Mapping the Haphazard Diffusion of Knowledge in the Biomedical Community*, 44 Ariz. L. Rev., 373, 380, (2002) noting that "evidence-based medicine attempts to improve decision making by practicing physicians."

In addition, the VRAG discussed in Chapters 6 and 7 was developed by two groups of Canadian psychiatric researchers studying the problem of why clinical predictions of repeated violent behavior among institutionalized violent offenders were wrong more often than not.[191] They found that clinical decision makers tend to erroneously assume the representativeness of events by ignoring sample sizes and base rates.[192] Clinicians, like other people, tend to think they have more information than they really do. Clinicians (again, like other people) are poor at making extreme judgments; they tend to have more confidence in predictive variables with extreme values than is warranted.[193] In other words, although it is more difficult to predict statistically rare events (e.g., violence), clinical judgments frequently fail to take that into account.[194]

Making the probabilistic nature of the evaluation task explicit tends to reduce the frequency of these errors.[195] Repetition and feedback also assist people in incorporating base rates into their reasoning.[196] Moreover, presenting probabilistic evidence in frequentist terms sometimes makes it more comprehensible.[197] However, even when clinicians are provided with more information than the actuarial instrument, clinical judgment fails to surpass the actuarial accuracy.[198]

Egocentric biases: self-serving, overconfidence, and cognitive dissonance

Behavioral economists have not been slow to note that when people must make impartial judgments about a course of action, self-interest has a way of creeping in – unconsciously – to the decision process. Research in this area includes studies in which, for example, participants who believed that a particular trait – introversion or extroversion – was more conducive to success would modify their descriptions of themselves in the favorable direction, and the first memories they would generate

191 See VERNON L. QUINSEY ET AL., VIOLENT OFFENDERS: APPRAISING AND MANAGING RISK 69 (1998), explaining how the statistical base-rate problem affects predictions of dangerousness.

192 Daniel Kahneman and Amos Tversky, *Subjective Probability: A Judgment of Representativeness*, 3 COGNITIVE PSYCHOL. 430 (1972). These shortcuts are not consciously employed but rather operate on a subliminal level to affect decision. *Id.*

193 H. Einhorn and R. Hogarth, *Confidence in Judgment: Persistence of the Illusion of Validity*, 85 PSYCHOL. REV. 395 (1978).

194 See John W. Parry et al., *Am. Bar Ass'n. Comm'n. on Mental Health and Physical Disability Law, National Benchbook on Psychiatric and Psychological Evidence and Testimony*, 20 (1998) (hereinafter *Benchbook*), noting that "it is difficult to predict with certainty statistically rare events."

195 See Gerd Gigerenzer, *From Tools to Theories: A Heuristic of Discovery in Cognitive Psychology*, 98 PSYCHOL. REV., 254–67 (1991).

196 Ralph Hertwig and Andreas Ortmann, *Experimental Practices in Economics: A Methodological Challenge for Psychologists?* 24 BEHAVIORAL & BRAIN SCI. 383, 387–88 (2001), noting that "experience can substantially improve Bayesian reasoning" and that "biases diminish in magnitude with sufficient experience although not necessarily after only a few trials."

197 See GERD GIGERENZER, CALCULATED RISK (2002).

198 See, e.g., Dawes, et al., (*Heuristics & Biases*), *supra* note 9, p. 721, "Even when given an information edge, the clinical judge still fails to surpass the actuarial method; in fact, access to additional information often does nothing to close the gap between the two methods."

were those that supported the characteristic.[199] Somehow, the information is processed in a way that makes the outcome more desirable to the decision maker. People who received positive feedback on a personality test, for example, were more likely to agree with a study showing that the test was valid than those who received negative feedback.[200] People have been shown to manipulate statistical inferences in ways consistent with the self-serving bias.[201] Self-enhancing interpretations of outcomes, by attributing more control over the situation than is warranted for positive outcomes and by overly attributing the bad outcomes to chance, may also impede decision making.[202]

These effects are less prominent in the decision-reaching stage than they are at the decision-justification stage.[203] But, across cultures, people appear to overestimate their ability to provide correct answers to questions.[204] In addition, overconfidence bias may afflict experts more than novices, and groups are more prone to it than individuals.[205]

Several explanations have been offered for this phenomenon. One explanation for overconfidence is that people "confuse easily drawn inferences for easily

199 *See* Sanitioso et al., *Motivated Recruitment of Autobiographical Memory*, 59 J. PERSONALITY AND SOCIAL PSYCHOL., 229–41 (1990).

200 *See* Pyszczynski et al, *Maintaining Consistency Between Self-Serving Beliefs and Available Data: A Bias in Information Evaluation*, 11 PERSONALITY & SOC. PSYCHOL. BULL. 179–90 (1985).

201 *See* Pittman, *supra* note 181, p. 562, discussing studies showing that although people usually ignore base rates, participants used base-rate information, "but only when they were playing the role of a person who wished to come to a conclusion that could only be reached through the use of base-rate information."

202 This is known as the fundamental attribution error, or a "tendency to attribute behavior exclusively to the actor's dispositions and to ignore powerful situational determinants of the behavior." RICHARD NISBETT AND LEE ROSS, HUMAN INFERENCE: STRATEGIES AND SHORTCOMINGS OF SOCIAL JUDGMENT, 31 (1980). *See* MAX H. BAZERMAN, JUDGMENT IN MANAGERIAL DECISION MAKING, 98–99 (3d ed., 1994), noting that "positive illusions lead organizational members to claim an inappropriately large proportion of the credit for positive outcomes, to overestimate their value to the organization, and to set objectives that have little chance of success"; K. D. Markman et al., *The Impact of Perceived Control on the Imagination of Better and Worse Possible Worlds* 21 PERSONALITY & SOC. PSYCHOL. BULL., 588–95 (1995), participants in a computer "wheel of fortune" game given control over either where the wheel started or which of two wheels would be theirs and then experiencing either a near big win or a near big loss attributed more control to the win than the loss scenario; N. D. Weinstein, *Unrealistic Optimism About Future Life Events* 39 J. PERSONALITY AND SOCIAL PSYCHOL, 806–20 (1980), people think they are more likely to experience positive outcomes than are others; S. E. Taylor and J. D. Brown, *Illusion and Well-Being Revisited: Separating Fact from Fiction*, 116 PSYCHOL. BULL., 193–210 (1994), documenting unrealistically positive self-evaluations, exaggerated perceptions of control, and unrealistic optimism; *Why Do People Need Self-Esteem? Converging Evidence that Self-Esteem Serves an Anxiety Buffering Function*, 63 J. PERSONALITY & SOC. PSYCHOL., 913, 913–21 (1992), arguing that self-deception sustains the illusion of control and diminishes anxiety.

203 *See* Pittman, *supra* note 181, p. 566, noting that these motivationally activated illusions are more likely to predominate once a person has decided to act than in the process of making a decision.

204 *See* J. Frank Yates, et al., *Probability Judgment Across Cultures*, in HEURISTICS & BIASES, *supra* note 9, p. 271, citing studies showing that – with the exception of Japanese and Singaporeans – Asians are even more overconfident than Westerners.

205 *See* Philip E. Tetlock, *Accountability: A Social Magnifier of the Dilution Effect*, 57 J. PERSONALITY & SOC. PSYCH. 388, 419 (1989), noting that "groupthink promoted rigid and self-righteous patterns of thinking."

remembered facts."[206] Another is the possibility that people selectively focus on evidence that is consistent with their first impression and ignore inconsistent evidence.[207] A third is that overconfidence is a buffer against anxiety.[208] A number of studies have challenged the existence and extent of the overconfidence bias. For example, Peter Justin claimed that design flaws exaggerated the experimental findings of overconfidence.[209] Further studies, however, taking these design flaws into account still showed an overconfidence effect.[210]

One cannot say that people always exhibit overconfidence, however. As noted previously, sometimes people exhibit underconfidence.[211] Difficulty of the task also appears to be a moderator: easy choices appear to produce underconfidence, whereas difficult choices appear to produce overconfidence.[212] This effect has been studied in general-knowledge questions[213] and in clinical diagnoses.[214] People may express very high confidence in their choice even when they acknowledge that they are frequently wrong in their assessments.[215] One of the explanations for this phenomenon is a "tendency to prefer an individual or 'inside' view rather than a statistical or 'outside' view" because it is more vivid.[216]

As discussed, in previous chapters, once a decision has been made, cognitive-dissonance theory suggests that people tend to take further actions that justify

---

206 *See* Hart Blanton, et al. *Overconfidence as Dissonance Reduction*, 37 J. Expt'l Soc. Psychol. 373, 374, citing studies.

207 *See* Eddie Harmon-Jones and Judson Mills, *An Introduction to Cognitive Dissonance Theory and an Overview of Current Perspectives on the Theory*, in Cognitive Dissonance: Progress on a Pivotal Theory in Social Psychology, 3–33 (Eddie Harmon-Jones and Judson Mills, eds., 1999), citing studies demonstrating that people selectively seek information that will decrease expected post-decision dissonance.

208 *See* Jeff Greenberg et al., *Why Do People Need Self-Esteem? Converging Evidence that Self-Esteem Serves an Anxiety Buffering Function*, 63 J. Personality & Soc. Psychol., 913–21 (1992), arguing that self-deception sustains the illusion of control and diminishes anxiety.

209 *See* Peter Justin, *The Overconfidence Phenomenon as a Consequence of Informal, Experimenter-Guided Selection of Almanac Items*, in Judgment in Managerial Decision Making, 544, 553 (Max Bazerman, 4th ed., 1998), arguing that design flaws in experiments inflated the overconfidence result.

210 *See* Joshua Klayman, et al., *Overconfidence: It Depends on How, What, and Whom You Ask*, 79 Org. Behav. & Hum. Decision Processes, 216, 217 (1999), finding "systemic difference between subjective confidence judgments and observed accuracy ... overall, confidence tends to exceed accuracy."

211 *See* Griffen and Tversky, *supra* note 39, p. 230, noting a pattern of overconfidence and underconfidence in the research literature.

212 *Id.* at 242, discussing the effect of difficulty of the task on the confidence people have in their choice.

213 *See e.g.*, S. Lichtenstein, et al., *Calibration and Probabilities: The State of the Art in 1980*, in Heuristics and Biases, note 9, p. 306–34, literature review.

214 *See* J. F. Yates, et al., *Measuring and Analyzing Probability Judgment in Medicine*, 28 Philippine J. Internal Med. (Suppl. 1), 21–32 (1990), testing overconfidence in medical diagnoses.

215 *See* Gerd Gigerenzer, et al., *Probabilistic Mental Models: A Brunswickian Theory of Confidence*, in 98 Psychol. Rev., 506–28 (1991), noting the disconnect between people's confidence in their choices and their own assessments of their error rates.

216 *See* Griffen and Tversky, *supra* note 39, p. 248, noting additionally that "people's performance on the frequency task leaves much to be desired" in that the "degree of underestimation in judgments of frequency was comparable, on average, to the degree of overconfidence in individual judgments of probability."

and reinforce those decisions.[217] Information supporting their decision is likely to have a disproportionate impact on their assessment. One explanation is that inconsistency – in beliefs, attitudes, opinions, information, and actions – makes people uncomfortable, so that they attempt to reduce the inconsistency.[218]

There is a large body of literature discussing this phenomenon, and the research has been critiqued and validated in hundreds of studies, using multiple methodologies.[219] These studies conclude that information contradicting a choice is likely to be ignored.[220] People also tend to take further actions that justify and reinforce decisions that they have already made.[221] A robust research program indicates that a cognitive discrepancy generates dissonance.

Conclusion

Law concerns human behavior, and science has much to tell us on that subject. But, an uncritical use of science can lead law badly astray. Law and economics' basic premise, that human rationality is governed by consistent self-maximizing choices, is demonstrably false in numerous situations. But, although the existence of systematic departures from the predictions of a rational actor model of behavior is not really controversial, and a number of heuristics has been identified, the attempt at providing an overarching theory is still in progress.

217 *See* Leon Festinger, A Theory of Cognitive Dissonance (1957). Festinger's theory provoked a great deal of controversy, but the empirical basis for it appears to have survived the controversy. *See, e.g.*, Dawes, *supra* note 55, pp. 557–61, detailing the controversy and concluding that "cognitive dissonance theory is resilient."

218 *See* Pittman, *supra* note 184, pp. 557–61, describing cognitive-dissonance theory and experimental studies of the phenomenon and concluding that "cognitive dissonance theory is resilient." An example is that smoking and the knowledge that smoking causes cancer are dissonant with each other; from knowing that smoking causes cancer, logically one shouldn't smoke, but many do. *See* Daniel J. O'Keefe, Persuasion Theory and Research, 62 (1990). People experiencing dissonance usually have more than one factor pulling in each direction, so that there would be, in the example, a cluster of factors that support smoking (e.g., beliefs that it relieves anxiety, tastes good, looks sophisticated, on the one hand) and contradict it (e.g., the expense, social opprobrium, and cancer causation, on the other hand). These factors are in conflict – one cluster is consonant with smoking and the other is dissonant – and choice between courses of action depends on the relative weights the chooser accords them. Once an initial choice has been made, the smoker will attempt to reduce dissonance in a number or ways, including selective exposure to new information that may increase dissonance.

219 *See, e.g., Introduction,* Cognitive Dissonance: Progress on a Pivotal Theory in Social Psychology, 3 (Eddie Harmon-Jones and Judson Mills, eds., 1999), noting that cognitive-dissonance theory "has generated hundreds and hundreds of studies, from which much has been learned about the determinants of attitudes and beliefs, the internalization of values, the consequences of decisions, the effects of disagreement among persons, and other important psychological processes."

220 *See* Max H. Bazerman, Judgment in Managerial Decision making, 35, noting the "tendency to ignore disconfirming information." This conclusion is one of the strongest implications of the theory. *See* Pittman, *supra* note 184, p. 561, citing studies showing that "a preferred, perhaps *the* preferred mode of dissonance reduction may be simply to ignore inconsistency until it fades away."

221 *See* G. Whyte, *Escalating Commitment in Individual and Group Decision Making: A Prospect Theory Approach,* 54 Org. Behav. & Hum. Dec. Proc., 430–5 (1993), finding a tendency to escalate commitment in individuals and groups.

Sound interdisciplinary application of scientific research requires evaluation of the strengths and weaknesses of a series of experiments – the research program – in terms of underlying theory, experimental design, statistical assumptions and analysis, and interdisciplinarity. It is in this aspect of interdisciplinarity that the research program of social psychologists has been (at least until recently) notably lacking. Neuroscience and evolutionary biology have been largely ignored as has complexity theory.

Support theory, for example, which relies on vividness of description, fails to explain "vividness" or why that should matter, or to draw on the neuroscience of memory, which might provide some insight. As a result, although moderating factors – contexts – that may affect heuristic use have been identified, as have some debiasing strategies, what this means to real-world decision making remains controversial. Moreover, complexity theory implies that any claims for predictability – whether emanating from law and economics or behavioral economics – should be viewed with skepticism. The lesson for lawyers is that while social science has much to offer law, its uncritical use should be avoided. A legal scholar should not simply cite a particular bias in support of an argument, for example, without acknowledging the strengths and weaknesses of the underlying research program. On the other hand, legal theorizing that fails to draw on the rich insights of social psychology is a paltry version of its potential. A more sophisticated view of science can only improve the discourse of law.

10

Evaluating battered woman syndrome

Domestic violence is all too often the hidden fulcrum catapulting litigants into court.[1] Far too often it remains a concealed force. Lawyers may fail to raise domestic violence as an issue, unaware of its impact on their clients' decisions. Judges may refuse to consider domestic violence, finding it irrelevant even when it could explain the reasonableness of a defendant's actions. Courts display an extraordinary reluctance to grapple with its implications. This is especially apparent in the homicide justification of self-defense.[2]

1 The Department of Justice estimates that 22 percent of women in federal prisons and 43 percent of women in state prisons have been victims of domestic violence. *See Statistics Packet, Nat'l Clearinghouse for the Defense of Battered Women*, Phila., Pa. (3d ed., 1994). A more recent study indicates that as many as 60 percent of women in state prisons were abused sexually or physically prior to incarceration. *See* U.S. Departmentt of Justice, Bureau of Statistics, *Women Offenders* 10/3/2000, http://www.ojp.usdoj.gov/bjs/pub (last visited 11/17/05).

2 Self-defense is a form of justification and traditionally is explained as an absence of moral blameworthiness, resulting in legal exoneration. Justification defenses exonerate someone who has killed another human being from criminal consequences. *See* J. L. Austin, *A Plea for Excuses*, in 57 PROCEEDINGS OF THE ARISTOTELIAN SOCIETY, 1 (1957), noting that regarding justification, "we accept responsibility but deny that it was bad," and distinguishing excuse, where "we admit that it was bad but don't accept full, or even any, responsibility." The distinction between justification and excuse is "between warranted action and unwarranted action for which the actor is not to blame." Kent Greenawalt, *The Perplexing Borders of Justification and Excuse*, 84 COLUM. L. REV. 1897, 1927 (1984) arguing that the "criminal law should not attempt to distinguish between justification and excuse in a fully systematic way." Professor Greenawalt argues that the distinction between justification and excuse is incoherent because in both instances, the result is legal exoneration. Some excuses, such as the "heat of passion" or "extreme emotional disturbance" defenses may result in partial rather than complete exoneration. Provocation and diminished responsibility are excuses that lead to partial exoneration in the Commonwealth. *See, e.g.,* "The Law Commission Partial Defenses to Murder" (*Law. Com. No. 290*) (HMSO; London, 2004). Although states differ somewhat in their requirements for self-defense, in general, four requirements must be met: (1) a belief that deadly force is necessary against an imminent threat of death or severe bodily harm; (2) a proportionate use of force in response to the threat; (3) absence of aggression on the part of the defendant; and (4) a retreat to the greatest degree reasonably possible. The Maryland Pattern Jury Instructions exemplify this notion, requiring – in pertinent part – that "before using deadly force, the Defendant is required to make all reasonable effort to retreat. The Defendant does not have to retreat if the Defendant was in his own home, or retreat was unsafe, or the avenue to retreat was unknown to the Defendant." Maryland State Bar Ass'n., *Maryland Criminal Pattern Jury Instructions*, 4:17.14 at 277.2.8 (1986, 1995 Supp.) (quoted in *Marr v. State*, 759 A. 2d, 327, 344 (Md. App., 2000). Some states impose a duty to retreat only when the accused is at fault in provoking the attack. *See, e.g., State v. Seals,* 2005 WL 2243687 (slip op.) Ohio App. Dist. (a defendant who started a fight could not be acting in self-defense); *Sands v. Commonwealth,* 2000 WL App. 1665041 (Va. App. 2000)

Complicating these issues of admissibility are competing visions of equality under the law. A defining aspect of justice is the requirement of equal treatment under the law. Equality under the law is far from a self-defining concept, however, and much legal debate has focused on its definition, with some arguing for formal equality and others for substantive equality.[3] Evidence law, no less than other legal rules, is subject to the debate about what constitutes equality.

The courts' failure to recognize the impact of domestic violence in making their evidentiary rulings can have drastic effects. Judges frequently misapply evidentiary rules, ignore established precedent, and circumvent criteria for scientific validity. On one hand, circumstances that are normally admissible in male-on-male violence cases become suddenly irrelevant and the context distorted in domestic female-to-male violence cases.[4] On the other hand, the widely adopted solution to the perceived unfairness of the traditional rules when applied to battered women who kill is the admission, by legislative or judicial fiat, of expert battered woman syndrome testimony.[5] This solution, however, is problematic in that such syndrome testimony

drawing a distinction between justified self-defense, for which no duty to retreat is imposed and excused self-defense for which a duty to retreat to the greatest extent possible is imposed, together with an announcement by the accused of a desire for peace. Evidence relevant to self-defense will relate to these factors.

3 Conceptions of formal equality require that judges apply rules of law in the same way to men and women and assume that everyone subject to the rules is in fundamentally the same position, regardless of status, including gender. *See* MARTHA A. FINEMAN, THE ILLUSION OF EQUALITY: THE RHETORIC AND REALITY OF DIVORCE REFORM, 3 (1991) discussing competing conceptions of equality. Proponents of substantive equality argue that even where rules are applied evenly across genders, the results of applying such gender-neutral rules may actually perpetuate unequal results. *See* Holly Maguigan, *Battered Women and Self-Defense: Myths and Misconceptions in Current Reform Proposals*, 140 U. PA. L. REV., 379, 383 (1991).

4 *See* Janet Parrish, *Trend Analysis: Expert Testimony on Battering and Its Effects in Criminal Cases*, 11 WIS. WOMEN'S L. J. 75, 79–80 (1996); Anna Carline, 26 LIVERPOOL L. REV., 13, 14–15 (2005) arguing that in the United Kingdom, "in relation to domestic homicide, women were more likely to be convicted, at the first instance, for murder, whereas men were much more successful at pleading provocation." *Cf. R. v. Ahluwalia*, 1992 WL 895579 (CA Crim. Div., 1993, Cr. L. R. 63), acknowledging that "in the case of abused wives, the act could be the result of a 'slowburn' reaction rather than an immediate loss of self control," for provocation, but nonetheless upholding the jury instructions that defined provocation as "a sudden and temporary loss of control" and allowing appeal on the basis of diminished responsibility due to depression, which the defense had failed to raise at trial.

5 *See, e.g.,* IND. CODE §§ 35–41–1-3.3 and 35–41–3-11, providing a procedural framework for using the "effects of battery" as evidence either "that the defendant was not responsible as a result of mental disease or defect" under the insanity statute or to claim that she "used justifiable reasonable force" under the law of self-defense; CA EVID. CODE §1107 (Stats. 1991 ch. 812 §1), expert testimony on battered woman syndrome admissible to show not only the effects of domestic violence on beliefs and perceptions but also on the "behavior of victims" of domestic violence; WYO. STAT. §. 6–1-203(b) "If a . . . person raises the affirmative defense of self-defense, the person may introduce expert testimony that the person suffered from [battered woman] syndrome, to establish the necessary requisite belief of an imminent danger of death or great bodily harm as an element of the affirmative defense, to justify the person's use of force"; Mo. Stat. § 563.033 "Evidence that the actor was suffering from the battered spouse syndrome shall be admissible upon the issue of whether the actor lawfully acted in self-defense or defense of another."; *People v. Humphrey*, 921 P. 2d, 1, 7 (1996), acknowledging that "expert testimony on domestic violence refers to more than a woman's

lacks empirical support and has been widely castigated as unscientific. Moreover, not only do juries refuse to buy the story battered woman syndrome presents,[6] but battered woman syndrome also casts women in a demeaning light that does not reflect reality.[7]

However, there is an alternative to both of these unwarranted extremes. Evidence rules invite expert testimony that would assist the jury in determining a factual issue in the case.[8] A crucial factual issue in a self-defense case is the reasonableness of the accused's conduct under the circumstances. Reasonableness can only be assessed with reference to the parties' relationship to each other and the community at large. Because there are widespread misconceptions about the prevalence and circumstances of domestic violence,[9] expert testimony about the demographics of domestic violence, its frequency, its under-reporting, the incidence of women killed in attempting to separate from abusive intimates, and the ineffectiveness of escape routes (including paucity of community support, police, and justice responses to victims seeking assistance) would indeed assist the jury.[10] In addition, for a subset

psychological reactions to violence" and should be admissible to explain the objective reasonableness of her conduct; *Bonner v. State*, 740 So. 2d, 439, 440–41 (Ala. App., 1998), battered woman" syndrome testimony allowed to explain conduct and coping mechanisms of battered women; *State v. Hill*, 339 S.E. 2d, 121, 122 (S.C., 1986), expert testimony relating battered women's syndrome to defendant's state of mind is critical to establishing self-defense. In Canada also, battered woman syndrome testimony is considered relevant to self-defense. See *R. v. Lavallee*, [1990] 1 S.C.R. 852 (Canada), upholding testimony of battered woman syndrome. In contrast to the United States and Canada, the United Kingdom appears to admit battered woman syndrome testimony and PTSD testimony as diminished responsibility defenses (*e.g.,* provocation). See Carline, note 4, p. 16. As in the United States, however, such testimony comes into evidence with virtually no examination of its scientific basis. See, e.g., *R. v. Howell*, 1997 WL 1106087, 1 Cr. App. R. (S.) 229, expert testimony on battered woman syndrome is "understood increasingly on an international level"; *R. v. Anderson*, 2000 WL 1841670 (CA Crim. Div.), upholding sentence based on expert report of battered woman syndrome as partial defense to murder; *R. v. Lawrenson*, 2003 WL 21917383 (CA Crim. Div., 1 Cr. App. R.(S.) 5), upholding sentence of manslaughter based on expert battered woman syndrome reports; *R. v. Fell*, 2000 WL 571218CA (Cr. Div., 2000 2 Cr. App. R. (S.) 464), quashing four-year sentence for manslaughter and commuting it to parole for the year served based on expert reports finding battered woman syndrome.

6 See Parrish, *supra* note 4, pp. 86–7, observing that juries overwhelmingly convict even when battered woman syndrome testimony is admitted, and that those convictions are overwhelming affirmed on appeal.

7 See Elizabeth Schneider, *Describing and Changing: Women's Self-Defense Work and the Problem of Expert Testimony on Battering*, 14 WOMEN'S RTS. L. REP., 213, 216 (1992), observing that battered woman syndrome simply replaces one stereotype with another.

8 See, e.g., FED. R. EVID. 702.

9 See *State v. Kelly*, 478 A. 2d, 364, 378 (N.J., 1984), expert social-context testimony about battered women admissible as "an area where the purported common knowledge of the jury may be very much mistaken, an area where jurors' logic, drawn from their own experience, may lead to a wholly incorrect conclusion, an area where expert knowledge would enable the jurors to disregard their prior conclusions as being common myths rather than common knowledge."

10 For a description of the depth of public misconceptions about domestic violence, See Martha Mahoney, *Legal Images of Battered Women: Redefining the Issue of Separation*, 90 MICH. L. REV. 1, 10–13 (1991), arguing that denial of the existence and prevalence of domestic violence is so prevalent that even women that have experienced abuse often deny that they were battered women.

of women who were not only subjected to domestic violence but who also suffered from post-traumatic stress disorder (PTSD) as a result of the abuse, expert testimony should be admissible to explain their actions. This testimony, however, should be limited to scientifically sound information.

Competing conceptions of equality

The guarantee of equal protection under the law is often explained as requiring that similarly situated people be treated similarly. This begs some obvious questions. What is similar treatment and who are similarly situated people? What does it mean that women are entitled to the same rights as men? Do gender differences make people differently situated, or should the same charge – homicide, for example – trigger the same rules across genders? Or should the goal rather be to achieve similar treatment? Is it necessary to recognize gender differences to assure that women have equal legal status with men? The answers to these questions form the basis of competing visions of equality.

Proponents of formal equality insist that equal treatment under the law requires evidentiary rules to apply in a neutral, gender-blind manner. Thus, in the context of homicide, women who kill must be subject to the same rules and use the same defenses as men who kill. Any other result, argue proponents of this approach, gives women a "license to kill."[11]

The goal of formal rights proponents is to include battered women, like all criminal defendants, within the traditional framework of the criminal law to guarantee their equal rights to trial. The argument is that if legal rules were really neutral and if they were really applied in an even-handed manner, equality goals (e.g., justice) would be met.[12] Thus, to meet the aspirations of formal equality – that neutral rules should be applied in an even-handed manner – women who assert self-defense to homicide ought to be subject to the same evidentiary rules applied in the same way as men who kill. One prominent feminist critique is that new self-defense rules are unnecessary for battered women; the impediment to fairness is that existing rules are not applied in an even-handed manner.[13]

The critique of the formal equality approach centers on two factors. First, some critics argue that the criminal law paradigm is a male-violence paradigm

11 *See, e.g.*, ALAN M. DERSHOWITZ, THE ABUSE EXCUSE AND OTHER COP-OUTS, SOB STORIES AND EVASIONS OF RESPONSIBILITY, 3 (1994), asserting that "legal tactic[s] by which criminal defendants claim a history of abuse as an excuse for violent retaliation . . . is quickly becoming a license to kill."
12 *See* Fineman, *supra* note 3, p. 3, discussing competing conceptions of equality and concluding that rules are neither neutral nor applied evenly.
13 *See, e.g.*, Elizabeth M. Schneider, *Resistance to Equality*, 57 U. PITT. L. REV., 477, 490 (1996), "cases involving battered women who kill fall within traditional frameworks of defenses or excuses, but are nonetheless viewed as different or exceptional by judges who apply the law to these cases"; Maguigan, *supra* note 3, p. 383, "the most common impediments to fair trials for battered women are the result not of the structure or content of existing law, but of its application by trial judges."

with little application to women's lives.[14] Second, some critics contend that even the traditional male-oriented rules are not evenly applied to women. To remedy these shortcomings, these critics maintain that a focus on substantive equality is necessary.[15]

Substantive equality insists that the legitimacy of any legal action depends on its consequences. Inequality in relationships among people may require different treatment for people of different genders to end up in the same position.[16] Result-oriented rules proponents contend that women and men are in fundamentally different situations and have different perceptions and different needs, and that these situations must be taken into account in any system of justice.[17] This is the impetus for statutes and court rules permitting battered woman syndrome testimony – for example, based on the perception that gender-neutral legal rules have systematically excluded women's explanations. Relational feminists argue that legal rules ought to accommodate the inequalities and interdependence of human beings.[18] One way of putting this is that "women suffer in ways that men do not, and that the gender-specific suffering that women endure is routinely ignored or trivialized in the larger (male) legal culture."[19] These scholars argue that women's stories about the reasonableness of their conduct need to be heard, and that legal doctrine must

14 *See, e.g.,* Stephen J. Schulhofer, *The Feminist Challenge in Criminal Law,* 143 U. Pa. L. Rev., 2151–52 (1995), arguing that "criminal law is, from top to bottom, preoccupied with male concerns and male perspectives" and that "sometimes equality cannot be achieved by treating two groups of people the same way."

15 *See, e.g.,* Sarah M. Buel, *Effective Assistance of Counsel for Battered Women Defendants: A Normative Construct,* 26 Harv. Women's L. J., 217 (2003), contending that to meet requirements of substantive equality, the law must recognize gender differences.

16 *See* Ann C. Scales, *The Emergence of Feminist Jurisprudence: An Essay,* in New Approaches to Equality and Sameness, 41 (Weisberg, ed., 1993), advocating that law be created from the constantly changing differences among people. The famous language of *Carolene Products,* note 4, arguably endorsed such a principle, suggesting that heightened scrutiny should be applied to laws affecting "discrete and insular minorities." *United States v. Carolene Prod. Co.,* 304 U.S. 144, 153, note 4 (1938). This theory stresses the idea that "culture and social practice subordinate women under laws that are formally neutral." Stephen J. Schulhofer, *The Feminist Challenge in Criminal Law,* 143 U. Pa. L. Rev., 2151, 2152 (1995).

17 Some scholars argue, for example, that danger is different for men and women and that the legal system's failure to recognize the difference results in pervasive unfairness. *See* Elizabeth M. Schneider et al., *Representation of Women Who Defend Themselves,* in Women's Self-Defense Cases: Theory and Practice, 4 (Elizabeth Bochnak, ed., 1981), arguing that "due to a variety of societally-based factors, a woman may reasonably perceive imminent and lethal danger in a situation in which a man might not." *See* Robert F. Schopp et al., *Battered Woman Syndrome, Expert Testimony, and the Distinction Between Justification and Excuse,* 1994 U. Ill. L. Rev., 45, 98 (1994), The Model Penal Code requires only a belief in the necessity of deadly force (rather than a reasonable belief), but the circumstances the defendant knows in forming that belief are equally important here.

18 *See* Deborah Rhode, Justice and Gender, 309 (1989), noting that relational feminist work insists that women's communitarian values be implemented. *Cf.* Renee Romkins, *Ambiguous Responsibilities: Law and Conflicting Expert Testimony on the Abused Woman Who Shot Her Sleeping Husband,* 25 Law and Soc. Inq., 355, 382 (2000), discussing the Netherlands conviction of an abused woman convicted of murdering her spouse "as a consequence of the law's tendency to initially disqualify women's day-to-day experiences as legally irrelevant."

19 Robin L. West, *The Difference in Women's Hedonic Lives: A Phenomenological Critique of Feminist Legal Theory,* 15 Wis. Women's L. J. 149, 150 (2000), arguing that women's injuries are not

accommodate the "interplay between human agency and social structure."[20] At the very least, the argument goes, if the consequences of legal rules disadvantage women over men, the rules ought to be changed.[21]

The critique of the substantive equality approach centers on the "slippery slope" of applying different standards to different groups of people in a melting-pot society, where the individual conduct at issue is virtually the same.[22] If different individuals are subjected to different standards by virtue of their group membership, the argument goes, then the common political culture is weakened.[23] Another criticism of the substantive-equality approach is that it may backfire on the voiceless group, emphasizing stereotypes and demonizing the minority.

Although both formal and substantive-equality paradigms have insights – and both have flaws – neither is sufficient. Using the insights of both formal and substantive equality, however, and insisting on substantiated, empirically based argument permits the court to transcend these limitations. If courts were required to take seriously their gatekeeping responsibilities, they would demand empirical support for the assertions of experts in their courtrooms. Sound decision making should be based on empirical knowledge rather than speculation.

Self-defense is a justification to homicide because self-preservation is an important value. The justification of self-defense reflects a moral entitlement to repel wrongful violence when there is no viable alternative. This value has not only a philosophical but also a biological basis because the survival instinct is demonstrably present in all organisms.[24] The limitation is that survival of the accused must really have been at stake. As close as we can tell, her conduct must have been necessary for her self-preservation. Because of the difficulty of assessing necessity in hindsight, the ordinary person standard is a proxy for the actuality. The question is, therefore, not whether it was really a kill-or-be-killed situation but whether a

recognized by the legal system and that one of the prime ways in which a woman's injuries are discounted as deserved or private is the context of domestic violence.

20 See Linda C. McClain, *Toward a Formative Project of Securing Freedom and Equality*, 85 CORNELL L. REV., 1221, 1235 (2000), contending that any system hoping to achieve gender equality must "pay heed to the multiple and overlapping forms of disadvantage and discrimination that women suffer."

21 See, e.g., Deborah Tuerkheimer, *Recognizing and Remedying the Harm of Battering*, 94 J. L. AND CRIMINOLOGY, 959–62 (2004), arguing that a criminal law that fails to recognize inherent gender differences is unjust.

22 Of course, the female half of the population hardly qualifies as a "melting pot," but the argument is that if you use special rules for women, you must use them for other minorities (and, hence, the slippery slope). For an excellent discussion of the "cultural defense" arguments, see Holly Maguigan, *Cultural Evidence and Male Violence: Are Feminist and Multiculturalist Reformers on a Collision Course in Criminal Courts?*," 70 N.Y.U. L. REV., 36, 96 (1995).

23 See Andrew E. Taslitz, *What Feminism Has to Offer Evidence Law*, 28 SW. U. L. REV., 171, 186 (1999), contending that battered woman syndrome testimony, by creating "different standards for different types of persons, . . . lessens the possibility of a common political culture to which a citizen can belong."

24 See N. Hughes-Jones, *Inter-Group Aggression: The Multi-Individual Organism and the Survival Instinct*, 16 INDEX MEDICUS 231, April–June 2000.

reasonable person would have thought it to be so under the circumstances that then existed. For that, the context of the relationship between the batterer and the accused is important (and will be the subject of lay witness testimony).

This relationship did not exist in a vacuum, however, but within a broader social realm. Thus, when reasonableness of a party's conduct is at issue, as it is in self-defense, this means that the story must be told with enough of the background for the jury to make the required factual evaluation. Expert testimony can provide that background, demonstrating the interdependence of the individuals involved with their larger society, a foundational insight of relational feminists. This expert testimony must be scientifically valid to be helpful, and the jury should be guided as to its significance. Thus, scientifically valid expert testimony ought to be combined with jury instructions linking the relevance of the testimony to the legal standards that must be met.

Evidence of self-defense

Despite differences in phrasing, self-defense in most jurisdictions requires proof of the following four elements: reasonable belief that force is necessary against an imminent threat of harm; use of proportionate force in responding to the threatened harm; absence of aggression on the part of the defendant; and retreat to the greatest degree reasonably possible.[25] Evidence to support each of these elements must meet the admissibility criteria of the court to be considered by the factfinder. The evidentiary framework thus determines which of the elements will be provable in court and, consequently, whether the defendant will be exonerated from criminal culpability.

Although the prosecution must prove that the accused did not kill in self-defense,[26] the judge must be convinced that a prima facie case of self-defense[27] had been made before expert testimony relevant to self-defense will be admitted or the jury charged with a self-defense instruction.[28] The trial court will neither

---

25 *See* 67 A.L.R. 5th 657; some courts also require evidence of an overt act of aggression on the part of the deceased. *See* Parrish, note 4, p. 112, citing Indiana and Ohio. The Model Penal Code provides that "the use of force upon or toward another person is justifiable when the actor believes that such force is immediately necessary for the purpose of protecting himself against the use of unlawful force by the other person on the present occasion." Model Penal Code sec. 3.04.

26 *See Commonwealth v. Yanoff*, 690 A. 2d, 260, 264 (Pa. Super. Ct., 1997), burden of proof on prosecution.

27 To make out a prima facie case of self-defense, there must be some factual evidence that the elements of self-defense are present. That means, essentially, that before any expert testimony will be allowed, the defendant (or another lay witness) will have to testify to the facts that comprise the claim.

28 Evidence proffered to show self-defense must be "evidence having any tendency to make the existence of any fact that is of consequence to the determination of the action more probable or less probable than it would be without the evidence." FED. R. EVID., 401. This broad rule of relevance is tempered by the limitation of the unfair-prejudice doctrine that may operate to exclude even relevant evidence. FED. R. EVID. 403. This is a balancing test, requiring the court to

permit expert testimony nor provide instructions to the jury unless it first determines that the circumstances warrant it.[29] But, in assessing whether self-defense testimony should be admitted or a jury charge given, domestic violence is often ignored.[30] Judges, defense counsel, and prosecution are all implicated in ignoring the significance of domestic violence.[31]

Reasonable belief that force is necessary against imminent threat of harm

Proximity of threatened harm is required for self-defense in every jurisdiction.[32] The foundational idea is that self-defensive conduct must be necessary for self-preservation.[33] Necessity is central to arguments about imminence and reasonableness. The traditional view of the basis for the imminence requirement is that "when an attack against private individuals is imminent, the police are no longer in

weigh the probative value against the danger of unfair prejudice, generally by way of emotional appeals. Undue prejudice is explained by the Advisory Committee Notes as "an undue tendency to suggest decision on an improper basis, commonly, though not necessarily, an emotional one." FED. R. EVID. 403, advisory committee note.

29 See, e.g., Sands v. Commonwealth, 2000 WL 1665041 (Va. App., 2000), reversing trial court's refusal to give self-defense charge due to trial court's perception that there was no evidence of self-defense – although the deceased had battered the accused for years, had held her hostage in her home on the day of the incident, had threatened that he intended to kill her – because the accused shot her husband during a lull in the fighting.

30 See, e.g., State v. Head, 2000 WL 1708513, 2 (Wis. Ct. App., 2000), narrowing the timeline for imminence to the morning of the shooting and affirming exclusion of domestic-violence evidence and refusal to instruct jury on self-defense, where accused could show only that on the morning in question, the decedent had been lying in bed, threatened to "take care of you guys," and "whipped the covers aside and rolled across with his fist" because there was no specific threat against the accused and the threat was "not accompanied by violence at that time."

31 See, e.g., Boykins v. State, 995 P. 2d 474 (Nev. 2000), reversing and remanding because trial court failed to properly instruct that evidence related to battering should be considered for evidence of defendant's state of mind; Commonwealth v. McFadden, 587 A. 2d, 740 (Pa. Super. Ct., 1991), remanding for ineffective assistance of counsel where, despite evidence of domestic violence, counsel failed to ask for a self-defense instruction; Commonwealth v. Stonehouse, 555 A. 2d, 772, 785 (Pa., 1989), failure to request jury instruction linking experience of domestic violence to self-defense is ineffective assistance of counsel; People v. Bolden, 84 Cal. Rptr. 2d, 111, 116 (Cal. Ct. App., 2000), affirming exclusion of evidence that accused had suffered injuries at the hands of the deceased because it saw the situation as mutual combat, and "[t]here are many explanations for bruises and even for a black eye"; Phillips v. Woodford, 267 F. 3d, 966, and note 4 (2001), taking the position that a history of mutual combat means that the accused cannot claim self-defense; Commonwealth v. Singh, 582 A. 2d, 1312, 1313 (Pa., 1990), (J. Zappala dissenting), majority's refusal to hear appeal was mistaken because by failing to request jury instructions linking testimony about domestic violence to self-defense, "the jury was never given guidance as to the legal significance of the history of abuse . . . [and] was required to address the relevance of the husband's prior acts of violence against the Appellant in a vacuum."

32 The Model Penal Code, for example, provides that "the use of force . . . is justifiable when the actor believes that such force is immediately necessary . . . on the present occasion." Model Penal Code, Sec. 3.04 (1). There appears to be some difference in the way courts interpret "immediate" and "imminent" in that "states that define the harm threatened as imminent are more likely than those requiring immediacy to receive expert testimony on the theory that it is relevant to the jury's assessment of the reasonableness of the defendant's judgment about the proximity of the harm threatened." Parrish, note 4, p. 120.

33 See Model Penal Code, Sec. 3.04, Comment 2, "Prevailing rules respecting self-defense, both common law and statutory, similarly demanded belief in the necessity of the defensive action."

a position to intervene and exercise the state's function of securing public safety."[34] This concept is often translated into a temporal requirement because temporal imminence of attack means that the state cannot protect the attacked individual.

A temporal proximity requirement is one of the biggest stumbling blocks for women who assert self-defense to a charge of killing their batterers. Without a showing of temporal proximity – whether imminent or immediate – the defendant may not be able to introduce a history of domestic violence, expert testimony about the context of her actions, or obtain any jury instruction on self-defense. First, there is the question of alternative conduct: calling for help or just walking away.[35] More fundamentally, each of these cases presents the issue of why the accused did not just leave the relationship, rather than staying in a "kill or be killed" situation.[36] Necessity as well as the credibility of a woman's self-defense claim is implicated in the question of why she did not leave the relationship. Judges (and probably juries too) consistently demand an answer to the question, although this question unfairly focuses responsibility on the woman rather than on the batterer.[37]

Alternatively, the killing may have occurred during a lull in the fighting (i.e., the sleeping-man paradigm).[38] If the judge does not perceive the danger as imminent, no expert testimony about domestic violence will be admitted into evidence and no self-defense instruction given.[39]

But – from a relational perspective – time is not the only basis for imminence. There are situations other than temporal necessity in which the state may be similarly powerless – or disinclined – to intervene. Notably, it is permissible to kill a putative kidnapper or rapist without any need to show necessity, presumably because the law

---

34 George P. Fletcher, *Domination in the Theory of Justification and Excuse*, 57 U. Pitt. L. Rev., 553, 570 (1996), arguing that a history of domestic violence is irrelevant to self-defense.

35 *See State v. Harris*, 711 So. 2d, 266 (La., 1998), affirming conviction on finding that testimony from victim's family members that accused had provoked the decedent's violence was harmless error because the accused "offered no explanation as to why she did not simply depart as she had in the past, especially considering that she had to pass within feet of an exterior door on her way to the closet where she retrieved the gun" after having been thrown to the floor and assaulted.

36 *See* Schneider, *supra* note 13, p. 477, "the lurking question behind any public or private discussion of battered women is 'Why didn't she leave?'"

37 *See, eg., Dunn v. Roberts*, 963 F. 2d, 308, 313–14 (10th Cir., 1992), "The mystery in this case, as in all battered woman cases, is why Petitioner remained with [her batterer] despite repeated abuse." The phenomenon of separation assault has been explained by evolutionary biologists as "adaptive problems of male reproductive competition and potential misdirection of paternal investments in species." Margo Wilson et al., *Familicide: The Killing of Spouse and Children*, 21 Aggressive Behavior, 275 (1995). Although most states admit expert testimony on this question, some do not. Thirty-six states find battered woman syndrome testimony relevant to the question of why the defendant failed to leave the relationship; six do not.

38 This paradigm, contrary to popular misconceptions, appears to be the minority of actual cases. *See* Maguigan, *supra* note 3, p. 379, observing that the appellate decisions do not support the commonly encountered assertion that most battered women kill in nonconfrontational situations.

39 For example, in *Brown v. State*, 512 S.E. 2d, 260 (GA 1999), in a case involving defense of a child, the court declined to admit evidence of prior abuse because the child was not threatened on the day of the killing. *See, e.g., State v. Smith*, 864 P. 2d, 709 (1993), despite a long history of abuse, the court affirmed the trial court's denial of self-defense instruction because the deceased had not made threats on the evening of the incident.

assumes that one faces an absence of alternatives in those circumstances.[40] Limiting necessity to the temporal element ignores the problem of absent alternatives.[41] If there really is no escape, or if the accused reasonably perceives that there is none, and it is only a matter of time until the abuser will kill, then insisting on a temporal necessity seems rather beside the point of survival. The question should be whether the defense response was necessary under the circumstances – that is, whether the intrusions on the accused's freedom of person were so extreme as to be tantamount to kidnaping, terrorism, torture, and rape.[42]

Most states incorporate a reasonableness requirement into imminence in two respects: a requirement that the accused's perception of *danger* be reasonable and a requirement that her perception of *imminence* be reasonable.[43] There is some argument about whether the standard is or ought to be subjective or objective reasonableness or an amalgam of both; however, under either of these standards, what is reasonable depends on the circumstances at the time of the event. Past violence on the part of the deceased is part of the circumstances and is traditionally admissible.[44] When two men are engaged in a fight, for example, evidence about

---

40 *See* WAYNE R. LaFAVE AND AUSTIN W. SCOTT, JR., CRIMINAL LAW, 456, note 15 (2d ed., 1986), explaining that deadly force is permitted against "extreme intrusions on freedom of the person (*e.g.,* kidnapping and rape)" even without a threat of death or severe bodily harm.

41 *See* Benjamin C. Zipursky, *Self-Defense, Domination, and the Social Contract,* 57 U. PITT. L. REV., 579, 584 (1996), noting "that if, in fact, the defendant needed to kill in order to avert death or grievous bodily harm inflicted by the assailant, then she had a right to kill, regardless of whether a 'short time frame' or some other limitation was the reason for her need." Courts do not often see it this way. *See, e.g., Ha v. State,* 892 P. 2d, 184, 192 (Alaska App., 1995), opining that "inevitable harm is not the same as imminent harm."

42 *See* LaFave and Scott, *supra* note 40, p. 458 noting that "the proper inquiry is not the immediacy of the threat, but the immediacy of the response necessary in defense."

43 *See, e.g.,* CONN. GEN. STAT. ANN. §53A-19(A) (WEST, 1958); GA CODE ANN. § 26–902(A) (SUPP., 1976); IND. COND. ANN. § 35–41-3-2(A) (BURNS SUPP., 1977); LA REV. STAT. ANN. §14.20 (1) (WEST, 1974); WASH. REV. CODE ANN. § 9A.16.050(1) (1977).

44 In a self-defense case, the evidence of the character of the deceased is relevant to showing the likelihood that the deceased was the primary aggressor, as well as to show that the accused had a reasonable belief in the necessity of a forceful response. Rule 404 requires the exclusion of character evidence if its only relevance is to show circumstantially that particular conduct occurred on the occasion in question. FED. R. EVID. 404. The rule, however, does not apply to character evidence of the victim. Some states, such as Louisiana, limit this exception (i.e., permitting evidence of the victim's character) to instances where there has been an overt act by the victim or where there is evidence of domestic violence. *See* LA CODE EVID. 404A(2).

   Fed. R. Evid. 404(a)(2) provides:

   (a) Character evidence generally. Evidence of a person's character or a trait of character is not admissible for the purpose of proving action in conformity therewith on a particular occasion, except:...
   (2) Character of victim. Evidence of a pertinent trait of character of the victim of the crime offered by an accused, or by the prosecution to rebut the same....

   Although character evidence is admissible under Rule 404(b), it may be proffered only through opinion or reputation testimony rather than through testimony about specific instances, unless character of the deceased is an essential element of the defense. *See* FED. R. EVID. 405(a), (b); *State v. Rodrigue,* 734 So. 2d 608, 610 (La., 1999), remanding for new trial where court refused to admit character evidence in self-defense. In battered women's cases, the deceased's character is an essential element of the defense, so character evidence may come in through both lay and

the deceased's past threats of violence against the defendant are admissible under ordinary rules of evidence, to explain the circumstances.[45] The deceased's conduct before the killing is normally – that is, in male-on-male violence cases – considered relevant to the reasonableness of the defendant's actions.[46] The decedent's reputation for violence is routinely admissible, as are the deceased's specific acts of past violence.[47] Curiously, these details have a way of being left out of women's cases.[48]

> expert testimony. Thus, character evidence about the deceased ought to be freely admissible both as testimony about specific instances of his behavior and as general testimony about the behavior he exhibited.

45 *See, e.g., State v. Brooks,* 734 So. 2d, 1232 (La. App., 1999), previous threats by deceased admissible; *State v. Clark,* 570 N.W. 2d, 195 (N.D., 1997), prior threats are relevant to show reasonableness of defendant's belief in imminent danger; *People v. Bush,* 264 Cal. Rptr, 167, 175 (Cal. Ct. App., 1978), finding admissible prior threats by victim against defendant. Moreover, the prohibition on character evidence to show conduct does not include "habit" evidence, which is admissible to show conduct under Rule 406. Fed. R. Evid. 406 provides:

> Evidence of the habit of a person . . . whether corroborated, or not, and regardless of the presence of eyewitnesses, is relevant to prove that the conduct of the person . . . was in conformity with the habit or routine practice.

Habit evidence relates to semiautomatic behavior, however. *Washington St. Phys. Ins. Ex. and Ass'n v. Fisons Corp.,* 858 P. 2d, 1054 (Wash., 1993), citing McCormick's definition of "semi-automatic, almost involuntary and invariabl[y] specific responses to fairly specific stimuli." Thus, whereas evidence portraying the deceased's habitual carrying or use of knives or guns may be admissible under this rule, his routinely picking fights with weaker people might not be. *See, e.g., United States v. Yazzie,* 188 F. 3d, 1178, 1190 (10th Cir., 1999), deceased's habitual wearing of guns and knives was admissible, although evidence of his routinely starting fights with weaker people in bars was excluded as habit because "it did not represent a sufficiently semi-automatic reaction."

46 *See, e.g., Petty v. State,* 997 P. 2d, 800 (Nev., 2000), defendant shot unarmed victim in a fight over a pair of pants, but testimony concerning victim's reputation for violence nonetheless admissible to show defendant's reasonable belief in the necessity of using deadly force; *State v. Brooks,* 734 So. 2d, 1232 (La. App., 1999), in parking-lot shooting, testimony relevant to self-defense admissible although victim was unarmed, defendant was armed and fired first shots, but victim lunged at defendant after the warning shots were fired; *Nelson v. State,* 739 So. 2d, 1177 (Fla., 1999), self-defense testimony about victim's character admissible to show who was really aggressor in parking-lot confrontation in which defendant left parking lot, returned with gun, and shot victim; *Stobbart v. State,* 533 S.E. 2d, 379, 382 (Ga., 2000), allowing evidence of violent reputation and acts because justification defense is largely dependent on what defendant knows about victim.

47 *See, e.g., State v. Barnes,* 2000 Ohio App. Lexis 3294, specific acts by victim are admissible to show likelihood that victim was the aggressor, whether or not the acts were directed at the defendant; *State v. Day,* 2000 S.C. Lexis 160, prior act of violence by victim is admissible even though not directed at defendant to show reasonable apprehension of violence; *State v. Clark,* 570 N.W. 2d 195 (N.D., 1997), specific acts of violence on the part of the victim are admissible to show defendant's state of mind.

48 *See, e.g., State v. Vigil,* 794 P. 2d, 728 (N.M., 1990), upholding trial court's denial of requested instruction and finding no ineffective assistance for failure to call expert despite testimony that deceased had a history of battering the accused, had beaten her the morning of his death after she confronted him with evidence that he had been sexually abusing her minor daughter from a prior marriage; *Lane v. State,* 957 S.W. 2d, 584 (Tex. Ct. App., 1997), upholding failure to charge jury on self-defense although there was a history of abuse, and estranged husband threatened on the night of the incident that he would kill the accused, slit her open and pull her guts out, track her down and kill their daughter, and that she would be better off to kill herself first, because accused returned home from her daughter's house eight miles away where she had fled and thus the court found that the imminence requirement had not been met; *State v. Manning,* 598 N.E. 2d, 25, 30 (Ohio Ct. App., 1991), excluding evidence of decedent's prior conviction for domestic violence

Moreover, even if the history of domestic violence is admitted and a self-defense instruction given, the jury may be constrained by an imminence instruction based on temporal immediacy. An instruction limiting self-defense to temporal proximity rather than necessity and failing to explain that the evidence of past violence must be considered in making a reasonableness determination may skew the doctrine of self-defense. Imminence is a proxy for necessity: they are linked ideas. Because of this linkage, an instruction on necessity should supplement – or replace – the current imminence requirements. The point of self-defense is that the accused reasonably believed it necessary to respond to her batterer with force.[49] The jury instructions should specifically direct the jury to consider the history of domestic violence in this relationship, the decedent's past history of other violence, and expert testimony on the effects of a history of abuse.

Proportionality of force to threatened harm

Another facet of necessity is the requirement of proportionality. The traditional rule is that only equal force may be used in response to a threat.[50] Where excessive force is used, the accused is not entitled to self-defense.[51] The requirement of proportionality is often assessed with reference to the relative sizes of the accused and the deceased and the type of weapon used in response to the assault because the reasonableness of the threat is measured from the victim's perspective. A person who is quite small with respect to an attacker may be justified, for example, in shooting the deceased even though the initial attack was a punch or kick.[52] In male-on-male violence cases, differences in size routinely are taken into account in assessing the proportion of force used against the decedent.[53] This does not, however,

---

arrest warrant because such evidence "would only distract the jury from the critical question of [defendant's] guilt or innocence." *See also* Evan Stark, *Re-Presenting Woman Battering: From Battered Woman Syndrome to Coercive Control*, 58 ALBANY L. REV., 973, 981 (1995), contrasting "the scope of battering with its limited recognition in the courts."

49 *See Smith v. State*, 486 S.E. 2d, 819 (1997), requiring modification of self-defense jury instructions in battered woman self-defense case and proposing that the instructions explain that expert testimony "relates to the issue of the reasonableness of the defendant's belief that the use of force was immediately necessary even though no use of force against the defendant may have been, in fact, imminent."

50 *See State v. Gartland*, 694 A. 2d. 564, 570 (N.J. 1997), acknowledging the male prototype behind "the common law regime, [where] even if faced with immediate danger of death or great bodily harm, an individual could use only equal force to repel the danger."

51 JOSHUA DRESSLER, UNDERSTANDING CRIMINAL LAW, 200 (1999), (The proportionality rule provides that a person is not justified in using force that is excessive in relation to the harm threatened.)

52 *See, e.g., State v. Wanrow*, 559 P. 2d, 548 (Wash. 1977), self-defense must reflect the relative position of the accused – a weaker woman – with respect to her assailant – a stronger man.

53 *See, e.g., State v. Hudson*, 760 So. 2d, 591 (La. App., 2000), affirming conviction based on part on considerations of defendant's superior physical shape relative to deceased; *State v. Barnes*, 2000 Ohio App. Lexis 3294, size differential between defendant and deceased relevant to reasonableness of belief in imminent danger.

always appear to be the case in battered-women cases, where size differential is often ignored (at least in many of the reported cases).[54]

The requirement of proportionality is malleable, however, and in some typically male violence cases, it is dispensed with entirely. For example, under the "castle doctrine," the force used to defend oneself at home need not be proportionate to the threat of harm.[55] Deadly force may be used against an intruder to counter any level of unlawful force. Although abused women are predominantly attacked in their home – which is, therefore, the locus of most battered women's self-defense cases – this factor consistently is ignored by the courts. The primary reason for this is that the castle doctrine does not apply to cohabitants.[56] This exception means a woman who is attacked by an intimate in her home must retreat even though she would not if a stranger had attacked, even if the threats to her were just as real.

Nor does the amount of force need to be proportionate in defending oneself against a sexual assault, which is another frequent precipitating factor in the cases of battered women who kill.[57] A sexual assault is deemed the equivalent of a threat of deadly harm and so can be responded to in kind. In domestic violence situations,

54 See, e.g., Commonwealth v. Miller, 634 A. 2d, 614 (Pa. Super. Ct., 1993), in which court held accused to a standard of proportionality because the deceased was unarmed, although the deceased had been carrying the murder knife in his pocket, immediately before the knife fell out of his pocket, he threatened to kill the accused, and they both grappled for it before she stabbed him. Although the accused in Miller claimed self-defense and her lawyer failed to present any evidence on battering, the appellate court declined to find ineffective assistance based on its validation of the trial court's interpretation that the accused had stabbed an unarmed man. See also State v. Gibson, 761 So. 2d, 670 (La. Ct. App., 2000), no self-defense where accused stabbed her boyfriend while he was choking her, because it was not clear that he was still choking her when she reached for the knife; Reynolds v. State, 2000 WL 761001, 1 (Miss. Ct. App.), finding, without any question of the relative sizes of accused and deceased, that it was a jury question whether "a steak knife was disproportionate to assault by telephone." But see State v. Wanrow, assessing the reasonableness of the accused's response in light of her diminutive size and physical handicaps as compared to the deceased who was a large, visibly intoxicated man.

55 The Model Penal Code provides that deadly force is justifiable if the actor reasonably believes "that such force is necessary to protect himself against death, serious bodily harm, kidnapping or sexual intercourse compelled by force or threat . . . " Model Penal Code, Sec. 3.04(b). However, deadly force is not permitted if "the actor knows that he can avoid the necessity of using such force with complete safety by retreating . . . except that (1) the actor is not obliged to retreat from his dwelling . . . " Model Penal Code, Sec. 3.04 (b) (ii). The use of deadly force is justifiable if "the use of force other than deadly force to prevent the commission or the consummation of the crime would expose the actor or another in his presence to substantial danger of serious bodily harm." Model Penal Code, Sec. 34.06(30(d)(ii) (2). This is known as the defense of premises or "castle doctrine."

56 Cf. State v. Gartland, 694 A. 2d, 564, 572 (N.J., 1997), reversing conviction for failure to instruct the jury that they needed to consider whether the accused could safely escape under the circumstances, but nonetheless finding trial court correctly instructed the jury that the accused had a duty to retreat from her home if she could do so safely, even from her own separate bedroom that she did not share with her husband.

57 See People v. Garcia, 1 P. 3d, 214, 221 (Colo. App., 1999), reversing and remanding conviction of battered wife for second-degree murder where court failed to give proper instructions, including an instruction that "one may justifiably use deadly force to prevent a sexual assault."

however, where the parties are intimates, this factor appears to be ignored, even when a sexual assault was the precipitating event in the chain leading to the decedent's demise.

Absence of aggression on part of defendant

The element of absence of aggression is routinely considered to be a requirement that the defendant did not start the conflict.[58] This may be problematic in light of a common misperception that battered women provoke the violence against them.[59] Some jurisdictions require an overt act by the decedent on the particular occasion, others merely require evidence that the decedent was the aggressor. This reflects a preference for the innocent party when two individuals seek to fulfill their self-preservation imperatives. Many courts interpret this requirement quite broadly in male conflicts, permitting a time line that encompasses the past acts and reputation of the victim in determining who was the likely aggressor on this occasion.[60] In domestic violence situations, however, courts are more likely to narrow their focus to the question of who instigated the immediate quarrel in which the deceased was killed.[61] What many courts fail to recognize is that domestic violence situations are not one-time encounters but ongoing relationships. Broadening the time frame of

58 The Model Penal Code does not require that the self-defender be the initial aggressor. Model Penal Code, Sec. 3.04, provides that "the use of force upon or toward another person is justifiable when the actor believes that such force is immediately necessary for the purpose of protecting himself against the use of unlawful force by such other person on the present occasion." Many jurisdictions, however, do impose such a requirement. See, e.g., State v. Millett, 273 A. 2d, 504, 509–10 (Me., 1971), "self-defense is designed to afford protection to one who is beset by an aggressor and confronted by a necessity not of his own making." Moreover, the Model Penal Code does preclude self-defense if "the actor, with the purpose of causing death or serious bodily harm, provoked the use of force against himself in the same encounter," a requirement that may essentially amount to the same thing.

59 See, e.g., State v. Harris, 711 So. 2d, 266 (La., 1998), affirming conviction despite "harmless error" of admitting decedent's family's testimony that the accused had provoked her husband's violence.

60 See, e.g., Petty v. State, 997 P. 2d, 800 (Nev., 2000), defendant shot unarmed victim in a fight over a pair of pants, but testimony concerning victim's reputation for violence nonetheless admissible to show defendant's reasonable belief in the necessity of using deadly force; Nelson v. State, 739 So. 2d, 1177 (Fla., 1999), self-defense testimony about victim's character admissible to show who was really aggressor in parking-lot confrontation in which defendant left parking lot, returned with gun, and shot victim.

61 See Brooks v. State, 630 So. 2d, 160 (Ala. Ct. App., 1993), refusing to overturn conviction despite evidence of history of abuse, despite the batterer having assaulted her on the morning of the killing, despite the decedent's threats that morning that he was going to kill the accused, because she could have remained inside her temporary refuge rather than emerging and telling her husband to "stay back" whereupon he lunged at her and she shot him; Lane v. State, 957 S.W. 584 (Tex. Ct. App., 1997), finding no immediate necessity in the accused's conduct where she drove eight miles to where the decedent was sleeping, despite verbal threats by the decedent that he would kill her, slit her open and pull her guts out, and despite a prior history of domestic violence; People v. Bogan, 732 N.E. 2d, 643 (Ill. Ct. App., 2000), affirming conviction, in a case without expert testimony, on instructions of use of force in self-defense – requiring imminence – and by an aggressor, despite extensive evidence of prior domestic violence, and death threats and assaults during the day of the killing, but where the accused responded to an immediate attack with a vacuum cleaner by stabbing the decedent.

their focus to encompass the ongoing nature of domestic violence would sharpen their vision.

Moreover, women who defy the passive-victim stereotype by actively defending themselves in the course of a battering relationship are often seen as undeserving of a self-defense instruction.[62] They are perceived to be engaging in mutual combat or provocation (and, therefore, are not "innocent"). Rather, they may be attempting to survive in the face of a society that offers little help or protection.[63]

Defendant retreated to greatest degree reasonably possible

Like proportionality, the duty to retreat is based on the necessity requirement.[64] Under the common-law doctrine of justified homicide, a defender must retreat or lack an opportunity to retreat.[65] Although most jurisdictions no longer explicitly impose a duty to retreat, the possibility of escape is relevant to the necessity of the accused's action.[66] The alternative of escape, like the imminence requirement, addresses the reasonableness of the accused's belief in the necessity of using force against an attacker.

Moreover, although most jurisdictions do not require retreat in the face of a deadly attack, many courts and juries nonetheless impose a type of duty to retreat

---

62 The prosecutor's closing argument in *Day* provides a good example of this misconception that true victims are passive: "Valoree's in mutual combat here. It's Valoree and Steve in the ring again, just like happened so many other times. She's in it and this other is a lie." *People v. Day,* 2 Cal. Rptr. 2d, 916, 922 (1992), reversing trial court's exclusion of battered woman syndrome testimony, finding it admissible to dispel misconceptions that "a woman in a battering relationship is free to leave at any time . . . that women are masochistic . . . and that they intentionally provoke their husbands." Defense counsel also characterized the defendant's experience as "mutual combat." *Id.* at 923. The appellate court recognized that expert testimony "would have disabused the jury of the notion that because a woman strikes back at her batterer, she is engaging in '"mutual combat."'" *Id.*

63 *See* Schneider, *supra* note 13, pp. 497–8 (1996), arguing that women cannot be categorized simplistically as victims or agents because they are often both simultaneously, and observing that "women who are battered are also survivors, active help-seekers who find little help and protection from the state, with extraordinary abilities to strategize in order to keep themselves and their families safe under terrible circumstances."

64 The Model Penal Code prohibits the use of deadly force against an aggressor if an actor "knows that he can avoid the necessity of using such force with complete safety by retreating." Model Penal Code, Section 3.04(2)(b)(ii). This is a version of the minority rule; most jurisdictions do not require retreat from an aggressor. *See* Dressler, note 52, p. 227. But in the majority of jurisdictions, "a nonaggressor is permitted to use deadly force to repel an unlawful deadly attack, even if he is aware of a place to which he can retreat in complete safety." *Id.,* 204.

65 *See* Greenawalt, *supra* note 2, p. 7, "Under the English common law doctrine of justified homicide, one of the elements of necessity is that a defender must 'retreat to the wall' (or lack an opportunity to retreat)."

66 *See Allen v. State,* 871 P. 2d, 79, 93 (Okla. Ct. Crim. App., 1994), acknowledging that although "a party has no obligation to retreat from a confrontation . . . the possibility of escape should be a recognized factor in determining whether deadly force was necessary to avoid death or great bodily harm"; *State v. Gibson,* 761 So. 2d, 670, 676 (La. Ct. App., 2000), "Although there is no unqualified duty to retreat, the possibility of escape is a factor in determining whether or not the defendant had a reasonable belief that deadly force was necessary to avoid the danger."

by imposing a duty to escape an abusive relationship.[67] The duty to escape an abusive relationship is the root of the often unspoken question "Why didn't she just leave?"[68] The idea is either that the accused is lying about the reality of the abuse (because why would any sane person stay in a dangerous situation?) or that she provoked the abuse (implying that she is masochistic and enjoyed the abuse).[69] Although most states permit expert testimony on battering and its effects as relevant to the question of why the defendant did not leave the relationship, six states reject such evidence.[70] Notably, in bar-room brawls, no one asks why the accused put himself in danger in the first place by going into a situation where such occurrences are common or why he didn't just leave a situation that was becoming dangerous before he had to respond to an attack.

Even in the minority of jurisdictions that have a retreat requirement, no retreat duty is imposed when the defender is at home when attacked, unless the parties are cohabitants.[71] Thus, in a duty-to-retreat jurisidiction, battered women are not

---

67 *See* Holly Maguigan, *Cultural Evidence and Male Violence: Are Feminist and Multiculturist Reformers on a Collision Course in Criminal Courts?*, 70 N.Y.U. L. Rev., 36, 82, note 171 (1995), observing that "[m]any people, including judges, tend to confuse the question of leaving the abusive relationship with the question of the defendant's duty to retreat on the occasion of homicide" and proposing that expert testimony be admissible to help the jury to understand why the two should not be conflated. *See also Harris,* 711 So. 2d, at 270, where the court, in affirming conviction, remarked that the accused "offered no explanation as to why she did not simply depart as she had in the past, especially considering that she had to pass within feet of an exterior door on her way to the closet where she retrieved the gun." The court also upheld the trial court's upward deviation from state sentencing guidelines because "the defendant could have easily escaped as she had in the past, if she were truly concerned about her safety."

68 This question surfaces also in the imminence/necessity requirement, demonstrating the linkage of the issues, particularly in battered women self-defense cases. *See, e.g., Gartland,* 694 A. 2d, 476, observing that "jurors may confuse the question of leaving the abusive partner with the duty to retreat on the occasion." Notably, the imminence/necessity/duty to leave issue is one that even counsel for the defense often fail to recognize. *See, e.g., Commonwealth v. Miller,* 634 A. 2d, 614, 619 (Pa. Super. Ct., 1993), reversing for ineffective assistance where counsel failed to proffer expert testimony to explain – *inter alia* – why accused battered woman did not leave the relationship; *Commonwealth v. Stonehouse,* 555 A. 2d, 772 (Pa. Super. Ct., 1989), finding reversible error in defense counsel's failure to request jury instruction and present expert testimony to rebut myths about the reasonableness of the defendant's conduct, including her choice to stay in an abusive relationship.

69 *See, e.g., State v. Harris,* 711 So. 2d, 266 (La., 1998), affirming manslaughter conviction on finding that admitting testimony of deceased's relatives that accused had provoked battering incidents was harmless error because "the undisputed facts of the homicide, and not the complained of evidence ... kept the jury from acquitting." In *Harris,* there was testimony of a history of abuse in the case but, curiously, self-defense was apparently not raised. The deceased had been battering the accused on the night of the incident, he left the room, and while he was gone, the accused went into a different room and armed herself with a gun. *Id.* at 268. When the deceased re-entered the room, the accused shot him.

70 *See* Parrish *supra* note 4, p. 122, noting that thirty-four states consider expert testimony to be relevant to the question of why the accused did not leave the relationship and that six states, including Alabama, Illinois, Michigan, Montana, Ohio, and Washington, do not.

71 *See* Greenawalt, *supra* note 2, p. 9. Moreover, in some jurisdictions, under the defense of premises doctrine, even without any perceived threat of death or bodily harm, a defender in his own home "may use deadly force against an aggressor who is making ... an unlawful, felonious, or violent entry into such premises." *Id.* Indeed, in some jurisdictions, the defense of premises doctrine has been extended to defense of vehicles. *See, e.g.,* La. Rev. Stat. Ann. § 14:20(3) (West, Supp. 1998),

permitted to claim they killed their batterer in self-defense if they could have escaped on that occasion.[72] Because judges and juries often are not aware of the limited escape opportunities feasible, they may assume she could have just walked out the door, called the police, or sought refuge in a battered woman's shelter.[73] An expert may be needed to testify about the paucity of such options.

Battered woman syndrome evidence

To counteract the perceived unfairness of formal rules in the cases of battered women who kill, legislatures and courts have mandated admissibility about domestic violence in the guise of battered woman syndrome testimony.[74] At least twelve states have statutes mandating admissibility of expert testimony on battered woman syndrome in self-defense cases.[75] Thirty-nine states permit such expert testimony.[76] The reason for such widespread admissibility may stem "from a belated effort to make amends for prior societal and legal insensitivity."[77] Generally, battered woman syndrome testimony is admissible as relevant to self-defense without any examination of its scientific validity.[78]

Once courts are convinced that there is evidence of a battering relationship and self-defense is at issue, most courts – state and federal – admit expert testimony about battering as relevant to the issue of the reasonableness of the defendant's belief that force was necessary and to her perception of imminent danger.[79] A majority

homicide is justifiable if "committed against a person whom one reasonably believes to be likely to use any unlawful force against a person present [in a motor vehicle] . . . while committing or attempting to commit a burglary or robbery" of the vehicle.

72 *But see Weiand v. State*, 732 So. 2d, 1044 (Fla., 1999), overruling prior case law regarding duty to retreat and holding that there is no duty to retreat from the residence even for cohabitants.

73 *See, e.g., People v. Garcia*, 1 P. 3d, 214, 220 (Col. Ct. App., 1999), reversing conviction of battered woman for failure to instruct jury that defendant had no duty to retreat, in light of the prosecutor's comments the accused could have "gone to another safe house or woman's center . . gone to a hotel . . . or to friends . . . or for a long run."

74 *See* Boykins, 995 P. 2d, p. 476, observing that 69 percent of states find expert testimony admissible "to explain battering and its effects generally," citing Parrish.

75 *See* Parrish, *supra* note 4, p. 99.

76 *See* Boykins, 995, P. 2d, p. 476, citing Parrish.

77 *See* Robert P. Mosteller, *Syndromes and Politics in Criminal Trials and Evidence Law*, 46 Duke L. J. 461, 466, noting the impact of political concerns on evidence law.

78 *See* Parrish, *supra* note 4, p. 113, noting that only fourteen states require some evidence that battered woman syndrome is generally accepted in the scientific community, and nine states have explicitly rejected the need for such a showing. This is the unfortunate state of affairs in most of the Commonwealth countries as well. *See* note 2. There, however, battered woman syndrome is considered relevant to provocation rather than self-defense. *See, e.g., R. v. Smith*, 2002 WL 31676314 (CA Crim. Div., 2002 EWCA Crim., 2671), battered woman syndrome was relevant to provocation rather than diminished responsibility.

79 *See* Parrish, *supra* note 4, p. 121, noting that only Georgia and Wyoming have found battered woman syndrome testimony not to be relevant to reasonableness; nineteen states find expert testimony relevant to the defendant's perception of temporal proximity to danger; six find it relevant to the defendant's credibility; and two find it relevant in assessing proportionality of force used. Most states, however, do not permit experts to testify to "ultimate issue" of reasonableness or self-defense; fourteen states permit such testimony; nineteen do not.

of states also find battered woman syndrome testimony relevant to the question of why the defendant failed to leave the relationship; some also find it relevant to her state of mind at the time of the killing.[80]

What is battered woman syndrome? examining the hypothesis

Lenore Walker, a clinical psychologist, developed a theory that typified women's reactions to domestic violence as a psychological condition she termed "the battered woman's syndrome."[81] According to this theory, domestic violence occurs in cycles, typified by three phases.[82] The first is a tension-building phase, followed by a violent incident in which the batterer expresses uncontrollable rage, and a third phase in which the batterer expresses profound regret and intentions to reform.[83] During the first two phases of the cycle, the victim experiences a state of fear and anxiety that Walker calls "cumulative terror."[84] The third stage, or "honeymoon phase," is typified by "extremely loving behavior" that lulls a woman into believing that the abuser has reformed.[85] Learned helplessness, or a false perception that there is no escape, is characteristic of Walker's syndrome theory, and typifies the first two stages.[86]

Thus, Dr. Walker's hypothesis is that women in battering relationships experience a cycle of violence, an experience that they are bound to repeat because "learned helplessness" makes it impossible for them to escape the relationship.[87] Although one might be able, at least in principle, to test such a theory, one would have to define descriptive terms, such as "battered woman," for the hypothesis to explain anything.[88] To determine whether there are precise logical consequences to

---

80 *See, e.g., State v. B.H.,* 870 A. 2d, 273, 280 (N.J., 2005), upholding expert testimony on battered woman syndrome as a form of PTSD; *Harris v. State,* 2004 WL 2418073, slip op., Ala. Crim. App. Ct., October 24, 2004, finding ineffective assistance not to have proffered PTSD testimony as mitigation. *But see Harrington v. State,* 858 So. 2d, 278 (Ala., 2002), rehearing denied (2003), holding harmless error to exclude expert testimony on battered woman syndrome and PTSD.

81 Lenore Walker, The Battered Woman (1979). Walker expanded her theory in Lenore Walker, The Battered Woman Syndrome (1984).

82 *See* Lenore Walker, The Battered Woman Syndrome, 95–6 (1984).

83 *See id.* p. 96.

84 *See id.*

85 *See id.,* p. 96.

86 *See id.,* p. 86.

87 In explaining the genesis of her battered woman syndrome theory, Dr. Walker wrote:

> Remembering the earlier studies of Martin Seligman and his dogs who developed learned helplessness from exposure to non-escapable random and variable aversive stimulation, I hypothesized that battered women may also have lost their ability to predict that what they did would protect themselves from further harm if they perceived the abuse as non-escapable, random and variable punishment. I liked this theory because it explained how women could function so well in one setting and be so ineffective at home in stopping the violence. It also helped explain why women didn't leave; they developed coping strategies that helped them minimize the pain and danger from the abuse at the cost of escape skills.

> Lenore E. Walker, *The Transmogrification of a Feminist Foremother,* in Women and Therapy, 517–29 (1995).

88 For an explanation of the importance of the clear articulation of terms in hypothesis testing, *see* Ernst Nagel, The Structure of Science: Problems in the Logic of Scientific

the hypothesis that are incompatible with alternative hypotheses, the terms of the hypothesis must be precisely defined.

This, however, Dr. Walker failed to do. Dr. Walker's primary study, performed in 1984, consisted of a structured questionnaire administered to 400 self-referred women living in six states.[89] For purposes of her hypothesis, Dr. Walker defines a battered woman as a woman "18 years of age or over, who is or has been in an intimate relationship with a man who repeatedly subjects or subjected her to forceful physical/and or psychological abuse."[90] The vagueness of this definition is illustrated by the definitions of "repeatedly" as "more than once" and "abuse" as "extreme verbal harassment and expressing comments of a derogatory nature with negative value judgments" as well as physical assaults.[91] Almost any couple who had occasional spats could, under this definition, be considered to have a battering relationship. The fallacy of using such a broad definition (that nearly any relationship could fall within) is that such a theory becomes fundamentally untestable.[92]

Moreover, the research identified no control groups with which to compare the responses. This made it impossible to determine how the responses of even these broadly defined women differed from those who were not so defined. Without controls, the hypothesis cannot be critiqued and loses its ability to explain anything. The absence of controls thus violates a fundamental principle of hypothesis testing.

Further, the subjects of the study were asked about only four incidents of domestic violence (i.e., the first, second, worst, and latest) and were asked to characterize the assailants' behavior before and after each incident.[93] On the basis of the subjects' numerical assessment of these incidents, the interviewer recorded whether "evidence of tension building or loving contrition" existed.[94] This violates principles of social science research in that it is the interviewer's expectations that color the responses.

What data support or undermine the theory?

The primary trouble with the data Walker collected from the 200-page questionnaires she used in her studies is that they do not support the author's conclusion

---

EXPLANATION, 7–8 (1961); David L. Faigman, *To Have and Have Not: Assessing the Value of Social Science to the Law as Science and Policy*, 38 EMORY L. J. 1005, 1054 (1989), observing that a "hypothesis can be tested only by making explicit the behaviors and observations upon which it is based."

89 Walker (1984), p. 202.

90 *Id.*, p. 203.

91 *Id.*

92 Karl Popper explained that the rationality of a hypothesis consists of "stating one's problem clearly ... and examining its various proposed solutions *critically*." KARL L. POPPER, THE LOGIC OF SCIENTIFIC DISCOVERY, 16 (rev. ed., 1992).

93 Walker (1984), p. 96.

94 Walker (1984), p. 96.

that a three-part cycle characterizes battering relationships.[95] Even assuming the questions were properly phrased so as not to be leading – which does not appear to be the case – and the interviewers did not skew their responses – again, a questionable assumption – the research does not provide data that support Dr. Walker's hypothesis of a cycle of violence. Walker herself has acknowledged that her data do not show a common cycle in all relationships or even a pattern of three distinct phases where such a cycle does exist.[96] Her 1984 research shows that fewer than 38 percent of the women interviewed had experienced the alleged cycle of violence.[97] That means that well over half of her subjects are not "characteristic." Dr. Walker makes no attempt to account for the data that undermine her hypothesis.

What assumptions are being made?

Not only is Dr. Walker's hypothesis virtually untestable and her data contradictory to her conclusions, but a fundamental assumption of the study design was flawed. The surveys were administered to women who were self-referred or patients in Dr. Walker's clinic.[98] To demonstrate what the study purports to show, the surveys would have to be administered to "typical" battered women – that is, women who are representative of the population being studied. The fallacy of the research design is that women who describe themselves as "battered" may not be representative of battered women generally.[99]

Moreover, the researcher's study becomes suspect as biased when the researcher gives selective attention to expected behavior.[100] This affects the study in two ways: first, the researcher may look for data that confirm (and ignore data that refute) the hypothesis; and second, the study subjects (who, because they are self-selected, know the study is about battered women) may report data to the researchers that they believe the researcher wishes to hear.[101] Thus, both the study design and execution are based on mistaken assumptions of representativeness and freedom from bias.

In addition, the concept of learned helplessness, central to Walker's theory, hypothesizes that, like dogs exposed to electric shock every time they attempt to leave their cages so that they eventually refuse to leave even in the absence of shock, women learn to become helpless and refuse to leave an abusive relationship. This theory of learned helplessness assumes that women are – at least, at some point prior to the time they kill their batterer – free to leave. This assumption is highly

---

95 See Lenore E. Walker, *Psychology and Law, Symposium: Women and the Law*, 20 PEPPERDINE L. REV., 1170, 1184 (1993), now arguing that four patterns are common.

96 See id.

97 Walker (1984), pp. 96–7.

98 Walker (1984).

99 See Mahoney, *supra* note 10, pp. 28–32, explaining that women who have been battered often resist labeling themselves as such and only can be categorized on the basis of the types of conduct to which they have been subjected.

100 See Faigman, *supra* note 88, p. 1055.

101 See id., pp. 1062–3, discussing the problems of bias.

questionable in light of what we know about separation assault.[102] Women who are killed by their batterers are overwhelmingly attempting to separate from the relationship.

Is the methodology sound?

Walker conducted two separate studies of battered women. Each study was based on a survey questionnaire. The first study interviewed 100 women who were self-referred volunteers or taken from Walker's practice.[103] The second study, consisting of 400 women, was entirely self-referred.[104] One of the fundamentals of survey design is that the survey population (i.e., the women interviewed) be representative of the target population (i.e., battered women generally).[105] Walker made no claims to representativeness of the sample surveyed.[106] In addition, control groups – one of the hallmarks of science – were absent from the studies.[107] Assessment of social science data involves examining the statistical choices made by the researcher. Without control groups and some attempt at unbiased selection, there is no way to disprove the null hypothesis (i.e., that the results were due to chance). Walker explained that her decision to omit controls was based on considerations of time and expense because the research was intended to be merely preliminary to more rigorous studies.[108] Unfortunately, those more rigorous studies have never been done.

How strong is the link between data and hypothesis?

Social science evidence presents particular concerns about scientific validity. Such evidence is frequently gleaned from surveys, which are conducted for the purpose of collecting data.[109] Courts have rarely questioned the scientific validity of survey evidence (on other than relevance grounds), generally finding it admissible under Rule 703, Federal Rules of Evidence[110] Nonetheless, expert testimony based on

---

102 *See* Margo Wilson, et al., *Lethal and Nonlethal Violence Against Wives*, CANADIAN J. CRIM., 331 (1995); Mahoney, *supra* note 10, pp. 70–79.

103 *See* Walker, (1979) xiii.

104 *See* Walker, (1984) 95.

105 *See* Shari S. Diamond, *Reference Guide on Survey Research*, in FEDERAL JUDICIAL CENTER, MANUAL ON SCIENTIFIC EVIDENCE, 225, 236 (1994).

106 Representativeness is the ability of measurements to fairly describe the target population. For a discussion of representativeness, the importance of random sampling methods, including choice of target population and sampling frame, *See* David H. Kaye and David H. Freedman, *Reference Guide on Statistics*, in FEDERAL JUDICIAL CENTER, MANUAL ON SCIENTIFIC EVIDENCE, 343–6 (1994).

107 Control or comparison groups and control questions "are the most reliable means for assessing response levels against the baseline level of error associated with a particular question." Diamond, *supra* note 105, p. 252.

108 Walker (1984), p. 203.

109 *See* Shari S. Diamond, *Reference Guide on Survey Research*," in FEDERAL JUDICIAL CENTER, MANUAL ON SCIENTIFIC EVIDENCE, 225 (1994), although the source of data may be individuals, "survey applies to any description or enumeration, whether or not an individual is the source of the information" and thus may encompass enumerating inanimate objects such as the number of trees destroyed in a fire.

110 Facts or data "of a type reasonably relied upon by experts in the particular field" are recognized under the rule. FED. R. EVID. 703.

surveys must meet the standards of scientific validity to be admissible.[111] Accordingly, experts relying on surveys must be prepared to account for their underlying hypothesis, their methodology (including sampling design, target population, survey instrument, and interviewer training), assumptions, results (including rates and patterns of missing data), and statistical analyses reflected in the surveys.[112] For social science testimony to meet standards of scientific validity, the research must have attempted to minimize biases in the selection of problems, the focus of research conclusions, the identification of relevant facts, and the assessment of data.

Dr. Walker's research suffers from problems in each of these areas. The presence of too many gaps in her analysis make this syndrome testimony wholly unreliable. Dr. Walker's broadly framed hypothesis is virtually untestable. Her data, methodology, and assumptions all reveal fatal flaws. Although other researchers have attempted to remedy these flaws, there remains no empirical support for the proposition that the majority of battered women suffer from the symptoms Dr. Walker described. Further, it is rare that any testimony that the particular accused suffered from these symptoms is adduced.[113] Thus, its admissibility under the *Daubert* trilogy is highly questionable.

Currently, Dr. Walker argues that battered woman syndrome is a subspecies of PTSD.[114] This is misconceived, however, because neither she nor any other researcher has ever remedied the fundamental problems with her research: the absence of empirical support for the syndrome.[115] Notably, Dr. Walker does not proffer any new studies for her assertion that "Battered Woman Syndrome is considered

---

111 *See Kumho Tire v. Carmichael,* 526 U.S. 136, 147 (1999).

112 *See* Diamond, *supra* note 105, pp. 231–3.

113 *See* Mary A. Dutton, *Understanding Women's Responses to Domestic Violence: A Redefinition of Battered Woman Syndrome,* 21 Hofstra L. Rev., 1191, 1198–9 (1993), explaining the conceptual problems of admitting battered woman syndrome as a subspecies of PTSD. It is apparently more common in the Commonwealth for the accused to seek diminished-capacity excuse through medical testimony about battered woman syndrome and PTSD. *See, e.g., R. v. Howell,* 1997 WL 1106087 (1998) 1 Cr. App. R. (S.) 229, medical witness testified that defendant suffered from battered woman syndrome.

114 *See* Lenore E. Walker, *Battered Women Syndrome and Self-Defense,* 6 Notre Dame J. Of L., Ethics and Pub. Pol'y, 321, 327 (1992). A number of courts have followed this lead. *See, e.g., Bechtel v. State,* 840 P. 2d, 1, 7 (Okla. Ct. Crim. App., 1992), acknowledging that battered woman syndrome is considered a subcategory of PTSD); *State v. Grecinger,* 569 N.W. 2d, 189, 193 (Minn., 1997), expert witness testified regarding battered woman syndrome, which she described as a subset of PTSD.

115 Although Professor Walker now contends that "[b]attered Woman Syndrome is considered a subcategory of the generic Post-Traumatic Stress Disorder," this claim has not been substantiated. Nonetheless, many courts appear to accept this unsupported notion. *See, e.g., State v. Engel,* 684 N.E. 2d, 1311, 1317 (Ohio 1997), testimony of clinical psychologist that defendant "is, indeed, suffering from all the symptoms of battered woman syndrome, including severe levels of type II PTSD" without examining the scientific basis of such testimony; *Vallinoto v. DiSandro,* 688 A. 2d, 830, 854, and note 28 (R.I., 1997), noting that "Rhode Island does not stand alone in its decision to allow social workers . . . to testify concerning treatment and diagnosis of emotional-trauma syndromes like PTSD"; *Bechtel v. State,* 840 P. 2d 1, 7 (Ok. Ct. Crim. App., 1992), opining that battered woman syndrome is considered a subcategory of PTSD; *State v. Grecinger,* 569 N.W. 2d, 189, 193 (Minn., 1997), expert witness testified regarding battered woman syndrome, which she described as a subset of PTSD. *But see Marley v. State,* 729 N.E. 2d, 1011, 1015 (Ind. Ct. App., 2000), admitting testimony about PTSD under Indiana's battering statute and acknowledging that PTSD, unlike battered woman syndrome, is a recognized mental disorder.

a subcategory of the generic Post-Traumatic Stress Disorder" but simply reiterates the old theory under a new guise.[116]

PTSD is well studied, has ample support, and some battered women may indeed suffer from it.[117] In cases where the accused suffers from the disorder, this testimony regarding her state of mind should be available as excuse testimony. Slipping battered woman syndrome into self-defense testimony as a subspecies of PTSD not only is unjustified from an empirical standpoint, it also conflates justification and excuse.

In sum, the problem with battered woman syndrome testimony is that it fails on validity grounds. It cannot meet the standards and methods of science. Such testimony cannot be helpful to the jury.

Transcending formal/substantive dichotomies: a plea for increased empiricism

The impetus for battered woman syndrome testimony is the insight that formal equality does not provide substantive equality in the instance of battered women. Battered woman syndrome is admissible to "aid the jury in determining whether a defendant's fear and claim of self-defense are reasonable."[118] The fact that battered woman syndrome is scientifically unsound does not negate the importance of explaining the circumstances of battered women in assessing the reasonableness of the accused's conduct. The solution to this conundrum is twofold. First, replace battered woman syndrome into its two – empirically sound – component parts: social context evidence and PTSD evidence; eliminate the unreliable syndrome testimony. Second, replace the imminence instruction – which is a special case – with necessity – which is the foundational idea. The reasons underlying the admissibility of battered woman syndrome testimony are sound. The problem is that the syndrome itself lacks empirical support. Replacing it with solid social context and PTSD evidence better meets the requirement for scientifically valid evidence without discarding the much-needed guidance relating to reasonableness of the accused's conduct.

Social context evidence

Expert testimony about domestic violence is necessary and helpful because to understand the abusive relationship circumstances in which the accused found herself, two things are needed: the particular relationship facts and the social, political, and economic contextual facts about domestic violence. Indeed, most courts recognize

---

116 *See, e.g., Boykins v. State*, 995 P. 2d 474, 476 (Nev., 2000), noting that Dr. Walker testified at trial and continued to describe the three-phase cycle of violence and a pattern of learned helplessness as a characteristic of battered women).

117 A clinical diagnosis requires that the patient meet a specific set of criteria in each symptom area. *See* American Psychiatric Association, Diagnostic and Statistical Manual of Mental Disorders IV (DSM-IV) p. 424.

118 *See State v. Edwards*, 2000 WL 308872, 3 (Mo. Ct. App.), reversing conviction for inadequate jury instructions and acknowledging that "the traditional concept of self-defense is based on one-time conflicts between persons of somewhat equal size and strength, and that when the defendant is a victim of long-term domestic violence suffering from battered spouse syndrome, such traditional concept does not apply."

this when admitting testimony about battering relationships.[119] Relationship facts are the evidence of what happened between the accused and the deceased, which will be provided by lay witnesses who were eyewitnesses to aspects of the relationship. The social-context testimony, provided by an expert witness, would explain the common social, political, and economic circumstances of battered women as a group.[120] Educating jurors about the dynamics of battering relationships generally is important to help the jury to assess the reasonableness of a woman acting in the accused's situation.

This kind of expert testimony about the circumstances of battered women is relevant to the objective reasonableness of the accused's conduct. As the Kelley court recognized, "external social and economic factors often make it difficult for some women to extricate themselves from battering relationships."[121] The courts' widespread admission of battered woman syndrome testimony recognizes that the experience of battered women transcends the particular woman's experience. Thus, it is as background information to evaluate the reasonableness of her conduct – the circumstances of the case – that testimony about the experience of battered women should be admitted, without the unsound syndrome testimony.

Reasonableness can only be assessed in relation to common experience. That is the function of the jury, to bring its common understanding to bear on the facts of the case. However, if the experience of battered women is not within the framework of the jury's experience, it will have difficulty assessing the reasonableness of her conduct. To understand the reasonableness of a battered woman's beliefs and conduct, social-context evidence is imperative. The accused did not act in a vacuum but rather in conjunction with pervasive overlapping social interests. Not only must the perspective of the individual be presented as evidence, but the perspective also must be explained in terms of the common experience of women in such situations. Social-context evidence is both essential to help the jury determine

119 *See* Parrish, note 4, p. 117 and note 111, citing cases. Although courts recognize the importance of context, they do so primarily when admitting battered woman syndrome testimony. The rationale for admitting social-context evidence is the same, however, and it should be similarly admissible.

120 *See, e.g.,* Victorian Law Reform Commission, *Defenses to Homicide, Final Report* (2004), noting the limitations of psychological testimony about battered woman syndrome and proposing adoption of legislation to clarify admissibility of a wider range of expert evidence about the social context of violent relationships.

121 *State v. Kelly,* 478 A. 2d, 364 (1984). Kelly involved the admissibility of battered woman syndrome testimony in the self-defense claims of a battered woman who stabbed her husband with scissors on the street as he ran toward her with his hands raised shortly after an attack where he had choked her, punched her in the face, and bit her leg. The court found expert testimony on battering to be admissible to show the objective reasonableness of the accused's actions and to dispel myths and misconceptions of the jury. Among the myths and misconceptions about battered women that the court identified were "beliefs that they are masochistic and actually enjoy their beatings, that they purposely provoke their husbands into violent behavior, and, most critically . . . that women who remain in battering relationships are free to leave their abusers at any time." The court was also persuaded that testimony about the psychological impact of the battering was important. Although the admissibility of this information was accomplished via the battered woman syndrome, the reasoning of the court is even more persuasive with respect to more scientifically valid social-context and PTSD evidence.

the reasonableness of a defendant's belief and actions and to answer the jury's underlying questions regarding credibility (i.e., if she was really battered, why did she stay?) and provocation (i.e., did she provoke the violence directed against her?). It also helps the jury understand the accused's options, the necessity of her actions, and whether her survival was really at stake when she killed her batterer.

Social-context evidence in the battered woman self-defense case is relevant to the necessity and reasonableness of the accused's beliefs and conduct. Because information about battering relationships and the alternatives to a violent response are not widely known, this information would enlighten rather than confuse the jury.[122] This kind of information is scientifically valid expert testimony (providing the expert can meet the required validity inquiry).[123]

This may be a novel kind of evidence for self-defense, but it is not altogether without precedent. First, social-context evidence has been a component of battered woman syndrome testimony from the start – and just because the syndrome evidence is baseless, that is no reason to toss out the sound evidence also.[124] Second, expert testimony about the general social context of a witness's perceptions is currently admissible in many different guises. It is admissible, for example, to impeach eyewitness testimony, at least in some jurisdictions.[125] The use of general observations drawn from social science to determine factual issues in a specific case is helpful to the jury because it brings to their attention factors beyond common knowledge.[126]

Moreover, social-context evidence provides the jury with background information to help the jury assess claims about reasonableness. The evidentiary basis on which such testimony is relevant is the same as that of syndrome testimony: to "explain why the abuse a woman suffered causes her to reasonably believe that her

---

122 Nor would expert social science testimony fall into the category of "undue prejudice." *See* Laurens Walker and John Monahan, *Social Frameworks: A New Use of Social Science in the Law*, 73 VA. L. REV., 559, 575–6, and note 48 (1987), observing that "To our knowledge, the charge of playing on the jurors' emotions has never been leveled against the introduction of a social framework" and noting that the paradigmatic example of undue prejudice is grisly photographic evidence of the crime. Further, any over-valuing of scientific expert testimony by the jury has been empirically disproven. *See id.*, 577, noting that juries "strongly tend to give less weight to the framework than the logic of inference suggests is due."

123 That is, social science research in general has an empirical basis that can at least in theory meet a *Daubert* inquiry. Whether the particular evidence adduced in a specific trial can meet such a standard must be determined in each case.

124 *See Kelly*, 478 A. 2d, 364, admitting battered woman syndrome testimony not only as testimony about psychological impacts of battering but also about the social and economic impacts, and to dispel myths and misconceptions of the jury. *See also R. v. M. (M.A.)*, (1998) 1 S.C.R. 123 (Can.), holding expert battered woman syndrome testimony admissible "to assist a jury in assessing the reasonableness of an accused's perceptions."

125 *See, e.g., United States v. Smithers*, 212 F. 3d, 306, 311 (6th Cir., 2000), noting a "jurisdictional trend" toward admitting expert testimony pertaining to eyewitness accuracy; *United States v. Hines*, 55 F. Supp. 2d, 62, 72 (D. Mass., 1999), admitting expert testimony on the reliability of eyewitness testimony.

126 Many courts acknowledge the admissibility of general social-context evidence when they are admitting battered woman syndrome testimony. *See, e.g., Commonwealth v. Hall*, 696 N.E. 2d, 151, 153 (Mass. Ct. App., 1998), admitting battered woman syndrome testimony not as "a diagnosis or an illness" but to explain the reasonableness of the accused's perception of threat.

life is in danger and that she must use deadly force to escape her batterer."[127] This information is beyond the ken of most people, judges and juries alike.

American families can be violent places,[128] and leaving is often not the solution because separation is fraught with danger.[129] Thus, a history of past domestic violence ought to be admissible, not as flawed battered woman syndrome testimony, but rather as a way of putting the reasonableness of the accused's actions in context. For example, social-context evidence may be key to explaining why a woman would be trapped in a violent situation and why being trapped in such a way was not a defect on her part. Women may be trapped, not psychologically but rather physically and economically, in an abusive relationship. They may have children that their flight would put in danger.

Explaining the circumstances that made a particular action reasonable is important to any objective system of justice. Moreover, the standard for self-defense in most jurisdictions requires a reasonable belief in the necessity of deadly force. Unless the factfinder is apprised of the circumstances, making a reasonableness determination is virtually impossible.

For the jury to decide whether the defendant acted as a reasonable woman in her situation would have acted, some chilling facts may need to be brought to the court's attention in a battered-spouse case. Although domestic violence constitutes the largest category of calls that police receive, police are notoriously reluctant to respond to such calls; when they do, only 10 to 18 percent of the abusers are arrested, despite grounds for arrest in 50 percent of the cases.[130] Arrest of the abuser frequently results in increased violence toward the woman. Shelters are often either

---

127 *People v. Minnis*, 455 N.E. 2d, 209, 219 (1983), explaining the basis for admissibility of battered woman syndrome testimony.

128 "[F]or the typical American woman, her home is the location where there is the most serious risk of assault." PHYSICAL VIOLENCE IN AMERICAN FAMILIES: RISK FACTORS AND ADAPTATIONS TO VIOLENCE, 98 (Murray A. Straus and Richard J. Gelles, eds., 1992), reporting the results of two surveys conducted ten years apart finding that the rates of husband-wife assault are "many times the female assault victimization rate outside the family" and that although women are seldom murder victims outside the family – 21 percent of stranger homicide victims – they represent 76 percent of spouse murder victims). In 2004, only 14 percent of murder victims were killed by a stranger, and the over whelming number of intimate homicides was perpetrated by men. www.ojp.usdoj.gov/bjs/cvict_c.htm#violent. For recent statistics on intimates' crimes, *see* http://www.fbi.gov./vcr/cius-03/pdf/03sec5.pdf.

129 *See* Mahoney, *supra* note 10, pp. 64–5, arguing that the concept of battered woman should be replaced with "separation assault," defined as " the attack on the woman's body and volition in which her partner seeks to prevent her from leaving, retaliate for the separation, or force her to return."

130 This is beginning to change. *See, e.g.,* FLA. STAT. §741.2901 (2005) (establishing a "pro-prosecution" policy empowering prosecutors to proceed, even over victim's objections); WISC. STAT. §968.075 (2003–2004) (requiring mandatory arrest of domestic abusers with physical injury or likelihood of continued abuse and requiring police to explain in writing any decision not to arrest). For a discussion of the move toward mandatory arrests, *see* Deborah Turkheimer, *Recognizing and Remedying the Harm of Battering: A Call to Criminalize Domestic Violence*, 94 J. CRIM. L. & CRIMINOLOGY 959 (2004). Perhaps because of this reluctance on the part of the police to respond to calls involving domestic violence and the paucity of arrests, studies estimate that only 10 percent of domestic-violence incidents are ever reported to the police. *See* Mary Ann Dutton, *Understanding Women's Responses to Domestic Violence: A Redefinition of Battered Woman Syndrome*, 21 HOFSTRA L. REV. 1191, 1213 (1993).

unavailable or unsafe.[131] Police, district attorneys, and judges all frequently attempt to dissuade victims from proceeding with criminal charges.[132] Judges often blame the victim, presuming provocation, and often fail to believe women without visible injuries.[133] It is interesting that women who kill a spouse are much more likely to be charged with murder than men who kill their wives – usually charged with manslaughter – and women's charges are much less likely to be reduced (18 versus 47 percent).[134] Batterers are rarely charged with felonies and sentences tend to be lenient.[135] In light of the high percentage of women who are murdered by their former partners after they leave abusive relationships, economic pressures, and the ineffectiveness of police intervention, leaving may simply not be an option.[136] The most recent studies indicate that women are killed by intimates far more often than men.[137]

Without social-context evidence, the jury will continue to struggle with their preconceptions and with the male paradigm in which the criminal law is cast. The point is that the wrong evidence (battered woman syndrome testimony) is being admitted, and even when the more useful (and reliable) social-context evidence is admitted, jury instructions are frequently inadequate.

Psychological impact evidence

Because of the lack of support for battered woman syndrome testimony, it should not be used – as many courts use it – to demonstrate the psychological impact of battering. Normally, state-of-mind evidence is an excuse defense rather than a justification (like self-defense). Although courts frequently discuss battered woman syndrome as affecting the accused's state of mind, in the United States, they normally admit battered woman syndrome testimony as justification rather than excuse testimony.[138] That is, battered woman syndrome testimony is usually offered to demonstrate honesty and reasonableness of the accused's belief in the necessity of using deadly force rather than to show that she suffered from an illness that would diminish her responsibility.[139]

---

131 *See* Gretchen P. Mullins, *The Battered Woman and Homelessness*, 3 J. L. AND POL'Y, 237, 249–50 (1994).

132 *See id. But see* FLA. STAT. § 741.2901 (2005) (pro-prosecution policy).

133 *See* Lynn H. Schafran, *There's No Accounting for Judges*, 58 ALB. L. REV., 1063–7 (1995), describing attitudes of judges toward male domestic violence and toward women).

134 *See* Parrish, SUPRA note 4, p. 141.

135 *See id.*

136 *See* Victoria Nourse, *Passion's Progress: Modern Law Reform and the Provocation Defense*, 106 YALE L. J., 1331 (1997).

137 *See* Bureau of Justice Statistics, U.S. Dep't. of Justice, *Domestic Violence: Violence Between Intimates*, 3 (1994); Bureau of Justice Statistics, U.S. Dep't. of Justice, *Violence Against Women*, 6 (1994). *See also* Turkheimer, *supra* note 130, at 966 (noting that 94% of intimate partner homicides are women).

138 The opposite appears to be true in the United Kingdom, where battered woman syndrome is more frequently used as part of a mitigation defense to reduce murder charges to manslaughter than as part of self-defense. *See supra* note 2.

139 *See, e.g., Commonwealth v. Hall*, 696 N.E. 2d, 151, 153 (Mass. Ct. App., 1998), admitting battered woman syndrome testimony not as "a diagnosis or an illness" but to explain the reasonableness

Many courts acknowledge that battered women may suffer from PTSD, and many experts that testify about battered woman syndrome attempt to characterize it – inaccurately – as a subspecies of PTSD.[140] PTSD is a disease known to afflict people – including women subjected to domestic violence – who have been threatened with death or who have suffered severe bodily harm.[141] PTSD is a type of sensory gating defect, in which sensory input is not filtered in a normal way.[142] As a result, people suffering with this disorder tend to respond to perceived events in an exaggerated manner.[143] This disorder arises when someone has experienced or witnessed an event involving death or severe injury and is characterized by a number of symptoms. First, there is avoidance of anything that reminds the sufferer of the original trauma. Second, the person suffering this disorder experiences hyperarousal – that is, an increased fight or flight response. Third, the afflicted suffers persistent re-experiencing of the traumatic event, which triggers increased arousal (fight or flight) and causes all the physical, emotional, and psychological responses that were experienced in the first traumatic event.

PTSD has been well researched, published, peer-reviewed, subjected to critique and error analysis, and meets standards of general consensus. Whether it is relevant in any case depends on its nexus with the facts, such as whether the accused exhibited such symptoms. In the appropriate case in which the accused has been diagnosed as suffering from PTSD, it may be appropriate to show the honesty of the accused's belief, a component of self-defense. It may also be appropriate as diminished capacity (excuse) evidence, as it appears to be used in the United Kingdom.

Evidence that a woman is suffering from PTSD as a result of the trauma of abuse may indeed be relevant to her conduct. It can explain why she reacted to a particular situation in the way she did. The increased fight-or-flight response may help to explain why the accused used more force than appears necessary, for example, or the reexperiencing phenomenon may explain why she killed during a lull in the fighting. Not all abused killers suffer from PTSD, but if statistics showing that 60 percent of rape victims suffer from it are anywhere close for battered women, a large percentage of them do. PTSD testimony should be available to them to explain their conduct.

As a brain dysfunction characterized by a particular set of symptoms, PTSD ought to be admissible whenever mental state is at issue. The disadvantage of this approach is that it relegates PTSD testimony in homicide cases to the category of

---

of the accused's perception of threat; *Bechtel v. State*, 840 P. 2d, 1, 7 (Okla. Ct. Crim App., 1992), noting that battered woman's syndrome is not a "mental disease."

140 *See, e.g., State v. Hines*, 696 A. 2d, 780 (N.J. Super. Cat., 1997), finding exclusion of expert testimony regarding PTSD reversible error where deceased father had history of sexually assaulting his accused daughter because it was necessary "to explain why defendant believed that the victim intended to rape her and that she needed to use force to avoid his assault."

141 *See* DSM IV, *supra* note 117, pp. 428–29.

142 *See id.*; Erica Beecher-Monas and Edgar Garcia-Rill, *Gatekeeping Stress: The Admissibility of Post-Traumatic Stress Disorder Evidence*, 24. U. Ark. Little Rock L. Rev. 9 (2001).

143 *See* DSM IV, *supra* note 117, pp. 428–29.

excuse, rather than justification, and perpetuates the myth of battered women as sick. There may well be times when a domestic-violence victim who has retaliated against her mate in self-defense suffers from PTSD. In those circumstances, it may well be that her heightened arousal symptoms from the PTSD caused her to perceive a minor threat as a major one. In those circumstances, if she can show that she suffers from PTSD, such a defense ought to be available to her.[144] On the other hand, it may well be that the threat she perceived really was a major threat to her survival because of the social context in which she lived. In that event, it is the social-context evidence that will explain her circumstances rather than the PTSD.

Conclusion

Neither formal equality goals nor substantive equality goals are met by the way domestic violence is currently handled in the courts. Evidence that would describe the violent situations that some women find themselves in – the kind of evidence that is routinely admissible in male-to-male violence – is frequently excluded. Syndrome evidence, on the other hand, which should be excluded for its lack of scientific validity, is routinely admissible. As a result, women who have been victimized by domestic violence are further victimized by the courts' mishandling of the evidence that would tell their story.

The increased empiricism demanded by the U.S. Supreme Court's transformative trilogy of *Daubert, Joiner,* and *Kumho Tire* (and amended Rule 702) may offer a way out of this conundrum in three ways. First, excluding the bogus science of battered woman syndrome restores the empirical basis for evidence presented to the factfinder. Second, social-context evidence about domestic violence educates the jury about the reasonableness of the defendant's response to danger and dispels prevalent misconceptions about the possibility of escape and the battered woman's responsibility for provoking her abuse. Third, in those cases in which the defendant also suffers from PTSD, expert testimony about the defendant's condition may help explain her actions. This perspective transcends the debate about formal and substantive equality by offering a way of incorporating the concerns and insights of both while accommodating the need for greater empiricism in the quest of providing justice for all.

144 *See Commonwealth v. Pitts*, 740 A. 2d 726 (Pa. Super. Ct., 1999), finding that expert testimony about dependant's PTSD stemming from having a gun pointed at him during previous robberies is relevant to show that the accused acted in self-defense in a road-rage case where the accused fired his gun at a driver who had shouted profanities at him.

Conclusion

Law's moral authority is based on the accuracy of its assumptions and predictions and how they are applied in crafting legislation, deciding disputes, and engaging in scholarly debate. Throughout, this book explored how scientific evidence has become a cornerstone in the construction and application of assumptions and predictions that are fundamental to the realization of justice in all of law's aspects, whether in legislation, adjudication, or scholarship. As we have canvassed, contests over what counts as genuine and reliable science, how those contests should get resolved, and who gets to resolve them are active and pervasive topics in the legal communities of the United States, England, and other Commonwealth jurisdictions. Allowing scientifically baseless or flawed evidence to poison or influence any of the law's processes is not only cynical, it also undermines law's moral authority. The very least that can be done in a system aspiring to do justice is to thoroughly test, carefully scrutinize, and properly limit data that carry the imprimatur of science.

A critical theme running throughout this book argues that although untrained in science, judges are fully capable of deciding what counts as science, and that it is their responsibility to do so. Too often, however, perhaps because of the daunting complexities of science, many shy from that duty, with dire consequences to the rule of law and those seeking justice within it. Conceiving the rule of law as a search for truth in a system that aspires to rationality has consequences. One of these is that implementing a structured-reasoning process improves judgment. Making judges the gatekeepers of relevant evidence is thus a facet of fundamental fairness and due process. In the context of scientific evidence, relevance means validity as well as fit. Judges must not abdicate this important responsibility.

Judges are relevance gatekeepers for good reason. They have training in critical thinking, they are accountable to reviewing courts and to legal commentators, and they get regular feedback about how well they have followed prescribed procedures and whether the procedures are appropriate and effective in the pursuit of justice. In a justice system in which the goal is accurate determinations, limiting evidence to relevant information is sound cognitive practice. To place this gatekeeping responsibility on the judge is not to denigrate the jury's ultimate province to find facts. For scientific evidence, a judge should have the censor's authority of the gatekeeping function, not because judges are innately more thoughtful or responsible than jurors but because a structured inquiry into scientific validity forces judges to confront the complexities of science and engage in what cognitive psychologists refer to as "active, open-minded thinking."

That leaves open the very practical question of how judges without a science education are to perform the gatekeeping role, an answer to which this book is dedicated. Many attempts at guidance have sprung up, the most influential of which is the Federal Judicial Center's *Reference Manual on Scientific Evidence.* However, although such reference tools are helpful in understanding what goes into optimal experimental design in several important areas of science, they do little to assist in the assessments of the imperfect scientific "truths" that legal actors need to make. Educating decision makers on how to evaluate the unavoidably imperfect science that can nonetheless constitute probative evidence is crucial if judges are to responsibly discharge their gatekeeping duties.

As will surprise no one, an all-inclusive set of rules that can be applied universally to determine scientific validity is a fantasy. Differences arise among scientists operating in various disciplines – and, of course, even within the same discipline – with respect to the amount of data and what proofs are needed to support a theory. The only overarching ingredient for good science – and, hence, the only essential method – is one that allows science to provide an explanation that is open to critique and revision.

Throughout this book, rather than rules, the underlying principles common to all fields of science have been emphasized. High empirical content is important. But, given the unavoidable gaps in our knowledge, how much empirical content should a judge demand for admissibility? Rather than rules, the heuristic followed in this book consists of a series of inquiries. For each proffered study, how valuable is the study on its own? What piece of the hypothetical puzzle does each study provide? How sound is the methodology underlying each study? What are the areas of uncertainty the study fails to address? Given the knowledge of the first study (or set of studies), how much more support does the second study (or set of studies) add to the expert's hypothesis? What information gaps does it fill? How much does the second study (or set) explain in the absence of the first study (or set)? How rare or unexpected are the results of each of the studies? In addition to the extent and strength of empirical support derived from data supplied in answers to such questions, consistency within the theory, with other current theories, and with the data is also important, as are the acceptability of underlying assumptions, whether each of the proffered studies is methodologically sound, and whether each contributes toward a plausible explanation.

A number of troubling areas in which scientific evidence is prevalent are illuminated by using this heuristic. In the United States, toxic torts have been a battleground about what counts as science. Toxic tort issues propelled both *Daubert* and *Joiner* into the U.S. Supreme Court. In applying the heuristic proposed by the Court, it becomes apparent that decisional analyses in toxic tort cases frequently founder along several rocky issues, including the admissibility and evaluation of animal studies, the impact of cumulative studies, and the use of statistical analysis. Too frequently, solid scientific evidence is excluded by judges who demand that the scientific witness's research meet standards few if any other scientists in the same scientific field would require. Locking the gate against scientifically solid information that fits the case impairs the delicate reasoning balance struck by the common law and impedes the jury's ultimate province to find facts.

In stark contrast, at the other end of the admissibility spectrum, is identification evidence in criminal prosecutions, where little scrutiny is given to the expert assertions that are frequently the focal point of the trial. In this context, the importance of empirical support for assumptions of uniqueness and the impact of probability theory on statements supporting uniqueness should become the focus of inquiry. How unlikely a coincidence of particular features might be is a question that must be based on the collection of data and the use of statistical analysis, which has been startlingly absent from this branch of courtroom science. Contrary to routine protocol in toxic tort trials, judges in criminal cases overwhelmingly permit experts to testify with little or no examination of the scientific basis for their testimony, a fact lamentably documented in the United States, United Kingdom, and Commonwealth countries as well.

The vulnerability of the rule of law to bogus evidence in criminal prosecutions is manifest: microscopic hair analysis, bitemark identification, voice spectrography, handwriting analysis, and even such time-honored prosecutorial tools of identification as fingerprinting have crept into evidence with dispositive – sometimes, fatal – results, supported by virtually no demonstration of their scientific bases. The inability of an identification technique to meet these tests should preclude admissibility. There can be no more demonstrable validation of commitment to the rule of law than an insistence that evidence admitted in trials affecting life and liberty have a legitimate, scientifically valid basis. In so insisting, courts can serve a major role in advancing the integrity of the factfinding process and concomitantly, in improving the quality of criminal justice and jurisprudence, a role that, to date, too many judges have declined to assume. Courts that cling to the rituals of discredited superstitions and admit unscientific evidence for reasons that cannot be justified on scientific grounds not only misread *Daubert* but also impede much-needed reform of the criminal justice system.

Equally dire is the struggle over what counts as science in capital sentencing proceedings, where many in the judiciary have flung wide the gates to crassly unscientific expert testimony. Failure to scrutinize expert testimony relating to future dangerousness is a massive, inexcusable failure of intellectual due process. In capital sentencing proceedings, experts are permitted to predict violence without any examination of the scientific validity of such assertions, despite widespread scientific disparagement of any ability to make such predictions. The tension between the scientific scrutiny required for admissibility in civil cases (in which money damages are at stake) and the unscientific predictions freely admissible in capital sentencing determinations (in which the issue is death) is, at the very least, scandalous.

A decision as important as a death sentence simply cannot be based on bunkum. Permitting expert witnesses to confuse the jury with wholly unscientific assertions cannot be tolerated in any community, much less a civilized country that prides itself on being governed by constitutional principles mandating due process of law to its citizens. Consequently, in addition to being sound cognitive practice and mandated by the rule of law, judicial gatekeeping to prevent jury confusion and to foreclose ritualistic bias is a minimum for fundamental fairness.

Clinical predictions of future dangerousness cannot meet these standards. Actuarial testimony is likewise highly suspect, even though it might infrequently and barely squeak through. Predicting violence, like predicting the weather, is at best subject to a large margin of error. Yet, despite its fragility, this kind of mis-nomered scientific testimony continues to prevail at capital-sentencing hearings. It is difficult to imagine the rule of law confronting a more critical setting requiring the most accurate scientific testimony. But, because evidentiary rules do not generally apply (and, even when they do, they are ignored in practice), testimony that a litigant on trial for his life is likely to be dangerous in the future goes unexamined. Particularly where a capital jury is charged with making reasoned moral judgments about the fate of a defendant rather than a factual determination, relevant and reliable information is crucial to their task. The dynamics of jury decision making in capital-sentencing decisions have demonstrated the importance of recognizing that the relevance requirement is a constitutional concern of fundamental fairness. In a system that strives for justice, it must be expected that judges will evaluate expert testimony that may fuel a determination of death with at least as much care as scientific testimony in civil cases is routinely scrutinized.

Although one might think that the problem of predicting future dangerousness is limited to capital trials (and, therefore, to the United States), expert testimony about sexual predation and recidivism is rampant in sexual-offender cases not only here but also in the United Kingdom and the Commonwealth countries. In the context of sexual-offender legislation, however, experts are more likely than in capital cases to base assertions of future dangerousness on actuarial instruments. Only rarely is any inquiry made into the scientific soundness of such instruments. That these predictions are admitted without serious judicial inquiry into their scientific validity is both astonishing and disheartening in a system that has as a fundamental tenet that only facts having rational probative value should be admissible in the search for truth.

Courtroom failures to scrutinize claims of scientific validity are not the only offenders of intellectual due process. Not infrequently in legal scholarship, self-styled "scientific evidence" is cited uncritically to support legal argument. This is especially true of social science evidence, which for years was described in judicial forums as "soft science" and either exempted or excluded entirely from scrutiny. With the advent of *Kumho Tire*, the U.S. Supreme Court held – and labored to make it plain to judges and lawyers – that the distinction between "hard" and "soft" science was illusory, and the only real difference – as well as the only justifiable one – was between scientifically valid and scientifically invalid data and theories. Here also, the heuristic presented in this book is offered as a useful assessment tool with which to reach a determination of the scientific validity of a proffered theory from the social sciences.

Cognitive illusions, such as hindsight bias, overconfidence, optimism, and the like, crop up in legal arguments about everything from antitrust to toxic torts. With little analysis of the research on which behavioral-decision theory is based, thousands of legal articles – and a few cases – have cited to various aspects of behavioral-decision theory as though it were accepted dogma. This is a shockingly unscientific approach to science. Similarly, but at the other end of the spectrum, are those who would adhere unskeptically to such frayed hypotheses as rational actor utility maximization, a theory from which even most economists have withdrawn their endorsements. Obviously, neither of these extremes is a sound solution. The rule of law, its systems, and those responsible for its continuing vitality can neither afford to ignore science nor to be uncritical in its use. In-depth interdisciplinary examination of evidence claiming to validate theoretical principles or posits of the social sciences is indispensable for scholars who expect that their arguments will affect the law.

References to framing effects, hindsight bias, overconfidence, and optimism bias pervade the legal literature. Occasionally, such references can even be found in court opinions. Jury studies and eyewitness unreliability studies are regular subjects of admissibility disputes. Behavioral studies are cited as support for everything from antitrust and environmental reform to failures in the securities markets. The lesson for lawyers is that whereas social science has much to offer law, its uncritical use is counterproductive and should be avoided. Legal scholarship should not cite a particular bias in support of an argument, for example, without acknowledging the strengths and weaknesses of the underlying research program that claims validity for the bias. On the other hand, legal theorizing that fails to draw on the rich insights of social psychology hamstrings its potential. A more sophisticated view and treatment of the insights science offers can only improve the discourse of law.

One form of social science testimony that has achieved astounding success in legislatures and courts alike is battered woman syndrome testimony. Battered woman syndrome testimony is controversial for a number of reasons. For openers, it perpetuates an offensive stereotype of a helpless, irrational woman reacting pathologically but self-interestedly, while it ignores the complexities of women's roles. And then it flunks out altogether, suffering the same inadequacies as its flawed siblings in the identification and prediction areas: battered woman's syndrome testimony lacks empirical support. Unhappily, although such testimony fails on scientific validity grounds, its admissibility is widespread, whereas important social-context evidence about domestic violence – which could educate a jury about the reasonableness of responses to danger and dispel prevalent misconceptions – is too frequently found inadmissible.

Domestic violence tends to be the hidden fulcrum that catapults litigants into court. Far too often it remains a concealed force. Lawyers fail to raise domestic violence as an issue, unaware of its impact on their clients' decisions. Judges refuse to consider domestic violence, finding it irrelevant even when it could explain the reasonableness (or not) of the warring litigants' actions. Courts display an extraordinary reluctance to grapple with its implications. This is especially apparent in the self-defense claim underpinning a homicide justification, the uncritical acceptance of which flatly ignores the increased empiricism demanded by the U.S. Supreme Court's transformative trilogy of *Daubert, Joiner,* and *Kumho Tire* (and amended Rule 702).

The authority of these decisions offers a way out of the conventional conundrum in three ways. First, excluding the bogus science of battered woman syndrome restores the empirical command of evidence presented to the factfinder. Second, social-context evidence about domestic violence educates a factfinder about the reasonableness of a victim's response to danger and dispels prevalent misconceptions about the possibility of escape and the battered woman's responsibility for "provoking" her abuse. Third, in those cases in which the victim also suffers from PTSD, expert testimony about her condition may help explain her actions. This perspective transcends the debate over formal and substantive equality by offering a way of incorporating the concerns and insights of both while accommodating the need for greater empiricism in the quest of providing justice for all.

In designing this heuristic and showing how it can be used in applications in specific areas that continue to roil the justice system, I hope to enable judges to make better admissibility decisions, lawyers to make better arguments about the science they bring into the courtroom, scholars to make more persuasive use of science in their critiques of the law, and anyone confronting unfamiliar information to better evaluate it and thereby to enhance law's moral authority and its endorsement by the society that has consented to its governance.

Index

abduction, 6
abduction theory, 6
accountability
  cognitive biases increased by, 23
  cognitive dissonance effect increased by, 23
  dilution effect and, 33
  feedback's importance for, 16
  for decision outcomes, 35
  for inferences, 33–34
  hypothesis testing and, 44
  individual decision making and, 16
  judgment improved by, 23, 34
  of judges, 16, 33
  of jurors, 33
Actual Innocence Project, 124
actuarial instruments
  admissibility and, 140–142
  and human judgment, 140
  brain dysfunction diagnosis by, 197
  components missing from, 166
  explanatory power of, 140
  future dangerousness predictions and, 162
  IQ tests, 164
  least-squares stepwise multiple regression
    analysis, 164
  multi-disciplinary teams v., 126
  multiple regression statistical tool, 163–164
  Receiver Operating Characteristic curve
    statistics of, 126
  relative accuracy of, 144
  risk analysis advantage of, 141
  sexual violence analysis via, 161
  testimony based on, 166
  theory underlying, 140
admissibility
  actuarial instruments and, 140–142
  assessing expert's conclusions for, 53–56
  battered women syndrome testimony, 219
  Burn's question on, 33

Canadian Supreme Court's criteria for, 11
consensus standard for, 5
court problems with standards of, 113
Daubert standards of, 95
determining, 6, 54
error rate importance to, 112
expert testimony and, 19
Frye v. United States and, 4
lawyers/judges determinations of, 63
of character evidence, 212
of mtDNA, 113
statistical significance and, 68
sufficiency conflation of, 82–84
adversarial system, 130, 132
AFIS. *See* Automated Fingerprint Identification
  System
aggression, absence of, 209
aggression, lack of, 209, 216–217
Aitken, C. G. G., 115
Aldridge, Peter, 98
American Academy of Forensic Sciences survey,
  102
American Psychiatric Association, 128
analogy-based reasoning, 8
anchoring heuristic, 151, 152
animal studies
  advantages of, 73
  arguments against, 72
  chemical exposure in, 71, 73
  court's rejection of, 72
  judges difficulties with, 71
  limitations of, 71
  misconceptions regarding usefulness of, 76
  rodent studies, 71
  rodent study, 71
  rule-of-thumb hierarchical ranking of, 70
  superiority of, 70
  toxicology's use of, 186
arguments. *See* scientific arguments

Aristotelian syllogism, 6
Ashbaugh, David R., 107
assessment(s)
    EPA risk, 69
    of arguments, 59
    of conclusions, 53–56
    of risk, 48
    of scientific validity, 51
    probabilistic, 65
    Supreme Court and general, 9
    violence risk, 166
assumptions
    criteria for basic, 51
    intellectual due process and, 51
    mtDNA's usefulness, 117–118
    randomness, 177
    reliance on, 50
    theories built on, 51
    understanding statistical, 62
Australia
    Alyce Chamberlin murder case of, 97
    convictions overturned in, 97–98
    expert testimony admissibility in, 13
    no reliability requirements of, 12
    probative value emphasis in, 13
    pseudo-science problems of, 99
    U.S. style legislation of, 13
Automated Fingerprint Identification System
        (AFIS), 106
availability heuristic, 151, 194, 198

Barefoot v. Estelle (Supreme Court decision),
        124
    and regime of evidentiary federalism,
        127–129
    Blackmun's dissenting opinion in, 129
    dilution effect and, 153
    evidentiary contradictions of, 127–131
    future dangerousness testimony and, 128
    group decision making dynamics and, 149
    psychiatric testimony in, 128
    rules of evidence changed since, 128
base rate
    defined,
    fallacy, 195
    neglect, 197
battered woman syndrome, 207. See also
        feminists; Walker, Lenore.
    as power struggle,
    as sub-species of PTSD, 224–225
    assessing scientific validity of, 220–221
    bogus science exclusion from, 231
    castle doctrine and, 215

cycle inconsistency in, 222
expert testimony permitted for, 218
formal v. substantive equality and, 225
learned helplessness as false perception in,
        220, 222
psychological impact evidence for, 229–231
questioning Walker's methodology regarding,
        223
reasonable assessment for, 226
scientific unsoundness of, 225
size differential considerations in, 215
social context evidence for, 225
testimony admissibility for, 219
Walker, Lenore, on, 220–221, 222–223, 225
battered woman/women
    characterization of,
    PTSD of, 230–231
    Walker's definition of, 221
batterers, lenient sentencing for, 229
battling, of experts, 19, 50
Bayes theorem, 24
Becker, Gary, 169
behavior, future
    impossibility of predicting, 138
    predicting weather v. predicting, 139
behavioral decision research
    between-subjects designs, 182, 183
    college students as subjects for, 177–181
    double-blind experiment control lack in, 185
    experimental design in, 176–181
    experimental design trade-offs, 183
    failing of, 189
    practical significance lack in, 188
    small effect sizes of, 188
    subject (people) variation influence on, 181
    within-subjects design, 182, 183
behavioral decision theorists
    claims of, 176
    heuristic choice of, 173
    human beings observations of, 170
    natural selection considerations of, 172
    questions asked by, 175
behavioral decision theory. See also decision
        making; decision theorists
    biological interactive systems and, 171
    law and economics v., 169–176
    methodology debate, 176
    strength/weakness of, 170
between-subjects designs, 182, 183
bias(es)
    cognitive illusions as,
    defining, 28, 149
    instinct and, 175

minimizing decision making, 22
of groups, 28
overconfidence, 27, 34, 152, 199
physical attractiveness bias, 24
self-serving, 199
biological information
examination of, 47
inferential synergy of combined, 48
biological significance, 64
biological systems
biological/statistical significance importance
to, 64
human-animal similarities of, 73
bitemark identification, 94, 96, 109–110
Kunco v. Commonwealth case and, 110
People v. Marx court case and, 109
State v. Krone case and, 110
Black, Bert, 99
Blackmun, Harry A., 124
Barefoot dissenting opinion by, 129
Daubert v. Merrell Dow Pharmaceuticals, Inc.
majority opinion of, 129
bounded rationality, 20–22, 169
unrealistic views of mind replaced by, 20
Bourke, Judy, 99
brain, human
actuarial instruments, measurement of, 126
as computer (metaphor), 44
nonlinearity of, 139
Brown, Malcolm, 101
Bukszar, E., 188
burden of proof, 67
Burns, Robert, 33

Canada
Daubert approved by courts of, 11
Supreme Court of, 11
cancer
causation issues, 77
EPA default position on, 77
rodent study extrapolations on, 71
Capital Juror Project, 133, 138
capital sentencing, 123
cognitive quirks impact on, 148–150
criminal sentencing v., 132
expert testimony proffered at, 133, 146
gatekeeping and, 131–133
heightened reliability standards of, 131
jury decision making for, 146, 149
overconfidence heuristic and, 150
systematic biases of concern in, 150–153
case-control studies, 68
castle doctrine, 215

causation
attribution of, 58
conundrum, 65
court's difficulty with, 57
Daubert and, 83
general, 58
human studies and, 70
Koch's postulates of, 58–59
making decisions about, 62
proving, 82
scientific uncertainty about, 58
specific, 58
Chamberlain, Alyce, 97
Chemical Institute of Toxicology report, 86
chemicals
animal studies and, 71, 73
EPA's regulation of, 49
illness caused by, 47
safety testing lack for, 80
choice shift, group polarization and, 29, 31
Christensen-Szalanski, J., 189
civil law, lower standards of, 65
clinical double-bind studies, 68
clinical predictions, 125
inaccuracies of, 125, 129
CODIS. *See* Combined DNA Index System
cognitive bias(es)
accountability's influence on, 23
dilution effect as, 23–26
cognitive dissonance, 27
accountability and, 23
decision making and, 201
defined, 150
juries and, 150
overconfidence and, 150
cognitive dissonance theory
resilience of,
cognitive illusions. *See also* social psychology
cognitive quirks
capital sentencing impacted by, 148–150
cognitive shortcuts, 148
coherence theory (of rationality), 19
cohort studies, 68
Cole, Simon A., 107
Combined DNA Index System (CODIS),
104
common law countries, 11–14
judges as gatekeepers in, 18
community notification statutes, 155
complex decisions, 20
complexity theory, 138–140, 173, 202
concern for accuracy (in common law), 19, 21,
27, 33, 107

conclusions, scientific
    conflicting, 38, 55
    languaging problem of, 55
    tentative phrases couching of, 55
confidence interval
    defined, 60
    scientist's use of, 66
confidence limits, 61
conflict, creating impression of, 67
Connolly, T., 188
Constitution (U.S.)
    Eighth Amendment, 135
    Fourteenth Amendment, 135
controls, importance of, 52
convictions
    foundationless evidence and, 95
    overturning of, 97
correspondence theory (of rationality), 19
court(s)
    admissibility standards, problems of, 113
    analysis standards, circumvented by, 95
    animal studies rejected by, 72
    causality difficulties of, 57
    causation conundrum in, 65
    certainty sought by, 54
    criminal evidence dilemma of, 96
    domestic violence issues of, 203
    epidemiological studies and, 69
    evidence excluded by, 65, 67, 84, 93
    expert testimony rejected by, 74, 131
    extrapolation struggles of, 76
    future dangerousness testimony exclusion by,
        130
    general acceptance test of,
    in vitro tissue culture studies, discomfort of,
        80
    lab standards/protocols issues of, 53
    pseudo-science admitted into, 99
    risk assessment/management by, 48
    scientific validity examined by, 11
    scientific validity not addressed by, 127
    State v. Council failure by, 120–121
courtroom disputes, scientific evidence focus in,
Cowans, Stephen, DNA evidence exoneration
    of, 108
Coyle, Marcia, 99, 102
Crane, Michael, 164. See also Kansas v. Crane
Criminal Cases Review Commission (England),
    12
criminal cases, judge testimony permissiveness
    in, 94
criminal laboratories, modernizing protocols
    of, 10

criminal sentencing, capital sentencing v., 132
Cummins, Harold, 100
cumulative studies, impact of, 57, 71, 233–234

Damaska, Mirjan, 130
data
    actuarial instruments for analyzing, 126
    conflicting, 49
    examining available, 47–49
    trimming, 63
data dredging experiments, 38
Daubert v. Merrell Dow Pharmaceuticals, Inc.
    decision, 4
    admissibility standards of, 95
    and causation, 83
    as constitutional minimum, 124, 133–137
    Blackmun's majority opinion in, 129
    Canada's approval of, 11
    circumventing mandate of, 111
    evidentiary contradictions of, 127–131
    expert testimony admissibility prior to,
    expert testimony influenced by, 129
    fingerprint challenge of, 105
    Frye's difference with, 10
    judicial analysis influenced by, 11
    junk science and,
    Kozinski's remand in, 10
    Rehnquist's dissent of, 7, 9–10
    relevance and,
    standards, 82
    structured analysis required under, 149
    Supreme Court (U.S.) guidelines for, 5
    Supreme Court's granting of certiorari in, 9
    unanswered questions of, 84
Dawes, Robyn, 171
death penalty
    future dangerousness and, 143
    jurisprudence, 134
    Supreme Court's minimal standard for, 136
decision making. See also behavioral decision
        theory; social psychology
    accountability in, 35
    aids to, 22
    Barefoot v. Estelle and dynamics of group, 149
    basis of sound, 208
    biological/evolutionary process consideration
        in, 171
    by judges, 14, 18, 46
    by juries, 14
    causation and, 62
    cognitive dissonance theory and, 201
    disbelief in rational choice models of, 21
    experimental settings v. real world, 186

group v. individual, 28
heuristics and, 20–21
increasing accuracy of, 34
individual biases in, 28, 149
inferences and, 21–22
minimizing biases in, 22
nonperfection in,
of groups, 27–32, 33, 149, 152
question variance for, 192
simplification of, 59
story model model of, 147–148
structural analysis advantages in, 126
decision theory, 170
defendant, lack of aggression by, 209, 216–217
defense of premises doctrine, 203
democratic system, rule of law in, 122
descriptive statistics, 60
Diagnostic and Statistical Manual (DSM-IV), 133
Diamond, Jared, 175, 196
dilution effect, 23–26, 33
    as cognitive bias, 149
    accountability and, 33
    Barefoot v. Estelle and, 153
    causes of, 24
    group processes lowering of, 26
    heuristics underlying, 24
    irrelevant information and, 149
DNA
    nuclear analysis of, 116
    PCR technique and, 104
    RFLP analysis of, 112
    STR of, 104
    VNTR of, 104
DNA Identification Act, 102
DNA typing. *See also* mitochondrial
        deoxyribonucleic acid; nuclear DNA
        analysis; restriction fragment length
        polymorphism DNA analysis
    as boon for defense/prosecution, 100–102
    as DNA "fingerprinting," 104
    as gold standard, 104
    Kron exoneration from, 110
    National Research Council reports on, 118
    theory behind, 115
    Virginia State Crime Lab errors with, 101
doctrine of relevance, 18
domestic violence
    cycles/phases of, 220
    expert testimony about, 225
    judge's/court's issues with, 203
    misconceptions about prevalence of, 205
    statistics on, 203

dose-response relationships, 53, 73
dual-process model of reasoning, 189–190
Due Process Clause (14th Amendment)
    right to fair hearings of, 134, 135
due process, free-standing, 135

economists, probability theory and, 171
effect size, 188–189, 191
egocentric biases, 26
Eighth Amendment (U.S. Constitution), 135
emotions
    framing effects and, 193
    nonrandomness of, 193
empirical support
    criminal evidence lacking in, 53
    expert's need for, 54
England
    Criminal Cases Review Commission of, 12
    no reliability requirements of, 12
    Royal Commission on Criminal Justice of, 12
    Sally Clark case of, 12
English law, admissibility of expert opinion
        testimony under, 11
Environmental Protection Agency (EPA)
    cancer default position of, 77
    chemicals regulated by, 49
    guidelines of, 5
    risk assessment, 69
    scientific claims evaluated by,
    target-organ studies position of, 77
EPA. *See* Environmental Protection Agency
epidemiological studies, 58, 64, 69
    courts and, 69
    limited availability of, 73
    meta-analysis technique, 180
    small sample size problems in, 177
epidemiologists, operational criteria of, 58
epistemology
    gatekeeper issue view of, 14
    naturalized,
    normative, 122
    reciprocal containment, 7
    social, 14
Epstein, Robert, 108
equality
    competing conceptions of, 206–209
    criticism of, 206–207
    formal equality issue, 208, 225
    gender and, 206
    justice and, 204
    substantive, 204, 206–207, 208, 225
equilibrium theory (of evolution), 173

error rates
  admissibility and, 112
  identification techniques for, 96
errors
  commission of statistical, 103
  random v. systematic, 60
Europe, inquisitorial adjudication system of,
    131
Everett, Ian, 108
evidence, criminal
  court's dilemma regarding, 96
  empirical support lacking in, 53
  failing to report contradictory, 63
  scientifically unsound, 95
  types of excluded, 123
evidence, hearsay, 123
evidence law, 204
evidence, rules of, 205
  abandoning strict adherence to, 124
  accuracy concerns, 19
  Barefoot v. Estelle's influence on, 128
  declining to apply, 132
  gender-blind, neutrality of, 206
  modernizing protocols of, 10
evidence, scientific
  cumulative impact of, 80–82
  exclusion of, 65, 67, 84, 93
  Frye v. United States and,
  litigation and, 8
  proffered probability statement for, 103
evidence, self-defense, 209–210
evidence, social context, 223
evidence-based medicine movement, 197
evidentiary federalism, 127–129
exemplary reasoning, 6
experiments
  data dredging, 38
  designing of, 52–53
  on humans, 58
experts, scientific
  admissibility inquiry of, 19
  assessing conclusions of, 53–56
  battling of, 19, 50
  categorical v. statistical articulation of results,
    142
  concerns regarding, 19
  conflicting conclusions of, 38, 55
  court-appointed/adversarial, 11
  cross-examination of, 12
  diagnosis/prediction variance of, 126
  empirical support needed by, 54
  excess leeway provided to, 99
  information gap influence on, 49

  jury education by, 166
  Netherland's appointment of, 57
  nontolerance for confusion created by, 145
  overconfidence bias and, 34
  perjury by, 97
  wrongness/rightness of, 96
extrapolation(s)
  animal to human, 72–73
  court struggles with, 76
  high dosage to low dosage, 73–77
  qualitative, 73
  quantitative, 73
  rebuttable presumption similarity to, 72
  rodent study, 71
  route of exposure, 78–80
  target organ, 77–78

F.B.I.
  CODIS of, 104
  fingerprint misidentification by, 109
  Justice Department report on, 97, 102–103
  STR loci (sites) used by, 104
  substandard forensic lab work by, 102
  whitepaper hair analysis commentary of,
    115
facts, scientific
  knowledge and, 50
  probabilistic nature of, 66
false positive
  false negative v., 102–103
  tests, 103
falsification
  of assertions, 161
  of incrimination, 112
  of null hypothesis, 170
  theory of, 7, 42, 44
Faulds, Henry, 106
FDA. *See* Food and Drug Administration
Federal Death Penalty Act of 1994, 133
Federal Judicial Center, 59
Federal Rules of Evidence (U.S.), 131
  1975 adoption of, 9
  amendment to, 4
  Australia's legislation similarity to, 13
  judges and, 4–5
feedback
  accountability's importance for, 16
feminists
  equal treatment under law issue, 204
  formal equality issue, 208, 225
  non-equal applications of rules, 206
  relational, 207, 209
  science critiqued by, 37

self-defense rules critique of, 206
substantive equality issue, 204, 206–207, 225
fingerprints/fingerprint technology, 94
    concerns for accuracy, 107
    Daubert's challenge to, 105
    discrepancies with, 112
    Faulds cautions regarding, 106
    Galton's statistical model for, 106
    Judge Pollack's effort regarding, 112
    lack of controlled studies regarding, 105
    Llera Plaza I court case and, 107
    matching process difficulties with, 107
    National Institute of Justice and, 107
    People v. Jennings court case and, 105
    problems with, 106
    reliability concerns about, 104–109
    zero error claims made regarding, 108
Food and Drug Administration (FDA), 68
forensic laboratories
    FBI substandard work in, 102
    mandatory regulation lacking in, 102
    methodological problems in, 101
    scientific standards ignored in, 96–97
forensic odontologists (bitemark experts), 97
forensic science, 95, 98
formaldehyde, example of toxic tort analysis, 84
Fourteenth Amendment (U.S. Constitution),
    135
framing effects heuristic, 190–193, 194
Frank, Jerome, 92
frequentist statistics, 21
Frye v. United States
    Daubert's difference with, 10
    Frye test, 4, 13
    New Zealand equivalence of, 13
    scientific evidence admissibility standard of, 8
fundamental fairness, 232
    as requirement of rationality, 136
    judicial gatekeeping as minimum for, 235
    rule of law requirement of, 130
future dangerousness predictions
    actuarial instruments used for, 162
    prior criminal records reliance of, 162
    under Hendricks/Crane, 156–158
future dangerousness testimony
    American Psychiatric Association's
        opposition to, 128
    as key to jury's life/death determination,
        castigation of, 129
    court exclusion of, 130
    death penalty and, 143
    forms of expert testimony about, 125–127
    in United Kingdom (U.K.), 155–156

juries influenced by, 142–143
lack of scientific basis for, 136
nonexamination of, 146
scientific validity lacking in, 156

Galton, Francis, 106
gambler's fallacy, 174
game theory, 21
gaps, in scientific knowledge, 51
gatekeepers
    appropriateness of role of, 10
    epistemology view of, 14
    judges as, 7, 11, 18, 35, 153, 232
    need for, 14
    Supreme Court (U.S.) divided on issue of,
        14
gatekeeping
    and capital sentencing, 131–133
    judicial, 153
Gaudette, B. D., 115
gender, equality and, 206
general causation, 58
general consensus standard. *See Frye* test
General Electric Co. v. Joiner, 4, 55, 81
    Daubert standards reiterated in, 129
    standards, 82
    unanswered questions of, 84
generalization
    inductive, 6
    probabilistic, 6
genocide, 196
Giannelli, Paul C., 120
Gibbons, Ann, 116, 117
Gigerenzer, Gerd, 171
global rationality, 20
Gregg v. Georgia, accurate sentencing
    information and, 135
Grieve, David L., 108
group dynamics, 152
group polarization, 29
    choice shift and, 29, 31
    diverse groups and absence of, 31
    group discussion influence on, 30
    individual changing view explanation of, 30
    persuasive argument theory explanation of,
        31
    studies of, 31
groups
    biases of, 28
    decisionmaking dynamics of, 27–32, 33, 152
    extreme judgments by, 29
    final judgments of, 28
    overconfidence bias and, 34

groups (*cont.*)
  polarizations' absence with diversity of, 31
  social loafing in, 32
guidelines
  of Environmental Protection Agency, 5
  of Supreme Court, 5

hair analysis, 94, 96
  F.B.I.'s whitepaper commentary on, 115
  mtDNA testing used in, 114
  State v. Council use of, 115, 117
  theory of, 114
  Williams v. Reynolds case and, 111
handwriting analysis, 94, 96
Hansen, Mark, 99
Hare Psychology Checklist-Revised (PCL-R),
  133
Hart, D. L., 104
Hastie, Reid, 138, 147, 171
hearsay evidence, 123
Hendricks, Leo, 163. *See also* Kansas v.
  Hendricks 157
heuristic(s)
  anchoring, 151, 152
  availability, 151, 194, 198
  behavioral decision theorists choice of, 173
  bias and, 175
  capital sentencing and overconfidence, 150
  cognitive psychologist's meaning of, 20–21
  decision making and, 20
  defined, 20
  dilution effect and, 24
  framing effects, 190–194
  instinct and, 175
  overconfidence, 150
  representative, 24–25, 151, 194, 198
  satisficing, 20
  social norms, 24, 25–26
  stereotyping outsiders, 196
  support theory for, 190
high-dosage extrapolations, 73–77
Higuchi, Russell, 117
Hill, Austin, 58
Holt, Sarah B., 105
homicide
  common law doctrine of justified, 217
  self-defense as justification for, 208
hot hand fallacy, 174
human beings
  decision theorist observation of, 170
  experimenting on, 58
  imperfect studies of, 185
  natural selection and, 172

self-serving bias of, 199
  short-cuts used by, 170
  stereotyping by, 196
human studies
  as "gold standard," 68
  causation and, 70
  inherent weaknesses of, 69
  rule-of-thumb hierarchical ranking of, 68
hung juries, 149
hypotheses
  careful construction of, 93
  determining validity of, 47
  testing of, 61
  theories v., 46–47
hypothesis testing. *See also* testability
  accountability in, 44
  effect of variables in, 44
  in scientific method, 36

identification techniques. *See also* bitemark
    identification; fingerprints/fingerprint
    technology; hair analysis; voice
    spectrography
  challenging previously accepted, 10
  DNA as, 47
  error rates for, 96
  problems of, 100
  types of, 94
in vitro tissue culture studies, 80
individual decision making
  accountability and, 16
  group decision making v., 27, 32
individual variation
  analysis of variance, 181
  consequence debates regarding, 182
  problems of, 181–184, 186
  statistical methods for dealing with, 181
individuals, unique identifying characteristics
    of, 47
inductive generalization, 6
inductive reasoning, 6
infant deaths, unexplained, 101. *See also* sudden
    infant death syndrome 98
inference(s)
  abduction and, 3
  accountability for, 33–34
  causal, 64
  components of scientific, 48
  decision making and, 21–22
  justifiable, 7
  making inappropriate, 63
  statistical, 41, 63
  unavoidability of, 51

inferential statistics, 60
inferential synergy, 48
information
    biological, 47
    cognitive shortcuts in processing, 21
    difficulty sorting, 23
    gaps in, 49
    heuristics and, 20
    irrelevant v. relevant, 24, 149
    judges screening irrelevant, 18
    juries need for relevant, 146
    non-exclusion of, 82
    post-decision dissonance decreased via,
        25–27
    rationality and accuracy of, 19
    reasoning based on trustworthy, 122
    relevance of, 33
Innocence Project, 100, 101
instinct, heuristics/biases and, 175
intellectual due process
    assumptions and, 51
    by judges, 5, 6
    limitation of, 135
    relevance as requirement of, 35
interdisciplinarity, 8
internal validity, 185
interviews, with death penalty jurors, 147, 151
involuntary commitment statutes, 157
IQ tests, 164

Janis, Irving, 152
Joiner. See General Electric Co. v. Joiner
judges
    accountability of, 16, 33
    admissibility determinations by, 6, 54, 63
    animal studies influence on, 71
    argument assessment by, 59
    as gatekeepers, 7, 11, 18, 35, 95, 153, 232
    as triers of science, 4
    Australia's probative value emphasis of, 13
    conflict's influence on, 67
    criminal case testimony permissiveness of, 94
    decision making by, 14, 18, 34, 46
    domestic violence issues of, 203
    educational needs of, 42
    evidence excluded by, 65, 67
    examining statistical inference by, 63
    expert's testimony consideration by, 46
    Federal Rules of Evidence and, 4–5
    intellectual due process provided by, 5, 6
    media's influence of, 151
    political pressure on federal, 18
    role of, 9

science difficulty of, 5
science thinking success of, 10
scientific testimony evaluated by, 4
scientific validity questioned by, 9
scientist's viewpoint v. viewpoint of, 66
screening irrelevant information by, 18
self-defense involvement of, 209
study types preferred by, 70
Supreme Court (U.S.) guidelines for, 5
testimony decisions of, 58, 96
unconscious decisions of, 15
judgment(s)
    accountability's improvement of, 23, 34
    actuarial instruments and human, 140
    group final, 28
    nonperfection of,
    self-belief in, 27
    shortcuts in making, 21
    structured reasoning's impact on, 16, 22–23
judicial analysis, *Daubert's* influence on, 11
judicial screening, 33–35
    of expert witnesses, 18, 27
junk science, *Daubert's* influence on,
juries. *See also* mock-juries
    capital sentencing by, 146, 149
    cognitive dissonance and, 150
    decision making by, 14
    duty to retreat imposition by, 217–218
    future dangerousness influence on, 142–143
    hung, 149
    information sorting difficulties of, 23
    physical attractiveness influence on, 24
    predictability and, 142
    reasoned moral response of, 132
    relevant information required by, 146
    scientific expert's education of, 142, 166
    screening irrelevant information from, 18
    self-defense constraints of, 214
    social environment influence on, 27
    studies of mock-juries, 31
    unconscious decisions of, 15
jurisprudence
    death penalty, 134
    transformation of, 129
jurors
    accountability of, 33
    cognitive dissonance of, 150
    experts rated by, 147
    interviews with death penalty, 147, 151
    overconfidence of, 150
    relevance of information to, 33
    self-belief of capital, 150
    skewed perceptions shared by, 151

jurors (*cont.*)
    underestimating years served, 15
    violence overestimation by, 143
jury instructions, importance of, 147
jury system, separation of powers doctrine and,
    17
justice
    as equal treatment under law, 204
    equality and, 204
Justice Department Report, 97, 102–103
justifiable inferences, 7
Justin, Peter, 200

Kahn, Patricia, 117
Kahnemann, Daniel, 190
Kansas Sexually Violent Predator Act ("Kansas
    Act"), 162. *See also* pedophilia 156
Kansas v. Crane, 156–158
Kansas v. Hendricks, 156, 157, 158
Kaye, David H., 116, 118
Kershaw, Sara, 109
killing, men v. women, 229
knowledge
    gaps in scientific, 51
    scientific dialogue and growth of, 45
    scientific facts and, 50
Koch, causation postulates of, 58–59
Koehler, Jonathan J., 98, 100, 115, 120, 190
Koenig, Bruce E., 96
Kozinski, Judge
    admissibility factor added by, 10
    Daubert remand of, 10
Kreuger, Joachim, 174
Kuhn, Thomas, 38
Kumbo Tire v. Carmichael, 5
    Daubert standards reiterated in, 129
Kunco v. Commonwealth case, 110

Lakatos, Imre, 38
law
    evidence, 204
    guaranteed equal protection under, 206
    human behavior research influence on,
        168–169
    justice as equality under, 204
    moral authority of, 232
    social psychology's importance to, 168
lawyers
    admissibility determinations of, 63
    examining statistical inference by, 63
least-squares stepwise multiple regression
    analysis, 164
legal paradigms, social construction of, 38

Lempert, Richard, 104
Lewontin, Richard C., 104
linear effects theory, 75
litigation
    appropriate inferences in context of, 51
    dosage issues/lab condition issues and, 76
    questionable science and, 8
Llera Plaza court case, 98, 107
    Judge Pollack's fingerprint analysis in, 112,
        113
loafing. *See* social loafing
logic. *See* scientific logic
low dosage extrapolations, 73–77

Maceo, Alice, 100
Marshal, Eliot, 117, 120
Marusic, Ana, 117
materiality, principle of, 122
Mayfield, Brandon, 109
McCartney, Carole, 97
medical research, control-based ranking used
    in, 185
Megans's Law, 155
men, killing of women v. killing of, 229
meta-analysis technique, 180
metaphors
    brain as computer, 44
    heart as pump, 44
    scientific theories and, 46
    scientific understanding aided by, 39, 51
methodology
    defined, 51
    protocols and standardization of, 52
    questioning soundness of, 56, 116
Midlo, Charles, 100
Minnesota Multiphase Personality Inventory
    (MMPI), 197
Minnesota Sex Offender Screening Test-Revised
    (MnSOST-R), 159
mitochondrial deoxyribonucleic acid (mtDNA)
    analysis, 113, 114
    assumptions regarding usefulness of, 117–118
    PCR technique used with, 118
    possible DNA contamination with, 118
MMPI. *See* Minnesota Multiphase Personality
    Inventory (MMPI)
MnSOST-R. *See* Minnesota Sex Offender
    Screening Test-Revised (MnSOST-R)
mock-juries, studies of, 31
Mohan court decision, 11
mtDNA. *See* mitochondrial deoxyribonucleic
    acid (mtDNA)
multiple regression statistical tool, 163–164

murder, rule of law and, 155
Murdock, John E., 102
myth, science v., 45

National Institute of Justice, 107
National Research Council, DNA reports by,
    118
natural selection, 172
naturalized epistemology, 7
nature never repeats assertion, 100
Netherlands, court appointed experts in, 57
Neufield, Peter, 100
New Zealand
    expert testimony admissibility in, 13
    Frye test equivalent of, 13
    no reliability requirements of, 12
nonscientists, reasoning process of, 6
normative epistemology, 122
nuclear DNA analysis, 116
null hypothesis, 44, 61, 62, 63
    defined, 61
    falsification of, 170
    importance of, 187

objectivity, scientific method and, 37
Occupational Safety and Health Administration
    (OSHA)
    formaldehyde exposure standards of, 86
outcomes, self-enhancing interpretations of,
    199
overconfidence
    cognitive dissonance and, 150
    of jurors, 150
overconfidence bias, 27, 34, 152, 199
overconfidence heuristic, 150

Paracelsus's maxim, 74
paradigms. *See* legal paradigms; scientific
    paradigms
pattern recognition, 197
PCR technique. *See* polymerase chain reaction
    technique
pedophilia, Kansas Sexually Violent Predator
    Act and, 157
Peirce, Charles Sanders, abduction theory of, 6
penile plethysmographs, 162
Pennington, Nancy, 138, 147
People v. Jennings court case, 105
People v. Marx bitemark case, 109
persuasive arguments theory, 29, 31, 148–150
Peterson, Joseph L., 102
phallometric studies, 161
    penile plethysmographs used in, 162

physical attractiveness, influence of, 24
policymakers, reliable information needed by,
    146
Pollack, Judge, 112, 113
polygraph technique,
polymerase chain reaction (PCR) technique,
    104, 118
Popper, Karl, 36, 39, 43
population genetics theory, 100
post-traumatic stress disorder (PTSD)
    battered woman and, 224–225, 230–231
    description of, 230
Powell, Lewis, 124
power
    defined, 42, 60
    significance levels and, 63
    toxic court cases and, 66
    truth and, 17
predator. *See* sexual predators
predictability
    and juries, 142
    inherent limits of, 140
    rare events and, 141
predictions
    clinical/actuarial, 125, 129
    complexity theory and inherent limits of,
        138–140, 202
    inaccuracy of violent behavior, 198
    rightness v. wrongness of, 148
prejudices (prior), tainting influence of, 126
preponderance standard, 82–84
probabilistic assessment, 65
probabilistic generalization, 6
probabilistic reasoning, 8, 39–43
probability, 62
    as physical quality, 40
    definition of, 40
    scientists and, 41
    statistical inference and, 41
    theory of, 40
probability theory, 40, 114, 171
proficiency testing, 102
proof, burden of, 67
proportionality, self-defense and, 214
prospect theory, 190, 191, 192
psychiatrists, *Barefoot v. Estelle* testimony by,
    128
psychologists, cognitive, heuristics and, 20–21
PTSD. *See* post-traumatic stress disorder

qualitative extrapolations, 73
quantitative extrapolations, 73
Quinie, Willard V.,

racial stereotyping, 197
random sampling, 25, 178
randomness assumptions, 177
randomness, statistical inference and, 41
Rapid Risk Assessment for Sexual Offense
    Recidivism (RRASOR), 159
rare events, predictability of, 141
rational choice, 24
rational utility theory, 171
rationality, 5
    accurate information prerequisite to, 19
    as goal of rule of law, 19
    asserting goals of, 6, 17
    bounded, 20, 22, 169
    constraints of, 38
    correspondence/coherence theory of, 19
    debatable meaning of, 36
    fundamental fairness requirement of, 136
    game theory assumption of,
    global, 20
    real world, 19
reasoning. See also structured reasoning
    "dual-process model" of, 189–190
    about biological systems, 64
    analogy-based, 8
    deductive, 45
    exemplary, 6
    inductive, 6
    metaphorical basis (proposed) for, 189
    probabilistic, 8, 39–43
    structured, 7, 140
    training's improvement of, 34
    trustworthy information based, 122
    underlying principles of, 5
Receiver Operating Characteristic curve
    statistics, 126
recidivism, violent, 156, 163
    base rate of, 156
    prediction of, 164
Reference Manual on Scientific Evidence
    (Federal Judicial Center), 233
regression analysis, 163
    VRAG and, 164
Rehnquist, William
    Daubert dissent of, 7, 9–10
    Joiner and, 83
relational feminists, 207, 209
relative risk, 60
relevance
    conditions of, 35
    criteria of, 130
    Daubert and,
    doctrine of, 18

due process and, 35
    screening for, 14
reliability, scientific, 4, 46
representative heuristic
    defined, 195
    original study of, 24–25, 151, 194
    research on, 198
research, laboratory v. field, 193–195. See also
    medical research; scientific research
restriction fragment length polymorphism
    (RFLP) DNA analysis, 112
retrials, bad lab practices leading to, 97
RFLP DNA analysis. See restriction fragment
    length polymorphism DNA analysis
rights, fundamental, 135
Risinger, D. Michael, 96
risk. See also violence risk assessments
    actuarial instrument improvement of, 141
    analysis, 141, 144, 159
    as probabilistic statement, 159
    as social construct, 141
    assessment v. management of, 48
    of violent recidivism, 156, 163
    relative, 60
Roberts, Paul, 94
rodent studies, 71
route of exposure, 78–80
Royal Commission on Criminal Justice, 12
RRASOR. See Rapid Risk Assessment for Sexual
    Offense Recidivism (RRASOR)
rule of law
    as safeguard, 17
    definition of, 6, 17
    fundamental fairness requirement of, 130
    in democratic system, 122
    murders/violent sex offenses and, 155
    truth/rationality goals of, 19, 122

Saks, Michael J., 98, 100, 114
Sally Clark case (England), 12, 97, 98
satisficing heuristics, 20
Scheck, Barry, 100
science. See also Reference Manual on Scientific
    Evidence (Federal Judicial Center)
    as charter of uncertainty (Frank), 92
    as collaborative enterprise, 81
    as creative process, 38
    as process movement, 92
    background assumptions of, 42
    determining what counts as, 122
    feminist critique of, 37
    idea construction process of, 47
    junk, 8

Kuhn's philosophy of, 38
litigation and questionable, 8
metaphor and, 39, 51
myth v., 45
Poppers' philosophy of, 36, 39, 43
probabilistic reasoning underlying, 39
questioning/critical attitude of, 38
value-laden nature of, 141
scientific analysis, theories as starting points for,
    46
scientific arguments
    cognitive shortcuts in evaluating, 148
    demystification of
    language/structure of
    theory/data juxtaposition in, 45
scientific dialogue, 45
scientific inferences, 48
scientific logic, nonspecialness of,
scientific method
    definitions of, 36
    hypothesis testing in, 36
    objectivity as goal of, 37
    Popper's debunking of, 36
    Supreme Court (U.S.) on, 36, 84
scientific noses, counting of, 6–11
scientific paradigms, social construction of, 38
scientific research
    behavioral decision, 176–181
    experimental settings v. real-world decision
        making, 186
    growing sophistication of, 49
    individual variation concern in, 181
    on self-perception, 174
scientific studies. See also animal studies;
    human studies
    in vitro tissue culture, 80
    battered women study (Walker, Lenore), 221
    biological significance studies, 64
    building/integrating influence of, 81
    case reports, 69
    case-control, 68
    clinical double-bind, 68
    cohort, 68
    controlling extrinsic variables in, 52
    epidemiological, 58, 64, 69
    inferential synergy of combining research
        from, 48
    judge preferences of, 70
    of group polarization, 31
    of mock-juries, 31
    on self-perception, 174
    phallometric studies, 161, 162
    post–decision dissonance study, 25–27

questioning methodology of, 56
repeating of, 60
structure-activity relationship, 80–81
target-organ, 77
toxicology, 52, 58, 78
scientific testimony, complexity of, 14–15
scientific validity
    assessing, 51
    battered woman syndrome and, 220–221
    challenging of, 10
    court's examination of, 11
    future dangerousness testimony and, 156
    judge's questioning of, 9
    proficiency testing/high lab standards and,
        102
    shared perceptions of, 38
    state's tests for, 4
scientists. See also nonscientists
    argument assessment by, 59
    basic premise agreement of, 42
    belief/reality disconnect of, 41
    confidence interval used by, 66
    differences among, 36–37
    evaluation process of, 39
    inaccuracies controlled/eliminated by, 62
    judge viewpoint v. viewpoint of, 66
    non-magic numbers used by, 63
    non-threshold response assumed by, 76
    Popper on task of, 43
    probability and, 41
    theories as understood by, 41
    valid causal inferences of, 64
screening. See judicial screening
self-categorization theory, 29
self-defense
    absent alternatives for, 212
    as justification for homicide, 208
    deceased's character relevance in, 212
    defendant's lack of aggression, 216–217
    defined, 214
    duty to retreat as, 217–219
    evidence of, 209–210
    excuse v. justified, 203
    feminist critique of rules of, 206
    "heat of passion," 203
    imminence requirement for, 203, 210–211,
        212
    judge involvement for, 209
    jury constraints with, 214
    personal size considerations for, 214–216
    proof requirements for, 209
    proportionality requirement for, 214
    temporal proximity requirement for, 211

self-perception, research on, 174
self-serving bias, 199
Sensbaugh, George, 116
sentencing hearings. *See also* capital sentencing;
    criminal sentencing
    as evidentiary free-for-alls, 123
    court's failure to address scientific validity at,
        127
    court's refusal to scrutinize expert testimony
        at, 131
    declining to apply rules of evidence at, 132
    hearsay evidence admitted at, 123
separation of powers doctrine, 17
sex offenders
    hearings for, 158–159
    incorrigibility of, 155
    MnSOST-R and, 159
sex offenses. *See also* Kansas Sexually Violent
        Predator Act ("Kansas Act"); predator,
        sexual
    rule of law and, 155
    statutes regarding, 156
    unpredictability of, 157
Sexual Offender Risk Assessment Guide
    (SORAG), 159
sexual predators
    community notification statutes and, 155
    defined, 156
    phallometric studies of, 161
sexual violence
    instruments used in assessing, 159
    phallometric studies and, 161
short term repeats (STR), 104
short-cuts, uncertainty and use of, 170
shortcuts, cognitive, 148
SIDS. *See* sudden infant death syndrome
significance
    statistical, 61
    testing, 67
social comparison theory, 29
social epistemology, 14
social influence network theory, 29
social loafing, in groups, 32
social norms heuristic, 24, 25–26
social psychology
    debates regarding, 23
    legal importance of, 168
    statistics used in, 176–178
SORAG. *See* Sexual Offender Risk Assessment
    Guide (SORAG)
specific causation, 58
St. Petersburg Paradox, 190
Stacey, Robert B., 107, 109

standard deviation, 60, 63, 176
standards
    admissibility consensus, 5
    civil law's lower, 65
    Daubert, 82
    forensic laboratories ignoring of, 96–97
    goal of scientific, 66
    Joiner, 82
    legal v. scientific, 65, 66
    preponderance as, 82–84
State v. Council
    admissibility standards problem in, 5
    court's failures in, 120–121
    hair identification used in, 115, 117
State v. Krone case, bitemark/DNA
    identification and, 110
statistical analysis, 60
statistical assumptions, 62
statistical inference, 41
statistical significance, 61
    admissibility and, 68
    biological significance and, 64
    importance of, 64
    legal burden of proof and, 67
    power and, 63
    unthinking use of, 67
statistical techniques, 181
statistical theory, 160
statistics
    errors in, 62
    frequentist, 21
    social psychologists use of, 176–178
statutes
    community notification, 155
    involuntary commitment, 157
    sexually violent predator, 156
stereotyping
    as human thought characteristic, 196
    racial, 197
    tainting influence of, 126
stereotyping outsiders heuristic, 196
Stoney, David A., 106
story model model, of decision making,
    147–148
STR. *See* short term repeats
structure-activity relationship studies, 80–81
structured reasoning, 7, 45, 140
    judgment improved by, 16, 22–23
students,(college) as research subjects, 177–181
studies. *See* scientific studies
substantive equality, 204, 206–207, 208, 225
sudden infant death syndrome (SIDS), 12
suffering, women's v. men's, 207

sufficiency, admissibility conflated with, 82–84
support theory, 175, 190, 194
 shortcoming of, 202
Supreme Court (Canada), admissibility criteria
  of, 11
Supreme Court (U.S.)
  and future dangerousness testimony, 127
  certiorari granted in *Daubert* by, 9
  Daubert guidelines of, 5
  death penalty minimal standards of, 136
  evidence excluded by, 93
  expert admissibility jurisprudence
   transformed by, 4
  gatekeeper quandary of, 14
  general assessment test dispatched by, 9
  guidelines for judges by, 5
  Kansas v. Crane examined by, 158
  Kansas v. Hendricks examined by, 156, 157
  on scientific method, 36, 84

target-organ studies, 77
testability
  as key precept, 43
  challenges to, 44
testimony, expert
  actuarial instrument based, 166
  Australia/New Zealand admissibility of,
   13
  based on hypothetical question, 128
  capital sentencing and, 133, 146
  court's refusal to scrutinize, 131
  court's rejection of, 74
  Daubert's influence on, 129
  domestic violence, 205, 225
  evidentiary rules and, 205
  future dangerousness, 125–127
  inadmissibility of, 83
  juries assisted by, 142
  jurors lack of confidence in, 147
  nonscrutinization of, 23
  on battering, 218
  polygraph technique and
  pre-*Daubert* admissibility of
  relevance/reliability screening of, 14, 144
  sex offender hearings and, 158–159
  transforming jurisprudence of, 129
  Wright v. Willamette Industries, Inc. and, 84
theories, scientific
  assumptions and, 51
  coherence theory, 19
  correspondence theory, 19
  determining validity of, 47
  DNA typing theory, 115

explanatory power of, 45–47
falsification theory, 42
game theory,
hair identification theory, 114
hypothesis v., 46–47
linear effects theory, 75
metaphor applied to, 46
methodology for gaining acceptance of,
 189
persuasive arguments theory, 29
Popper on, 43
population genetics theory, 100
probability theory, 40, 114
relative evaluation of, 42
science's questioning/criticism of, 38, 41, 46
self-categorization theory, 29
social comparison theory, 29
social influence network theory, 29
strength of, 45
testability of, 43
threshold theory, 74
thinking, by association, 25
Thompson, William C., 120
three-strikes rules, 162
threshold theory, 74
tort cases, proving causation in toxic, 57
toxicology studies, 52, 58, 78
  animals used in, 186
  meta-analysis technique, 180
  small effects size/large consequences of, 188
  small sample size problems in, 177
trials, criminal. *See also* retrials
  proffered probability statement at, 103
  types of evidence excluded from, 123
trimming, of data, 63
truth
  adversarial system perspective on, 130
  as contest for power, 17
  as goal of rule of law, 19, 122
  asserting goals of, 6, 17
  debatable meaning of
  evidentiary practice and, 124
  negotiating, 37
Tversky, Amos, 190
Twining, William, 94, 95

uncertainty, scientific
  about causation, 58
  rational decisions under conditions of, 58
United Kingdom (U.K.)
  convictions overturned in, 97–98
  future dangerousness predictions in,
   155–156

United States v. Lowe court case, DNA
    methodology and, 111

validity. *See* internal validity; scientific validity
variable number of random repeats (VNTR),
    104
variance, analysis of, 181
violence. *See also* domestic violence; sexual
    violence
    age influence on, 144
    American families and, 228
    inaccurate predictions regarding, 198
    jurors overestimation of, 143
    predicting probability of recurring, 161
    three-strikes rules and, 162
Violence Risk Assessment Guide (VRAG), 159
    author attributed accuracy of, 165
    hypothesis underlying, 163–165
    regression analysis and, 164
    violent conduct definitions, 163
violence risk assessments
    biological basis possibility for, 167
    uncertainty of, 166
Violent Crime Control and Law Enforcement
    Act (1994), 155
Virginia State Crime Lab, DNA typing errors by,
    101
VNTR. *See* variable number of random repeats
voice spectrography, 94, 96, 98
    discrediting of, 99
voiceprints, 96, 98

VRAG. *See* Violence Risk Assessment Guide
    (VARG)

Walker, C. P., 97
Walker, Lenore, 220–221, 222–223, 225
Wertheim, Kasey, 100
Whitaker, D. D., 96
Whitehurst, Frederic, 97
Williams v. Reynolds case, hair analysis and,
    111
Williams, R. L., 108
Wilson, Paul, 101
within-subjects design, 182, 183
witnesses, expert
    judicial screening of, 18
    oath required of, 19
women
    abusive relationship entrapment of, 228
    killing of men v. killing of, 229
    science critique by, 37
    suffering of, 207
Woods, Frank G., 106
Wright v. Willamette Industries, Inc., 84
    assessing expert's conclusions in, 89–92
    causation hypothesis, 85
    court's causation conundrum in, 92
    evidence availability, 86–87
    expert testimony and, 84, 89
    validity of assumptions in, 87–92

Zuckerman, Adrian, 94

Books in the Series (*continued from p. iii*)

Moffat: *Trusts Law: Text and Materials*
Norrie: *Crime, Reason and History*
O'Dair: *Legal Ethics*
Oliver: *Common Values and the Public-Private Divide*
Oliver & Drewry: *The Law and Parliament*
Picciotto: *International Business Taxation*
Reed: *Internet Law: Text and Materials*
Richardson: *Law Process and Custody*
Roberts & Palmer: *Dispute Process ADR and the Primary Forms of Decision Making*
Seneviratne: *Ombudsmen: Public Services and Administrative Justice*
Stapleton: *Product Liability*
Tamanaha: *Law as a Means to an End: Threat to the Rule of Law*
Turpin: *British Government and the Constitution: Text, Cases and Materials*
Twining: *Globalisation and Legal Theory*
Twining: *Rethinking Evidence: Exploratory Essays*
Twining & Miers: *How to Do Things with Rules*
Ward: *A Critical Introduction to European Law*
Ward: *Shakespeare and Legal Imagination*
Zander: *Cases and Materials on the English Legal System*
Zander: *The Law Making Process*